CLYMER™

HONDA

VT700 & 750 · 1983-1987

The world's finest publisher of mechanical how-to manuals

INTERTEC PUBLISHING

P.O. Box 12901, Overland Park, Kansas 66282-2901

Copyright ©1988 Intertec Publishing Corporation

FIRST EDITION
First Printing May, 1985
Second Printing November, 1985

SECOND EDITION
Updated by Ron Wright to include 1985-1987 models
First Printing June, 1988
Second Printing October, 1989
Third Printing October, 1990
Fourth Printing September, 1991
Fifth Printing October, 1992
Sixth Printing March, 1994
Seventh Printing July, 1995

Printed in U.S.A.

ISBN: 0-89287-408-2

MEMBER

COVER: Photographed by Michael Brown Photographic Productions, Los Angeles, California. Assisted by Tim Lunde. Motorcycle courtesy of Torrance Honda, Torrance, California.

CONTENTS

QUICK REFERENCE DATA

FLUID CAPACITIES

Fuel	
1983-1985	12.5 liters (3.3 U.S. gal., 2.75 Imp. gal.)
1986-on	12.0 liters (3.18 U.S. gal., 2.64 Imp. gal.)
Engine oil	
Oil and filter change	3.0 liter (3.2 U.S. qt., 2.6 Imp. qt.)
At overhaul	3.5 liter (3.7 U.S. qt., 3.1 Imp. qt.)
Final drive unit (oil change)	130 cc (4.4 oz.)

ENGINE OIL CAPACITY

Oil and filter change	3.0 liter (3.2 U.S. qt., 2.6 Imp. qt.)
At overhaul	3.5 liter (3.7 U.S. qt., 3.1 Imp. qt.)

FRONT FORK AIR PRESSURE

Normal	Maximum*
0-6 psi (0-0.4 kg/cm^2)	43 psi (4 kg/cm^2)

*Do not exceed the maximum air pressure or internal parts of the fork will be damaged.

TIRE INFLATION PRESSURE (COLD)

Tire size	Air pressure	
	Normal	Maximum load limit*
Front		
110/90-19	32 psi (2.25 kg/cm^2)	32 psi (2.25 kg/cm^2)
Rear		
140/90-15	32 psi (2.25 kg/cm^2)	40 psi (2.80 kg/cm^2)

* Up to maximum load limit of 200 lb. (89 kg) including total weight of motorcycle with accessories, rider(s) and luggage.

FRONT FORK OIL CAPACITY*

VT700C, VT750C	
1983-1985	467.5-472.5 cc (15.82-15.99 oz.)
1986-on	442.5-447.5 cc (14.99-15.16 oz.)

* Capacity for each fork leg.

BRAKE SPECIFICATIONS

Item	Specification	Wear limit
Master cylinder		
Cylinder bore ID		
1983-1985	15.870-15.913 mm (0.6248-0.6265 in.)	15.93 mm (0.627 in.)
1986-on	14.000-14.043 mm (0.5512-0.5529 in.)	14.055 mm (0.5533 in.)
Piston OD		
1983-1985	15.827-15.854 mm (0.6231-0.6242 in.)	15.82 mm (0.623 in.)
1986-on	13.957-13.984 mm (0.5495-0.5506 in.)	13.945 mm (0.5490 in.)
Front caliper		
Cylinder bore ID		
1983-1985	30.148-30.280 mm (1.1901-1.1921 in.)	30.290 mm (1.1925 in.)
1986-on	32.030-32.080 mm (1.2610-1.2630 in.)	32.090 mm (1.2634 in.)
Piston OD		
1983-1985	30.230-30.280 mm (1.1902-1.1913 in.)	30.10 mm (1.187 in.)
1986-on	31.948-31.998 mm (1.2578-1.2598 in.)	31.940 mm (1.2575)
Front brake disc thickness		
1983-1985	4.8-5.2 mm (0.19-0.20 in.)	4.0 mm (0.16 in.)
1986-on	4.5-5.2 mm (0.18-0.20 in.)	4.0 mm (0.16 in.)
Disc runout	—	0.3 mm (0.12 in.)
Rear brake drum ID		
1983-1985	160.0-160.3 mm (6.30-6.31 in.)	161 mm (6.34 in.)
1986-on	180 mm (7.09 in.)	181.0 mm (7.13 in.)
Rear brake shoe thickness		
1983-1985	4.9-5.0 mm (0.19-0.20 in.)	2.0 mm (0.08 in.)
1986-on	5.0 mm (0.20 in.)	2.0 mm (0.08 in.)

ANTIFREEZE PROTECTION AND CAPACITY

Temperature	Antifreeze-to-water ratio
Above −25° F (−32° C)	45/55
Above −34° F (−37° C)	50/50
Above −48° F (−44.5° C)	55/45
Coolant capacity	
1983-1985	
Total system	2.1 liters (2.22 qt.)
Radiator and engine	1.7 liters (1.8 qt.)
Reserve tank	0.4 liters (0.42 qt.)
1986-on	
Total	1.83 liters (1.92 qt.)
Radiator and engine	1.56 liters (1.64 qt.)
Reserve tank	0.27 liters (0.28 qt.)

TUNE-UP SPECIFICATIONS

Compression pressure	
(at sea level)	
1983-1985	12.0 $\pm$ 2.0 kg/cm² (171 $\pm$ 28 psi)
1986-on	13.0 $\pm$ 2.0 kg/cm² (185 $\pm$ 28 psi)
Spark plug type	
1983-1985	
Standard heat range	ND X24EPR-U9 or NGK DPR8EA-9
Cold weather*	ND X22EPR-U9 or NGK DPR7EA-9
Extended high-speed riding	ND X27EPR-U9 or NGK DPR9EA-9
1986-on	
Standard heat range	ND X22EPR-U9 or NGK DPR7EA-9
Cold weather*	ND X20EPR-U9 or NGK DPR6EA-9
Extended high-speed riding	ND X24EPR-U9 or NGK DPR8EA-9
Spark plug gap	0.8-0.9 mm (0.031-0.035 in.)
Ignition timing	"F" mark @ idle
Idle speed	
1983	900 $\pm$ 100 rpm
1984-1985	1,000 $\pm$ 100 rpm
1986-on	
49-state	1,000 $\pm$ 100 rpm
California	1,100 $\pm$ 100 rpm

* Cold weather climate—below 41° F (5° C).

CHAPTER ONE

GENERAL INFORMATION

This detailed, comprehensive manual covers Honda 700 and 750 cc water-cooled V-twins from 1983-on. The expert text gives complete information on maintenance, tune-up, repair and overhaul. Hundreds of photos and drawings guide you through every step. The book includes all you need to know to keep your Honda running right.

A shop manual is a reference. You want to be able to find information fast. As in all Clymer books, this one is designed with you in mind. All chapters are thumb tabbed. Important items are extensively indexed at the rear of the book. All procedures, tables, photos, etc., in this manual are for the reader who may be working on the bike or using this manual for the first time. All the most frequently used specifications and capacities are summarized on the *Quick Reference Data* pages at the front of the book.

Keep the book handy in your tool box. It will help you to better understand how the bike runs, lower repair and maintenance costs and generally improve your satisfaction with the bike.

Table 1 is at the end of this chapter.

MANUAL ORGANIZATION

All dimensions and capacities are expressed in English units familiar to U.S. mechanics as well as in metric units.

This chapter provides general information and discusses equipment and tools useful both for preventive maintenance and troubleshooting.

Chapter Two provides methods and suggestions for quick and accurate diagnosis and repair of problems. Troubleshooting procedures discuss typical symptoms and logical methods to pinpoint the trouble.

Chapter Three explains all periodic lubrication and routine maintenance necessary to keep the Honda running well. Chapter Three also includes recommended tune-up procedures, eliminating the need to constantly consult chapters on the various assemblies.

Subsequent chapters describe specific systems such as the engine, clutch, transmission, fuel, exhaust, cooling, suspension and brakes. Each chapter provides disassembly, repair and assembly procedures in simple step-by-step form.

If a repair is impractical for a home mechanic, it is so indicated. It is usually faster and less expensive to take such repairs to a dealer or competent repair shop.

Specifications concerning a particular system are included at the end of the appropriate chapter.

Some of the procedures in this manual specify special tools. In most cases, the tool is illustrated either in actual use or alone. Well equipped mechanics may find they can substitute similar tools already on hand or can fabricate their own.

NOTES, CAUTIONS
AND WARNINGS

The terms NOTE, CAUTION and WARNING have a specific meaning in this manual. A NOTE provides additional information to make a step or procedure easier or clearer. Disregarding a NOTE could cause inconvenience, but would not cause equipment damage or personal injury.

A CAUTION emphasizes areas where equipment damage could occur. Disregarding a CAUTION could cause permanent mechanical damage; however, personal injury is unlikely.

A WARNING emphasizes areas where personal injury or even death could result from negligence. Mechanical damage may also occur. WARNINGS *are to be taken seriously.* In some cases, serious injury or death has resulted from disregarding similar warnings.

Throughout this manual keep in mind 2 conventions. "Front" refers to the front of the bike. The front of any component, such as the engine, is the end which faces toward the front of the bike. The "left-" and "right-hand" sides refer to the position of the parts as viewed by a rider sitting on the seat facing forward. For example, the throttle control is on the right-hand side and the clutch lever is on the left-hand side. These rules are simple, but even experienced mechanics occasionally become disoriented.

SERVICE HINTS

Most of the service procedures covered are straightforward and can be performed by anyone reasonably handy with tools. It is suggested, however, that you consider your own capabilities carefully before attempting any operation involving major disassembly of the engine.

Some operations, for example, require the use of a press. It would be wiser to have these performed by a shop equipped for such work, rather than trying to do the job yourself with makeshift equipment. Other procedures require precise measurements. Unless you have the skills and equipment required, it would be better to have a qualified repair shop make the measurements for you.

There are many items available that can be used on your hands before and after working on your bike. A little preparation prior to getting "all greased up" will help when cleaning up later.

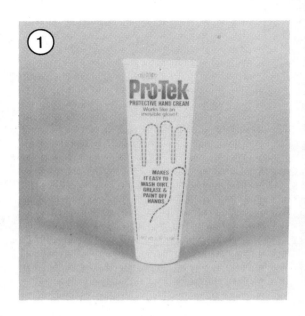

Before starting out, work Vaseline, soap or a product such as Pro-Tek (**Figure 1**) onto your forearms, into your hands and under your fingernails and cuticles. This will make cleanup a lot easier.

For cleanup, use a waterless hand soap such as Sta-Lube and then finish up with powdered Boraxo and a fingernail brush.

Repairs go much faster and easier if the bike is clean before you begin work. There are special cleaners, such as Gunk or Bel-Ray Degreaser, for washing the engine and related parts. Just spray or brush on the cleaning solution, let it stand, then rinse it away with a garden hose. Clean all oily or greasy parts with cleaning solvent as you remove them.

> *WARNING*
> *Never use gasoline as a cleaning agent. It presents an extreme fire hazard. Be sure to work in a well-ventilated area when using cleaning solvent. Keep a fire extinguisher, rated for gasoline fires, handy in any case.*

Special tools are required for some repair procedures. These may be purchased from a dealer or motorcycle shop, rented from a tool rental dealer or fabricated by a mechanic or machinist (often at a considerable savings).

Much of the labor charged for by mechanics to remove and disassemble other parts to reach the defective unit. It is usually possible to perform the preliminary operations yourself and then take the defective unit in to the dealer for repair.

1

Once you have decided to tackle the job yourself, read the entire section in this manual which pertains to it, making sure you have identified the proper one. Study the illustrations and text until you have a good idea of what is involved in completing the job satisfactorily. If special tools or replacement parts are required, make arrangements to get them before you start. It is frustrating and time-consuming to get partly into a job and then be unable to complete it.

Simple wiring checks can be easily made at home, but knowledge of electronics is almost a necessity for performing tests with complicated electronic testing gear.

During disassembly of parts keep a few general cautions in mind. Force is rarely needed to get things apart. If parts are a tight fit, such as a bearing in a case, there is usually a tool designed to separate them. Never use a screwdriver to pry parts with machined surfaces such as crankcase halves. You will mar the surfaces and end up with leaks.

Make diagrams (or take a Polaroid picture) wherever similar-appearing parts are found. For instance, crankcase bolts are often not the same length. You may think you can remember where everything came from, but mistakes are costly. There is also the possibility you may be sidetracked and not return to work for days or even weeks, in which interval carefully laid out parts may have become disturbed.

Tag all similar internal parts for location and mark all mating parts for position. Record number and thickness of any shims as they are removed. Small parts such as bolts can be identified by placing them in plastic sandwich bags. Seal and label them with masking tape.

Wiring should be tagged with masking tape and marked as each wire is removed. Again, do not rely on memory alone.

Protect finished surfaces from physical damage or corrosion. Keep gasoline and hydraulic brake and clutch fluid off painted surfaces.

Frozen or very tight bolts and screws can often be loosened by soaking with penetrating oil, such as WD-40 or Liquid Wrench, then sharply striking the bolt head a few times with a hammer and punch (or screwdriver for screws). Avoid heat unless absolutely necessary, since it may melt, warp or remove the temper from many parts.

No parts, except those assembled with a press fit, require unusual force during assembly. If a part is hard to remove or install, find out why before proceeding.

Cover all openings after removing parts to keep dirt, small tools, etc., from falling in.

When assembling 2 parts, start all fasteners, then tighten evenly.

Wiring connections and brake components should be kept clean and free of grease and oil.

When assembling parts, be sure all shims and washers are installed exactly as they came out.

Whenever a rotating part butts against a stationary part, look for a shim or washer. Use new gaskets if there is any doubt about the condition of the old ones. A thin coat of oil on gaskets may help them seal effectively.

Heavy grease can be used to hold small parts in place if they tend to fall out during assembly. However, keep grease and oil away from electrical and brake components.

High spots may be sanded off a piston with sandpaper, but fine emery cloth and oil will do a much more professional job.

Carbon can be removed from the heads, the piston crowns and the exhaust ports with a dull screwdriver. Do *not* scratch machined surfaces. Wipe off the surface with a clean cloth when finished.

The carburetors are best cleaned by disassembling them and soaking the parts in a commercial carburetor cleaner. Never soak gaskets and rubber parts in these cleaners. Never use wire to clean out jets and air passages; they are easily damaged. Use compressed air to blow out the carburetor *after* the float has been removed.

A baby bottle makes a good measuring device for adding oil to the final drive and front forks. Get one that is graduated in fluid ounces and cubic centimeters. After it has been used for this purpose, do not let a small child drink out of it as there will always be an oil residue in it.

Take your time and do the job right. Do not forget that a newly rebuilt engine must be broken in the same as a new one. Keep the rpm within the limits given in your owner's manual when you get back on the road.

TORQUE SPECIFICATIONS

Torque specifications throughout this manual are given in Newton meters (N•m) and foot-pounds (ft.-lb.). Newton meters have been adopted in place of meter kilograms (mkg) in accordance with the International Modernized Metric System. Tool manufacturers offer torque wrenches claibrated in Newton meters.

Existing torque wrenches calibrated in meter kilograms can be used by performing a simple conversion. All you have to do is move the decimal point one place to the right; for example,

4.7 mkg = 47 N•m. This conversion is accurate enough for mechanical work even though the exact mathematical conversion is 3.5 mkg = 34.3 N•m.

SAFETY FIRST

Professional mechanics can work for years and never sustain a serious injury. If you observe a few rules of common sense and safety, you can enjoy many hours servicing your own machine. If you ignore these rules you can hurt yourself or damage the bike.

1. Never use gasoline as a cleaning solvent.
2. Never smoke or use a torch in the vicinity of flammable liquids such as cleaning solvent in open containers.
3. If welding or brazing is required on the machine, remove the fuel tanks to a safe distance, at least 50 feet away.
4. Use the proper sized wrenches to avoid damage to nuts and injury to yourself.
5. When loosening a tight or stuck nut, think about what would happen if the wrench should slip. Be careful; protect yourself accordingly.
6. Keep your work area clean and uncluttered.
7. Wear safety goggles during all operations involving drilling, grinding or the use of a cold chisel.
8. Never use worn tools.
9. Keep a fire extinguisher handy and be sure it is rated for gasoline and electrical fires.

SPECIAL TIPS

Because of the extreme demands placed on a bike several points should be kept in mind when performing service and repair. The following items are general suggestions that may improve the overall life of the machine and help avoid costly failures.

1. Use a locking compound such as Loctite Lock N' Seal No. 2114 (blue Loctite) on all bolts and nuts, even if they are secured with lockwashers. This type of Loctite does not harden completely and allows easy removal of the bolt or nut. A screw or bolt lost from an engine cover or bearing retainer could easily cause serious and expensive damage before its loss is noticed.

When applying Loctite, use a small amount. If too much is used, it can work its way down the threads and stick parts together not meant to be stuck.

Keep a tube of Loctite in your tool box; when used properly it is cheap insurance.

2. Use a hammer-driven impact tool to remove and install all bolts and screws, particularly engine

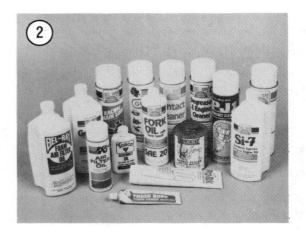

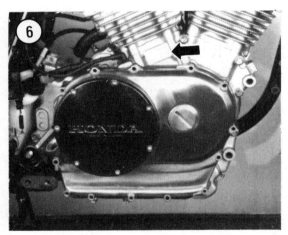

EXPENDABLE SUPPLIES

Certain expendable supplies are required during maintenance and repair work. These include grease, oil, gasket cement, wiping rags and cleaning solvent. Ask your dealer for the special locking compounds, silicone lubricants and other products (**Figure 2**) which make vehicle maintenance simpler and easier. Cleaning solvent or kerosene is available at some service stations or hardware stores.

PARTS REPLACEMENT

Honda makes frequent changes during a model year—some minor, some relatively major. When you order parts from the dealer or other parts distributor, always order by engine and frame number. Write the numbers down and carry them with you. Compare new parts to old before purchasing them. If they are not alike, have the parts manager explain the difference to you.

SERIAL NUMBERS

You must know the model serial number and VIN number for registration purposes and when ordering replacement parts.

The frame serial number is stamped on the right-hand side of the steering head (**Figure 3**). The vehicle identification number (VIN) is on the left-hand side of the steering head (**Figure 4**). On 1983-1985 models, the engine serial number is located on the lower left-hand side of the crankcase above the oil drain plug (**Figure 5**). On 1986 and later models, the engine serial number is located on the right-hand crankcase below the rear cylinder (**Figure 6**). The carburetor identification number is located on the rear of the carburetor body above the float bowl on the intake side as shown in **Figure 7**.

cover screws. These tools help prevent the rounding off of bolt heads and ensure a tight installation.

3. When replacing missing or broken fasteners (bolts, nuts and screws), especially on the engine or frame components, always use Honda replacement parts. They are specially hardened for each application. The wrong fastener bolt could easily cause serious and expensive damage, not to mention rider injury.

4. When installing gaskets in the engine, always use Honda replacement gaskets *without* sealer, unless designated. These gaskets are designed to swell when they come in contact with oil. Gasket sealer will prevent the gaskets from swelling as intended, which can result in oil leaks. These Honda gaskets are cut from material of the precise thickness needed. Installation of a too thick or too thin gasket in a critical area could cause engine damage.

TUNE-UP AND TROUBLESHOOTING TOOLS

Multimeter or Volt-ohm Meter

This instrument (**Figure 8**) is invaluable for electrical system troubleshooting and service. A few of its functions may be duplicated by homemade test equipment, but for the serious mechanic it is a must. Its uses are described in the applicable sections of the book.

Strobe Timing Light

This instrument is necessary for tuning. By flashing a light at the precise instant the spark plug fires, the position of the timing mark can be seen. Marks on the alternator flywheel line up with the stationary mark on the crankcase while the engine is running.

Suitable lights range from inexpensive neon bulb types to powerful xenon strobe lights. See **Figure 9**. Neon timing lights are difficult to see and must be used in dimly lit areas. Xenon strobe timing lights can be used outside in bright sunlight. Both types work on the bike; use according to the manufacturer's instructions.

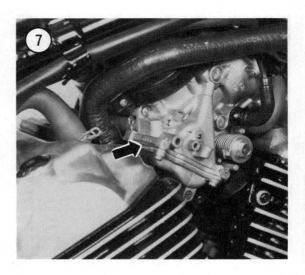

Portable Tachometer

A portable tachometer is necessary for tuning. See **Figure 10**. Ignition timing and carburetor adjustments must be performed at the specified engine speed. The best instrument for this purpose is one with a low range of 0-1,000 or 0-2,000 rpm and a high range of 0-4,000 rpm. Extended range (0-6,000 or 0-8,000 rpm) instruments lack accuracy at lower speeds. The instrument should be capable of detecting changes of 25 rpm on the low range.

Compression Gauge

A compression gauge measures the engine compression (**Figure 11**). They are available from motorcycle or auto supply stores and mail order outlets.

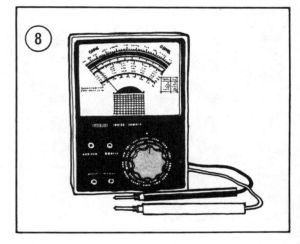

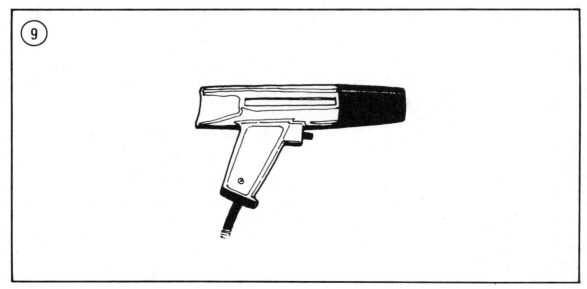

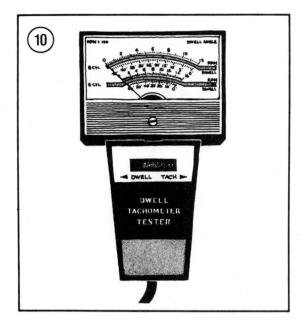

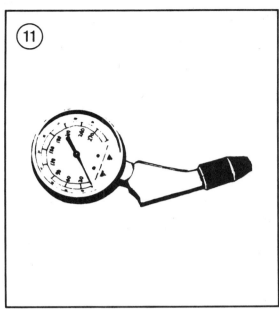

Table 1 HOME WORKSHOP TOOLS

Tool	Size or Specification
Screwdrivers	
Slot	5/16×8 in. blade
Slot	3/8×12 in. blade
Phillips	Size 2 tip, 6 in. blade
Pliers	
Gas pliers	6 in. overall
Vise Grips®	10 in. overall
Needlenose	6 in. overall
Channel lock	12 in. overall
Snap ring	–
Wrenches	
Box-end set	10-17, 20, 32 mm
Open-end set	10-17, 20, 32 mm
Crescent (adjustable)	6 and 12 in. overall
Socket set	1/2 in. drive ratchet with 10-17, 20, 32 mm sockets
Allen set	2-10 mm
Cone wrenches	–
Spoke wrench	–
Other Special Tools	
Impact driver	1/2 in. drive with ass't tips
Torque wrench	1/2 in. drive—0-100 ft.-lb.
Tire levers	For moped or motorcycle tires

CHAPTER TWO

TROUBLESHOOTING

Diagnosing mechanical problems is relatively simple if you use orderly procedures and keep a few basic principles in mind.

The troubleshooting procedures in this chapter analyze typical symptoms and show logical methods of isolating causes. These are not the only methods. There may be several ways to solve a problem, but only a systematic, methodical approach can guarantee success.

Never assume anything. Do not overlook the obvious. If you are riding along and the engine suddenly quits, check the easiest, most accessible problems first. Is there gasoline in the tank? Is the fuel shutoff valve in the ON position? Has a spark plug wire fallen off?

If nothing obvious turns up in a quick check, look a little further. Learning to recognize and describe symptoms will make repairs easier for you or a mechanic at the shop. Describe problems accurately and fully. Saying that "it won't run" isn't the same as saying "it quit at high speed and won't start" or that "it sat in my garage for 3 months and then wouldn't start."

Gather as many symptoms together as possible to aid in diagnosis. Note whether the engine lost power gradually or all at once. Remember that the more complicated a machine is, the easier it is to troubleshoot because symptoms point to specific problems.

After the symptoms are defined, areas which could cause the problems are tested and analyzed. Guessing at the cause of a problem may provide the solution, but it can easily lead to frustration, wasted time and a series of expensive, unnecessary parts replacements.

You do not need fancy equipment or complicated test gear to determine whether repairs can be attempted at home. A few simple checks could save a large repair bill and time lost while the bike sits in a dealer's service department. On the other hand, be realistic and don't attempt repairs beyond your abilities. Service departments tend to charge a lot for putting together a disassembled engine that may have been abused. Some dealers won't even take on such a job—so use common sense and don't get in over your head.

OPERATING REQUIREMENTS

An engine needs 3 basics to run properly: correct fuel-air mixture, compression and a spark at the correct time. If one or more are missing, the engine just won't run. The electrical system is the weakest link of the 3 basics. More problems result from electrical breakdowns than from any other source. Keep that in mind before you begin tampering with carburetor adjustments and the like.

If the bike has been sitting for any length of time and refuses to start, check and clean the spark plugs

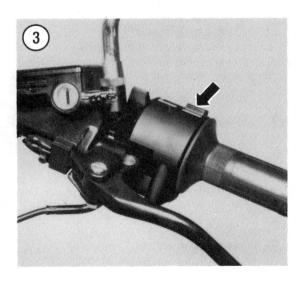

and then look to the gasoline delivery system. This includes the fuel tank, fuel shutoff valve, fuel line to the carburetor, the fuel pump and inline fuel filter. Gasoline deposits may have formed and gummed up the carburetor's jets and air passages. Gasoline tends to lose its potency after standing for long periods. Condensation may contaminate the fuel with water. Drain the old fuel and try starting with a fresh tankful.

EMERGENCY TROUBLESHOOTING

When the bike is difficult to start or won't start at all, it does not help to wear down the battery using the starter. Check for obvious problems even before getting out your tools. Go down the following list step by step. Do each one; you may be embarrassed to find your kill switch is stuck in the OFF position, but that is better than wearing down the battery. If it still will not start, refer to the appropriate troubleshooting procedure which follows in this chapter.

1. Is there fuel in the tank? Open the filler cap (**Figure 1**) and rock the bike. Listen for fuel sloshing around.

> *WARNING*
> *Do not use an open flame to check in the tank. A serious explosion is certain to result.*

2. Is the fuel shutoff valve (**Figure 2**) in the ON position?
3. Make sure the fuel pump is operating correctly; refer to Chapter Six. Also make sure the fuel filter is not clogged; replace if necessary.
4. Make sure the kill switch (**Figure 3**) is not stuck in the OFF position.
5. Are all 4 spark plug wires on tight? Make sure to check the spark plug wire that is buried in the deep well in each cylinder head. Push all of them on and slightly rotate them to clean the electrical connection between the plug and the connector.
6. Is the choke lever in the right position? The lever should be moved *up* for a cold engine and *down* for a warm engine.

ENGINE STARTING

An engine that refuses to start or is difficult to start is very frustrating. More often than not, the problem is very minor and can be found with a simple and logical troubleshooting approach.

The following items show a beginning point from which to isolate engine starting problems.

Engine Fails to Start

Perform the following spark test to determine if the ignition system is operating properly.

1. Remove only one of the spark plugs from one of the cylinders.

2. Connect the spark plug wire and connector to the spark plug and touch the spark plug's base to a good ground such as the engine cylinder head. Position the spark plug so you can see the electrodes.

WARNING
If it is necessary to hold the high voltage lead in Step 3, do so with an insulated pair of pliers. The high voltage generated by the CDI could produce serious or fatal shocks.

3. Crank the engine over with the starter. A fat blue spark should be evident across the plug's electrodes.

4. If the spark is good, check for one or more of the following possible malfunctions:
   a. Obstructed fuel line.
   b. Leaking head gasket(s).
   c. Low compression.

5. If spark is not good, check for one or more of the following:
   a. Weak ignition coil(s).
   b. Weak CDI pulse generator(s).
   c. Weak spark unit(s).
   d. Broken or shorted high tension lead to the spark plug(s).
   e. Loose electrical connections.
   f. Loose or broken ignition coil ground wire.

Engine Is Difficult to Start

Check for one or more of the following possible malfunctions:
   a. Fouled spark plug(s).
   b. Improperly adjusted choke.
   c. Contaminated fuel system.
   d. Improperly adjusted carburetors.
   e. Weak ignition coil(s).
   f. Weak CDI pulse generator(s).
   g. Weak spark unit(s).
   h. Incorrect type ignition coil(s).
   i. Poor compression.

Engine Will Not Crank

Check for one or more of the following possible malfunctions:
   a. Discharged battery.
   b. Defective starter motor.
   c. Seized piston(s).

d. Seized crankshaft bearings.
e. Broken connecting rod(s).
f. Locked-up transmission or clutch assembly.

ENGINE PERFORMANCE

In the following check list, it is assumed that the engine runs, but is not operating at peak performance. This will serve as a starting point from which to isolate a performance malfunction.

The possible causes for each malfunction are listed in a logical sequence and in order of probability.

Engine Will Not Start
Or Is Hard To Start

   a. Fuel tank empty.
   b. Fuel pump not operating properly.
   c. Obstructed fuel line, fuel shutoff valve or fuel filter.
   d. Sticking float valve in carburetor.
   e. Carburetor incorrectly adjusted.
   f. Improper choke operation.
   g. Fouled or improperly gapped spark plug(s).
   h. Ignition timing incorrect.
   i. Broken or shorted ignition coil(s).
   j. Weak or faulty spark unit(s) or pulse generator(s).
   k. Improper valve timing.
   l. Clogged air filter element.
   m. Contaminated fuel.

Engine Will Not Idle

   a. Carburetor incorrectly adjusted.
   b. Fouled or improperly gapped spark plug(s).
   c. Leaking head gasket(s).
   d. Ignition timing incorrect.
   e. Weak or faulty spark unit(s) or pulse generator(s).
   f. Improper valve timing.
   g. Obstructed fuel line or fuel shutoff valve.

Engine Misses at High Speed

   a. Fouled or improperly gapped spark plugs.
   b. Improper ignition timing.
   c. Improper carburetor main jet selection.
   d. Clogged jets in the carburetors.
   e. Weak ignition coil.
   f. Weak or faulty spark unit(s) or pulse generator(s).
   g. Improper valve timing.
   h. Obstructed fuel line or fuel shutoff valve.

Engine Overheating

a. Coolant level low.
b. Faulty temperature gauge or gauge sensor.
c. Thermostat stuck in the closed position.
d. Faulty radiator cap.
e. Passages blocked in the radiator, hoses or water jackets in the engine.
f. Fan blades cracked or missing.
g. Faulty fan motor.
h. Improper ignition timing.
i. Improper spark plug heat range.

Smoky Exhaust and Engine Runs Roughly

a. Carburetor mixture too rich.
b. Choke not operating correctly.
c. Water or other contaminants in fuel.
d. Clogged fuel line.
e. Clogged air filter element.

Engine Loses Power

a. Carburetor incorrectly adjusted.
b. Engine overheating.
c. Improper ignition timing.
d. Incorrectly gapped spark plugs.
e. Weak ignition coil(s).
f. Weak spark unit(s).
g. Weak CDI pulse generator(s).
h. Obstructed mufflers.
i. Dragging brake(s).

Engine Lacks Acceleration

a. Carburetor mixture too lean.
b. Clogged fuel line.
c. Improper ignition timing.
d. Dragging brake(s).

ENGINE NOISES

1. *Knocking or pinging during acceleration—* Caused by using a lower octane fuel than recommended. May also be caused by poor fuel. Pinging can also be caused by spark plugs of the wrong heat range. Refer to *Spark Plug Selection* in Chapter Three.

2. *Slapping or rattling noises at low speed or during acceleration—* May be caused by piston slap (excessive piston to cylinder wall clearance).

3. *Knocking or rapping while decelerating—* Usually caused by excessive rod bearing clearance.

4. *Persistent knocking and vibration—* Usually caused by excessive main bearing clearance.

5. *Rapid on-off squeal—* Compression leak around cylinder head gasket(s) or spark plugs.

EXCESSIVE VIBRATION

Usually this is caused by loose engine mounting hardware. If not, it can be difficult to find without disassembling the engine.

FRONT SUSPENSION AND STEERING

Poor handling may be caused by improper tire pressure, a damaged or bent frame or front steering components, a worn front fork assembly, worn wheel bearings or dragging brakes.

BRAKE PROBLEMS

Sticking disc brakes may be caused by a stuck piston(s) in a caliper assembly or warped pad shim(s).

A sticking drum brake may be caused by worn or weak return springs, dry pivot and cam bushings or improper adjustment. Grabbing brakes may be caused by greasy linings which must be replaced. Brake grab may also be due to an out-of-round drum. Glazed linings will cause loss of stopping power.

CHAPTER THREE

LUBRICATION, MAINTENANCE AND TUNE-UP

A motorcycle, even in normal use, is subjected to tremendous heat, stress and vibration. When neglected, any bike becomes unreliable and actually dangerous to ride.

To gain the utmost in safety, performance and useful life from the Honda V-twins it is necessary to make periodic inspections and adjustments. Frequently, minor problems are found during these inspections that are simple and inexpensive to correct at the time. If they are not found and corrected at this time they could lead to major and more expensive problems later on.

Start out by doing simple tune-up, lubrication and maintenance. Tackle more involved jobs as you become more acquainted with the bike.

This chapter explains lubrication, maintenance and tune-up procedures required for the Honda 700 and 750 cc V-twins.

Table 1 is a suggested factory maintenance schedule. **Tables 1-8** are located at the end of this chapter.

ROUTINE CHECKS

The following simple checks should be performed at each stop at a service station for gas.

Engine Oil Level

Refer to *Engine Oil Level Check* under *Periodic Lubrication* in this chapter.

Coolant Level

Check the coolant level when the engine has warmed up to normal operating temperature.

Check the level in the coolant reserve tank. The level should be between the UPPER and LOWER marks. See **Figure 1A** (1983-1985) or **Figure 1B** (1986-on). If necessary, add coolant to the reserve tank, not to the radiator, so the level is to the UPPER mark.

General Inspection

1. Quickly inspect the engine for signs of oil, fuel or coolant leakage.
2. Check the tires for embedded stones. Pry them out with your ignition key.
3. Make sure all lights work.

NOTE
At least check the brake light. It can burn out at any time. Motorists cannot stop as quickly as you and need all the warning you can give.

3

Tire Pressure

Tire pressure must be checked with the tires cold. Correct tire pressure varies with the load you are carrying. See **Table 2**.

Battery

Remove the left-hand side cover and check the battery electrolyte level. The level must be between the upper and lower level marks on the case (**Figure 2**).

For complete details see *Battery Removal, Installation and Electrolyte Level Check* in this chapter.

Check the level more frequently in hot weather; electrolyte will evaporate rapidly as heat increases.

Lights and Horn

With the engine running, check the following.
1. Pull the front brake lever on and check that the brake light comes on.
2. Push the rear brake pedal down and check that the brake light comes on soon after you have begun depressing the pedal.
3. Press the headlight dimmer switch to both the HI and LO positions and check to see that both headlight elements are working.
4. Turn the turn signal switch to the left and right positions and check that all 4 turn signals are working.
5. Push the horn button and make sure that the horn blows loudly.
6. If the horn or any of the lights failed to operate properly, refer to Chapter Seven.

PRE-CHECKS

The following checks should be performed prior to the first ride of the day.
1. Inspect all fuel lines and fittings for wetness.
2. Make sure the fuel tank is full of fresh gasoline.
3. Make sure the engine oil level is correct.
4. Inspect the coolant level in the coolant reserve tank.
5. Inspect the oil level in the final drive unit.
6. Check the operation of the clutch. Add hydraulic fluid to the clutch master cylinder or bleed the system if necessary.
7. Check the operation of the front brake. Add hydraulic fluid to the brake master cylinder if necessary.
8. Check the throttle and the rear brake pedal. Make sure they operate properly with no binding.
9. Inspect the front and rear suspension; make sure they have a good solid feel with no looseness.
10. Check tire pressure. Refer to **Table 2**.

11. Check the air pressure in the front forks. Refer to **Table 3**.

12. Check the exhaust system for damage.

13. Check the tightness of all fasteners, especially engine mounting hardware.

SERVICE INTERVALS

The services and intervals shown in **Table 1** are recommended by the factory. Strict adherence to these recommendations will ensure long service from the Honda. If the bike is run in an area of high humidity, the lubrication services must be done more frequently to prevent possible rust damage.

For convenience when maintaining your motorcycle, most of the services shown in the table are described in this chapter. However, some procedures which require more than minor disassembly or adjustment are covered elsewhere in the appropriate chapter.

TIRES AND WHEELS

Tire Pressure

Tire pressure should be checked and adjusted to maintain the smoothness of the tire, good traction and handling and to get the maximum life out of the tire. A simple, accurate gauge (**Figure 3**) can be purchased for a few dollars and should be carried in your motorcycle tool kit. The appropriate tire pressures are shown in **Table 2**.

Tire Inspection

The tires take a lot of punishment so inspect them periodically for excessive wear, cuts, abrasions, etc. If you find a nail or other object in the tire, mark its location with a light crayon prior to removing it. This will help locate the hole for repair. Refer to Chapter Nine for tire changing and repair information.

Check local traffic regulations concerning minimum tread depth. Measure the tread depth at the center of the tire tread using a tread depth gauge (**Figure 4**) or small ruler. Honda recommends that original equipment tires be replaced when the front tire tread depth is 1.5 mm (1/16 in.) or less, when the rear tread depth is 2.0 mm (3/32 in.) or less or when tread wear indicators appear across the tire indicating the minimum tread depth.

Rim Inspection

Frequently inspect the wheel rims. If a rim has been damaged it might have been enough to knock it out of alignment. Improper wheel alignment can

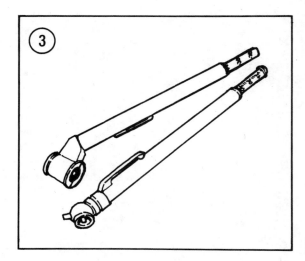

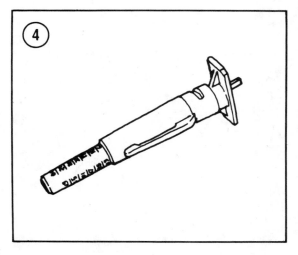

cause severe vibration and result in an unsafe riding condition. If the rim portion of the alloy wheel is damaged the wheel must be replaced as it cannot be repaired.

CRANKCASE BREATHER HOSE (U.S. MODELS ONLY)

Remove both side covers, seat and fuel tank. Inspect the breather hoses for cracks and deterioration and make sure that all hose clamps are tight.

EVAPORATIVE EMISSION CONTROL (1984-ON CALIFORNIA MODELS ONLY)

Inspect the hoses for cracks, kinks and deterioration. Make sure that all hoses are tight where they attach to the various components. For correct hose routing, refer to Chapter Six.

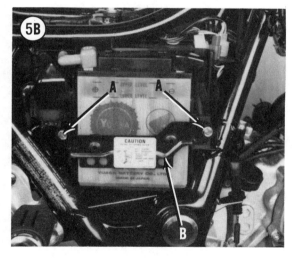

3

**SECONDARY AIR SUPPLY
SYSTEM (1986-ON CALIFORNIA
MODELS ONLY)**

Inspect all hoses for cracks, kinks and deterioration. Make sure that all hoses are tight where they attach to the various components. For correct hose routing, refer to Chapter Six.

BATTERY

**Removal, Installation and
Electrolyte Level Check**

The battery is the heart of the electrical system. It should be checked and serviced as indicated in

Table 1. The majority of electrical system troubles can be attributed to neglect of this vital component.

The electrolyte level should be maintained between the 2 marks on the battery case (**Figure 2**). If the electrolyte level is low, remove the battery from the bike so it can be thoroughly serviced and checked.

1. Place the bike on the centerstand.
2A. *1983-1985:* Perform the following.
   a. Remove the left-hand side cover and the seat.
   b. Remove the bolt (A, **Figure 5A**) securing the voltage regulator and battery holder plate (B, **Figure 5A**) and swing the holder plate out of the way.
2B. *1986-on:* Perform the following.
   a. Remove the right-hand side cover.
   b. Remove the battery holder bolts (A, **Figure 5B**) and remove the holder (B, **Figure 5B**).
3. Disconnect the negative (–) lead and then the positive (+) lead from the battery.
4. Unhook the battery vent tube from the battery. Leave it routed through the bike's frame.
5. Slide the battery out of the frame.
6. Wipe off any of the highly corrosive residue that may have dripped from the battery during removal.

*WARNING
Protect your eyes, skin and clothing. If electrolyte gets into your eyes, flush your eyes thoroughly with clean water and get prompt medical attention.*

*CAUTION
Be careful not to spill battery electrolyte on painted or polished surfaces. The liquid contains sulfuric acid that is highly corrosive and will damage the finish. If it is spilled, wash it off immediately with soapy water and thoroughly rinse with clean water.*

7. Remove the caps from the battery cells and add distilled water to correct the fluid level. Never add electrolyte (acid) to correct the level.

*NOTE
If distilled water has been added, reinstall the battery caps and gently shake the battery for several minutes to mix the existing electrolyte with the new water.*

8. After the fluid level has been corrected and the battery allowed to stand a few minutes, remove the

battery caps and check the specific gravity of the electrolyte in each cell with a hydrometer (**Figure 6**). See *Battery Testing* in this chapter.

9. After the battery has been refilled, recharged or replaced, install it by reversing these removal steps.

> *CAUTION*
> *If you removed the breather tube from the frame, be sure to route it so that residue will not drain onto any part of the bike's frame. The tube must be free of bends or twists as any restriction may pressurize the battery and damage it.*

Testing

Hydrometer testing is the best way to check battery condition. Use a hydrometer with numbered graduations from 1.100 to 1.300 rather than one with just color-coded bands. To use the hydrometer, squeeze the rubber ball, insert the tip into the cell and release the pressure on the ball. Draw enough electrolyte to float the weighted float inside the hydrometer. Note the number in line with the surface of the electrolyte; this is the specific gravity for this cell. Squeeze the rubber ball again and return the electrolyte to the cell from which it came.

The specific gravity of the electrolyte in each battery cell is an excellent indication of that cell's condition. A fully charged cell will read from 1.265-1.280, while a cell in good condition reads from 1.225-1.265 and anything below 1.225 is practically dead.

Specific gravity varies with temperature. For each 10° the electrolyte temperature exceeds 27° C (80° F), add 0.004 to readings indicated on the hydrometer. Subtract 0.004 for each 10° below 27° C (80° F). If the cells test in the poor range, the battery requires recharging. The hydrometer is useful for checking the progress of the charging operation. **Table 4** shows approximate state of charge.

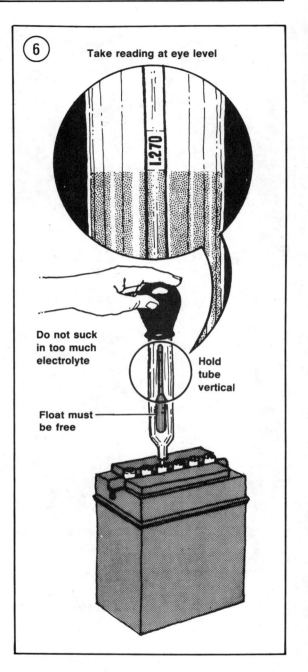

⑥

Take reading at eye level

1.270

Do not suck in too much electrolyte

Hold tube vertical

Float must be free

Charging

> *WARNING*
> *During the charging process, highly explosive hydrogen gas is released from the battery. The battery should be charged only in a well-ventilated area away from any open flames (including pilot lights on home gas appliances). Do not allow any smoking in the area. Never check the charge of the battery by*

arcing (connecting metal) across the terminals; the resulting spark can ignite the hydrogen gas.

> *CAUTION*
> *Always remove the battery from the bike before connecting the battery charger. Never recharge a battery in the bike's frame; the corrosive mist that is emitted during the charging process will damage the bike.*

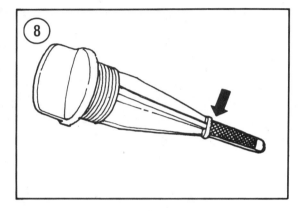

1. Connect the positive (+) charger lead to the positive (+) battery terminal (or lead) and the negative (–) charger lead to the negative (–) battery terminal (or lead).
2. Remove all vent caps from the battery, set the charger at 12 volts and switch the charger on. If the output of the charger is variable, it is best to select a low setting—1 1/2 to 2 amps.

CAUTION
The electrolyte level must be maintained at the upper level during the charging cycle; check and refill as necessary.

3. After the battery has been charged for about 8 hours, turn the charger off, disconnect the leads and check the specific gravity. It should be within the limits specified in **Table 4**. If it is and remains stable for 1 hour, the battery is considered charged.
4. Clean the battery terminals, electrical cable connectors and surrounding case and tray and reinstall them in the bike, reversing the removal steps. Coat the battery terminals with Vaseline or silicone spray to retard corrosion and decomposition of the terminals.

CAUTION
Route the breather tube so that it does not drain onto any part of the bike's frame. The tube must be free of bends or twists as any restriction may pressurize the battery and damage it.

New Battery Installation

The battery for these models has a unique shape to the lower case due to the bike's frame configuration. When replacing the battery make sure the new battery has the same lower case contour.

When replacing the old battery with a new one, be sure to charge it completely (specific gravity 1.260-1.280) before installing it in the bike. Failure to do so or using the battery with a low electrolyte level will permanently damage the new battery.

PERIODIC LUBRICATION

Oil

Oil is graded according to its viscosity, which is an indication of how thick it is. The Society of Automotive Engineers (SAE) system distinguishes oil viscosity by numbers. Thick oils have higher viscosity numbers than thin oils. For example, an SAE 5 oil is a thin oil while an SAE 90 oil is relatively thick.

Grease

A good quality grease (preferably waterproof) should be used. Water does not wash grease off parts as easily as it washes oil off. In addition, grease maintains its lubricating qualities better than oil on long and strenuous rides. In a pinch, though, the wrong lubricant is better than none at all. Correct the situation as soon as possible.

Engine Oil Level Check

Engine oil level is checked with the dipstick located at the rear of the right-hand crankcase/clutch cover (**Figure 7**).
1. Place the bike on level ground and on the centerstand.
2. Start the engine and let it idle for 2-3 minutes.
3. Shut off the engine and let the oil settle.
4. Unscrew the dipstick and wipe it clean. Reinsert the dipstick onto the threads in the hole; do not screw it in.
5. Remove the dipstick and check the oil level. The level should be between the 2 lines (**Figure 8**) and not above the upper one. If the level is below the lower line, add the recommended type engine oil to correct the level.

Engine Oil and Filter Change

The factory-recommended oil and filter change interval is listed in **Table 1**. This assumes that the motorcycle is operated in moderate climates. In extreme climates, oil should be changed every 30 days. The time interval is more important than the mileage interval because acids formed by combustion blow-by will contaminate the oil even if the motorcycle is not run for several months. If the motorcycle is operated under dusty conditions, the oil will get dirty more quickly and should be changed more frequently than recommended.

Use only a high-quality detergent motor oil with an API rating of SE or SF. The quality rating is stamped or printed on top of the can (**Figure 9**). Try to use the same brand of oil at each change. Use of oil additives is not recommended as it may cause clutch slippage. Refer to **Figure 10** for correct oil viscosity to use under anticipated ambient temperatures (not engine oil temperature).

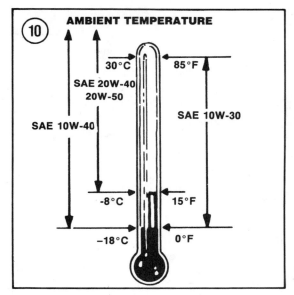

> *CAUTION*
> *Do not add any friction-reducing additives to the oil as they will cause clutch slippage. Also do not use an engine oil with graphite added. The use of graphite oil will void any applicable Honda warranty. It is not established at this time if graphite will build up on the clutch friction plates and cause clutch problems. Until further testing is done by the oil and motorcycle industries, do not use this type of oil.*

To change the engine oil and filter you will need the following:
  a. Drain pan.
  b. Funnel.
  c. Can opener or pour spout.
  d. 17 mm wrench (drain plug).
  e. Strap wrench for the oil filter.
  f. 3 quarts of oil.
  g. New oil filter.

There are a number of ways to discard the old oil safely. Some service stations and oil retailers will accept your used oil for recycling; some may even give you money for it. Never drain the oil onto the ground.

1. Start the engine and let it reach operating temperature; 15-20 minutes of stop-and-go riding is usually sufficient.

2. Turn the engine off and place the bike on the centerstand.

3. Place a drain pan under the engine. Place the drain pan so it is under the crankcase drain plug and the oil filter.

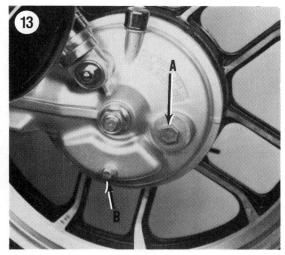

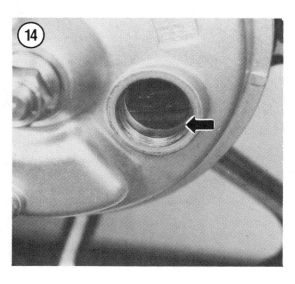

4. Remove the oil pan drain plug (**Figure 11**). Using a hammer and nail, carefully punch a hole in the bottom of the oil filter and allow the oil to drain out of the oil filter. Remove the oil filler cap (**Figure 7**); this will speed up the flow of oil.

5. Let the oil drain for at least 15-20 minutes. During this time, push the starter button a couple of times to help drain any remaining oil.

> *CAUTION*
> *Do not let the engine start and run without oil in the crankcase.*

6. Inspect the sealing washer on the crankcase drain plug. Replace if its condition is in doubt.

7. Install the oil pan drain plug and tighten to 35-40 N•m (25-29 ft.-lb.).

> *NOTE*
> *Before removing the oil filter, thoroughly clean off all road dirt and oil around it.*

8. Use a strap wrench and unscrew the oil filter from the crankcase (**Figure 12**).

> *CAUTION*
> *Prior to installing the oil filter, clean off the mating surface of the crankcase—do not allow any road dirt to enter into the oil system.*

9. Apply a light coat of new engine oil to the rubber seal on the new oil filter and screw on the oil filter. Tighten the oil filter to approximately 18 N•m (12 ft.-lb.).

10. Insert a funnel into the oil fill hole and fill the engine with the correct viscosity and quantity of oil. Refer to **Table 5**.

11. Screw in the oil filler cap securely.

12. Start the engine, let it run at moderate speed and check for leaks.

13. Turn the engine off and check for correct oil level; adjust as necessary.

Final Drive Oil Level Check

The final drive case should be cool. If the bike has been run, allow it to cool down (minimum of 10 minutes), then check the oil level. When checking or changing the final drive oil, do not allow any dirt or foreign matter to enter the case opening.

1. Place the bike on the centerstand on a level surface.

2. Wipe the area around the oil filler cap clean and unscrew the oil filler cap (A, **Figure 13**).

3. The oil level is correct if the oil is up to the lower edge of the filler cap hole (**Figure 14**). If the

oil level is low, add hypoid gear oil rated API GL-5 until the oil level is correct.

NOTE
On VT 700C models, use SAE 80 for all temperatures. On all other models, use SAE 90 for ambient temperatures above 5° C (41° F) or SAE 80 for ambient temperatures below 5° C (41° F).

4. Inspect the O-ring seal (**Figure 15**) on the oil filler cap. If it is deteriorated or starting to harden it must be replaced.
5. Install the oil filler cap.

Final Drive Oil Change

The factory-recommended oil change interval is listed in **Table 1**.
To drain the oil you will need the following:
a. Drain pan.
b. Funnel.
c. Approximately 120-130 cc (4.1-4.4 oz.) of hypoid gear oil.
Discard old oil as outlined under *Engine Oil and Filter Change* in this chapter.
1. Ride the bike until normal operating temperature is obtained. Usually 15-20 minutes of stop-and-go riding is sufficient.
2. Place the bike on the centerstand.
3. Place a drain pan under the drain plug.
4. Remove the oil filler cap (A, **Figure 13**) and the drain plug (B, **Figure 13**).
5. Let the oil drain for at least 15-20 minutes to ensure that the majority of the oil has drained out.
6. Inspect the sealing washer on the drain plug; replace the sealing washer if necessary.
7. Install the drain plug and tighten it securely.
8. Insert a funnel into the oil filler cap hole.
9A. On 700 cc models, add approximately 130 cc (4.4 oz.) of hypoid gear oil. If you are filling the final drive unit after an overhaul, the capacity is 150 cc (5.1 oz.). Remove the funnel and make sure the oil level is correct.
9B. On 750 cc models, add approximately 130 cc (4.4 oz.) of hypoid gear oil. If you are filling the final drive unit after an overhaul, the capacity is 170 cc (5.8 oz.). Remove the funnel and make sure the oil level is correct.

NOTE
On VT700C models, use SAE 80 for all temperatures. On all other models, use SAE 90 for ambient temperatures above 5° C (41° F) or SAE 80 for ambient temperatures below 5° C (41° F).

NOTE
In order to measure the correct amount of fluid, use a plastic baby bottle. These have measurements in cubic centimeters (cc) and fluid ounces (oz.) on the side.

10. Install the oil filler cap.
11. Test ride the bike and check for oil leaks. After the test ride recheck the oil level as described in this chapter and readjust if necessary.

Front Fork Oil Change

There is no factory-recommended fork oil change interval but it's a good practice to change the oil every 12,800 km (8,000 miles) or when it becomes contaminated.

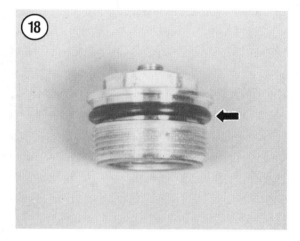

WARNING
Always bleed off all air pressure in Step 1; failure to do so may cause personal injury when disassembling the fork.

NOTE
Release the air pressure gradually in Step 1. If released too fast, fork oil will spurt out with the air. Protect your eyes and clothing accordingly.

1. Remove each fork top cover (**Figure 16**) and bleed off *all* air pressure from each fork by depressing the valve stem.

2. Place wood block(s) under the engine to support it securely with the front wheel off the ground.

3. Unscrew the fork top cap slowly as it is under pressure from the fork spring.

4. Place a drain pan under the drain screw and remove the drain screw (**Figure 17**). Allow the oil to drain for at least 5 minutes. *Never* reuse the oil.

CAUTION
Do not allow the fork oil to come into contact with any of the brake components.

5. Inspect the gasket on the drain screw; replace it if necessary. Install the drain screw.
6. Repeat Steps 3-5 for the other fork.
7. Refill each fork leg with the specified quantity of DEXRON automatic transmission fluid or 10W fork oil. Refer to **Table 6** for specified quantity.

NOTE
In order to measure the correct amount of fluid, use a plastic baby bottle. These have measurements in cubic centimeters (cc) and fluid ounces (oz.) on the side.

8. Inspect the O-ring seal (**Figure 18**) on the fork top cap; replace if necessary.
9. Install the fork top cap while pushing down on the spring. Start the fork top cap slowly; don't cross thread it. Tighten the fork top cap to 15-30 N•m (11-22 ft.-lb.).
10. Inflate the front forks to 0-40 kPa (0-6 psi). Do not use compressed air; only use a small hand-operated air pump.

WARNING
Never use any type of compressed gas as an explosion may be lethal. Never heat the fork assembly with a torch or place it near an open flame or extreme heat as this will also result in an explosion.

11. Install the fork top cover on each fork leg.
12. Road test the bike and check for leaks.

Throttle Control
Cable Lubrication

The throttle control cables should be lubricated at the interval indicated in **Table 1**. They should also be inspected at this time for fraying and the cable sheath should be checked for chafing. The cables are relatively inexpensive and should be replaced when found to be faulty.

The throttle control cables can be lubricated either with oil or with any of the popular cable lubricants and a cable lubricator. The first method requires more time and complete lubrication of the entire cable is less certain.

Examine the exposed end of the inner cable. If it is dirty or the cable feels gritty when moved up and down in its housing, first spray it with a lubricant/solvent such as LPS-25 or WD-40. Let this solvent drain out, then proceed with the following steps.

Oil method

1. Remove the screws that clamp the throttle control/switch housing together to gain access to the cable ends. Disconnect the cables from the throttle grip assembly (**Figure 19**).
2. Make a cone of stiff paper and tape it to the end of the cable sheath (**Figure 20**).
3. Hold the cable upright and pour a small amount of thin oil (SAE 10W-30) into the cone. Work the cable in and out of the sheath for several minutes to help the oil work its way down to the end of the cable.

NOTE
To avoid a mess, place a shop cloth at the end of the cable to catch the oil as it runs out.

4. Remove the cone, reconnect the cable and adjust the cable(s) as described in this chapter.

Lubricator method

1. Remove the screws that clamp the throttle control/switch housing together to gain access to the cable ends. Disconnect the cables from the throttle grip assembly (**Figure 19**).
2. Attach a lubricator following the manufacturer's instructions.
3. Insert the nozzle of the lubricant can in the lubricator, press the button on the can and hold it down until the lubricant begins to flow out of the other end of the cable.

NOTE
Place a shop cloth at the end of the cables to catch all excess lubricant that will flow out.

4. Remove the lubricator, reconnect the cables and adjust the cables as described in this chapter.

Speedometer Cable Lubrication

Lubricate the cable every year or whenever needle operation is erratic.
1. Unscrew the retaining collar (**Figure 21**) and remove the cable from the instrument.
2. Pull the cable from the cable sheath.
3. If the grease on the cable is contaminated, thoroughly clean off all old grease.
4. Thoroughly coat the cable with a good grade multipurpose grease and reinstall into the sheath.

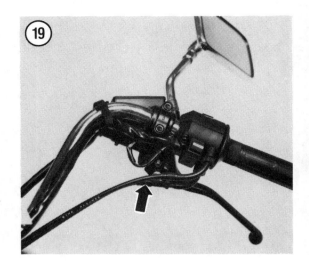

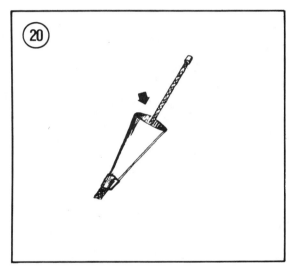

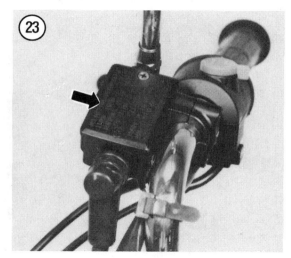

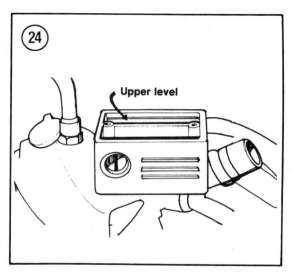

Upper level

5. Make sure the cable is correctly seated into the drive unit at the wheel.

6. Insert the cable into the instrument and screw the retaining collar on securely.

3

PERIODIC MAINTENANCE

Disc Brake Fluid Level

The fluid level in the front brake reservoir should be up to the upper mark within the reservoir. This upper level mark is only visible when the master cylinder top cover is removed. If the brake fluid level reaches the lower level mark (**Figure 22**), visible through the viewing port on the side of the master cylinder reservoir, the fluid level must be corrected by adding fresh brake fluid.

1. Place the bike on level ground and position the handlebars so the master cylinder reservoir is level.

2. Clean any dirt from the area around the top cover prior to removing the cover.

3. Remove the top cover (**Figure 23**) and the diaphragm. Add brake fluid until the level is to the upper level line (**Figure 24**) within the master cylinder body. Use fresh brake fluid from a sealed brake fluid container.

WARNING
Only use brake fluid from a sealed container clearly marked DOT 3 only (specified for disc brakes). Others may vaporize and cause brake failure. Do not intermix different brands or types of brake fluid as they may not be compatible. Do not intermix a silicone based (DOT 5) brake fluid as it can cause brake component damage leading to brake system failure.

CAUTION
Be careful when handling brake fluid. Do not spill it on painted or plated surfaces as it will destroy the surface. Wash the area immediately with soapy water and thoroughly rinse it off.

4. Reinstall the diaphragm and the top cover. Tighten the screws securely.

Disc Brake Lines

Check brake lines between the master cylinder and the brake calipers. If there is any leakage, tighten the connections and bleed the brakes as described in Chapter Eleven. If this does not stop the leak or if a brake line is obviously damaged, cracked or chafed, replace the brake line and bleed the system.

Disc Brake Pad Wear

Inspect the brake pads for excessive or uneven wear, scoring and oil or grease on the friction surface. Look at the pads from the top of the caliper assembly (**Figure 25**). Replace the pads if the wear line on the pads reaches the brake disc.

> *NOTE*
> *Always replace all pads in both caliper assemblies at the same time.*

If any of these conditions exist, replace the pads as described in Chapter Eleven.

Disc Brake Fluid Change

Every time the reservoir cap is removed, a small amount of dirt and moisture enters the brake fluid. The same thing happens if a leak occurs or any part of the hydraulic system is loosened or disconnected. Dirt can clog the system and cause unnecessary wear. Water in the brake fluid vaporizes at high temperature, impairing the hydraulic action and reducing the brake's stopping ability.

To maintain peak performance, change the brake fluid as indicated in **Table 1**. To change brake fluid, follow the *Bleeding the Brake System* procedure in Chapter Eleven. Continue adding new fluid to the master cylinder and bleeding out at the calipers until the fluid leaving the calipers is clean and free of contaminants.

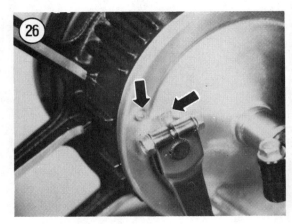

> *WARNING*
> *Only use brake fluid from a sealed container clearly marked DOT 3 only (specified for disc brakes). Others may vaporize and cause brake failure. Do not intermix different brands or types of brake fluid as they may not be compatible. Do not intermix a silicone based (DOT 5) brake fluid as it can cause brake component damage leading to brake system failure.*

Rear Drum Brake Lining

Check the rear brake linings for wear. If the arrow on the brake arm aligns with the raised index mark on the brake backing plate (**Figure 26**) when the brake pedal is applied, the brake linings require replacement.

If replacement is necessary, refer to Chapter Eleven.

Rear Brake Pedal Height Adjustment

The rear brake pedal should be adjusted as indicated in **Table 1**.

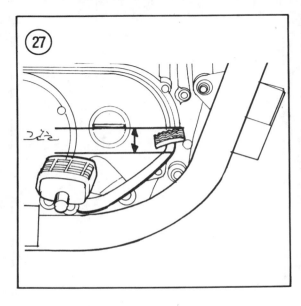

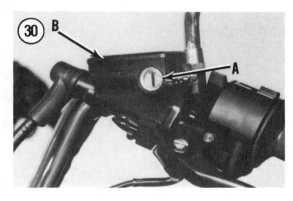

1. Place the bike on the centerstand.
2. Check that the brake pedal is in the at-rest position.
3A. *1983-1985:* Adjust the pedal height so that the brake pedal is 20 mm (3/4 in.) above the top surface of the front footpeg (**Figure 27**).
3B. *1986-on:* Adjust the pedal height so that the brake pedal is 35 mm (1 3/8 in.) above the top surface of the front footpeg (**Figure 27**).
4. To change height position, loosen the locknut and turn the adjuster bolt (**Figure 28**). Tighten the locknut.

Rear Brake Pedal Free Play

Free play is the distance the rear brake pedal travels from the at-rest position to the applied position when the pedal is depressed.

1. Place the bike on the centerstand with the rear wheel off the ground.

2. Adjust the brake pedal to the correct height as described in this chapter.

3. Turn the adjust nut on the end of the brake rod (**Figure 29**) until the pedal has 20-30 mm (3/4-1 1/4 in.) free play.

4. Rotate the rear wheel and check for brake drag.

5. Operate the brake pedal several times to make sure the pedal returns to the at-rest position immediately after release.

Clutch Fluid Level Check

The clutch is hydraulically operated and requires no routine adjustment.

The hydraulic fluid in the clutch master cylinder should be checked as listed in **Table 1** or whenever the level drops, whichever comes first. Bleeding the clutch system and servicing clutch components are covered in Chapter Five.

> *CAUTION*
> *If the clutch operates correctly when the engine is cold or in cool weather, but operates erratically (or not at all) after the engine warms up or in hot weather, there is air in the hydraulic line and the clutch must be bled. Refer to Chapter Five.*

The fluid level in the reservoir should be up to the upper mark within the reservoir. This upper level mark is only visible when the master cylinder top cover is removed. If the fluid level reaches the lower level mark (A, **Figure 30**), visible through the viewing port in the master cylinder reservoir, the fluid level must be corrected by adding fresh hydraulic (brake) fluid.

1. Place the bike on level ground and position the handlebars so the master cylinder reservoir is level.

2. Clean any dirt from the area around the top cover prior to removing the cover.

3. Remove the top cover (B, **Figure 30**) and the diaphragm. Add clutch fluid until the level is to the

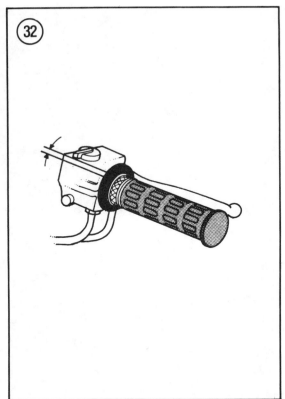

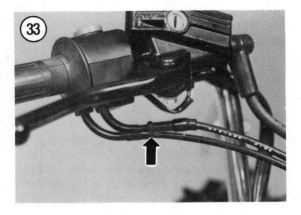

upper level line (**Figure 31**) within the master cylinder body. Use fresh hydraulic fluid from a sealed hydraulic fluid container.

> *WARNING*
> *Only use hydraulic fluid from a sealed container clearly marked DOT 3. Do not intermix different brands or types of hydraulic fluid as they may not be compatable. Do not intermix a silicone based (DOT 5) hydraulic fluid as it can cause clutch component damage leading to clutch release system failure.*

> *CAUTION*
> *Be careful when handling hydraulic fluid. Do not spill it on painted or plated surfaces as it will destroy the surface. Wash the area immediately with soapy water and thoroughly rinse it off.*

4. Reinstall the diaphragm and the top cover. Tighten the screws securely.

Clutch Hydraulic Lines

Check clutch lines between the master cylinder and the clutch slave cylinder. If there is any leakage, tighten the connections and bleed the

clutch as described in Chapter Five. If this does not stop the leak or if a clutch line is obviously damaged, cracked or chafed, replace the clutch line and bleed the system.

Throttle Adjustment and Operation

The throttle grip should have 2-6 mm (1/8-1/4 in.) rotational free play (**Figure 32**). If adjustment is necessary, loosen the locknut and turn the adjuster (**Figure 33**) at the throttle grip in or out to achieve proper free play rotation. Tighten the locknut.

> *NOTE*
> *Minor adjustments can be made at the throttle grip. Major adjustments can be made where the throttle cables attach to the carburetor assembly (**Figure 34**).*

Check the throttle cables from grip to carburetor. Make sure they are not kinked or chafed. Replace as necessary.

Make sure the throttle grip rotates freely from a fully closed to fully open position. Check with the handlebar at center, at full right and at full left. If necessary, remove the throttle grip and apply a lithium base grease to it.

3

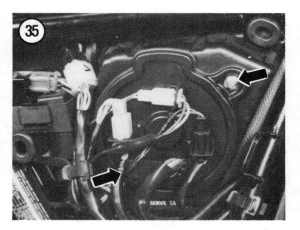

Air Filter
(1983-1985)

The air filter element should be removed and cleaned as indicated in **Table 1**.

The air filter removes dust and abrasive particles from the air before the air enters the carburetors and engine. Without the air filter, very fine particles could enter into the engine and cause rapid wear of the piston rings, cylinder and bearings and might clog small passages in the carburetors. Never run the bike without the air filter element installed.

Proper air filter servicing can do more to ensure long service from your engine than almost any other single item.

1. Remove the right-hand side cover.
2. Remove the screws securing the air filter cover (**Figure 35**).
3. Remove the air filter element holder and the air filter element from the air box.
4. Wipe out the interior of the air box with a shop rag dampened with cleaning solvent. Remove any

foreign matter that may have passed through a broken element.

5. Slide the outer holder off of the element (**Figure 36**) then slide the element off of the inner holder (**Figure 37**).

6. Clean the outer and inner holders in cleaning solvent. Make sure all of the openings are clean and free from dirt to allow maximum air flow. Thoroughly dry both holders with compressed air.

7. Clean the element gently in cleaning solvent until all dirt is removed. Thoroughly dry the element in a clean shop cloth until all solvent residue is removed. Let it dry for about one hour.

NOTE
Inspect the element; if it is torn or broken in any area it should be replaced. Do not run with a damaged element as it may allow dirt to enter the engine.

8. Pour a small amount of SAE 80 gear oil or foam air filter oil onto the air filter element and work it

into the porous foam material. Do not oversaturate the element as too much oil will restrict air flow. The element will be discolored by the oil and should have an even color indicating that the oil is distributed evenly. If foam air filter oil was used, let the element dry for another hour prior to installation. If installed too soon, the chemical carrier in the foam air filter oil will be drawn into the engine and may cause damage.

9. Install the air filter element onto the inner holder then install this assembly into the outer holder.

10. Install the air filter element assembly into the air box.

11. Inspect the gasket on the air filter cover. If it is damaged in any way, replace the gasket.

12. Install the air filter cover and secure it with the screws.

13. Install the right-hand side cover.

Air Filter (1986-on)

The air filter should be removed and replaced as indicated in **Table 1**.

The air filter removes dust and abrasive particles from the air before the air enters the carburetors and engine. Without the air filter, very fine particles could enter into the engine and cause rapid wear of the piston rings, cylinder and bearings and might clog small passages in the carburetors. Never run the bike without the air filter element installed.

These models use a non-serviceable paper air filter element. Replacement of the element at the proper time can do more to ensure long service from your engine that almost any other single item.

1. Carefully pry the plugs (**Figure 38**) out of the air filter case bolts.

2. Remove the 2 air filter case bolts (**Figure 39**).

3. Remove the air filter decorative plate (**Figure 40**).

4. Remove the air filter cover (**Figure 41**).

5. See **Figure 42**. Remove the 3 screws (A) and remove the holder (B). Lift the air filter element (C) out of the case.

6. Replace the element at the intervals specified in **Table 1**.

> *CAUTION*
> *If the air filter element was removed before the replacement interval, inspect the element. If it is torn or broken in any area it should be replaced. Do not run the engine with a damaged element as it may allow dirt to enter the engine.*

7. Install the element by reversing these steps. Note the following.

8. When installing the decorative plate, insert the tab on the right-hand side of the plate (**Figure 43**) into the notch in the air filter cover. Then push the plate against the cover and install the 2 case bolts.

Fuel Filter

The separate inline fuel filter used on this model removes particles in the fuel which might otherwise enter the carburetors. This could cause the float needle(s) to stay in the open position or clog one of the jets. Refer to Chapter Six for replacement procedure.

Fuel Line Inspection

Inspect the fuel lines from the fuel tanks to the carburetor. If any are cracked or starting to deteriorate they must be replaced. Make sure the small hose clamps are in place and holding securely.

> *WARNING*
> *A damaged or deteriorated fuel line presents a very dangerous fire hazard to both the rider and the bike if fuel should spill onto a hot engine or exhaust pipe.*

Cooling System Inspection

At the interval indicated in **Table 1**, the following items should be checked. If you do not have the test equipment, the tests can be done by a Honda dealer, automobile dealer, radiator shop or service station.

1. Have the radiator cap pressure tested (**Figure 44**). The specified radiator cap relief pressure is 0.75-1.05 kg/cm² (10.7-14.9 psi). The cap must be able to sustain this pressure for 6 seconds. Replace the radiator cap if it does not hold pressure or if the relief pressure is too high or too low.

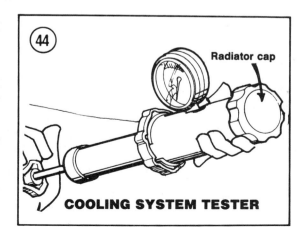

Radiator cap

COOLING SYSTEM TESTER

2. Leave the radiator cap off and have the entire cooling system pressure tested (**Figure 45**). The entire cooling system should be pressurized up to, but not exceeding, 1.05 kg/cm² (14.9 psi). The system must be able to sustain this pressure for 6 seconds. Replace or repair any components that fail this test.

NOTE
CAUTION
If test pressure exceeds the specifications the radiator may be damaged.

3. Test the specific gravity of the coolant with an antifreeze tester (**Figure 46**) to ensure adequate temperature and corrosion protection. Never let the mixture become less than 40% antifreeze or corrosion protection will be impaired.
4. Check all cooling system hoses for damage or deterioration. Replace any hose that is questionable. Make sure all hose clamps are tight.
5. Carefully clean any road dirt, bugs, mud, etc. from the radiator core. Use a whisk broom, compressed air or low-pressure water. If the radiator has been hit by a small rock or other item, *carefully* straighten out the fins with a screwdriver.

NOTE
If the radiator has been damaged across approximately 20% or more of the frontal area, the radiator should be recored or replaced.

Coolant Change

The cooling system should be completely drained and refilled at the interval indicated in **Table 1**.

CAUTION
Use only a high quality ethylene glycol antifreeze specifically labeled for use with aluminum engines. Do not use an alcohol-based antifreeze.

In areas where freezing temperatures occur, add a higher percentage of antifreeze to protect the system to temperatures far below those likely to occur. **Table 7** lists the recommended amount of antifreeze for protection at various ambient temperatures. The following procedure must be performed when the engine is cool.

CAUTION
Be careful not to spill antifreeze on painted surfaces as it will destroy the surface. Wash immediately with soapy water and rinse thoroughly with clean water.

1. Place the bike on the centerstand.
2. Remove the seat and both side covers.
3. Remove the main fuel tank as described in Chapter Six.
4. Remove the radiator filler neck cover. See **Figure 47** (1983-1985) or **Figure 48** (1986-on).
5. *1983-1985:* Remove the Allen set screw on the side of the radiator cap.
6. Remove the radiator cap (**Figure 49**). This will speed up the draining process.
7. *1983-1985:* Loosen the bleed bolt on the thermostat cover (**Figure 50**).

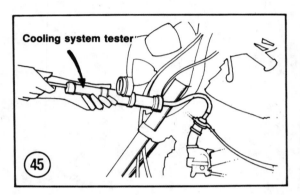

Cooling system tester

45

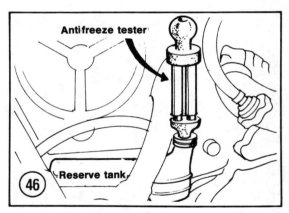

Antifreeze tester

Reserve tank

46

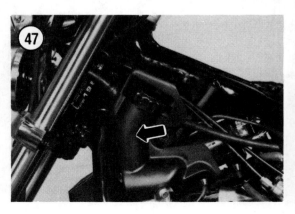

47

8. Place a drain pan under the frame on the left-hand side of the bike under the water pump. Remove the drain screw (**Figure 51**) and sealing washer on the water pump cover. Do not install the drain screw yet.

9. Take the bike off the centerstand and tip the bike from side to side to drain any residual coolant from the cooling system. Place the bike back onto the centerstand.

10. Install the drain screw and sealing washer on the water pump cover. Tighten the bleed screw on the thermostat housing (1983-1985).

11. Refill the radiator. Add the coolant through the radiator filler neck, not the reserve tank. Use the recommended mixture of antifreeze and distilled water; see **Table 7**. Do not install the radiator cap at this time.

12. Start the engine and let it run at idle speed until the engine reaches normal operating temperature. Make sure there are no air bubbles in the coolant and that the coolant level stabilizes at the correct level. Add coolant as necessary.

13. Install the radiator cap.

14. Add coolant to the reserve tank to the correct level.

15. Install the radiator filler neck cover.

16. Install the fuel tank as described in Chapter Six.

17. Test ride the bike and readjust the coolant level in the reserve tank if necessary.

Wheel Bearings

There is no factory-recommended mileage interval for cleaning and repacking the wheel bearings. They should be serviced whenever they are removed from the wheel hub or whenever there is the likelihood of water contamination. The correct service procedures are covered in Chapter Nine and Chapter Ten.

Steering Head Adjustment Check

The steering head is fitted with assembled bearings. It should be checked as indicated in **Table 1**.

Place the bike up on wood block(s) so that the front wheel is off the ground. Hold onto the front fork tubes and gently rock the fork assembly back and forth. If you can feel looseness, the steering stem must be disassembled and adjusted; refer to Chapter Nine.

Front Suspension Check

1. Apply the front brake and pump the forks up and down as vigorously as possible. Check for smooth operation and check for any oil leaks.

2. Make sure the upper and lower fork bridge bolts are tight (**Figure 52**).

3. Make sure the bolts securing the handlebar holders (**Figure 53**) are tight and that the handlebar is secure.

4A. *1983-1985:* Make sure the front axle and axle pinch bolt are tight (**Figure 54**).

4B. *1986-on:* Make sure the front axle holder nuts (**Figure 55**) are tight.

> *CAUTION*
> *If any of the previously mentioned bolts and nuts are loose, refer to Chapter Nine for correct procedures and torque specifications.*

Rear Suspension Check

1. Place the bike on the centerstand.

2. Push hard on the rear wheel (sideways) to check for side play in the rear swing arm bushings.

3. Check the tightness of the upper and lower mounting bolts or nuts (**Figure 56**) on each shock absorber.

4. Make sure the rear axle nut is tight (**Figure 57**).

5. Check the tightness of the rear brake torque arm bolt (**Figure 58**). Make sure the cotter pin is in place.

> *CAUTION*
> *If any of the previously mentioned bolts and nuts are loose, refer to Chapter Ten for correct procedures and torque specifications.*

Nuts, Bolts and Other Fasteners

Constant vibration can loosen many of the fasteners on the motorcycle. Check the tightness of all fasteners, especially those on:

   a. Engine mounting hardware.
   b. Engine crankcase covers.
   c. Handlebar and front forks.
   d. Gearshift lever.
   e. Brake pedal and lever.
   f. Exhaust system.

Sidestand Rubber

The rubber pad on the sidestand kicks the sidestand up if you should forget. If it wears down to the molded line (**Figure 59**), it will no longer be effective and must be replaced.

Remove the bolt and replace the rubber pad with a new one. Be sure the new rubber pad is marked "Over 260 lbs. Only."

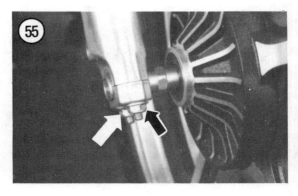

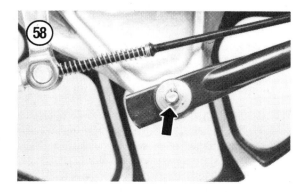

**Crankcase Breather
(1983-1985 U.S. Models Only)**

At the interval indicated in **Table 1** or sooner if a considerable amount of riding is done at full throttle or in the rain, the residue in the breather drain tube should be drained.

Remove the drain plug (**Figure 60**) and drain out all residue. Install the cap; make sure the clamp is tight.

Refer to Chapter Six for complete details on the breather system.

TUNE-UP

A complete tune-up should be performed at the interval indicated in **Table 1** for normal riding. More frequent tune-ups may be required if the bike is ridden primarily in stop-and-go traffic. The purpose of the tune-up is to restore the performance lost due to normal wear and deterioration of parts.

Table 8 summarizes tune-up specifications.

The spark plugs should be routinely replaced at every tune-up. In addition, this is a good time to clean the air filter element. Have the new parts on hand before you begin.

The cam chain tensioners are completely automatic and do not require any periodic adjustment. There are no provisions for tensioner adjustment on the engine.

The engine is equipped with a hydraulic valve adjuster train system and requires no periodic valve adjustment. The only time any type of adjustment is necessary is after a cylinder head overhaul; see Chapter Four.

The air filter element should be cleaned or replaced prior to doing other tune-up procedures, as described in this chapter.

Because different systems in an engine interact, the procedure should be done in the following order:

a. Clean or replace the air filter element.
b. Run a compression test.
c. Check or replace the spark plugs.
d. Check the ignition timing.
e. Synchronize the carburetors.
f. Adjust the carburetor idle speed.

To perform a tune-up on your Honda, you will need the following tools:

a. 18 mm spark plug wrench.
b. Socket wrench and assorted sockets.
c. Compression gauge.
d. Spark plug wire feeler gauge and gapper tool.
e. Ignition timing light.
f. Tune-up tachometer.
g. Manometer (carburetor synchronization tool).

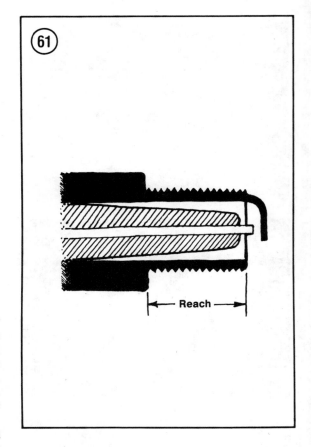

Compression Test

At every other tune-up check cylinder compression. Record the results and compare them at the next tune-up. A running record will show trends in deterioration so that corrective action can be taken before complete failure occurs.

The results, when properly interpreted, can indicate general cylinder, piston ring and valve condition.

1. Warm the engine to normal operating temperature. Shut off the engine. Make sure that the choke valve and throttle valve are completely open.
2. Place the bike on the centerstand.
3. Disconnect the spark plug wires from all spark plugs.
4. Remove only one of the spark plugs from each cylinder. Remove the one next to the exhaust pipe outlet as it will be easier to connect a tester to that hole. Leave the other spark plug in place as it is necessary to seal off the cylinder.
5. Connect the compression tester to one cylinder following manufacturer's instructions.
6. Using the starter, crank the engine over until there is no further rise in pressure. Maximum pressure is usually reached within 4-7 seconds of engine cranking.

NOTE
Do not turn the engine over more than absolutely necessary. When spark plug leads are disconnected, the electronic ignition will produce the highest voltage possible and the coils may overheat and be damaged.

7. Remove the tester and record the reading.

8. Repeat Step 5 and Step 6 for the other cylinder.

When interpreting the results, actual readings are not as important as the difference between the readings. Readings should be between the limits specified in **Table 8**. A maximum difference of 4 kg/cm^2 (57 psi) between the 2 cylinders is acceptable. Greater differences indicate worn or broken rings, leaking or sticking valves, a blown head gasket(s) or a combination of all.

If compression readings do not differ between the 2 cylinders by more than 10 psi, the rings and valves are in good condition.

If a low reading (10% or more) is obtained on one of the cylinders, it indicates valve or ring trouble. To determine which, insert a small funnel into the spark plug hole and pour about a teaspoon of engine oil through it onto the top of the piston. Turn the engine over once to clear some of the excess oil, then take another compression test and record the reading. If the compression returns to normal, the valves are good but the rings are defective on that cylinder. If compression does not increase, the valves require servicing. A valve could be hanging open or a piece of carbon could be on a valve seat.

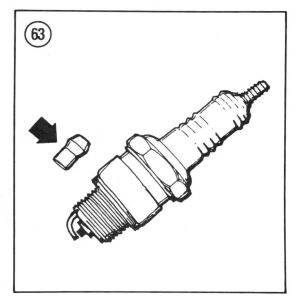

the portion of the insulator within the cylinder after the plug has been in service.

In areas where seasonal temperature variations are great, the factory recommends a "2-plug system"—cold plugs for hard summer riding and hot plugs for slower winter operation.

The reach (length) of a plug is also important. A longer than normal plug could interfere with the valves and pistons, causing permanent and severe damage. Refer to **Figure 61**. The recommended spark plugs are listed in **Table 8**.

Spark Plug Removal/Cleaning

There are 2 spark plugs per cylinder. Be sure to use a spark plug wrench with a rubber insert that grabs onto the spark plug. Do not use a deep socket as it will be difficult to remove and install the spark plugs in the deep wells.

1. Grasp the spark plug lead (A, **Figure 62**) as near to the plug as possible and pull it off the plug. If the boot is stuck to the plug, twist it slightly to break it loose.

2. Blow away any dirt that has accumulated in the spark plug wells. This is especially true for the spark plugs that are buried deep in the cylinder head (B, **Figure 62**).

CAUTION
The dirt could fall into the cylinders when the plugs are removed, causing serious engine damage.

3. Remove spark plugs with an 18 mm spark plug wrench.

NOTE
If plugs are difficult to remove, apply penetrating oil around base of plugs and let it soak in about 10-20 minutes.

4. Inspect spark plug carefully. Look for a plug with broken center porcelain, excessively eroded electrodes and excessive carbon or oil fouling. Replace such plugs. If deposits are light, the plug may be cleaned in solvent with a wire brush or in a special spark plug sandblast cleaner. Regap the plug as explained in this chapter.

Spark Plug Gapping and Installation

New plugs should be carefully gapped to ensure a reliable, consistent spark. You must use a special spark plug gapping tool with a wire feeler gauge.

Be sure to replace all 4 spark plugs at the same time; all 4 plugs must be of the same heat range.

1. Remove the new plugs from the box. Do *not* screw in the small piece that is loose in each box (**Figure 63**); it is not used.

Spark Plug Selection

Spark plugs are available in various heat ranges, hotter or colder than plugs originally installed at the factory.

Select plugs of a heat range designed for the loads and temperature conditions under which the bike will be run. The use of incorrect heat ranges can cause seized pistons, scored cylinder walls or damaged piston crowns.

In general, use a hot plug for low speeds, low engine loads and low temperatures. Use a cold plug for high speeds, high engine loads and high temperatures. The plug should operate hot enough to burn off unwanted deposits, but not so hot that it is damaged or causes preignition. A spark plug of the correct heat range will show a light tan color on

2. Insert a wire feeler gauge between the center and the side electrode of each plug (**Figure 64**). The correct gap is 0.8-0.9 mm (0.031-0.035 in.). If the gap is correct, you will feel a slight drag as you pull the wire through. If there is no drag or the gauge won't pass through, bend the side electrode *with the gapping tool* (**Figure 65**) to set the proper gap.

3. Put a *small* drop of oil or aluminum anti-seize compound on the threads of each spark plug.

NOTE
On spark plugs that are buried in a deep well, make sure that the gasket is firmly attached to the spark plug so it will not fall off in the well. If installing a used gasket that will not stay on the spark plug, apply a light coat of cold grease to the gasket and install it on the spark plug.

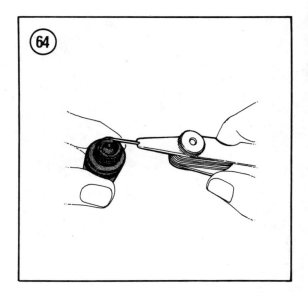

4. Install the spark plug into a spark plug wrench (and extension for some installations).

5. Screw each spark plug in by hand until it seats. Very little effort is required. If force is necessary, you have a plug cross-threaded; unscrew it and try again.

6. Tighten the spark plugs an additional 1/2 turn after the gasket has made contact with the head. If you are reinstalling old, regapped plugs and are reusing the old gasket, only tighten an additional 1/4 turn.

NOTE
Do not overtighten. This will only squash the gasket and destroy its sealing ability.

7. Install each spark plug lead; make sure the lead is on tight.

8. On spark plugs that are buried deep in the cylinder head, make sure that the rubber boot surrounding the spark plug lead is seated correctly (B, **Figure 62**). They are designed to keep out moisture and dirt.

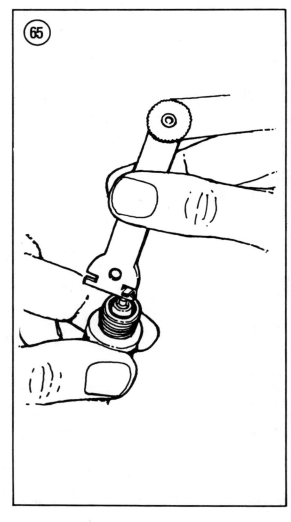

Reading Spark Plugs

Much information about engine and spark plug performance can be determined by careful examination of the spark plugs. This information is only valid after performing the following steps.

1. Ride the bike a short distance at full throttle in any gear.

2. Turn the engine kill switch to the OFF position before closing the throttle and simultaneously pull in the clutch or shift to NEUTRAL; coast and brake to a stop.

3. Remove the spark plugs and examine them. Compare them to **Figure 66**. If the insulator is

SPARK PLUG CONDITION

(66)

NORMAL

- Identified by light tan or gray deposits on the firing tip.
- Can be cleaned.

GAP BRIDGED

- Identified by deposit buildup closing gap between electrodes.
- Caused by oil or carbon fouling. If deposits are not excessive, the plug can be cleaned.

OIL FOULED

- Identified by wet black deposits on the insulator shell bore and electrodes.
- Caused by excessive oil entering combustion chamber thorugh worn rings and pistons, excessive clearance between valve guides and stems, or worn or loose bearings. Can be cleaned. If engine is not repaired, use a hotter plug.

CARBON FOULED

- Identified by black, dry, fluffy carbon deposits on insulator tips, exposed shell surfaces and electrodes.
- Caused by too cold a plug, weak ignition, dirty air cleaner, too rich a fuel mixture, or excessive idling. Can be cleaned.

LEAD FOULED

- Identified by dark gray, black, yellow, or tan deposits or a fused glazed coating on the insulator tip.
- Caused by highly leaded gasoline. Can be cleaned.

WORN

- Identified by severely eroded or worn electrodes.
- Caused by normal wear. Should be replaced.

FUSED SPOT DEPOSIT

- Identified by melted or spotty deposits resembling bubbles or blisters.
- Caused by sudden acceleration. Can be cleaned.

OVERHEATING

- Identified by a white or light gray insulator with small black or gray brown spots and with bluish-burnt appearance of electrodes.
- Caused by engine overheating, wrong type of fuel, loose spark plugs, too hot a plug, or incorrect ignition timing. Replace the plug.

PREIGNITION

- Identified by melted electrodes and possibly blistered insulator. Metallic deposits on insulator indicate engine damage.
- Caused by wrong type of fuel, incorrect ignition timing or advance, too hot a plug, burned valves, or engine overheating. Replace the plug.

3

white or burned, the plug is too hot and should be replaced with a colder one.

A too-cold plug will have sooty or oily deposits ranging in color from dark brown to black. Replace with a hotter plug and check for too-rich carburetion or evidence of oil blow-by at the piston rings.

If the plug has a light tan or gray colored deposit and no abnormal gap wear or electrode erosion is evident, the plug and the engine are running properly.

If the plug exhibits a black insulator tip, a damp and oily film over the firing end and a carbon layer over the entire nose, it is oil fouled. An oil fouled plug can be cleaned, but it is better to replace it.

If any one plug is found unsatisfactory, discard and replace all plugs.

Ignition Timing

The Honda V-twins are equipped with a capacitor discharge ignition (CDI) system. This system uses no breaker points and is non-adjustable. The timing should be checked to make sure all ignition components are operating correctly.

Incorrect ignition timing can cause a drastic loss of engine performance and efficiency. It may also cause overheating.

Before starting on this procedure, check all electrical connections related to the ignition system. Make sure all connections are tight and free of corrosion and that all ground connections are tight.

1. Start the engine and let it reach normal operating temperature. Shut the engine off.
2. Place the bike on the centerstand.
3. Remove the timing cover on the right-hand rear crankcase cover (**Figure 67**).
4. Connect a portable tachometer following the manufacturer's instructions. The bike's tachometer is not accurate enough in the low rpm range for this adjustment.
5. Connect a timing light to one of the spark plugs on the front cylinder following the manufacturer's instructions.
6. Fill in the timing marks on the pulse generator rotor with white grease pencil or typewriter white correction fluid. This will make the marks more visible.
7. Start the engine and let it idle at the speed listed in **Table 8**.
8. Aim the timing light at the timing hole in the crankcase cover and pull the trigger. If the timing mark "F" aligns with the fixed pointer on the crankcase cover (**Figure 68**), the timing is correct.

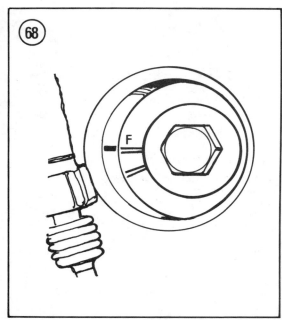

9. If the timing is incorrect, refer to Chapter Seven and check the spark units and the pulse generator. There is no method for adjusting ignition timing.
10. Shut off the engine and disconnect the timing light and portable tachometer. Install the timing cover.

Carburetor Idle Mixture

The idle mixture (pilot screw) is preset at the factory and is *not* to be reset. This pertains to both carburetors. Do not adjust the pilot screws unless the carburetors have been overhauled; refer to Chapter Six.

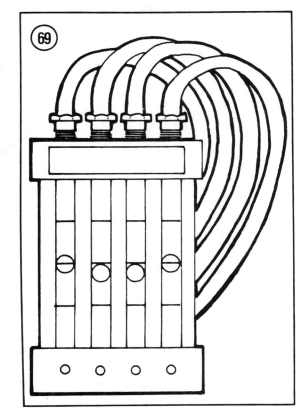

This procedure requires special tools. You will need a mercury manometer (carb-sync tool). This is a tool that measures the manifold vacuum for both cylinders simultaneously. A carb-sync tool (**Figure 69**) can be purchased from a Honda dealer, motorcycle supply store or mail order firm.

3

NOTE
When purchasing this tool, check that it is equipped with restrictors. These restrictors keep the mercury from being drawn into the engine when engine rpm is increased during the adjustment procedure. If the mercury is drawn into the engine the tool will have to be replaced.

1. Start the engine and let it warm up to normal operating temperature. Ten minutes of stop-and-go riding is usually sufficient. Shut off the engine.
2. Place the bike on the centerstand.
3. Remove both side covers and the seat.
4. Remove the fuel tank as described in Chapter Six. There should be enough fuel left in the float bowls to run the bike for this procedure.

WARNING
*Do **not** rig up a temporary fuel supply as this presents a real fire danger. If you start to run out of fuel during the test, shut off the engine and momentarily install the fuel tank to refill the carburetor float bowls, then proceed with the test.*

5A. *1983-1985:* Remove the vacuum plug, consisting of a screw and flat washer, from each cylinder head (**Figure 70**).
5B. *1986-on:* Remove the vacuum plug (consisting of a screw and flat washer) from the front cylinder head (**Figure 71**). Disconnect the vacuum hose (**Figure 72**) from the rear cylinder head.
6. Install the vacuum line adapters into the vacuum hole in each cylinder head.

NOTE
Most carb-sync tools are made for 4-cylinder engines. Use the vacuum lines for No. 1 (front cylinder) and No. 2 (rear cylinder).

7. Connect the vacuum lines from the carb-sync tool, following the manufacturer's instructions. Most carb-sync tools have the cylinder number on them adjacent to each tube containing mercury.

Carburetor Synchronization

When the carburetors are properly synchronized the engine will warm up faster and there will be an improvement in throttle response, performance and mileage.

Prior to synchronizing the carburetors, the air filter element must be clean and valve clearances must be properly adjusted. The ignition timing must also be checked to make sure all components are operating correctly.

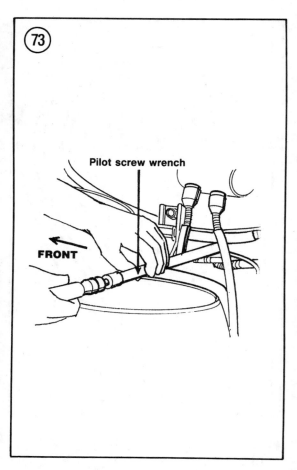

Pilot screw wrench

FRONT

NOTE
The left-hand carburetor has no synchronization screw. The right-hand carburetor must be synchronized to it. The left-hand side refers to a rider sitting on the seat facing forward.

8. Start the engine and let it idle at the idle speed listed in **Table 8.** If necessary, adjust the idle speed as described under *Idle Speed Adjustment* in this chapter.

9. If the difference in gauge readings is 40 mm Hg (1.6 in. Hg) or less between the 2 cylinders, the carburetors are considered synchronized. If not, proceed as follows.

NOTE
*On 1986-on models, the Honda pilot screw wrench (No. 07908-4220201) is required for adjustment. See **Figure 73.***

10. Turn the synchronization adjusting screw on the right-hand carburetor. See **Figure 74** (1983-1985) or **Figure 75** (1986-on).

NOTE
***Figure 74** and **Figure 75** are shown with the carburetor assembly removed for clarity. Do not remove the carburetor assembly for this procedure.*

CAUTION
If your carb-sync tool is not equipped with restrictors, open and close the throttle very gently to avoid sucking mercury into the engine. If this happens, it will not harm the engine but will render the tool useless.

NOTE
To gain the utmost in performance and efficiency from the engine, adjust the carburetors so that the gauge readings are as close to each other as possible.

11. Shut off the engine and remove the vacuum lines and adapters. Install the screws and washers into the vacuum ports in the cylinder heads. Make sure they are in tight to prevent a vacuum leak. On 1986-on models, reconnect the vacuum line (**Figure 72**) at the rear cylinder.

12. Install the fuel tank, if removed.

13. Install the seat and side covers.

14. Restart the engine and readjust the idle speed, if necessary, as described in this chapter.

Idle Speed Adjustment

Before making this adjustment, the air filter element must be clean, the carburetors must be synchronized and the engine must have adequate compression. Otherwise, this procedure cannot be done properly.

1. Attach a portable tachometer following the manufacturer's instructions.

NOTE
The bike's tachometer is not accurate enough in the low rpm range for this adjustment.

2. Start the engine and let it warm up to normal operating temperature.

3A. *1983-1985:* Set the idle speed by turning the large black plastic idle speed stop screw (**Figure 76**) in to increase or out to decrease idle speed. The correct idle speed is listed in **Table 8**.

3B. *1986-on:* Set the idle speed by turning the large black plastic idle speed stop screw (**Figure 77**) in to increase or out to decrease idle speed. The correct idle speed is listed in **Table 8**.

NOTE
Figure 77 shows the idle speed stop screw on 1986-on models with the air filter case removed for clarity. Do not remove the air filter case when performing this adjustment.

4. Open and close the throttle a couple of times. Check for variations in idle speed and readjust if necessary.

WARNING
*With the engine idling, move the handlebar from side to side. If idle speed increases during this movement, the throttle cables may need adjusting or they may be incorrectly routed through the frame. Correct this problem immediately. Do **not** ride the bike in this unsafe condition.*

5. Shut off the engine and disconnect the portable tachometer.

Table 1 SERVICE INTERVALS *

Every 600 miles **(1,000 km) or 6 months**	• Check engine oil level • Check battery specific gravity and electrolyte level • Check hydraulic fluid level in brake master cylinder • Check hydraulic fluid level in clutch master cylinder • Lubricate rear brake pedal and shift lever • Lubricate side and center stand pivot points • Inspect front steering for looseness • Check wheel bearings for smooth operation • Check wheel runout
Every 4,000 miles **(6,400 km)**	• Clean air cleaner element (1983-1985) • Replace spark plugs • Check and adjust throttle operation and free play • Adjust rear brake pedal heigt and free play • Clean fuel shutoff valve and filter • Check hydraulic fluid level in brake master cylinder • Check hydraulic fluid level in clutch master cylinder • Inspect brake pads and linings for wear • Inspect crankcase breather hose for cracks or loose • hose clamps; drain out all residue • Inspect fuel line for chafed, cracked or swollen ends • Check engine mounting bolts for tightness • Check all suspension components
Every 8,000 miles **(12,800 km)**	• Check ignition timing • Check and adjust the carburetors • Check and synchronize the carburetors • Check and adjust the choke • Run a compression test • Change engine oil and filter • Inspect fuel lines for wetness or damage • Inspect the radiator for damage or leakage • Inspect entire brake system for leaks or damage • Change front fork oil • Inspect oil level in final drive unit • Inspect wheel bearings • Inspect and repack the steering head bearings • Inspect evaporative emission control system • Lubricate the speedometer drive cable • Lubricate final drive splines • Check and adjust headlight aim
Every 12,00 miles **(19,200 km)**	• Replace air cleaner element (1986-on) • Change hydraulic fluid in clutch master cylinder • Change hydraulic fluid in brake master cyinder

(continued)

Table 1 SERVICE INTERVALS* (continued)

Every 24,000 miles (38,000 km)	• Replace fuel filter • Change oil in final drive unit • Change hydraulic fluid in clutch master cylinder • Change coolant
Every 4 years	• Replace all hydraulic brake hoses • Replace the hydraulic clutch hose assembly

* This Honda factory maintenance schedule should be considered as a guide to general maintenance and lubrication intervals. Harder than normal use and exposure to mud, water, sand, high humidity, etc. will naturally dictate more frequent attention to most maintenance items.

Table 2 TIRE INFLATION PRESSURE (COLD)

Tire size	Air pressure	
	Normal	Maximum load limit*
Front 110/90-19	32 psi (2.25 kg/cm²)	32 psi (2.25 kg/cm²)
Rear 140/90-15	32 psi (2.25 kg/cm²)	40 psi (2.80 kg/cm²)

* Up to maximum load limit of 200 lb. (89 kg) including total weight of motorcycle with accessories, rider(s) and luggage.

Table 3 FRONT FORK AIR PRESSURE

Normal	Maximum*
0-6 psi (0-0.4 kg/cm²)	43 psi (4 kg/cm²)

* Do not exceed the maximum air pressure or internal parts of the fork will be damaged.

Table 4 STATE OF CHARGE

Specific Gravity	State of Charge
1.110-1.130	Discharged
1.140-1.160	Almost discharged
1.170-1.190	One-quarter charged
1.200-1.220	One-half charged
1.230-1.250	Three-quarters charged
1.260-1.280	Fully charged

Table 5 ENGINE OIL CAPACITY

Oil and filter change	3.0 liter (3.2 U.S. qt., 2.6 Imp. qt.)
At overhaul	3.5 liter (3.7 U.S. qt., 3.1 Imp. qt.)

Table 6 FRONT FORK OIL CAPACITY *

VT700C, VT750C	
1983-1985	467.5-472.5 cc (15.82-15.99 oz.)
1986-on	442.5-447.5 cc (14.99-15.16 oz.)

* Capacity for each fork leg.

Table 7 ANTIFREEZE PROTECTION AND CAPACITY

Temperature	Antifreeze-to-water ratio
Above −25° F (-32° C)	45/55
Above −34° F (−37° C)	50/50
Above −48° F (−44.5° C)	55/45
Coolant capacity	
1983-1985	
Total system	2.1 liters (2.22 qt.)
Radiator and engine	1.7 liters (1.8 qt.)
Reserve tank	0.4 liters (0.42 qt.)
1986-on	
Total	1.83 liters (1.92 qt.)
Radiator and engine	1.56 liters (1.64 qt.)
Reserve tank	0.27 liters (0.28 qt.)

Table 8 TUNE-UP SPECIFICATIONS

Compression pressure (at sea level)	
1983-1985	12.0 ± 2.0 kg/cm² (171 $\pm$ 28 psi)
1986-on	13.0 ± 2.0 kg/cm² (185 $\pm$ 28 psi)
Spark plug type	
1983-1985	
Standard heat range	ND X24EPR-U9 or NGK DPR8EA-9
Cold weather *	ND X22EPR-U9 or NGK DPR7EA-9
Extended high-speed riding	ND X27EPR-U9 or NGK DPR9EA-9

(continued)

Table 8 TUNE-UP SPECIFICATIONS (continued)

Spark plug type (continued)	
1986-on	
Standard heat range	**ND X22EPR-U9 or NGK DPR7EA-9**
Cold weather*	**ND X20EPR-U9 or NGK DPR6EA-9**
Extended high-speed riding	**ND X24EPR-U9 or NGK DPR8EA-9**
Spark plug gap	**0.8-0.9 mm (0.031-0.035 in.)**
Ignition timing	**"F" mark @ idle**
Idle speed	
1983	**900 ± 100 rpm**
1984-1985	**1,000 ± 100 rpm**
1986-on	
49-state	**1,000 ± 100 rpm**
California	**1,100 ± 100 rpm**

* Cold weather climate—below 41° F (5° C).

3

CHAPTER FOUR

ENGINE

The engine in the Honda 700-750 cc V-twin is a water-cooled, 4-stroke engine with a single overhead camshaft per cylinder. The crankshaft is supported by 2 main bearings and the camshafts are chain-driven from the sprockets on each end of the crankshaft. The camshafts operate rocker arms above each of the 3 valves per cylinder. There is a hydraulic valve adjuster system that eliminates the need for valve adjustment. The only difference between the 700 cc and the 750 cc engine is in the cylinder bore dimension.

Engine lubrication is by wet sump, with the oil supply housed in the crankcase. The chain-driven oil pump supplies oil under pressure throughout the engine.

The starter motor is located just behind the rear cylinder and drives the starter clutch on the alternator side of the engine.

This chapter provides complete service and overhaul procedures for the Honda 700-750 cc V-twin engine. Although the clutch and the transmission are located within the engine, they are covered separately in Chapter Five to simplify the presentation of this material.

Service procedures for all models are virtually the same. Where differences occur, they are identified.

Table 1 provides complete engine specifications. **Tables 1-11** are located at the end of this chapter.

ENGINE PRINCIPLES

Figure 1 explains how the engine works. This will be helpful when troubleshooting or repairing your engine.

HYDRAULIC VALVE ADJUSTER SYSTEM

The hydraulic valve adjuster system is designed to create an automatic zero valve clearance setting throughout the engine's rpm range and to eliminate any routine valve adjustment. Valve clearance remains the same whether the engine is cold or hot. The system is basically a tensioning system and does not contain hydraulic valve lifters like those used in many automobile engines.

Each rocker arm is installed on an eccentric rocker arm shaft. The rocker arm shaft has a notch on the top of it where an assist shaft and spring are positioned. There is also a notch on the bottom of the rocker arm shaft that accepts the hydraulic tappet. The hydraulic tappets are supplied with air-bled engine oil from the defoaming chambers in the cylinder head cover. The combined effort of these components maintains zero valve clearance.

Refer to **Figure 2** for the following operation principle of the system.

4-STROKE OPERATING PRINCIPLES

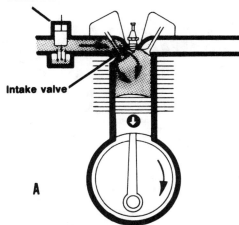

A

As the piston travels downward, the exhaust valve is closed and the intake valve opens, allowing the new air-fuel mixture from the carburetor to be drawn into the cylinder. When the piston reaches the bottom of its travel (BDC), the intake valve closes and remains closed for the next 1 1/2 revolutions of the crankshaft.

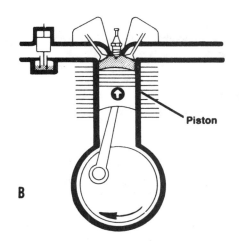

B

While the crankshaft continues to rotate, the piston moves upward, compressing the air-fuel mixture.

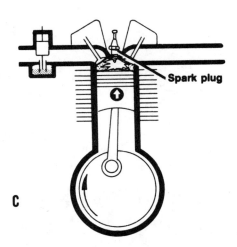

C

As the piston almost reaches the top of its travel, the spark plug fires, igniting the compressed air-fuel mixture. The piston continues to top dead center (TDC) and is pushed downward by the expanding gases.

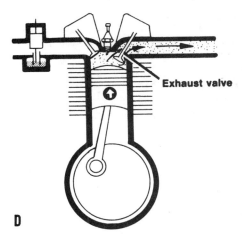

D

When the piston almost reaches BDC, the exhaust valve opens and remains open until the piston is near TDC. The upward travel of the piston forces the exhaust gases out of the cylinder. After the piston has reached TDC, the exhaust valve closes and the cycle starts all over again.

1. When there is no cam lift on the rocker arm, the hydraulic tappet, assist shaft and spring are in the at-rest position (A, **Figure 2**).

2. As the cam lobe starts to lift the rocker arm, the eccentric rocker arm shaft also moves.

3. This movement of the rocker arm begins to compress the hydraulic tappet, the assist shaft and the spring.

4. When the hydraulic tappet is compressed, the oil pressure in the tappet high pressure chamber increases and moves the check ball onto its seat and to the closed position.

5. When the cam lobe reaches its maximum lift, the oil pressure within the tapped high pressure chamber is very high and keeps the check ball closed.

6. As the rocker arm is pressing on the tappet, some of the oil within the high pressure chamber is forced out. This allows the plunger in the tappet to absorb some of the load when the cam lobe is at its maximum lift (B, **Figure 2**).

7. As the cam lobe moves past its maximum lift, the valve spring apply force on the other end of the rocker arm and moves the rocker arm back in the other direction.

8. As the rocker arm shaft moves back in the other direction the spring within the tappet pushes the plunger upward (C, **Figure 2**).

9. The oil pressure within the high pressure chamber has now decreased, allowing the check ball to leave its seat. The displaced oil can now re-enter, after leaving the defoaming chambers, into the high pressure chamber.

10. And the sequence starts all over again. The combination of all of these parts interacting with each other maintains zero clearance at all engine speeds—up to 8,000 rpm.

SERVICING ENGINE
IN FRAME

The following components can be serviced while the engine is mounted in the frame. The bike's frame is a great holding fixture for breaking loose stubborn bolts and nuts.

a. Partial clutch assembly (1983-1985)
b. Complete clutch assembly (1986-on)
c. Alternator and starter gears
d. Carburetor assembly

ENGINE
REMOVAL/INSTALLATION

WARNING
The engine weighs approximately 78 kg (171.6 lb.). Due to this weight it is essential that a minimum of 2, preferably 3, people be available for the removal and installation procedure.

1. Place the bike on the centerstand and remove the seat and the side covers.
2. Disconnect the battery negative and positive leads.

3. Remove the main fuel tank as described in Chapter Six.
4. Drain the engine oil as described in Chapter Three.
5. Drain the engine coolant as described in Chapter Three.
6. Remove the radiator as described in Chapter Eight.
7. Disconnect the spark plug wires and tie them up out of the way.
8. Remove the rear brake pedal as described in Chapter Eleven.
9. Remove the exhaust system as described in Chapter Six.
10. Remove the carburetor assembly as described in Chapter Six. After the carburetor assembly has been removed, insert a clean shop cloth into the intake ports to prevent the entry of foreign matter and coolant.
11. Remove the thermostat assembly and the coolant metal pipes and hoses as described in Chapter Eight.
12. Disconnect the engine breather hose from the cylinder head cover (**Figure 3**).
13. Remove the ignition coils as described in Chapter Seven.
14. Remove the alternator as described in this chapter.
15A. *1983-1986:* Remove all clutch components that can be removed with the engine in the frame, refers to Chapter Five.
15B. *1987:* Remove the clutch as described in Chapter Five.
16. Remove the clutch slave cylinder as described in Chapter Five.
17. Use a large screwdriver on the pry point on each side of the gearshift spindle guide plug (**Figure 4**) and remove the plug. This is a metal plug with an O-ring seal and is difficult to remove.
18. Remove the gearshift spindle (**Figure 5**).
19. Disconnect the engine ground strap, the thermo sensor wire, the neutral/OD switch wire, the oil pressure sender wire, the pulse generator and the tachometer sending unit wire connector.
20. On models so equipped, disconnect all tubes relating to the fuel evaporation canister. Refer to Chapter Six.
21. Take a final look all over the engine to make sure everything has been disconnected.
22. To remove the fuel pump, perform the following.

    a. Remove the plastic cover over the fuel pump.
    b. Disconnect the electrical connector (A, **Figure 6**) going to the fuel pump.

c. Remove the fuel pump and its rubber mount (B, **Figure 6**) out of the retaining tab on the frame. It is not necessary to remove the fuel pump, just move it out of the way to gain access to the engine mounting bolt and nut behind it.

23. Remove the bolts (A, **Figure 7**) securing the sub-frame.

24. Remove the front through-bolt (B, **Figure 7**) and remove the sub-frame. Don't lose the spacer on the right-hand side.

25. Loosen, but do not remove, the rear through-bolts and nuts (**Figure 8**).

26. Place two 4×6 and one 2×4 piece of wood on their sides under the engine. This stack-up of wood fits snugly under the crankcase.

WARNING
Due to the weight of the engine the following steps must be taken slowly and carefully to avoid dropping the engine out of the frame, causing damage to the engine and injury to yourself and your helpers.

27. Remove the front through-bolt. The nuts were removed from this through-bolt when the sub-frame was removed. Don't lose the spacer on the left-hand side.

28. Remove the upper and then the lower rear through-bolts. The engine should now be resting on the stack-up of wood blocks.

WARNING
The engine assembly is very heavy. This final step requires a minimum of 2, preferably 3, people to safely remove the engine from the frame.

29. Carefully and slowly pivot the engine (on the wood blocks) out of the right-hand side of the frame in order to gain access to all sides. Move it out far enough so that everyone can get a good handhold on the engine.

30. Slide the engine out of the open frame area on the right-hand side.

31. Place the engine in an engine stand or take it to a work bench for further disassembly.

32. Install by reversing these removal steps, noting the following.

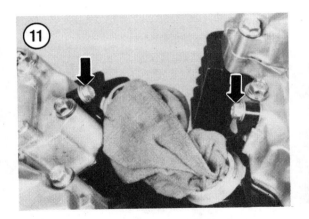

4

NOTE
Due to the weight of the complete engine assembly, it is suggested that all components removed for engine removal be left off until the crankcase assembly is reinstalled into the frame. If you choose to install a completed engine assembly, it requires a minimum of 3 people.

33. Install all through-bolts in from the left-hand side.
34. On the front through-bolt, install the left-hand spacer (**Figure 9**) and the right-hand spacer (**Figure 10**).
35. Tighten the bolts and nuts to the torque specifications listed in **Table 2** or **Table 3**.
36. Fill the crankcase with the recommended type and quantity of engine oil and coolant. Refer to Chapter Three.
37. Start the engine and check for leaks.

CYLINDER HEAD COVER AND CAMSHAFT (1983-1985)

There are 2 camshafts and 2 cam chains. Each cylinder has one camshaft that operates all 3 valves

for that cylinder. There are 2 intake valves and one exhaust valve per cylinder.

There is a cam chain sprocket on the left-hand side of the crankshaft and a separate timing sprocket that is splined onto the crankshaft on the right-hand side. Both cam chains are the Hy-Vo type and the engine must be removed and disassembled to remove the chains.

The gaskets used on the upper covers are not the reusable type. The gaskets on the cylinder head cover and cam sprocket cover have an adhesive coating on each side and "self-destruct" when any part is removed from the engine. Purchase these gaskets before doing any upper-end service on the engine.

Either cylinder head cover and camshaft can be removed without removing these items from the other cylinder. If both cylinders are going to be disassembled, perform the procedures in the order given.

Rear Cylinder Head Cover and Camshaft Removal

1. Remove the engine as described in this chapter.
2. Place a clean shop cloth into the intake ports of both cylinders to prevent the entry of small parts and foreign matter.
3. Remove the bolts securing the external oil pipe to each cylinder head (**Figure 11**) and to the crankcase (**Figure 12**). Don't lose the sealing washers on each side of the fitting where the bolts attach. Remove the oil pipe.

NOTE
The spark plug sleeve must be removed for cam chain removal. The sleeve can be removed 2 different ways as described in Step 4A or Step 4B.

4A. Remove the spark plug sleeve (**Figure 13**) on each cylinder head as follows.

a. Use a bolt with a dimension across the flats of the head of 1 1/16 in.

b. Install the bolt head into the sleeve with the threaded portion sticking out.

c. Attach Vise-Grips to the bolt threads and unscrew the sleeve from the cylinder head.

4B. Remove the spark plug sleeve (**Figure 13**) on each cylinder head as follows.

a. Use a K & N rotor puller (**Figure 14**), part No. 82-0150.

b. Install the puller *backwards* into the sleeve (**Figure 15**).

c. Use an open end wrench on the puller and unscrew the sleeve from the cylinder head.

5. Remove the bolts, cap nuts and washers (**Figure 16**) securing the cam sprocket cover and remove the cover and gasket. Don't lose the locating dowels.

6. Remove the bolts, cap nuts and washers (**Figure 17**) securing the cylinder head cover and remove the cover and gasket. Discard the gasket.

7A. If the camshaft holder is going to be disassembled, remove the springs and assist shafts (A, **Figure 18**) from the camshaft holder.

7B. If the camshaft holder is not going to be disassembled, leave the springs and assist shafts (A, **Figure 18**) in the camshaft holder. This will make installation easier.

8. Remove all 4 spark plugs. This will make it easier to rotate the engine by hand in the following steps.

9. Remove the timing hole cover cap (**Figure 19**).

10. Using a 17 mm socket, rotate the engine using the primary drive gear bolt (**Figure 20**).

NOTE
Figure 19 and Figure 20 are shown with additional components removed from the engine for clarity.

11. Rotate the engine *clockwise* until the "R-T" mark (**Figure 21**) aligns with the fixed pointer on the crankcase cover.

12. Before removing any parts, perform the following to inspect cam chain length.

a. Measure the amount that wedge "B" protrudes above the top surface of the cam chain tensioner (**Figure 22**).

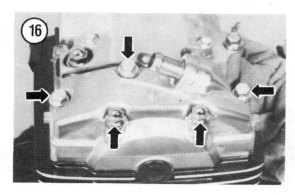

b. If the dimension exceeds the service limit of 9.0 mm (0.35 in.) the cam chain has stretched and must be replaced.

13. To achieve the minimum amount of cam chain tension for cam removal and installation perform the following.

a. Push wedge "B" down and pull wedge "A" straight up until the hole in wedge "A" is exposed.

b. Install a 2 mm pin or piece of wire in the hole in wedge "A". This will hold wedge "A" in the up position.

14. Remove the bolts and washers (B, **Figure 18**) securing the camshaft holder.

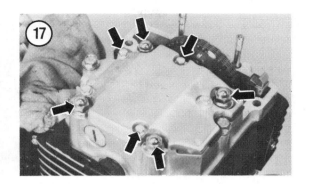

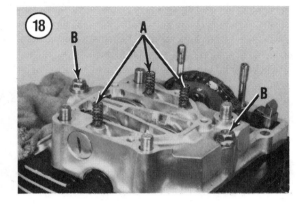

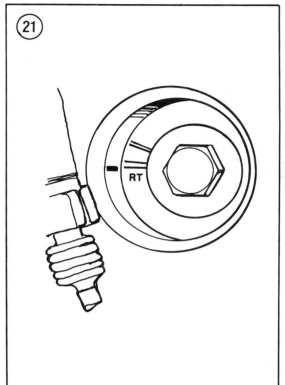

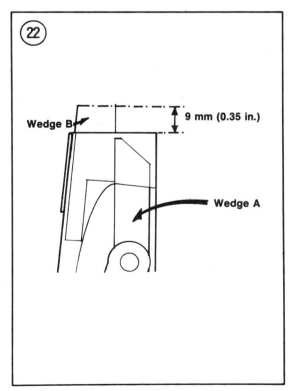

9 mm (0.35 in.)

Wedge B

Wedge A

4

15. Partially pull the camshaft holder up.

16. Look between the camshaft holder and the cylinder head and locate the 3 hydraulic tappets. They are next to 3 of the crankcase studs. Carefully remove the camshaft holder but keep the hydraulic tappets and shims in place in the cylinder head.

> *CAUTION*
> *If the hydraulic tappets and any shims come out of their receptacle in the cylinder head, reinstall them into their correct receptacle in the cylinder head. They must be kept in their respective pairs otherwise the **Hydraulic Tappet Shim Adjustment** procedure will have to be performed before the camshaft holder can be installed.*

17. Remove the hydraulic tappets and shim(s) (A, **Figure 23**) from the cylinder head. Place each tappet and its shim(s) into a container and mark its location — i.e. intake/ left-hand side, intake/ right-hand side and exhaust. Remember the right-hand side refers to the engine in the bike's frame, not as it sits on your workbench.

> *NOTE*
> *The shim will stick either to the base of the tappet or in the receptacle in the cylinder head. Make sure no shims are left in the cylinder head. The receptacle in the cylinder head has a machine-recessed dimple in it. If you look into the receptacle and it looks smooth, chances are there still is a shim in there.*

18. Remove the dowel pins from the crankcase studs in the cylinder head.

19. Remove the rubber grommets (A, **Figure 24**) at each end of the camshaft from the cylinder head.

20. Remove the exposed cam sprocket bolt (B, **Figure 24**).

21. Rotate the engine *clockwise* 360° and remove the other exposed sprocket bolt.

22. Rotate the engine *clockwise* 180°.

23. Slide the cam sprocket and cam chain off the shoulder on the cam.

24. Slide the cam out of the cam sprocket and remove the cam.

25. Remove the cam sprocket and tie a piece of wire to the cam chain. Tie the other end of the wire to an external part of the engine so the cam chain will not fall down into the crankcase.

Front Cylinder Head Cover and Camshaft Removal

1. Perform Steps 1-3 of *Rear Cylinder Head and Camshaft Removal* in this chapter.

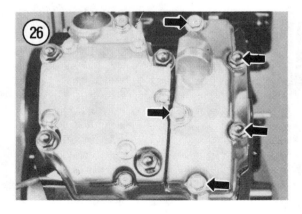

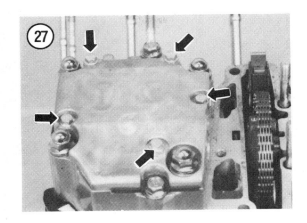

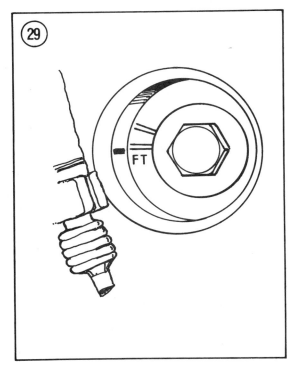

NOTE
The spark plug sleeve must be removed for cam chain removal. The sleeve can be removed 2 different ways.

2A. Remove the spark plug sleeve (**Figure 25**) on each cylinder head as follows.

   a. Use a bolt with a dimension across the flats of the head of 1 1/16 in.

   b. Install the bolt head into the sleeve with the threaded portion sticking out.

   c. Attach Vise-Grips to the threads of the bolt and unscrew the sleeve from the cylinder head.

2B. Remove the spark plug sleeve (**Figure 25**) on each cylinder head as follows.

   a. Use a K & N rotor puller (**Figure 14**), part No. 82-0150.

   b. Install the puller *backwards* into the sleeve (**Figure 15**).

   c. Use an open end wrench on the puller and unscrew the sleeve from the cylinder head.

3. Remove the bolts, cap nuts and washers (**Figure 26**) securing the cam sprocket cover and remove the cover and gasket. Don't lose the locating dowels.

4. Remove the bolts, cap nuts and washers (**Figure 27**) securing the cylinder head cover and remove the cover and gasket.

5A. If the camshaft holder is going to be disassembled, remove the springs and assist shafts (A, **Figure 28**) from the camshaft holder.

5B. If the camshaft holder is not going to be disassembled, leave the springs and assist shafts (A, **Figure 28**) in the camshaft holder. This will make installation easier.

6. Rotate the engine *clockwise* until the "F-T" mark (**Figure 29**) aligns with the fixed pointer on the crankcase cover.

7. Before removing any parts, perform the following to inspect cam chain length.

   a. Measure the amount that wedge "B" protrudes above the top surface of the cam chain tensioner (**Figure 22**).

   b. If the dimension exceeds the service limit of 9.0 mm (0.35 in.), the cam chain has stretched and must be replaced.

8. To achieve the minimum amount of cam chain tension for cam removal and installation perform the following.

   a. Push wedge "B" down and pull wedge "A" straight up until the hole in wedge "A" is exposed.

   b. Install a 2 mm pin or piece of wire in the hole in wedge "A". This will hold wedge "A" in the up position.

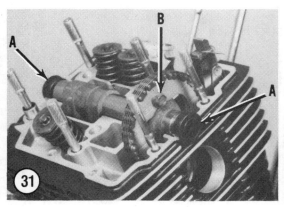

9. Remove the bolts and washers securing the camshaft holder (B, **Figure 28**).

10. Partially pull the camshaft holder up.

11. Look between the camshaft holder and the cylinder head and locate the 3 hydraulic tappets. They are next to 3 of the crankcase studs. Carefully remove the camshaft holder but keep the hydraulic tappets and shims in place in the cylinder head.

> *CAUTION*
> *If the hydraulic tappets and any shims come out of their receptacle in the cylinder head, reinstall them into their correct receptacle in the cylinder head. They must be kept in their respective pairs, otherwise the **Hydraulic Tappet Shim Adjustment** procedure will have to be performed before the cylinder head cover can be installed.*

12. Remove the hydraulic tappets and shim(s) (A, **Figure 30**) from the cylinder head. Place each tappet and its shim(s) into a container and mark its location (i.e. intake/ left-hand side, intake/ right-hand side and exhaust). Remember the right-hand side refers to the engine in the bike's frame, not as it sits on your workbench.

> *NOTE*
> *The shim will stick either to the base of the tappet or in the receptacle in the cylinder head. Make sure no shims are left in the cylinder head. The receptacle in the cylinder head has a machined recessed dimple in it. If you look into the receptacle and it looks smooth, chances are there still is a shim in there.*

13. Remove the locating dowels (B, **Figure 30**) from the crankcase studs in the cylinder head.

14. Remove the rubber grommets (A, **Figure 31**), at each end of the camshaft, from the cylinder head.

15. Remove the exposed cam sprocket bolt (B, **Figure 31**).

> *CAUTION*
> *If the front cylinder head cover and camshaft are removed, Step 16 and Step 17 will require the aid of a helper. When rotating the engine in the following steps, have the helper pull up on the cam chain for the front cylinder and keep it properly meshed with the sprocket on the crankshaft. This is necessary to avoid letting the chain bunch up and damage the crankcase and chain.*

16. Rotate the engine *clockwise* 360° and remove the other exposed sprocket bolt.

17. Rotate the engine *clockwise* 180°.

18. Slide the cam sprocket and cam chain off the shoulder on the cam.

19. Slide the cam out of the cam sprocket and remove the cam.

20. Remove the cam sprocket and tie a piece of wire to the cam chain. Tie the other end of the wire to an external part of the engine so the cam chain will not fall down into the crankcase.

> *CAUTION*
> *If the crankshaft must be rotated when the camshafts are removed, pull up on the cam chains and keep them taut while rotating the crankshaft. Make certain that the chains are positioned onto the crankshaft sprockets. If this is not done, the chains may become kinked and may damage both the chains and the sprockets on the crankshaft.*

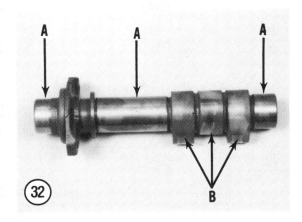

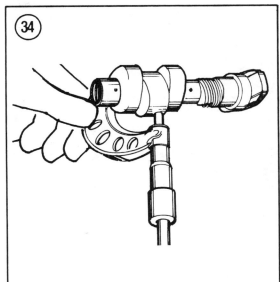

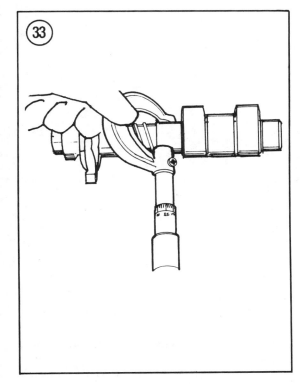

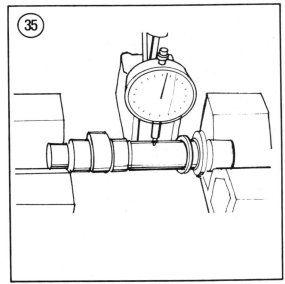

Inspection

1. Check the camshaft bearing journals (A, **Figure 32**) for wear and scoring.

2. Even though the camshaft bearing journal surface appears to be satisfactory, with no visible signs of wear, the camshaft bearing journal must be measured with a micrometer as shown in **Figure 33**. Replace the camshaft(s) if worn beyond the service limits listed in **Table 1**.

3. Check the camshaft lobes for wear (B, **Figure 32**). The lobes should not be scored and the edges should be square. Slight damage may be removed with a silicone carbide oilstone. Use No. 100-200 grit initially, then polish with a No. 280-320 grit.

4. Even though the camshaft lobe surface appears to be satisfactory, with no visible signs of wear, the camshaft lobes must be measured with a micrometer as shown in **Figure 34**. Replace the camshaft(s) if worn beyond the service limits listed in **Table 1**.

5. Measure the runout of the camshaft with a dial indicator and V-blocks as shown in **Figure 35**. Use 1/2 of the total runout and compare to the service limits listed in **Table 1**.

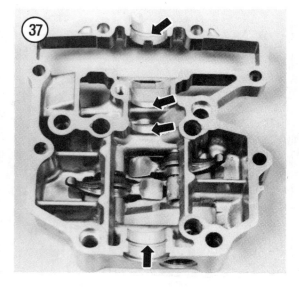

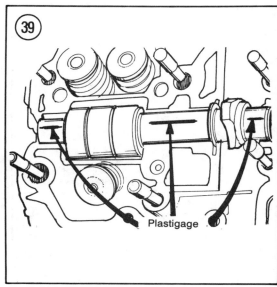

6. Check the camshaft bearing journals in the cylinder head (**Figure 36**) and camshaft holder (**Figure 37**) for wear and scoring. They should not be scored or excessively worn. If necessary, replace the cylinder head and cam holder as a matched pair.

7. Inspect the sprocket mounting flanges (**Figure 38**) on the camshaft for fractures or wear; replace if necessary.

8. Inspect the cam sprockets for wear; replace if necessary.

Camshaft Bearing Clearance Measurement

This procedure requires the use of a Plastigage set. The camshaft must be installed into the head. Before installation, wipe all oil residue from each cam bearing journal and bearing surface in the head and all camshaft holders. Perform this measurement on one cylinder at a time.

1. Install the camshaft into the cylinder head with the lobes facing down.

2. Install all camshaft holder locating dowels into position in the cylinder head.

3. Wipe all oil from cam bearing journals before using the Plastigage material.

4. Place a strip of Plastigage material on top of each cam bearing journal, parallel to the cam, as shown in **Figure 39**. Place the camshaft holder in position.

5. Install all camshaft holder bolts and nuts that hold the camshaft holder in place. Install finger-tight at first, then tighten in a crisscross pattern to the final torque specification listed in **Table 2**.

> *NOTE*
> *Do not rotate either camshaft with the Plastigage material in place.*

6. Gradually remove the bolts in a crisscross pattern. Remove the camshaft holder carefully.

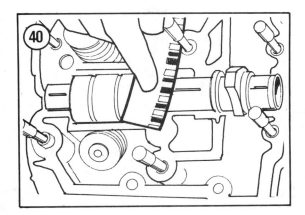

7. Measure the width of the flattened Plastigage according to manufacturer's instructions (**Figure 40**).

8. If the clearance exceeds the wear limit in **Table 1**, measure the camshaft bearing journals with a micrometer and compare to the wear limits in **Table 1**. If the camshaft bearing journal is less than the dimension specified, replace the cam. If the cam is within specifications, the cylinder head and camshaft holders must be replaced as a matched set.

> *CAUTION*
> *Remove all particles of Plastigage from all camshaft bearing journals and camshaft holder. Be sure to remove this material from the groove in the camshaft holder groove. This material must not be left in the engine as it can plug up an oil control orifice and cause severe engine damage.*

Front Cylinder Head Cover and Camshaft Installation

If both cylinder head covers and camshaft holders have been removed, install the front camshaft and holder first then the rear. Each camshaft is marked with an "F" (front) (**Figure 41**) or "R" (rear) on the sprocket boss. Be sure to install the camshaft in the correct cylinder head.

> *CAUTION*
> *If the rear cylinder head cover and camshaft have been removed, the following steps will require the aid of a helper. When rotating the engine in the following steps, have the helper pull up on the cam chain for the rear cylinder and keep it properly meshed with the sprocket on the crankshaft. This is necessary to avoid letting the chain bunch up and damage the crankcase and chain.*

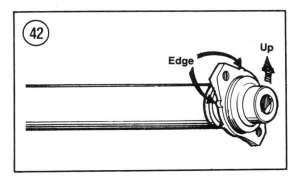

1. Coat all camshaft lobes and bearing journals with molybdenum disulfide grease or assembly oil.

2. Also coat the bearing surfaces in the cylinder head and camshaft bearing holders.

3. Position the cam sprocket with the index marks facing toward the left-hand side and with the index marks up and down (90° from the top surface of the cylinder head).

4. Temporarily install the cam chain onto the cam sprocket.

5. Install the cam into the sprocket and cam chain and fill the cam lobe oil cavity in the cylinder head with fresh engine oil.

6. Position the cam with the lobes facing down and the raised edges on the cam sprocket mounting flange facing up (**Figure 42**).

> *CAUTION*
> *If the rear cylinder head cover and camshaft have been removed, the following steps will require the aid of a helper. When rotating the engine in the following steps, have the helper pull up on the rear cam chain and keep it properly meshed with the sprocket on the crankshaft. This is necessary to avoid causing damage to the crankcase and chain.*

7. Using a 17 mm socket on the primary gear bolt (**Figure 20**), rotate the engine *clockwise* until the "F-T" mark (**Figure 29**) aligns with the fixed pointer on the crankcase cover.

8. Carefully pull the cam chain off of the cam sprocket and rotate the cam sprocket until the index marks are parallel to the top surface of the cylinder head (A, **Figure 43**).

9. Pull the cam chain and sprocket up onto the shoulder on the camshaft. Again check the alignment of the index marks as noted in Step 8. If the alignment is incorrect, correct it at this time.

10. Temporarily install the sprocket bolt into the exposed hole (B, **Figure 43**).

11. Rotate the engine *clockwise* 360° and install the other cam sprocket bolt.

12. Rotate the engine *clockwise* 360° and check for correct cam sprocket alignment as described in Step 7 and Step 8; readjust if necessary.

> *CAUTION*
> *Very expensive damage could result from improper camshaft and chain alignment. Recheck your work several times to be sure alignment is correct.*

13. Remove the exposed cam sprocket bolt and apply Loctite Lock N' Seal to the bolt threads and to the underside of the bolt head. Install the bolt and tighten to the torque specifications listed in **Table 2**.

14. Rotate the engine *clockwise* one full turn (360°). Remove the exposed cam sprocket bolt and apply Loctite Lock N' Seal to the bolt threads and to the underside of the bolt head. Install this bolt and tighten to the torque specifications listed in **Table 2**.

15. Clean all oil residue from the rubber grommets and apply a light coat of liquid gasket seal to the portion that fits into the cylinder head.

16. Install the rubber grommets in the cylinder at each end of the camshaft (A, **Figure 31**).

17. Place wood blocks under the crankcase so the front cylinder head is almost horizontal.

> *CAUTION*
> *The hydraulic tappets must be bled of all air before installation, otherwise they will not function properly.*

18. Inspect and bleed the hydraulic tappets as described in this chapter.

19. Install the tappet shim(s) into their correct receptacle in the cylinder head (**Figure 44**).

20. Keep the hydraulic tappet vertical and install the tappets into their correct receptacles in the cylinder head (**Figure 45**).

21. Install the locating dowels (B, **Figure 30**) onto the crankcase studs in the cylinder head.

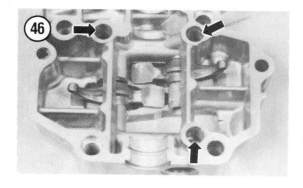

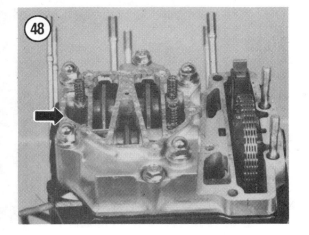

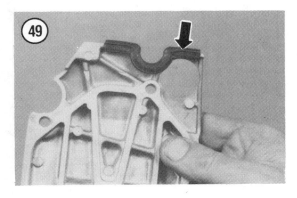

CAUTION
*In the following step, do **not** apply the liquid gasket sealer to the area around each hydraulic tappet receptacle (**Figure 46**).*

22. Clean the mating surfaces of the cylinder head and the camshaft holder with contact cleaner. Apply a light coat of liquid gasket sealer to the mating surface of the camshaft holder.

23. Install the camshaft holder, 8 mm bolts, 10 mm cap nuts and washers. Tighten the bolts and nuts in a crisscross pattern in 2-3 stages to the torque specifications listed in **Table 2**.

24. Make sure the assist shafts and springs (A, **Figure 28**) are in place. They were installed during the rocker arm installation procedure.

25. Fill both de-foaming chambers (**Figure 47**) with fresh engine oil. These chambers must be full of oil so the bleed hole in each tappet will be covered with oil. This is necessary so that air will not enter the high pressure chamber in the tappet.

26. Clean any oil residue from the mating surfaces of the cylinder head cover and the camshaft holder with contact cleaner.

27. Remove the protective sheet from each side of the new gasket and install the gasket (**Figure 48**).

28. Install the rubber seal (**Figure 49**) to the front of the cylinder head cover.

29. Install the cylinder head cover and tighten the 6 mm bolts in a crisscross pattern in 2-3 stages to the torque specification listed in **Table 2**.

30. Install the locating dowels and then the camshaft sprocket cover on the chain side. Install the 8 mm bolts, cap nuts and washers (**Figure 26**) and tighten in a crisscross pattern in 2-3 stages to the torque specification listed in **Table 2**.

31. If only the front cover and camshaft were removed, perform Steps 31-35 of *Rear Cylinder Head Cover and Camshaft Installation* in this chapter.

Rear Cylinder Head Cover and Camshaft Installation

Each camshaft is marked with an "F" (front) or "R" (rear) (**Figure 50**) on the sprocket boss. Be sure to install the camshaft in the correct cylinder head.

1. Coat all camshaft lobes and bearing journals with molybdenum disulfide grease or assembly oil. Also coat the bearing surfaces in the cylinder head and camshaft bearing holders.

2. Position the cam sprocket with the index marks facing toward the left-hand side and with the index marks up and down (90° from the top surface of the cylinder head).

3. Temporarily install the cam chain onto the cam sprocket.

4. Install the cam into the sprocket and cam chain (**Figure 51**) and fill the cam lobe oil cavity in the cylinder head with fresh engine oil.

5. Position the cam with the lobes facing down (**Figure 52**) and the raised edges on the cam sprocket mounting flange facing up (**Figure 42**).

6. Using a 17 mm socket, rotate the engine using the primary drive gear bolt (**Figure 20**).

7. Rotate the engine *clockwise* until the "R-T" mark (**Figure 21**) aligns with the fixed pointer on the crankcase cover.

8. Carefully pull the cam chain off of the cam sprocket and rotate the cam sprocket until the index marks are parallel to the top surface of the cylinder head (A, **Figure 53**).

9. Pull the cam chain and sprocket up onto the shoulder on the camshaft. Again check the alignment of the index marks as noted in Step 8. If the alignment is incorrect, correct it at this time.

10. Temporarily install the sprocket bolt into the exposed hole (B, **Figure 53**).

11. Rotate the engine *clockwise* 360° and install the other cam sprocket bolt (**Figure 54**).

12. Rotate the engine *clockwise* 360° and check for correct cam sprocket alignment as described in Step 7 and Step 8; readjust if necessary.

CAUTION
Very expensive damage could result from improper camshaft and chain alignment. Recheck your work several times to be sure alignment is correct.

13. Remove the exposed cam sprocket bolt and apply Loctite Lock N' Seal to the bolt threads and to the underside of the bolt head. Install this bolt and tighten to the torque specifications listed in **Table 2**.

14. Rotate the engine *clockwise* one full turn (360°). Remove the exposed cam sprocket bolt and apply Loctite Lock N' Seal to the bolt threads and to the underside of the bolt head. Install this bolt and tighten to the torque specification listed in **Table 2**.

15. Clean all oil residue from the rubber grommets and apply a light coat of liquid gasket seal to the portion that sits into the cylinder head.

16. Install the rubber grommets in the cylinder at each end of the camshaft (A, **Figure 24**).

17. Place wood blocks under the crankcase so the rear cylinder head is almost horizontal.

NOTE
When the crankcase is blocked up this way, some of the oil in the de-foaming

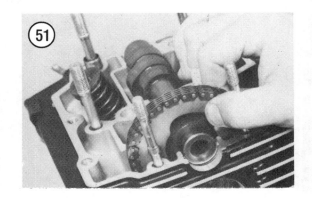

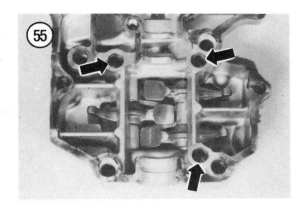

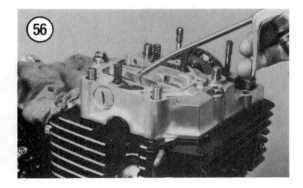

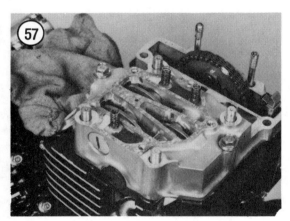

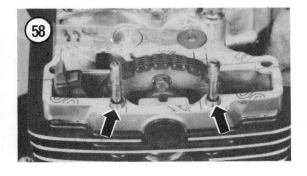

chambers of the front cylinder will run out. Don't worry—the loss of oil is minimal and will not affect the front cylinder's hydraulic tappets.

> *CAUTION*
> *The hydraulic tappets must be bled of all air before installation, otherwise they will not function properly.*

18. Inspect and bleed the hydraulic tappets as described in this chapter.

19. Install the tappet shim(s) into their correct receptacle in the cylinder head (**Figure 44**).

20. Keep the hydraulic tappet vertical and install the tappets into their correct receptacles in the cylinder head (A, **Figure 23**).

21. Install the locating dowels (B, **Figure 23**) onto the crankcase studs in the cylinder head.

> *CAUTION*
> *In the following step, do **not** apply the liquid gasket sealer to the area around each hydraulic tappet receptacle (**Figure 55**).*

22. Clean the mating surfaces of the cylinder head and the camshaft holder with contact cleaner. Apply a light coat of liquid gasket sealer to the mating surface of the cylinder head cover.

23. Install the camshaft holder, 8 mm bolts, 10 mm cap nuts and washers. Tighten the bolts and nuts in a crisscross pattern in 2-3 stages to the torque specifications listed in **Table 2**.

24. Make sure the assist shafts and springs (A, **Figure 18**) are in place. They were installed during the rocker arm installation procedure.

25. Fill both de-foaming chambers (**Figure 56**) with fresh engine oil. These chambers must be full of oil so the bleed hole in each tappet will be covered with oil. This is necessary so that air will not enter the high pressure chamber in the tappet.

26. Clean the mating surfaces of the cylinder head cover and the camshaft holder with contact cleaner.

27. Remove the protective sheets from each side of the new gasket and install the gasket (**Figure 57**).

28. Install the rubber seal (**Figure 49**) to the rear of the cylinder head cover.

29. Install the cylinder head cover and tighten the 6 mm bolts in a crisscross pattern in 2-3 stages to the torque specification listed in **Table 2**.

30. Install the locating dowels (**Figure 58**) and then the camshaft holder on the chain side. Install the 8 mm bolts, cap nuts and washers (**Figure 16**) and

tighten in a crisscross pattern in 2-3 stages to the torque specification listed in **Table 2**.

31. Inspect the O-ring seals (**Figure 59**) on the spark plug sleeve. Replace if they are hard or starting to deteriorate.

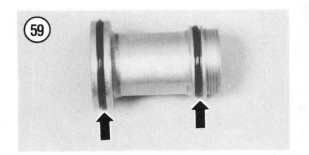

NOTE
Steps 31-35 pertain to both the front and rear cylinders.

32. Install the spark plug sleeve into the cylinder head and tighten securely. Use the same tool set-up used for removal.
33. Install the external oil pipe to each cylinder head and to the crankcase. Install a sealing washer (**Figure 60**) on each side of the fitting where the bolts attach. Refer to **Figure 11** and **Figure 12**. Tighten the bolts to the torque specification listed in **Table 2**.
34. Install the engine as described in this chapter.
35. Make sure the O-ring seals are in place on the coolant pipes. Install the coolant pipes and thermostat as described in Chapter Eight.

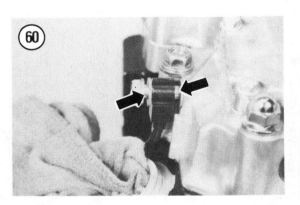

CYLINDER HEAD COVER AND CAMSHAFT (1986-ON)

There are 2 camshafts and 2 cam chains. Each cylinder has one camshaft that operates all 3 valves for that cylinder. There are 2 intake valves and one exhaust valve per cylinder.

There is a cam chain sprocket on the left-hand side of the crankshaft and a separate timing sprocket that is splined onto the crankshaft on the right-hand side. Both cam chains are the Hy-Vo type and the engine must be removed and disassembled to remove the chains. Purchase new gaskets before doing any upper-end service on the engine. A tube of silicone sealer (clear) will also be required during reassembly.

Either cylinder head cover and camshaft can be removed without removing these items from the other cylinder. If both cylinders are going to be disassembled, perform the procedures in the order given.

Rear Cylinder Head Cover and Camshaft Removal

1. Remove the engine as described in this chapter.
2. Place a clean shop cloth into the intake ports of both cylinders to prevent the entry of small parts and foreign matter.

3. Remove the bolts securing the external oil pipe to each cylinder head (**Figure 61**). Then remove the 2 oil pipe attaching bolts between the cylinders. See **Figure 62** and **Figure 63**. Then remove the oil pipe bolt at the lower crankcase (**Figure 64**) and remove the oil pipe. Don't lose the sealing washers on each side of the fitting where the banjo bolts attach.
4. Remove the water pipe and hoses from the engine (**Figure 65**).
5. On California models, remove the secondary air pipes from the cylinder heads.

NOTE
The spark plug sleeve must be removed for cam chain removal. The sleeve can be removed 2 different ways, depending on what tools are available. Refer to Step 6A or Step 6B.

6A. Remove the spark plug sleeve (**Figure 66**) on each cylinder head as follows.
   a. Select a bolt head that is 1 1/16 in. across the flats of the head.
   b. Thread two nuts onto the bolt. Then tighten the nuts against each other to lock them.
   c. Install the bolt head into the sleeve with the threaded portion sticking out.
   d. Use a wrench on the nuts and unscrew the sleeve from the cylinder head.
6B. Remove the spark plug sleeve (**Figure 66**) on each cylinder head as follows.

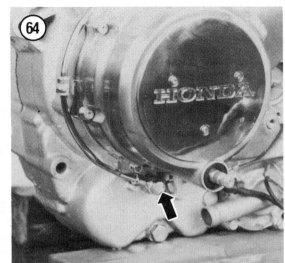

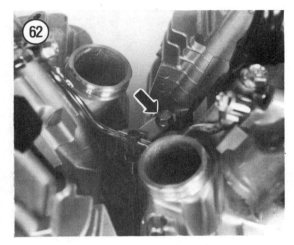

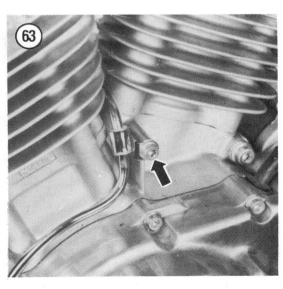

a. Use a K & N rotor puller (A, **Figure 67**), part No. 82-0150. Remove the puller bolt and install it backwards in the puller as shown in B, **Figure 67**. Tighten the bolt securely in the puller.

b. Install the puller *backwards* into the sleeve (**Figure 68**).

c. Use an open end-wrench on the puller bolt and unscrew the sleeve (**Figure 69**) from the cylinder head.

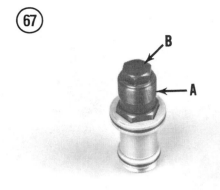

7. Remove the bolts, cap nuts and washers (**Figure 70**) securing the cylinder head cover. Do not remove the 3 assist shaft caps (**Figure 71**). Remove the water pipe.

CAUTION
*When removing the cylinder head cover in Step 8, the hydraulic tappets and shims may pull out of the cylinder head and fall through the chain tunnel and into the lower crankcase. To ease removal, tilt the engine approximately 40° to the left or right and remove the cylinder head cover. **Figure 72** shows the position of the tappets and shims. Immediately after removing the cylinder head cover, check the tappet positions. If a tappet or shim is missing, do not tilt the engine upright until you can locate and remove the missing part. Tilting the engine upright when a tappet or shim is dislodged may cause the part to fall into the engine.*

8. Remove the cylinder head cover (**Figure 73**).

CAUTION
*If the hydraulic tappets and any shims pull out of their receptacle in the cylinder head, reinstall them immediately. They must be kept in their respective pairs, otherwise the **Hydraulic Tappet Shim Adjustment** procedure will have to be performed before installation.*

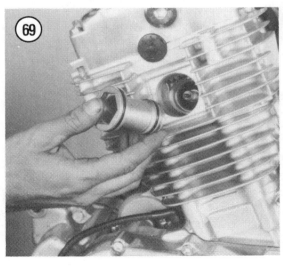

9. Remove the hydraulic tappets (**Figure 73**) and shims (**Figure 74**) from the cylinder head. Place each tappet and its shim(s) into a container and mark its location (i.e. intake/left-hand side, intake/right-hand side and exhaust). Remember the right-hand side refers to the engine in the bike's frame, not as it sits on your workbench.

10. Remove the 2 dowel pins (**Figure 75**).

4

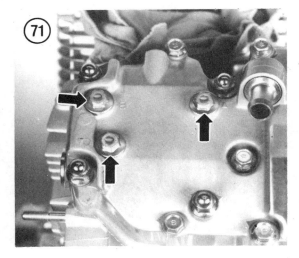

11. Remove the rubber grommets at each end of the camshaft from the cylinder head. See **Figure 76** and **Figure 77**.

12. Remove all 4 spark plugs. This will make it easier to rotate the engine by hand in the following steps.

> *CAUTION*
> *To prevent damaging the plastic timing hole cover cap (**Figure 78**) in Step 13, use a large flat-tipped screwdriver or a wide thin piece of metal.*

13. Remove the timing hole cover cap (**Figure 78**).

14. Using a 17 mm socket, rotate the engine using the primary drive gear bolt (**Figure 79**).

15. Rotate the engine *clockwise* until the "R-T" mark (**Figure 80**) aligns with the fixed pointer on the crankcase cover.

16. Before removing any parts, perform the following to inspect cam chain length.
　　a. Measure the amount that wedge "B" (**Figure 81**) protrudes above the top surface of the cam chain tensioner. See **Figure 82**.
　　b. If the dimension exceeds the service limit of 9.0 mm (0.35 in.) the cam chain has stretched and must be replaced.

17. To achieve the minimum amount of cam chain tension for cam removal and installation perform the following.
　　a. Push wedge "B" down and pull wedge "A" straight up until the hole in wedge "A" is exposed.
　　b. Install a 2 mm pin or piece of wire in the hole in wedge "A". This will hold wedge "A" in the up position. See **Figure 83**.

18. Remove the exposed cam sprocket bolt (**Figure 84**).

19. Rotate the engine *clockwise* 360° and remove the other exposed sprocket bolt.

20. Slide the cam sprocket and cam chain off the shoulder on the cam (**Figure 85**).

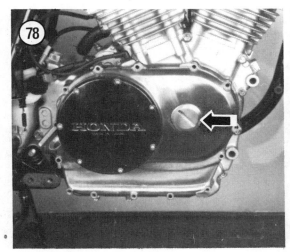

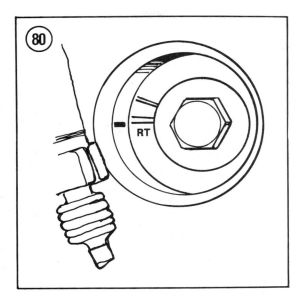

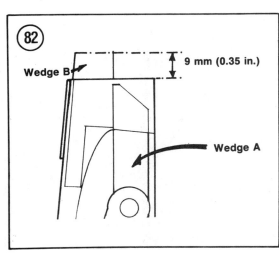

9 mm (0.35 in.)

Wedge B

Wedge A

4

21. Rotate the engine *clockwise* 180°.

22. Slide the cam out of the cam sprocket and remove the cam.

23. Remove the cam sprocket (**Figure 86**) and tie a piece of wire to the cam chain. Tie the other end of the wire to an external part of the engine so the cam chain will not fall down into the crankcase.

Front Cylinder Head Cover and Camshaft Removal

1. Perform Steps 1-6 of *Rear Cylinder Head and Camshaft Removal* in this chapter.

2. Remove the bolts, cap nuts and washers (**Figure 87**) securing the cylinder head cover. Do not remove the 3 assist shaft caps (circles, **Figure 87**). Remove the water pipe.

> *CAUTION*
> *When removing the cylinder head cover in Step 3, the hydraulic tappets and shims may pull out of the cylinder head and fall through the chain tunnel and into the lower crankcase. To ease removal, tilt the engine approximately 40° to the left or right and remove the cylinder head cover. **Figure 72** shows the position of the tappets and shims. Immediately after removing the cylinder head cover, check the tappets. If a tappet or shim is missing, do not tilt the engine upright until you can locate and remove the missing part. Tilting the engine upright may cause the part to fall into the engine.*

3. Remove the cylinder head cover (**Figure 88**).

4. Remove the hydraulic tappets (**Figure 72**) and shims (**Figure 74**) from the cylinder head. Place each tappet and its shim(s) into a container and mark its location (i.e. intake/left-hand side, intake/right-hand side and exhaust). Remember the right-hand side refers to the engine in the bike's frame, and not as it sits on your workbench.

5. Remove the 2 dowel pins (**Figure 75**).

6. Remove the rubber grommets at each end of the camshaft from the cylinder head. See **Figure 76** and **Figure 77**.

7. Remove all 4 spark plugs. This will make it easier to rotate the engine by hand in the following steps.

> *CAUTION*
> *To prevent damaging the plastic timing hole cover cap (**Figure 78**) in Step 8, use a large flat-tipped screwdriver or a wide thin piece of metal.*

8. Remove the timing hole cover cap (**Figure 78**).

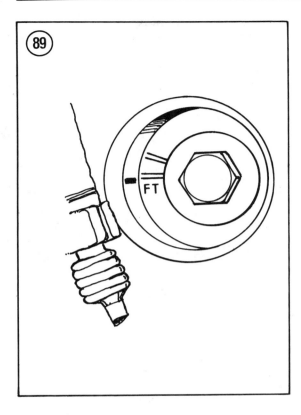

b. If the dimension exceeds the service limit of 9.0 mm (0.35 in.), the cam chain has stretched and must be replaced.

12. To achieve the minimum amount of cam chain tension for cam removal and installation perform the following.

  a. Push wedge "B" down and pull wedge "A" straight up until the hole in wedge "A" is exposed.

  b. Install a 2 mm pin or piece of wire in the hole in wedge "A". This will hold wedge "A" in the up position. See **Figure 83**.

13. Remove the exposed cam sprocket bolt (**Figure 84**).

4

CAUTION
If the rear cylinder head cover and camshaft are removed, Step 14 and Step 15 will require the aid of a helper. When rotating the engine in the following steps, have the helper pull up on the cam chain for the front cylinder and keep it properly meshed with the sprocket on the crankshaft. This is necessary to avoid letting the chain bunch up and damage the crankcase and chain.

14. Rotate the engine *clockwise* 360° and remove the other exposed sprocket bolt.

15. Rotate the engine *clockwise* 180°.

16. Slide the cam sprocket and cam chain off the shoulder on the cam (**Figure 85**).

17. Slide the cam out of the cam sprocket and remove the cam.

18. Remove the cam sprocket (**Figure 86**) and tie a piece of wire to the cam chain. Tie the other end of the wire to an external part of the engine so the cam chain will not fall down into the crankcase.

CAUTION
If the crankshaft must be rotated when the camshafts are removed, pull up on the cam chains and keep them taut while rotating the crankshaft. Make certain that the chains are positioned onto the crankshaft sprockets. If this is not done, the chains may become kinked and may damage both the chains and the sprockets on the crankshaft.

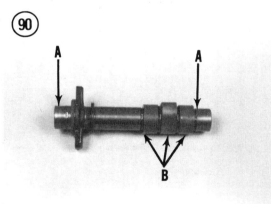

9. Using a 17 mm socket, rotate the engine using the primary drive gear bolt (**Figure 79**).

10. Rotate the engine *clockwise* until the "F-T" mark (**Figure 89**) aligns with the fixed pointer on the crankcase cover.

11. Before removing any parts, perform the following to inspect cam chain length.

  a. Measure the amount that wedge "B" (**Figure 81**) protrudes above the top surface of the cam chain tensioner. See **Figure 82**.

Inspection

1. Check the camshaft bearing journals (A, **Figure 90**) for wear and scoring.

2. Even though the camshaft bearing journal surface appears to be satisfactory, with no visible signs of wear, the camshaft bearing journal must be

measured with a micrometer as shown in **Figure 91**. Replace the camshaft(s) if worn beyond the service limits listed in **Table 1**.

3. Check the camshaft lobes for wear (B, **Figure 90**). The lobes should not be scored and the edges should be square. Slight damage may be removed with a silicon carbide oilstone. Use No. 100-200 grit initially, then polish with a No. 280-320 grit.

4. Even though the camshaft lobe surface appears to be satisfactory, with no visible signs of wear, the camshaft lobes must be measured with a micrometer as shown in **Figure 92**. Replace the camshaft(s) if worn beyond the service limits listed in **Table 1**.

5. Measure the runout of the camshaft with a dial indicator and V-blocks as shown in **Figure 93**. Use 1/2 of the total runout and compare to the service limits listed in **Table 1**.

6. Check the camshaft bearing journals in the cylinder head (**Figure 94**) and camshaft holder (**Figure 95**) for wear and scoring. They should not be scored or excessively worn. If necessary, replace the cylinder head and cam holder as a matched pair.

7. Inspect the sprocket mounting flanges (**Figure 96**) on the camshaft for fractures or wear; replace if necessary.

8. Inspect the cam sprockets (**Figure 97**) for wear; replace if necessary.

Camshaft Bearing Clearance Measurement

This procedure requires the use of a Plastigage set. The camshaft must be installed into the head. Before installation, wipe all oil residue from each cam bearing journal and bearing surface in the head and all camshaft holders. Perform this measurement on one cylinder at a time.

1. Install the camshaft into the cylinder head with the lobes facing down.

2. Install all camshaft holder locating dowels into position in the cylinder head.

3. Wipe all oil from cam bearing journals before using the Plastigage material.

4. Place a strip of Plastigage material on top of each cam bearing journal, parallel to the cam, as shown in **Figure 98**.

5. Install the cylinder head cover into position.

6. Install all cylinder head bolts and nuts. Install finger-tight at first, then tighten in a crisscross pattern to the final torque specification listed in **Table 3**.

NOTE
Do not rotate either camshaft with the Plastigage material in place.

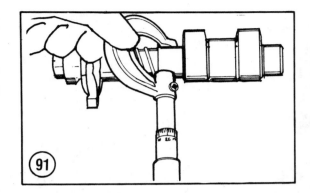

(91)

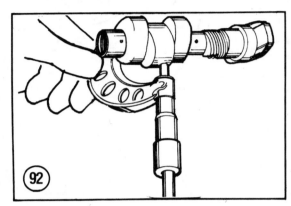

(92)

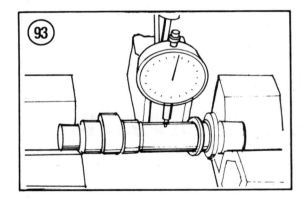

(93)

(94)

7. Gradually remove the bolts and nuts in a crisscross pattern. Remove the cylinder head cover carefully.

8. Measure the width of the flattened Plastigage according to manufacturer's instructions (**Figure 99**).

9. If the clearance exceeds the wear limit in **Table 1**, measure the camshaft bearing journals with a micrometer and compare to the wear limits in **Table 1**. If the camshaft bearing journal is less than the dimension specified, replace the cam. If the cam is within specifications, the cylinder head cover and cylinder head must be replaced as a matched set.

> *CAUTION*
> *Remove all particles of Plastigage from all camshaft bearing journals and camshaft holder. Be sure to remove this material from the groove in the camshaft holder groove. This material must not be left in the engine as it can plug up an oil control orifice and cause severe engine damage.*

Camshaft Installation
Service Notes

1. If both cylinder head covers and camshaft holders have been removed, install the front camshaft and cylinder head cover first. Each camshaft is marked with an "F" (front) (**Figure 100**) or "R" (rear) on the sprocket boss. Be sure to install the camshaft in the correct cylinder head.

2. If only one cylinder head cover was removed, the opposite cylinder head cover must be removed so that its camshaft position can be checked. It is not necessary to remove the spark plug sleeve or camshaft to check camshaft position.

96

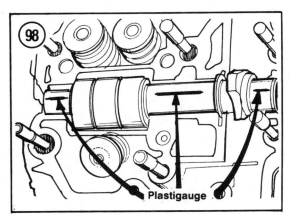

**Front Cylinder Head Cover and
Camshaft Installation**

1. If the rear cylinder head cover was not removed, perform the following.

    a. Remove the rear cylinder head cover as described in this chapter. Do not remove the rear cylinder head camshaft.

    b. Using a 17 mm socket on the primary gear bolt, rotate the engine *clockwise* until the "R-T" mark (**Figure 101**) aligns with the fixed pointer on the crankcase cover.

    c. Check the "R" identification mark on the camshaft flange (**Figure 100**). If the "R" mark faces up, rotate the engine *clockwise* 495° and proceed to Step 2. If the "R" mark faces down (cannot be seen), rotate the engine *clockwise* 135° and proceed to Step 2.

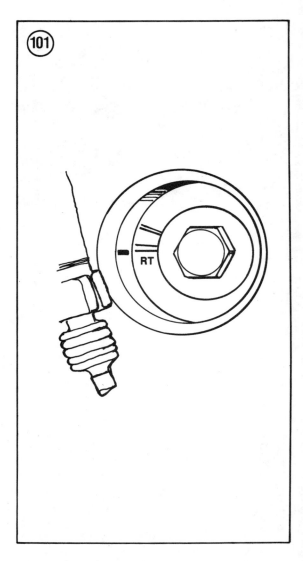

> *CAUTION*
> *If the rear cylinder head cover and camshaft have been removed, the following steps will require the aid of a helper. When rotating the engine in the following steps, have the helper pull up on the cam chain for the rear cylinder and keep it properly meshed with the sprocket on the crankshaft. This is necessary to avoid letting the chain bunch up and damage the crankcase and chain.*

2. Using a 17 mm socket on the primary gear bolt (**Figure 102**), rotate the engine *clockwise* until the "F-T" mark (**Figure 103**) aligns with the fixed pointer on the crankcase cover.

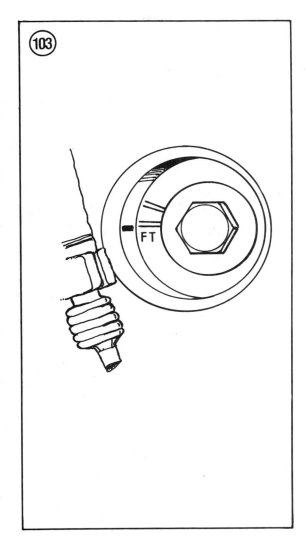

3. Coat all camshaft lobes and bearing journals with molybdenum disulfide grease or assembly oil.

4. Also coat the bearing surfaces in the cylinder head and camshaft bearing holders.

5. Position the cam sprocket with the index marks facing toward the left-hand side.

6. Temporarily install the cam chain onto the cam sprocket (**Figure 104**).

7. Install the cam into the sprocket and cam chain.

8. Position the cam with the lobes facing down and the "F" mark on the flange facing up (**Figure 100**).

9. Carefully pull the cam chain off of the cam sprocket and rotate the cam sprocket until the index marks are parallel to the cylinder head surface (**Figure 105**).

10. Pull the cam chain and sprocket up onto the shoulder on the camshaft. Again check the alignment of the index marks as noted in Step 9.

If the alignment is incorrect, correct it at this time.

11. Temporarily install the sprocket bolt into the exposed hole (**Figure 106**).

12. Rotate the engine *clockwise* 360° and install the other cam sprocket bolt.

13. Rotate the engine *clockwise* 360° and check for correct cam sprocket alignment as described in Step 2 and Step 9; readjust if necessary.

> *CAUTION*
> *Very expensive damage could result from improper camshaft and chain alignment. Recheck your work several times to be sure alignment is correct.*

14. Remove the exposed cam sprocket bolt and apply Loctite Lock N' Seal to the bolt threads and to the underside of the bolt head. Install the bolt and tighten to the torque specifications listed in **Table 3**.

15. Rotate the engine *clockwise* one full turn (360°). Remove the exposed cam sprocket bolt and apply Loctite Lock N' Seal to the bolt threads and to the underside of the bolt head. Install this bolt and tighten to the torque specifications listed in **Table 3**.

16. Remove the 2 mm pin securing the cam chain tensioner wedge "B" (**Figure 107**).

17. Clean all oil residue from the rubber grommets and apply a light coat of liquid gasket seal to the portion that sits into the cylinder head.

18. Install the rubber grommets in the cylinder at each end of the camshaft. See **Figure 108** and **Figure 109**.

19. Place wood blocks under the crankcase so the front cylinder head is almost horizontal.

> *CAUTION*
> *The hydraulic tappets must be bled of all air before installation, otherwise they will not function properly.*

20. Inspect and bleed the hydraulic tappets as described in this chapter.

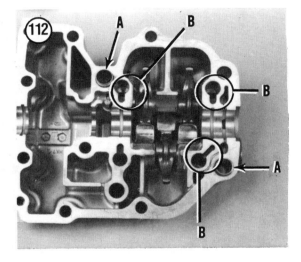

21. Install the tappet shims into their correct receptacle in the cylinder head (**Figure 110**).

22. Keep the hydraulic tappets vertical and install the tappets into their correct receptacles in the cylinder head (**Figure 111**).

23. Install the locating dowels (A, **Figure 112**).

24. Install the rocker arm assemblies, if removed, as described under *Rocker Arm Assemblies* in this chapter.

25. If the rear cylinder camshaft was removed, install it as described under *Rear Cylinder Head Cover and Camshaft Installation* before installing the front cylinder head cover. When the rear cylinder camshaft is correctly installed, proceed with Step 26.

CAUTION
*In the following step, do **not** apply the liquid gasket sealer to the area around each hydraulic tappet receptacle (B, **Figure 112**) or tappet failure may occur.*

26. Clean the mating surfaces of the cylinder head and the cylinder head cover with contact cleaner. Apply a light coat of liquid gasket sealer to the mating surface of the cylinder head cover.

27. Fill the cam lobe oil cavity in the cylinder head with fresh engine oil (**Figure 113**).

28. Using a 17 mm socket on the primary gear bolt, rotate the engine *clockwise* until the "F-T" mark (**Figure 103**) aligns with the fixed pointer on the crankcase cover.

29. Install the front cylinder head cover as follows.
   a. Remove the rocker arm shaft covers (**Figure 114**).
   b. Install the front cylinder head cover.

c. Check the position of the rocker arm shafts. The slot in the end of each shaft must face straight up (90°) as shown in **Figure 115**. If the slots are not positioned correctly, repeat Step 28.

30. Insert the water pipe into the cylinder head (**Figure 116**).

31. Install the cylinder head cover bolts and cap nuts. Tighten the bolts and nuts in a crisscross pattern in 2-3 stages to the torque specifications listed in **Table 3**.

32. If the rear cylinder was *not* disassembled, perform Steps 27-37 of *Rear Cylinder Head Cover and Camshaft Installation*.

Rear Cylinder Head Cover and Camshaft Installation

1. If the front cylinder head cover was not removed, perform the following.

   a. Remove the front cylinder head cover as described in this chapter. Do not remove the front cylinder head camshaft.

   b. Using a 17 mm socket on the primary gear bolt (**Figure 102**), rotate the engine *clockwise* until the "F-T" mark (**Figure 103**) aligns with the fixed pointer on the crankcase cover.

   c. Check the "F" identification mark on the camshaft flange (**Figure 100**). If the "F" mark faces up, rotate the engine *clockwise* 225° (180° plus 45°) and proceed to Step 2. If the "F" mark faces down (cannot be seen), rotate the engine *clockwise* 585° (360° plus 180° plus 45°) and proceed to Step 2.

   CAUTION
   If the front cylinder head cover and camshaft have been removed, the following steps will require the aid of a helper. When rotating the engine in the following steps, have the helper pull up on the cam chain for the rear cylinder and keep it properly meshed with the sprocket on the crankshaft. This is necessary to avoid letting the chain bunch up and damage the crankcase and chain.

2. Using a 17 mm socket on the primary gear bolt (**Figure 102**), rotate the engine *clockwise* until the "R-T" mark (**Figure 101**) aligns with the fixed pointer on the crankcase cover.

3. Coat all camshaft lobes and bearing journals with molybdenum disulfide grease or assembly oil.

4. Also coat the bearing surfaces in the cylinder head and camshaft bearing holders.

5. Position the cam sprocket with the index marks facing toward the left-hand side.

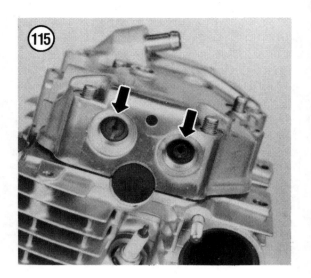

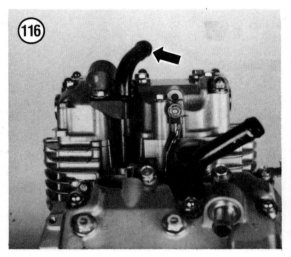

6. Temporarily install the cam chain onto the cam sprocket (**Figure 104**).

7. Install the cam into the sprocket and cam chain.

8. Position the cam with the lobes facing down and the "R" mark on the flange facing up (**Figure 100**).

9. Carefully pull the cam chain off of the cam sprocket and rotate the cam sprocket until the index marks are parallel to the cylinder head surface (**Figure 105**).

10. Pull the cam chain and sprocket up onto the shoulder on the camshaft. Again check the alignment of the index marks as noted in Step 10. If the alignment is incorrect, correct it at this time.

11. Temporarily install the sprocket bolt into the exposed hole (**Figure 106**).

12. Rotate the engine *clockwise* 360° and install the other cam sprocket bolt.

13. Rotate the engine *clockwise* 360° and check for correct cam sprocket alignment as described in Step 2 and Step 9; readjust if necessary.

CAUTION
Very expensive damage could result from improper camshaft and chain alignment. Recheck your work several times to be sure alignment is correct.

14. Remove the exposed cam sprocket bolt and apply Loctite Lock N' Seal to the bolt threads and to the underside of the bolt head. Install the bolt and tighten to the torque specifications listed in **Table 3**.

15. Rotate the engine *clockwise* one full turn (360°). Remove the exposed cam sprocket bolt and apply Loctite Lock N' Seal to the bolt threads and to the underside of the bolt head. Install this bolt

and tighten to the torque specifications listed in **Table 3**.

16. Remove the 2 mm pin securing the cam chain tensioner wedge "B" (**Figure 107**).

17. Clean all oil residue from the rubber grommets and apply a light coat of liquid gasket seal to the portion that seats into the cylinder head.

18. Install the rubber grommets in the cylinder at each end of the camshaft. See **Figure 108** and **Figure 109**.

19. Place wood blocks under the crankcase so the rear cylinder head is almost horizontal.

CAUTION
The hydraulic tappets must be bled of all air before installation, otherwise they will not function properly.

20. Inspect and bleed the hydraulic tappets as described in this chapter.

21. Install the tappet shims into their correct receptacle in the cylinder head (**Figure 110**).

22. Keep the hydraulic tappets vertical and install the tappets into their correct receptacles in the cylinder head (**Figure 111**).

23. Install the locating dowels (A, **Figure 112**).

24. Install the rocker arm assemblies, if removed, as described under *Rocker Arm Assemblies* in this chapter.

CAUTION
*In the following step, do **not** apply the liquid gasket sealer to the area around each hydraulic tappet receptacle (B, **Figure 112**) or tappet failure may occur.*

25. Clean the mating surfaces of the cylinder head and the cylinder head cover with contact cleaner. Apply a light coat of liquid gasket sealer to the mating surface of the cylinder head cover.

26. Fill the cam lobe oil cavity in the cylinder head with fresh engine oil (**Figure 113**).

27. Using a 17 mm socket on the primary gear bolt, rotate the engine *clockwise* until the "R-T" mark (**Figure 101**) aligns with the fixed pointer on the crankcase cover.

28. Install the rear cylinder head cover as follows.
    a. Remove the rocker arm shaft covers (**Figure 114**).
    b. Install the rear cylinder head cover (**Figure 117**).
    c. Check the position of the rocker arm shafts. The slot in the end of each shaft must face straight up (90°) as shown in **Figure 115**. If the slots are not positioned correctly, repeat Step 27.

29. Insert the water pipe into the cylinder head (**Figure 118**).

30. Install the cylinder head cover bolts and cap nuts. Tighten the bolts and nuts in a crisscross pattern in 2-3 stages to the torque specifications listed in **Table 3**.

31. If the front cylinder was *not* disassembled, perform Steps 28-31 of *Front Cylinder Head Cover and Camshaft Installation*.

NOTE
Steps 32-37 pertain to both the front and rear cylinders.

32. Inspect the O-ring seals (**Figure 119**) on the spark plug sleeve. Replace O-ring seals if they are hard or starting to deteriorate.

33. Install the spark plug sleeve into the cylinder head and tighten securely. Use the same tool set-up used for removal.

34. Install the external oil pipe to each cylinder head and to the crankcase. Install a sealing washer on each side of the fitting where the bolts attach. Tighten the bolts to the torque specification listed in **Table 3**.

35. On California models, install the secondary air pipes.

36. Install the engine as described in this chapter.

37. Make sure the O-ring seals are in place on the coolant pipes.

CYLINDER HEADS

Removal/Installation

Either cylinder head can be removed without first removing the other cylinder head. If both cylinder heads are going to be removed, either cylinder head can be removed first. This procedure pertains to both cylinder heads.

1. Remove the engine as described in this chapter.

2. Remove the cylinder head cover, camshaft holder and camshaft for the specific cylinder as described in this chapter.

3. Remove the bolts (**Figure 120**) securing the cam chain tensioner and pull the cam chain tensioner assembly up out of the cylinder head (**Figure 121**).

4. Loosen the head by tapping around the perimeter with a rubber or plastic mallet.

CAUTION
Remember, the fins on the cylinder head are fragile and may be damaged if tapped or pried too hard. Never use a metal hammer. These fins are more for cosmetic value than cooling and are not as fragile as those on an air cooled engine, but they still may break.

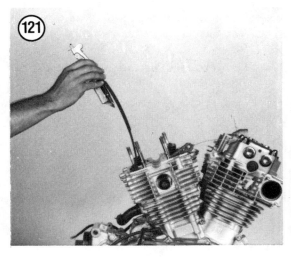

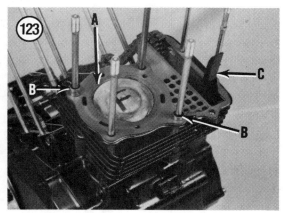

5. Untie the wire securing the cam chain and retie it to the cylinder head. Lift the cylinder head (**Figure 122**) straight up and off the crankcase studs. Pull the cam chain and wire through the opening in the cylinder head and retie the cam chain up to one of the crankcase studs.

> *NOTE*
> *If both heads are going to be removed, mark them with an "F" (front cylinder) or "R" (rear cylinder) so they will be reinstalled onto the correct position on the engine.*

6. Remove the head gasket, dowel pins and the cam chain guide.

7. Place a clean shop rag into the cam chain opening in the cylinder to prevent entry of foreign matter.

8. Install by reversing these removal steps, noting the following.

9. Clean the cylinder head mating surfaces of any gasket material.

10. See **Figure 123** (1983-1985) or **Figure 124** (1986-on). Install a new head gasket (A) and locating dowels (B).

11. Install the cam chain guide. See C, **Figure 123** or C, **Figure 124**.

12. Install the bolts (**Figure 120**) securing the cam chain tensioner and tighten the bolts securely.

13. Install the bolt and nuts securing the cylinder head. Tighten the bolts in 2-3 stages in a crisscross pattern to the torque specifications listed in **Table 2** or **Table 3**.

14. Repeat this procedure for the other cylinder head if necessary.

Inspection

1. Remove all traces of gasket material from the cylinder head (A, **Figure 125**) and the cylinder mating surfaces.

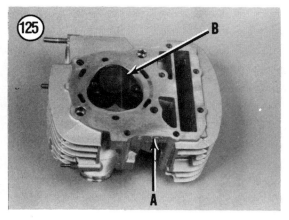

2. *Without* removing the valves, remove all carbon deposits from the combustion chambers (B, **Figure 125**) with a wire brush. A blunt screwdriver or chisel may be used if care is taken not to damage the head, valves and spark plug threads.

3. After all carbon is removed from the combustion chambers and valve intake and exhaust ports, clean the entire head in solvent.

4. Clean away all carbon on the piston crowns. Do not remove the carbon ridge at the top of the cylinder bore.

5. Check for cracks in the combustion chamber (B, **Figure 125**) and exhaust ports (**Figure 126**). A cracked head must be replaced.

6. After the head has been thoroughly cleaned, place a straightedge across the gasket surface (**Figure 127**) at several points. Measure warp by inserting a flat feeler gauge between the straightedge and the cylinder head at each location. There should be no warpage. If a small amount is present, the head can be resurfaced by a Honda dealer or qualified machine shop.

7. Check the valves and valve guides as described in this chapter.

8. Inspect the cam chain tensioner and cam chain guide for wear (**Figure 128**).

9. Inspect the spring and all moving parts of the cam chain tensioner assembly (**Figure 129**) for wear or damage. If any parts are worn the assembly must be replaced.

VALVES AND VALVE COMPONENTS

Removal

Refer to **Figure 130** for this procedure.

1. Remove the cylinder head(s) as described in this chapter.

2. Compress springs with a valve spring compressor tool (**Figure 131**). Remove the valve

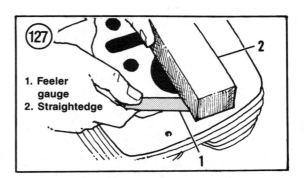

1. Feeler gauge
2. Straightedge

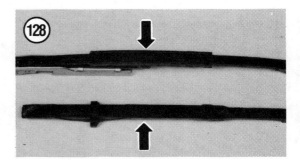

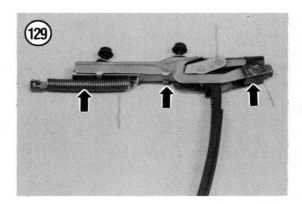

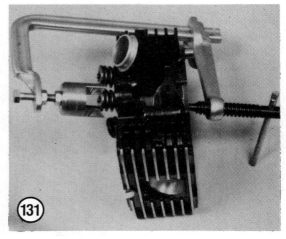

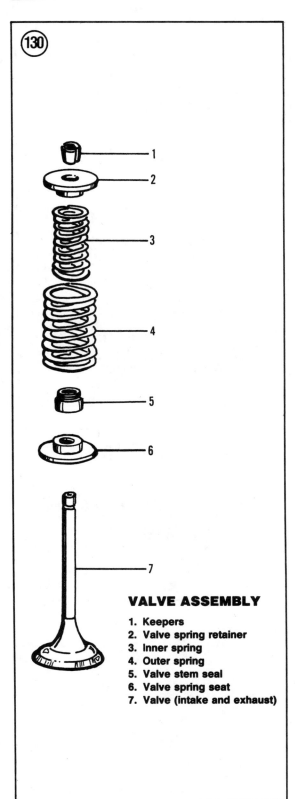

VALVE ASSEMBLY

1. Keepers
2. Valve spring retainer
3. Inner spring
4. Outer spring
5. Valve stem seal
6. Valve spring seat
7. Valve (intake and exhaust)

keepers and release compression. Remove the valve compressor tool.

CAUTION
To avoid loss of spring tension, do not compress the springs any more than necessary to remove the keepers.

3. Before removing the valves, remove any burrs from the valve stem (**Figure 132**). Otherwise, the valve guides will be damaged.
4. Remove the valve keepers, valve spring retainer and both inner and outer springs (**Figure 133**).
5. Remove the valve seal/ring and the valve spring seat.

Inspection

1. Clean all valves with a wire brush and solvent.
2. Inspect the contact surface of each valve for burning. Minor roughness and pitting can be removed by lapping the valve as described in this chapter. Excessive unevenness of the contact

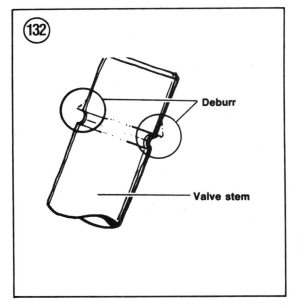

surface is an indication that the valve is not serviceable.

> *NOTE*
> *The contact surface of the valve **cannot** be ground. The valve must be replaced if this area shows more than normal damage.*

3. Measure valve stems for wear (**Figure 134**). Compare with specifications in **Table 1**.
4. Remove all carbon and varnish from the valve guides with a stiff spiral wire brush.

> *NOTE*
> *The next step assumes that all valve stems are within specifications.*

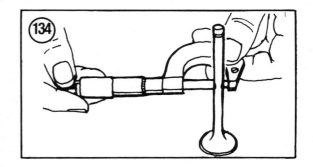

5. Insert each valve in its guide. Hold the valve just slightly off its seat and rock it sideways in 2 directions (**Figure 135**). If it rocks more than slightly, the guide is probably worn and should be replaced. If a dial indicator is available, a more accurate measurement can be made as shown in **Figure 136**. Replace any guides that exceed the valve stem-to-guide clearance specified in **Table 1**. If the guides must be replaced, take the cylinder head to a dealer or machine shop for guide replacement.
6. Measure the valve spring heights with a vernier caliper (**Figure 137**). All should be the length specified in **Table 1** with no bends or other distortion. Replace defective springs as a set.
7. Check the valve spring retainer and valve keepers. If they are in good condition, they may be reused.
8. Inspect valve seats. If worn or burned, they must be reconditioned. This should be performed by your dealer or a qualified machine shop. Seats and valves in near-perfect condition can be reconditioned by lapping with a fine carborundum paste. Lapping, however, is always inferior to precision grinding.

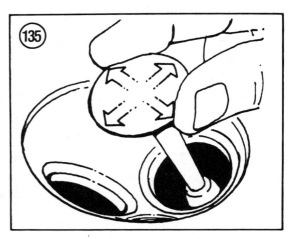

Installation

1. Install the valve spring seat (A, **Figure 138**).
2. Remove the ring from the valve seal. This will make valve seal installation much easier.
3. Install a new valve seal (B, **Figure 138**) and then install the ring onto the valve seal.
4. Coat the valve stems with molybdenum disulfide grease. To avoid damage to the valve stem seal, turn the valve slowly while inserting the valve into the cylinder head.

> *NOTE*
> *The exhaust valve springs have a stripe of green paint on them.*

Valve   Dial gauge

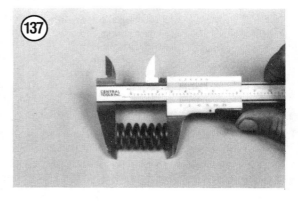

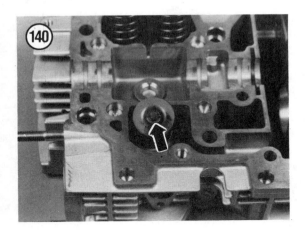

5. Install the valve springs with the narrow pitch end (end with coils closest together) facing the head (**Figure 139**). Install the upper valve spring retainers.

6. Push down on upper valve spring retainers with the valve spring compressor and install valve keepers.

> *CAUTION*
> *To avoid loss of spring tension, do not compress the springs any more than necessary to install the keepers.*

7. After all keepers have been installed, gently tap the valve stems (**Figure 140**) with a plastic mallet to make sure the keepers are properly seated.

Valve Guide Replacement

When guides are worn so that there is excessive stem-to-guide clearance or valve tipping, they must be replaced. Replace all, even if only one is worn. This job should only be done by a dealer, as special tools are required.

Valve Seat Reconditioning

This job is best left to your dealer or local machine shop. They have the special equipment and knowledge for this exacting job. You can still save considerable money by removing the cylinder heads and taking just the heads to the shop.

Valve Lapping

Valve lapping is a simple operation which can restore the valve seal without machining if the amount of wear or distortion is not too great.

> *CAUTION*
> *Avoid excessive lapping as it will wear off the special surface coating on the valve face. If this happens the valves will burn prematurely.*

1. Coat the valve seating area in the head with a lapping compound such as Carborundum or Clover Brand.

2. Insert the valve into the cylinder head.

3. Wet the suction cup (**Figure 141**) of the lapping stick and stick it onto the head of the valve. Lap the valve to the seat by rotating the lapping stick in both directions. Every 5 to 10 seconds, rotate the valve 180° in the valve seat; continue lapping until

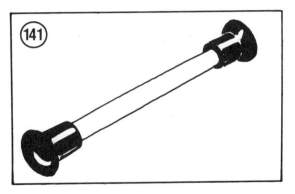

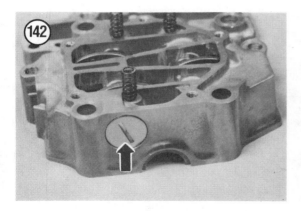

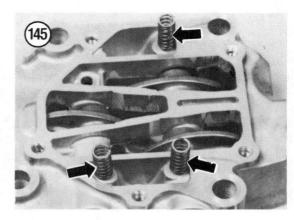

the contact surfaces of the valve and the valve seat are a uniform grey. Stop as soon as they are, to avoid removing too much material.

4. Thoroughly clean the valves and cylinder head in solvent to remove all lapping compound. Any compound left on the valves or the cylinder head will end up in the engine and will cause rapid valve stem and guide wear.

5. After the lapping has been completed and the valve assemblies have been reinstalled into the head, the valve seal should be tested. Check the seal of each valve by pouring solvent into each of the intake and exhaust ports. The solvent should not flow past the valve seat and the valve head. Perform on all sets of valves. If fluid leaks past any of the seats, disassemble that valve assembly and repeat the lapping procedure until there is no leakage.

ROCKER ARM ASSEMBLIES
(1983-1985)

The rocker arm assemblies (rocker arms, shafts and camshaft holder) for the front and rear cylinders are identical (same Honda part No.) but they will develop different wear patterns during

use. It is recommended that the rocker arm assemblies from one head be disassembled, inspected and then assembled to avoid the intermixing of parts.

Disassembly

1. Remove the camshaft and camshaft holder as described in this chapter.

2. Unscrew the plug from the camshaft holder (**Figure 142**) from the side opposite the cam chain.

3. On the side next to the cam chain, screw in a 6 mm bolt (**Figure 143**) into each plug and remove both rocker arm holder plugs (**Figure 144**).

4. Remove the assist shafts and springs (**Figure 145**).

5. Using a rubber mallet, tap on the ends of the camshaft holder and the rocker arm shafts will partially work their way out of the camshaft holder.

6. Withdraw each rocker arm shaft and rocker arm (**Figure 146**). Place each set in a container and keep them separate as they must be reinstalled in the correct position. Mark the exhaust, intake (away from the cam chain) and intake (next to cam chain).

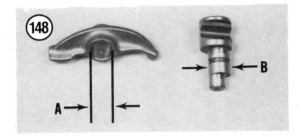

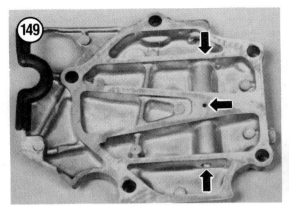

4

Inspection

1. Wash all parts in cleaning solvent and dry thoroughly.

2. Inspect the rocker arm pad where it rides on the cam lobe and where it rides on the valve stem (**Figure 147**). If the pad is scratched or unevenly worn, inspect the cam lobe for scoring, chipping or flat spots. Replace the rocker arm if defective.

3. Measure the inside diameter of the rocker arm (A, **Figure 148**) with an inside micrometer and check against dimensions in **Table 1**. Replace if worn to the service limit or greater.

NOTE
Even though all 3 rocker arm shafts are different in appearance, the inspection dimension is the same for all 3.

4. Inspect the rocker arm shaft for signs of wear or scoring. Measure the outside diameter where the rocker arm rides (not the larger portion that rides in the camshaft holder) (B, **Figure 148**) with a micrometer and check against dimensions in **Table 1**. Replace if worn to the service limit or less.

5. Inspect each assist shaft for wear or bending; replace if necessary.

6. Measure the freelength of each assist spring. Replace all 3 as a set even if only one has sagged to the service limit dimension given in **Table 1**.

7. Inspect the oil flow holes (**Figure 149**) in the cylinder head cover and the camshaft holder (**Figure 150**). Blow them out with compressed air to make sure they are open. They must be clean for proper oil flow to the assist shafts and springs.

8. Inspect the O-ring seal on each plug. Replace if they have started to harden or deteriorate.

Assembly

1. Coat the rocker arm shaft and rocker arm bore with molybdenum disulfide grease.

CAUTION
*In the following steps be sure to install the correct rocker arm into the correct position in the camshaft holder. Refer to **Figure 146**.*

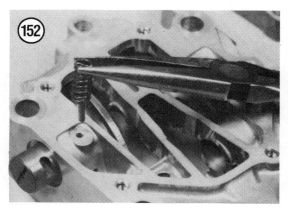

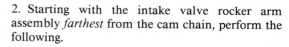

2. Starting with the intake valve rocker arm assembly *farthest* from the cam chain, perform the following.

   a. Partially install the intake rocker arm shaft and align the rocker arm with the shaft. Push the rocker arm shaft in sufficiently to hold the rocker arm in place.

   b. Align the assist shaft notch (A, **Figure 151**) in the rocker arm with the assist shaft hole (B, **Figure 151**) in the camshaft holder.

   c. Recheck the alignment (**Figure 152**) and push the rocker arm shaft in all the way.

   d. Install the assist shaft and assist spring (A, **Figure 153**).

   e. After the assist shaft and spring are installed, use a screwdriver in the slot in the end of the rocker arm shaft to carefully turn the rocker arm shaft (B, **Figure 153**) back and forth about 8-10° from the 1 o'clock position. Check that the rocker arm shaft and rocker arm move

correctly and that the assist shaft and spring move up and down.

   f. Move the slot in the end of the rocker arm shaft to the 1 o'clock position. At this point the assist shaft should be in the down position.

3. On the intake valve rocker arm assembly *next* to the cam chain, perform the following.

   a. Partially install the rocker arm shaft and align the rocker arm with the shaft. Push the rocker arm shaft in sufficiently to hold the rocker arm in place.

   b. Align the assist shaft notch (A, **Figure 154**) in the rocker arm with the assist shaft hole (B, **Figure 154**) in the camshaft holder.

   c. Recheck the alignment and push the rocker arm shaft in all the way.

   d. Install the assist shaft and assist spring (A, **Figure 155**).

   e. After the assist shaft and spring are installed use a screwdriver in the slot in the end of the rocker arm shaft to carefully turn the rocker arm shaft (B, **Figure 155**) back and forth about

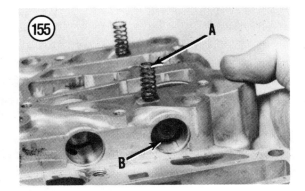

4

8-10° from the 11 o'clock position. Check that the rocker arm shaft and rocker arm move correctly and that the assist shaft and spring moves up and down.

   f. Move the slot in the end of the rocker arm shaft to the 11 o'clock position. At this point the assist shaft should be in the down position.

4. On the exhaust rocker valve arm assembly, perform the following.

   a. Partially install the exhaust rocker arm shaft and align the rocker arm with the shaft. Push the rocker arm shaft in sufficiently to hold the rocker arm in place.

   b. Align the assist shaft notch (A, **Figure 156**) in the rocker arm with the assist shaft hole (B, **Figure 156**) in the camshaft holder.

   c. Recheck the alignment and push the rocker arm shaft in all the way.

   d. Install the assist shaft and assist spring (**Figure 157**).

   e. After the assist shaft and spring are installed, use a screwdriver in the slot in the end of the rocker arm shaft to carefully turn the rocker arm shaft (**Figure 158**) back and forth about 8-10° from the 1 o'clock position. Check that the rocker arm shaft and rocker arm move

correctly and that the assist shaft and spring move up and down.

   f. Move the slot in the end of the rocker arm shaft to the 1 o'clock position. At this point the assist shaft should be in the down position.

5. Repeat the disassembly, inspection and assembly procedures for the other cylinder head camshaft holder assembly.

ROCKER ARM ASSEMBLIES (1986-ON)

The rocker arm assemblies (rocker arms, shafts and camshaft holder) for the front and rear cylinders are identical (same Honda part No.) but they will develop different wear patterns during use. It is recommended that the rocker arm assemblies from one head be disassembled, inspected and then assembled to avoid the intermixing of parts.

Disassembly

1. Remove the cylinder head cover as described in this chapter.

2. Lift the rocker arm shaft stopper pin (**Figure 159**) out of the cylinder head cover.

> *NOTE*
> *Loosen the assist shaft caps slowly in Step 3 as the springs under the caps may fly out.*

3. Remove the 3 assist shaft caps (**Figure 160**) from the cylinder head cover.
4. Remove the 3 assist springs and assist shafts. See **Figure 161** and **Figure 162**.
5. Unscrew the 3 shaft hole plugs from the cylinder head cover. See **Figure 163** and **Figure 164**.

> *NOTE*
> *Place each rocker arm shaft and rocker arm set in a container and keep them separate. All 3 rocker arms are different from each other and must be reinstalled in the correct position.*

6. Remove the intake rocker arm shafts. On the cam chain side, screw a 6 mm bolt (**Figure 165**) into the end of the rocker arm and pull it out of the rocker arm cover. Remove the opposite rocker arm by pulling it out of the cover as shown in **Figure 166**.
7. Remove the exhaust rocker arm shaft by pulling it out of the cover as shown in **Figure 167**.
8. Lift the rocker arms (**Figure 168**) out of the cylinder head cover.

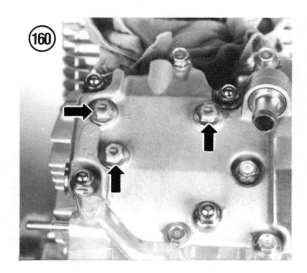

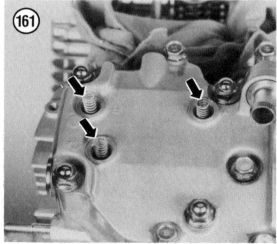

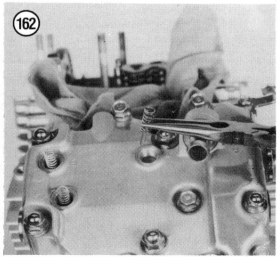

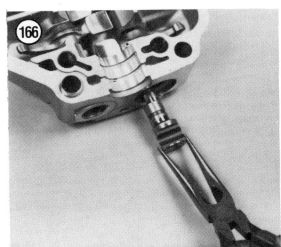

4

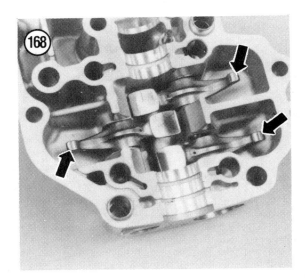

Inspection

1. Wash all parts (**Figure 169**) in cleaning solvent and dry thoroughly.

2. Inspect the rocker arm pad where it rides on the cam lobe and where it rides on the valve stem (**Figure 170**). If the pad is scratched or unevenly worn, inspect the cam lobe for scoring, chipping or flat spots. Replace the rocker arm if defective.

3. Measure the inside diameter of the rocker arm (A, **Figure 171**) with an inside micrometer and check against dimensions in **Table 1**. Replace if worn to the service limit or greater.

NOTE
Even though all 3 rocker arm shafts are different in appearance, the inspection dimension is the same for all 3.

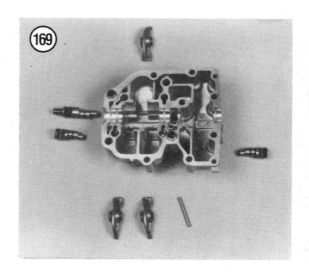

4. Inspect the rocker arm shaft for signs of wear or scoring. Measure the outside diameter where the rocker arm rides (not the larger portion that rides in the camshaft holder) (B, **Figure 171**) with a micrometer and check against dimensions in **Table 1**. Replace if worn to the service limit or less.

5. Inspect each assist shaft (**Figure 172**) for wear or bending; replace as necessary.

6. Measure the free length of each assist spring (**Figure 173**). Replace all 3 as a set even if only one has sagged to the service limit dimension given in **Table 1**.

7. Inspect the oil flow holes (**Figure 174**) in the cylinder head cover. Blow them out with compressed air to make sure they are open. They must be clean for proper oil flow to the assist shafts and springs.

8. Inspect the O-ring seal on each plug (**Figure 175**). Replace if they have started to harden or deteriorate.

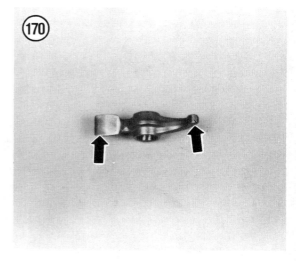

Assembly

1. Coat the rocker arm shaft and rocker arm bore with molybdenum disulfide grease.

CAUTION
In the following steps be sure to install the correct rocker arm into the correct position in the camshaft holder. Refer to **Figure 176** *(intake) and* **Figure 177** *(exhaust).*

2. Install the exhaust rocker arm and shaft as follows.

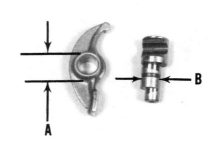

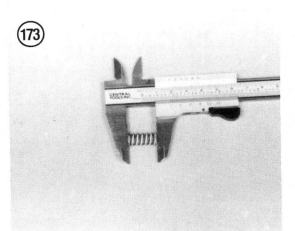

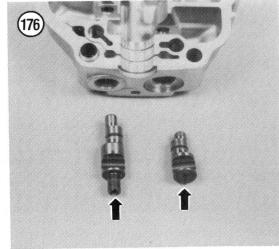

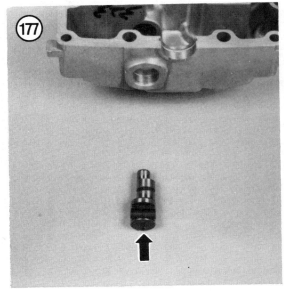

4

a. Install the exhaust rocker arm (**Figure 178**) into the cylinder head cover.

b. Insert the exhaust rocker arm shaft into the cylinder head cover as shown in **Figure 167**.

c. Install the rocker arm shaft stopper pin (**Figure 159**).

3. Install the intake rocker arms and shafts as follows.

a. Install the intake rocker arm (closest to cam chain) into the cylinder head cover. See **Figure 179**.

b. Insert the intake rocker arm shaft into the cylinder head cover as shown in **Figure 180**.

c. Install the intake rocker arm (farthest from cam chain) into the cylinder head cover. See **Figure 181**.

d. Insert the intake rocker arm shaft into the cylinder head cover as shown in **Figure 182**.

4. Check that the alignment slot in the end of each rocker arm shaft faces 90° (straight up) as shown in **Figure 183**.

CAUTION
*If the alignment slot positioning is incorrect, the assist springs and shafts cannot be properly installed. Rotate the rocker arm shafts to obtain the correct alignment as shown in **Figure 183**.*

5. Install and tighten the cylinder head cover before installing the assist shafts and springs. Install as described in this chapter for 1986 and later models.

6. Turn the assist spring onto the assist shaft, if removed (**Figure 172**).

7. Install the assist shafts and springs into the cylinder head cover (**Figure 184**). The springs

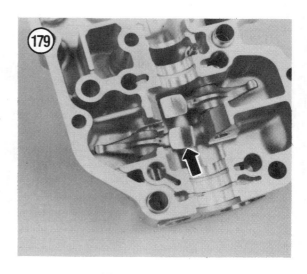

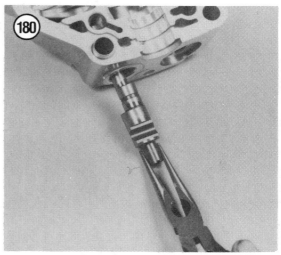

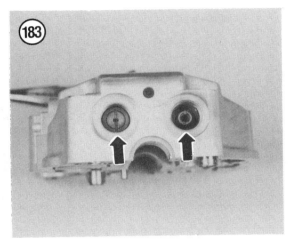

should protrude above the cylinder head cover as shown in **Figure 185**.

8. Replace the assist cap O-rings if hard or worn.

9. Install the assist shaft caps (**Figure 186**). Tighten the caps to the torque specifications in **Table 3**.

10. Repeat the disassembly, inspection and assembly procedures for the other cylinder head camshaft holder assembly.

HYDRAULIC TAPPET

Inspection

1. Inspect the exterior of the tappet (**Figure 187**) for wear or damage; replace if necessary.

2. Measure the free length of the tappet as follows.

  a. Bleed the tappet as described in this chapter.

  b. Remove the tappet from the container used for bleeding.

  c. Keep the tappet upright and place it on a flat surface and under a dial gauge.

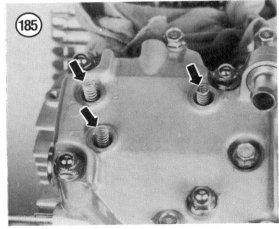

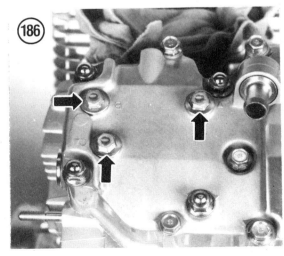

d. Still keeping the tappet upright, try to quickly compress the tappet with your fingers (**Figure 188**).

e. You should be able to compress the tappet between 0-0.2 mm (0-0.0078 in.). If it compresses more than the specified dimension, the tappet must be replaced.

3. If the tappet is okay, it must be bled again before installation.

Bleeding

For proper operation, the hydraulic tappets must be free of air in the high pressure chamber. A special Honda tool, Hydraulic Tappet Bleeder, Honda part No. 07973-ME90000 (1983-1985)/part No. 07973-MJ00000 (1986-on) or an improvised tool set-up may be used.

> *CAUTION*
> *Be sure to note the correct location in the cylinder head from where the tappet and shim(s) were removed.*

1. Remove the tappet and shim(s) from the cylinder head as described in this chapter.

2. Fill a wide mouth plastic or glass jar (it has to be transparent) with kerosene. Fill the jar with enough kerosene so the tappet is completely covered.

> *CAUTION*
> *The tappet must be kept submerged and upright during this procedure.*

3A. If the special tool is used, perform the following.

a. Place the tappet right side up within the special tool.

b. Place the special tool and tappet into the jar filled with kerosene.

c. Hold the tappet and special tool upright, push down on the special tool and pump the tappet as shown in **Figure 189**.

d. Continue to pump until air bubbles stop coming from the high pressure chamber in the tappet.

3B. If the special tool is not available, perform the following.

a. Insert a 1/16 in. drill bit into the opening in the top of the tappet.

b. Place the tappet and drill bit into the jar filled with kerosene (**Figure 190**).

c. Hold the tappet upright, push down on the drill bit with a piece of metal or wood dowel and pump the tappet as shown in **Figure 191**.

d. Continue to pump until air bubbles stop coming from the high pressure chamber in the tappet.

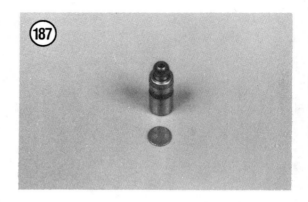

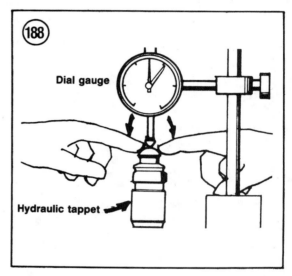

Dial gauge

Hydraulic tappet

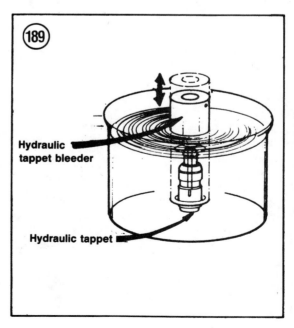

Hydraulic tappet bleeder

Hydraulic tappet

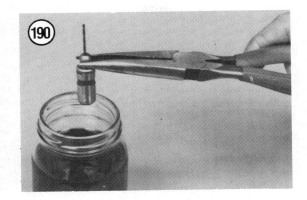

NOTE
The small amount of kerosene left in the high pressure chamber of the tappets will not contaminate the engine's oil.

4. Remove the tappet from the jar filled with kerosene and keep the tappet in the upright position. If the tappet is laid down on an angle or on its side, air will enter the high pressure chamber and the tappet will have to be bled again.
5. Reinstall the tappet and shim(s) into the correct receptacle in the cylinder head as described in this chapter.
6. Repeat this procedure for all tappets.

Tappet Shim Adjustment

In order to achieve zero clearance in the valve train, the tappet must provide the correct amount of pressure on the rocker arm. To compensate for manufacturing tolerances in various parts, shims are added to the base of each tappet. Measuring the stroke of the assist shaft will determine the number of shim(s) required to achieve the correct pressure.

This procedure is *not* a routine adjustment but has to be performed *only* when any of the following parts are replaced.
    a. Camshaft holder (1983-1985).
    b. Cylinder head cover (1986-on).
    c. Cylinder head.
    d. Valve, valve guide or valve seat (reground).
    e. Rocker arm and rocker arm shaft.
    f. Camshaft.
1. Remove the camshaft cover (1983-1985) or cylinder head cover (1986-on) as described in this chapter.
2. Remove the tappets as described in this chapter.
3. Bleed the tappets as described in this chapter.
4. Remove all shims from the receptacles in the cylinder head.
5. Install the tappets into their correct receptacles in the cylinder head. See **Figure 192** (1983-1985) or **Figure 193** (1986-on).
6A. *1983-1985:* Install the camshaft holder and secure it with the 8 mm bolts and 10 mm cap nuts (**Figure 194**). Tighten the bolts and nuts to the torque specifications listed in **Table 2**.
6B. *1986-on:* Install the cylinder head cover and secure it with the 6 mm, 8 mm and 10 mm bolts and nuts (**Figure 195**). Tighten the bolts and nuts to the torque specifications listed in **Table 3**.

7. Using the 17 mm bolt on the primary drive gear (**Figure 196**), rotate the engine *clockwise* until the timing marks align with the fixed pointer on the crankcase cover. Refer to the following.

    a. **Figure 197**: front cylinder "F-T".

    b. **Figure 198**: rear cylinder "R-T".

8. Install a dial gauge to the camshaft holder.

NOTE
*The assist shafts are installed in Step 9 without their springs. See **Figure 199**.*

9. Install one of the assist shafts into the hole in the camshaft holder (1983-1985) or cylinder head cover (1986-on).

10. Place the dial indicator over the assist shaft and place the pointer of the dial indicator onto the top of the assist shaft (**Figure 200**).

11. Zero-in the dial on the dial indicator.

12. Have an assistant rotate the crankshaft 2 complete revolutions using the 17 mm bolt on the primary drive gear.

13. Record the stroke dimension of the assist shaft during these 2 revolutions.

14. Refer to the dimensions listed in **Table 4** to determine the number of shim(s) required under that tappet.

15. Repeat this procedure for all tappets affected by any replaced parts.

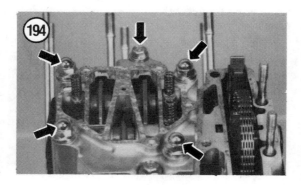

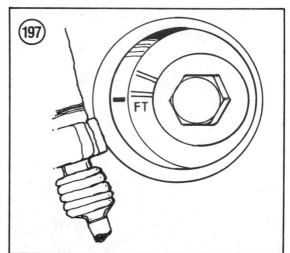

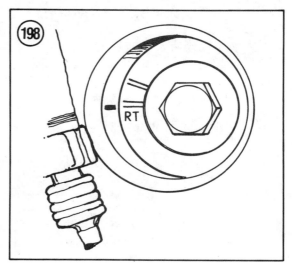

16. After the shims have been added to all tappets in one cylinder head, repeat this procedure and check that the stroke is within the 0-1.20 mm (0-0.047 in.) range.

CYLINDER

Removal

1. Remove the cylinder head as described in this chapter.
2. If both cylinders are going to be removed, they should be marked with an "F" (front cylinder) or "R" (rear cylinder) as shown in **Figure 201**. This will avoid any mix-up upon installation.
3. Loosen the cylinder by tapping around the perimeter with a rubber or plastic mallet. If necessary, *gently* pry the cylinder loose with a broad-tipped screwdriver.
4. Pull the cylinder straight up and off of the crankcase studs. Work the cam chain wire through the opening in the cylinder.
5. Remove the cylinder base gasket and discard it. Remove the dowel pins from the crankcase studs.
6. Install a piston holding fixture under the piston (**Figure 202**) to protect the piston skirt from damage. This fixture may be purchased or may be a homemade unit of wood. See **Figure 203** for dimensions.

Inspection

The following procedure requires the use of highly specialized and expensive measuring instruments. If such equipment is not readily available, have the measurements performed by a dealer or qualified machine shop.

1. Do not remove or damage the carbon ridge around the top of the cylinder bore. If the cylinders, pistons, and rings are found to be dimensionally correct and can be reused, removal

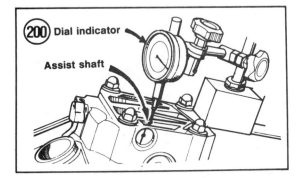

Dial indicator

Assist shaft

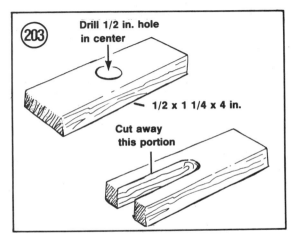

Drill 1/2 in. hole in center

1/2 x 1 1/4 x 4 in.

Cut away this portion

of the carbon ridge from the top of the cylinder bores or the ring from the top of pistons will promote excessive oil consumption.

2. Soak with solvent any old cylinder head gasket material on the cylinder. Use a broad-tipped *dull* chisel and gently scrape off all gasket residue. Do not gouge the sealing surface as oil and air leaks will result.

3. Measure the cylinder bore with a cylinder gauge or inside micrometer at the points shown in **Figure 204**. Measure in 2 axes—in line with the piston-pin and at 90° to the pin. If the taper or out-of-round is 0.10 mm (0.004 in.) or greater, the cylinder must be rebored to the next oversize and a new piston installed. There are 2 oversize piston sizes available (0.25 mm and 0.50 mm oversize).

NOTE
The new piston should be obtained before the cylinder is rebored so that the piston can be measured. Slight manufacturing tolerances must be taken into account to determine the actual size and working clearance.

4. Check the cylinder wall (**Figure 205**) for scratches. If evident, the cylinder should be rebored.

Installation

1. Check that the top surface of the crankcase and the bottom surface of the cylinder are clean before installing a new base gasket.

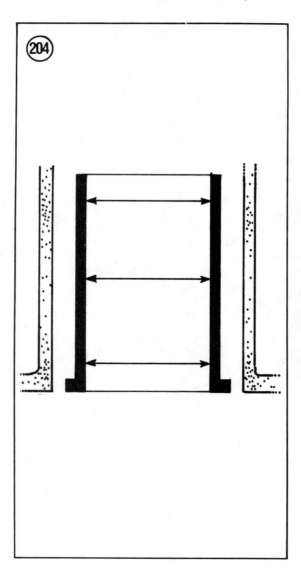

2. Install a new cylinder base gasket (A, **Figure 206**) and locating dowels (B, **Figure 206**) to either the crankcase or to the base of the cylinder.

3. Make sure the piston holding fixture is still under the piston (C, **Figure 206**).

4. Make sure the end gaps of the piston rings are *not* lined up with each other. They must be staggered. Lightly oil the piston rings and the inside of the cylinder bores with assembly oil.

5. Install the cylinder and slide it down onto the crankcase studs (**Figure 207**).

> *CAUTION*
> *The side rings of the oil ring assembly are very thin. Be very careful that the cylinder does not snag one of these rings during installation.*

6. Start the cylinder down over the piston. Compress each piston ring with your fingers as it enters the cylinder.

7. Slide the cylinder down until it bottoms on the piston holding fixture (**Figure 208**).

8. Remove the piston holding fixture and slide the cylinder down into place on the crankcase.

9. Carefully feed the cam chain and wire up through the opening in the cylinder and tie it to the engine (**Figure 209**).

10. Install the cylinder head as described in this chapter.

11. Follow the *Break-in Procedure* in this chapter if the cylinder was rebored or honed or a new piston or piston rings were installed.

12. Repeat this procedure for the other cylinder if necessary.

PISTON PIN AND PISTON RINGS

Piston Removal

1. Remove the cylinder head as described in this chapter.

2. Mark the top of each piston with an "F" (front cylinder) or "R" (rear cylinder) so they will be reinstalled in their correct cylinder. Refer to **Figure 210**.

3. Remove the cylinder as described in this chapter.

4. Remove the piston rings as described in this chapter.

> *NOTE*
> *Wrap a clean shop cloth under the piston so the piston pin clip will not fall into the crankcase.*

5. Remove the piston pin clips (**Figure 211**) from each side of the piston with a small screwdriver or scribe. Hold your thumb over one edge of the clip when removing it to prevent it from springing out.

6. Use a proper size wooden dowel or socket extension and push out the piston pin.

CAUTION
Be careful when removing the pin to avoid damaging the connecting rod. If it is necessary to gently tap the pin to remove it, be sure that the piston is properly supported.

7. If the piston pin is difficult to remove, heat the piston and pin with a small butane torch. The pin will probably push right out. If not, heat the piston to about 60° C (140° F), i.e., until it is too warm to touch, but not excessively hot. If the pin is still difficult to push out, use a special tool as shown in **Figure 212**.

Piston Inspection

1. Carefully clean the carbon from the piston crown with a chemical remover or with a soft scraper. Do not remove or damage the carbon ridge around the circumference of the piston above the top ring. If the pistons, rings and cylinders are found to be dimensionally correct and can be reused, removal of the carbon ring from the top of pistons or carbon ridge from the top of cylinder bores will promote excessive oil consumption.

CAUTION
Do not wire brush piston skirts.

2. Examine each ring groove for burrs, dented edges and wide wear. Pay particular attention to the top compression ring groove, as it usually wears more than the others.
3. Measure piston-to-cylinder clearance as described in this chapter. If damage or wear indicates piston replacement, select a new piston as described under *Piston Clearance Measurement* in this chapter.
4. Oil the piston pin and install it in the connecting rod bearing. Slowly rotate the piston pin and check for radial and axial play (**Figure 213**). If there is play, the piston pin should be replaced, providing the rod bore is in good condition.
5. Measure the piston pin bore (**Figure 214**) with a snap gauge and measure the outside diameter of the piston pin with a micrometer (**Figure 215**). Compare against dimensions given in **Table 1**. A machinist can do this for you if you do not have the measuring tools. Replace the piston and piston pin as a set if either is worn.
6. Check the piston skirt for galling and abrasion which may have been caused by piston seizure. If light galling is present, smooth the affected area with No. 400 emery cloth and oil or a fine oilstone.

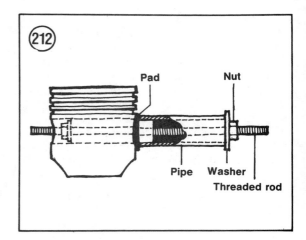

Pad   Nut
Pipe   Washer
Threaded rod

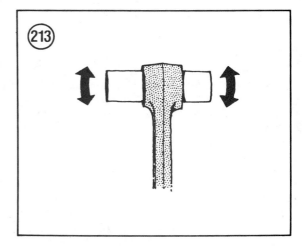

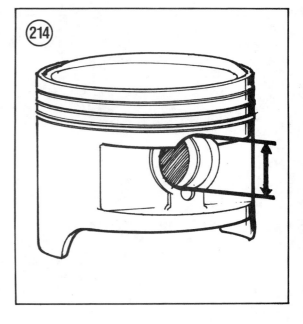

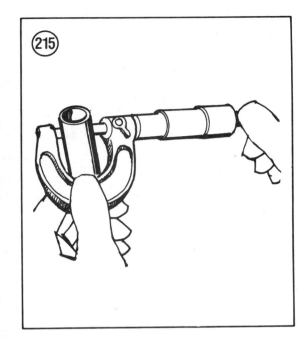

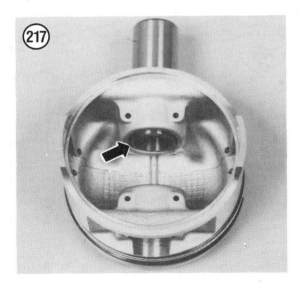

However, if galling is severe or if the piston is deeply scored, replace it.

Piston Clearance Measurement

1. Make sure the piston and cylinder walls are clean and dry.

2. Measure the inside diameter of the cylinder bore at a point 13 mm (1/2 in.) from the upper edge with a bore gauge.

3. Measure the outside diameter of the piston across the skirt (**Figure 216**) at right angles to the piston pin. Measure at a distance 10 mm (0.4 in.) up from the bottom of the piston skirt.

4. Piston clearance is the difference between the maximum piston diameter and the minimum cylinder diameter. Subtract the dimension of the piston from the cylinder dimension. If the clearance exceeds the dimension listed in **Table 1** the cylinder should be rebored to the next oversize and a new piston installed.

> *NOTE*
> *The new piston should be obtained before the cylinder is rebored so that the piston can be measured. Slight manufacturing tolerances must be taken into account to determine the actual size and working clearance.*

5. To establish a final overbore dimension with a new piston, add the new piston skirt measurement to the specified piston-to-cylinder clearance. This will determine the dimension for the cylinder overbore size. Remember, do not exceed the cylinder maximum inside diameter listed in **Table 1**.

6. There are 2 oversize piston sizes available (0.25 mm and 0.50 mm oversize).

Piston Installation

1. Apply molybdenum disulfide grease to the inside surface of the connecting rod small end. Apply fresh engine oil to the piston pin and piston pin bore.

2. Insert the piston pin into the piston until its end extends slightly beyond the inside of the boss (**Figure 217**).

3. Align the piston with the IN mark (**Figure 218**) toward the other cylinder (facing toward the carburetors).

4. Be sure to install the piston to the correct connecting rod as marked during removal. Line up the piston pin with the holes in the piston and connecting rod and push the pin into the piston until its ends are even with the clip grooves.

> *NOTE*
> *If the piston pin does not slide in easily, heat the piston until it is too warm to touch but not excessively hot (60° C/140° F). Continue to drive the piston pin while holding the piston so the rod does not have to take any shock. Drive the piston pin in until it is centered in the rod. If the pin is still difficult to install, use the special tool used during the removal sequence.*

> *NOTE*
> *In the next step, install the clips with the gap away from the cutout in the piston (**Figure 219**).*

5. Install new piston pin clips in the ends of the pin boss (**Figure 211**). Make sure they are seated in the grooves.

6. Check installation by rocking the piston back and forth around the pin axis and from side to side along the axis. It should rotate freely back and forth but not from side to side.

7. Repeat for the piston in the other cylinder.

8. Install the rings as described in this chapter.

9. Install the cylinders and cylinder heads as described in this chapter.

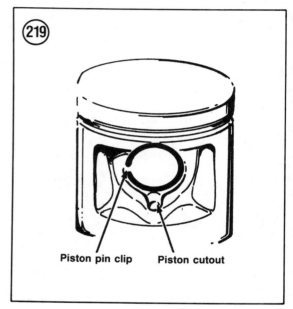

Piston pin clip   Piston cutout

Piston Ring
Removal/Inspection/Installation

> *WARNING*
> *The edges of all piston rings are very sharp, especially the flat rings of the oil ring assembly. Be careful when handling them to avoid cut fingers.*

1. Measure the side clearance of each ring in its groove with a flat feeler gauge (**Figure 220**) and compare with dimensions listed in **Table 1**. If the clearance is greater than specified, the rings must be replaced. If the clearance is still excessive with the new rings, the piston must be replaced.

2. Remove the top ring with a ring expander tool or by spreading the ring ends with your thumbs and lifting the ring up and over the piston (**Figure 221**). Repeat for the remaining rings.

3. Carefully remove all carbon from the ring grooves. Inspect grooves carefully for burrs, nicks

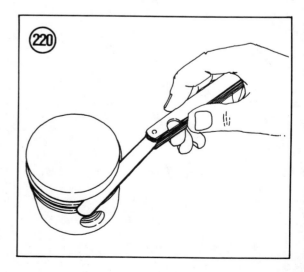

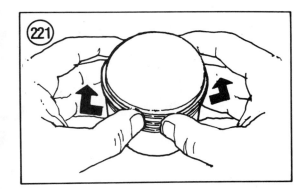

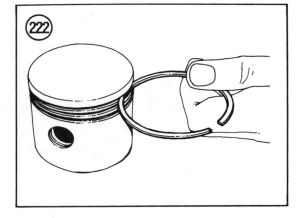

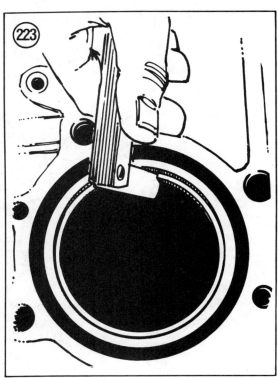

or broken and cracked lands. Recondition or replace the piston if necessary.

4. Roll each ring around its piston groove as shown in **Figure 222** to check for binding. Minor binding may be cleaned up with a fine-cut file.

5. Measure the rings for wear as shown in **Figure 223**. Place each ring, one at a time, into the cylinder and push it in about 20 mm (3/4 in.) with the crown of the piston to ensure that the ring is square in the cylinder bore. Measure the gap with a flat feeler gauge and compare with dimensions listed in **Table 1**. If the gap is greater than specified, the ring(s) should be replaced. When installing new rings, measure their end gap in the same manner. If the gap is less than specified, carefully file the ends with a fine-cut file until the gap is correct.

6. Install the piston rings in the order shown in **Figure 224**.

NOTE
Install all rings with their markings facing up.

7. Install the piston rings—first the bottom, then the middle, then the top ring—by carefully spreading the ends with your thumbs and slipping the ring over the top of the piston. Remember that the piston rings must be installed with the marks on them facing up toward the top of the piston.

8. Make sure the rings are seated completely in their grooves all the way around the piston and that the end gaps are distributed around the piston

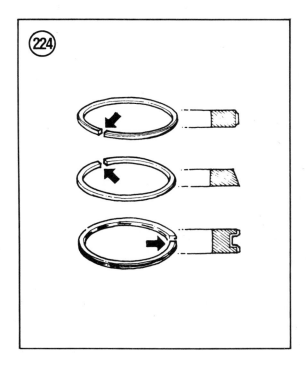

as shown in **Figure 225**. The important thing is that the ring gaps are not aligned with each other when installed.

9. If new rings are installed, measure the side clearance of each ring in its groove with a flat feeler gauge (**Figure 220**) and compare to dimensions listed in **Table 1**.

OIL PUMP DRIVE SPROCKETS AND DRIVE CHAIN

Removal/Installation

1. Remove the clutch as described in Chapter Six.
2. Remove the internal oil line (**Figure 226**) from the crankcase. Don't lose the O-ring seals on each end of the line.

NOTE
If the O-rings are not on the oil line when it is removed, check the receptacles in the crankcase. Remove them and install them onto the oil line to prevent losing them.

3. Remove the bolt and washer (A, **Figure 227**) securing the oil pump driven sprocket.
4. As an assembly, slide off the oil pump driven sprocket (B, **Figure 227**), the drive chain (C, **Figure 227**), the oil pump drive sprocket and clutch outer housing bushing (D, **Figure 227**).
5. Inspect the drive chain and both sprockets (**Figure 228**) for wear or damage; replace as a set if necessary.
6. Install by reversing these removal steps, noting the following.

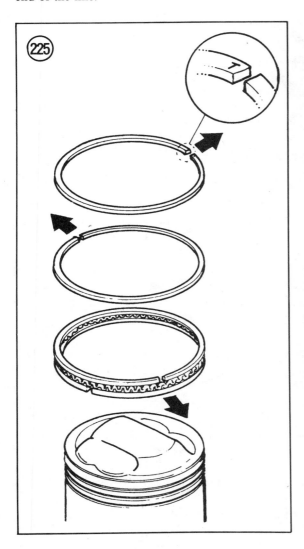

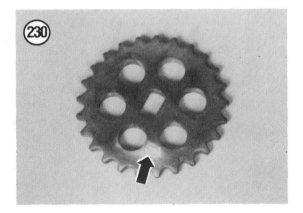

7. Install the clutch outer housing bushing (**Figure 229**) onto the transmission mainshaft before installing the sprockets and drive chain.

8. Position the oil pump driven sprocket with the IN mark (**Figure 230**) facing in toward the crankcase and align the flats on the sprocket with the flats on the oil pump shaft.

9. Tighten the driven sprocket bolt to the torque specification listed in **Table 2** or **Table 3**.

10. Install an O-ring seal (**Figure 231**) onto both ends of the internal oil line and install the oil line into the receptacles in the crankcase.

OIL PUMP

The oil pump is mounted within the crankcase. The engine must be removed from the frame and the crankcase disassembled to gain access to the oil pump.

Removal

1. Remove the engine as described in this chapter.

2. Separate the crankcase as described in this chapter.

3. Remove the bolts (**Figure 232**) securing the oil pump assembly to the left-hand crankcase.

> *NOTE*
> *Figure 232 is shown with the crankshaft and transmission assemblies removed for clarity. It is not necessary to remove any of these assemblies for this procedure.*

4. Remove the locating dowel and O-ring seal (**Figure 233**) from the left-hand crankcase.

5. Remove the oil strainer, O-ring seal and the oil pump relief valve pipe from oil pump assembly.

Installation

1. To prime the oil pump, add clean engine oil into one of the openings in the oil pump. Add oil until the oil drains out of the other opening.

2. Install the O-ring seal (**Figure 234**) onto the oil pump body and then install the oil strainer (**Figure 235**) into the O-ring seal.

3. Install the oil pump relief valve pipe (**Figure 236**) onto the oil pump body.

4. Install a new O-ring seal (**Figure 233**) onto the locating dowel and install the dowel into the crankcase.

5. Install the oil pump assembly into the left-hand crankcase.

6. Install the mounting bolts and tighten to the torque specifications listed in **Table 2** or **Table 3**.

7. Assemble the crankcase and install the engine as described in this chapter.

8. Refill the engine with the recommended viscosity and quantity of engine oil as described in Chapter Three.

9. Start the engine and check for leaks.

Disassembly/Inspection/Assembly

> *NOTE*
> *Replacement parts are not available for the oil pump. If any of the external or internal components are worn or damaged, the entire oil pump assembly must be replaced.*

1. Inspect the outer cover and body for cracks.

2. Remove the bolts (**Figure 237**) securing the pump cover to the pump body. Remove the pump cover.

3. Withdraw the oil pump drive shaft, spacer and pin. Don't lose the pin; it will slide out of the shaft.

4. Remove the inner and outer rotors. Check all parts for scratches and abrasion.

5. Clean all parts in solvent and thoroughly dry with compressed air. Carefully scrub the strainer screen with a soft toothbrush; do not damage the screen.

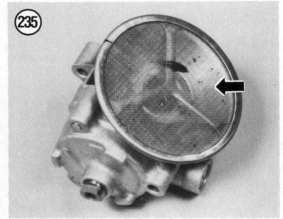

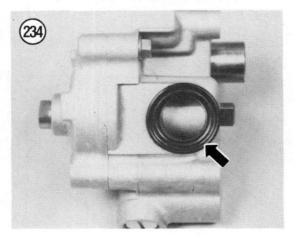

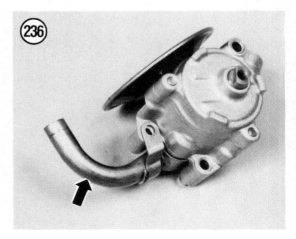

6. Coat all parts with fresh oil before installation.

7. Inspect the interior passageways of the oil pump body. Make sure that all oil sludge and foreign matter is removed.

8. Inspect the strainer screen for broken areas (**Figure 238**). This would allow small foreign particles to enter the oil pump and cause damage. If broken in any area, replace the strainer.

9. Install the outer rotor into the pump cover.

10. Check the clearance between the outer rotor and the body (**Figure 239**) with a flat feeler gauge. If the clearance is greater than the service limit in **Table 1** the oil pump must be replaced.

11. Install the inner rotor, the oil pump drive shaft and pin (**Figure 240**). Mesh the pin into the groove in the inner rotor and install the spacer onto the shaft.

12. Check the clearance between the inner tip and outer rotor (**Figure 241**) with a flat feeler gauge. If the clearance is greater than the service limit in **Table 1** the oil pump must be replaced.

13. Check the rotor end clearance with a straightedge and flat feeler gauge (**Figure 242**). If the clearance is greater than the service limit in **Table 1** the oil pump must be replaced.

4

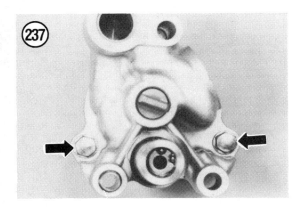

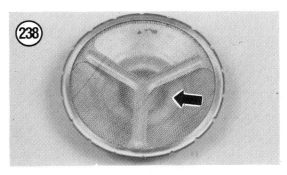

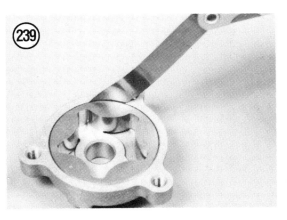

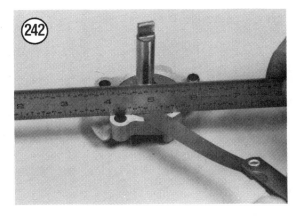

14. Install the location dowel (**Figure 243**) into the cover.

15. Install the body and tighten the screws (**Figure 237**) securely.

16. After the oil pump is assembled, turn the shaft and make sure the oil pump turns freely with no binding.

17. Install the oil pump as described in this chapter.

NOTE
*If the condition of the oil pump is doubtful, run the **Oil Pump Pressure Test** described in this chapter.*

Oil Pump Pressure Test

If the oil pump output is doubtful, the following test can be performed.

1. Warm the engine up to normal operating temperature (80° C/176° F). Shut off the engine.

2. Place the bike on the centerstand.

3. Check the engine oil level. It must be to the upper line; add oil if necessary. Do not run this test with the oil level low or the test readings will be false.

4. Pull the rubber boot back from the oil pressure switch (**Figure 244**).

5. Remove the electrical wire from the oil pressure switch.

6. Remove the oil pressure switch from the crankcase.

7. Screw a portable oil pressure gauge into the switch hole in the crankcase.

NOTE
These can be purchased in an automotive or motorcycle supply store or from a Honda dealer. The Honda parts are No. 07506-3000000 (Oil Pressure Gauge) and No. 07510-4220100 (Oil Pressure Gauge Attachment).

8. Start the engine and run it at 6,000 rpm. The standard pressure is 4.7-6.1 kg/cm² (52.7-72.5 psi) at 6,000 rpm and at 80° C (176° F). If the pressure is less than specified the oil pump must be replaced.

9. Remove the portable oil pressure gauge.

10. Apply Loctite Lock N' Seal to the switch threads before installation. Tighten the switch to the torque specifications listed in **Table 2** or **Table 3**.

11. Install the electrical wire to the top of the switch. This connection must be free of oil to make good electrical contact.

12. Slide the rubber boot back into place on the switch.

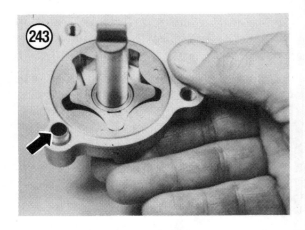

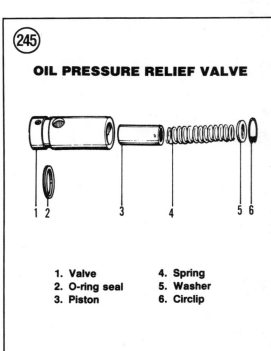

OIL PRESSURE RELIEF VALVE

1. Valve
2. O-ring seal
3. Piston
4. Spring
5. Washer
6. Circlip

OIL PRESSURE RELIEF VALVE

Refer to **Figure 245** for this procedure.

Disassembly/Inspection/Assembly

1. Remove the oil pump as described in this chapter.

2. Remove the circlip (**Figure 246**) securing the pressure relief valve.

3. Remove the washer, spring and check valve.

4. Wash all parts in solvent and thoroughly dry with compressed air.

5. Inspect the check valve and the cylinder that it rides in for scratches or wear; replace if defective.

6. Make sure the spring is not broken or distorted; replace if necessary.

7. Make sure the holes in the valve are not clogged.

8. Install the check valve, spring, washer and circlip.

9. Install the oil pump as described in this chapter.

PRIMARY DRIVE GEAR

Removal/Installation

1. Perform Steps 1-6 of *Clutch Removal* in Chapter Five.

2. Remove the bolts (A, **Figure 247**) securing both pulse generator units to the crankcase.

3. Remove the bolt (B, **Figure 247**) securing the clip on the electrical harness to the crankcase. Remove the clip.

4. Remove the pulse generator units and rubber grommet (C, **Figure 247**) from the right-hand crankcase.

5. To keep the primary drive gear from turning, insert a copper washer (or penny) into mesh with the primary drive gear and the clutch outer housing gear (**Figure 248**).

6. Remove the bolt (A, **Figure 249**) securing the pulse generator plate and the primary drive gear.

7. Remove the pulse generator plate (B, **Figure 249**) and the primary drive gear (C, **Figure 249**).

8. Before installing the pulse generator plate, fill in the timing marks (**Figure 250**) with white grease pencil or typewriter white correction fluid. This will make it easier to see the timing marks.

9. Install by reversing these removal steps, noting the following.

10. Align the flat on the crankshaft splines with the flat section on the primary drive gear and the pulse generator plate and install both parts.

11. Use the same tool set-up used in Step 5 to keep the primary drive gear from turning and tighten the bolt to the torque specifications listed in **Table 2** or **Table 3**.

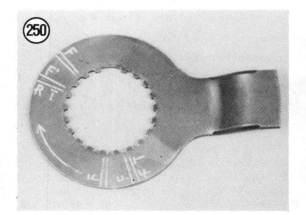

CRANKCASE AND CRANKSHAFT

Disassembly of the crankcase (splitting the cases) and removal of the crankshaft assembly requires that the engine be removed from the frame.

The crankcase is made in 2 halves of precision diecast aluminum alloy and is of the "thin-walled" type. To avoid damage, do not hammer or pry on any of the interior or exterior projected walls. These areas are easily damaged. The cases are assembled with a coat of gasket sealer between the 2 halves and dowel pins align the halves when they are bolted together.

The procedure which follows is presented as a complete, step-by-step major lower-end rebuild that should be followed if an engine is to be completely reconditioned. However, if you're replacing a known failed part, the disassembly should be carried out only until the failed part is accessible. There is no need to disassemble the engine beyond that point so long as you know the remaining components are in good condition and that they were not affected by the failed part.

Disassembly

1. Remove the engine as described in this chapter.

2. Before removing the clutch, loosen the bolt (**Figure 251**) securing the primary drive gear to the end of the crankshaft.

NOTE
*Wedge a soft copper washer (or penny) between the primary drive gear and the gear on the clutch outer housing to keep the primary drive gear from rotating during removal and installation of the bolt (**Figure 248**).*

3. Remove the clutch as described in Chapter Five.

NOTE
*Install the drive shaft universal joint onto the splined end of the output gear shaft (A, **Figure 252**). Place a large screwdriver or drift between the 2 sections of the universal joint (B, **Figure***

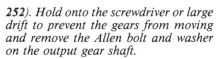

252). Hold onto the screwdriver or large drift to prevent the gears from moving and remove the Allen bolt and washer on the output gear shaft.

4. See **Figure 253**. Remove the following.

   a. *1983-on:* Remove the Allen bolt and washer (A) securing the output gear shaft.

   b. *1983-1985:* Remove the countershaft Allen bolt and washer (B).

5. Remove all exterior engine assemblies as described in this chapter and other related chapters.

   a. Cylinder head (this chapter).

   b. Cylinder (this chapter).

   c. Piston and piston pin (this chapter).

   d. Alternator (this chapter).

   e. External shift mechanism (Chapter Five).

   f. Water pump (Chapter Eight).

   g. Starter gears (this chapter).

   h. Starter motor (Chapter Seven).

6. Remove the front cylinder cam chain from the timing gear on the crankshaft (**Figure 254**) and remove the chain.

7. Remove the rear cylinder cam chain from the timing sprocket (**Figure 255**) and remove the chain.

8. Slide the timing sprocket (**Figure 256**) off of the crankshaft.

9. Remove the gearshift drum holder (**Figure 257**) from the left-hand crankcase.

10. Loosen the right-hand crankcase 6 mm and 8 mm bolts (**Figure 258**) in a crisscross pattern in 2-3 steps. Remove the bolts.

NOTE
*Note the location of the copper washer on the bolt (W, **Figure 258**).*

NOTE
*In **Figure 259** bolt C is used on 1983-1985 models only.*

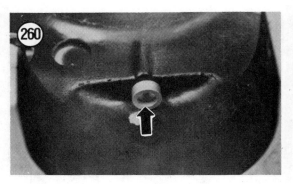

11. Loosen the left-hand crankcase 6 mm and 8 mm bolts (**Figure 259**) in a crisscross pattern in 2-3 steps. Remove the bolts.

12. Lay the crankcase assembly on 2 blocks of wood with the right-hand crankcase side up.

13. Using a soft-faced mallet, tap around the perimeter of the crankcase half and on the end of the crankshaft while pulling up on the right-hand crankcase half. Continue to tap until the crankcase halves separate.

14. Remove the right-hand crankcase half.

15. Remove the gearshift drum, shift forks and transmission shaft assemblies as described in Chapter Five.

16. Pull the crankshaft assembly straight up and out of the left-hand crankcase.

17. Remove the oil pump assembly as described in this chapter.

18. Remove the oil jet (**Figure 260**) from each crankcase half.

19. Remove the output gear case as described in this chapter.

20. If necessary, remove the neutral and the overdrive (OD) indicator switches (**Figure 261**) and the oil pressure switch (**Figure 262**) from the left-hand crankcase.

Crankcase Inspection

1. Clean both crankcase halves inside and out with cleaning solvent. Thoroughly dry with compressed air and wipe off with a clean shop cloth. Be sure to remove all traces of the old gasket material from the mating surfaces.

2. Check the transmission, shift drum and output gear ball bearings for roughness and play by

rotating them slowly by hand (**Figure 263**). If any roughness or play can be felt in a bearing, it must be replaced. Refer to *Crankcase Ball Bearing Replacement* in this chapter for the correct procedure.

NOTE
Inspection of the crankshaft main bearing is covered under **Crankshaft Inspection** *in this chapter.*

3. Carefully examine the cases for cracks and fractures. Also check the areas around the stiffening ribs, bearing bosses and threaded holes. If any damage is found, have it repaired by a shop specializing in the repair of precision aluminum castings or replace the crankcase halves as a set.

4. Make sure the crankcase studs are tight. If any are loose, tighten to the torque specification listed in **Table 2** or **Table 3**.

5. Inspect the camshaft drive chain and sprockets (**Figure 264**) for each cylinder. Check the sprockets for chipped or missing teeth; replace if necessary. If one of the sprockets is damaged chances are the drive chain will also be damaged. If any one of the 3 parts is worn or damaged, replace all 3 parts as a set.

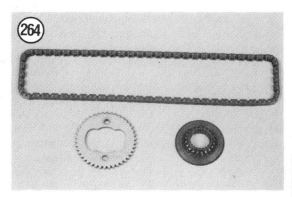

4

Crankcase Ball Bearing Replacement

The following special Honda tools may be required for left- and right-hand main bearing removal:

  a. *1983-1985:* Bearing remover (part No. 07936-3710600), remover handle (part No. 07936-3710100) and remover weight (part No. 07936-3710200).

  b. *1986-on:* Driver (part No. 07749-001000), main bearing remover attachment (part No. 07946-ME90100) and main bearing driver attachment (part No. 07946-ME90200).

1. On the right-hand crankcase, remove the screws (1983-1985) or bolts (1986-on) securing the bearing

retainers (**Figure 265**) and remove the bearing retainers.

2. The bearings are installed with a slight interference fit. The crankcase must be heated in an oven to about 100° C (212° F). An easy way to check the proper temperature is to drop tiny drops of water on the case. If they sizzle and evaporate immediately, the temperature is correct. Heat only one case at a time.

> *CAUTION*
> *Do not heat the cases with a torch (propane or acetylene). Never bring a flame into contact with the bearing or case. The direct heat will destroy the case hardening of the bearing and will likely cause warpage of the case.*

3. Remove the case from the oven and hold onto the crankcase with a kitchen potholder, heavy gloves or heavy shop cloths—it is *hot*.

4. Hold the case with the bearing side down and tap it squarely on a piece of soft wood. Continue to tap until the bearing(s) fall out. Repeat for the other half.

> *CAUTION*
> *Be sure to tap the crankcase squarely on the piece of wood. Avoid damaging the sealing surfaces of the crankcase.*

5A. On the right-hand crankcase half, if the bearings are difficult to remove, they can be gently tapped out with a socket or piece of pipe the same size as the bearing outer race.

5B. On the left-hand crankcase half, if the bearings are difficult to remove, special tools are required as the bearings are not accessible from the other side of the crankcase. Use the special Honda tools described in the introduction to this procedure.
   a. Attach the bearing remover to the bearing.
   b. Attach the remover handle and remover weight to the bearing remover.
   c. Move the weight up and down on the remover handle (similar to a body shop slide hammer) until the bearing is removed from the crankcase.
   d. If necessary, repeat this step for the other bearing.

NOTE
If the bearings or seals are difficult to remove or install, don't take a chance on expensive damage. Have the work performed by a dealer or competent machine shop.

6. While heating the crankcase halves, place new bearings in a freezer if possible. Chilling them will slightly reduce their overall diameter while the hot crankcase is slightly larger due to heat expansion. This will make installation easier.

7. Install the new bearing(s) in the heated cases. Press each bearing in by hand until it is completely seated. Do not hammer it in. If a bearing will not seat, remove it and cool it. Reheat the case and install the bearing again.

8. On bearings so equipped, install the bearing retainer and tighten the screws securely.

Assembly

Assemble all components into the right-hand crankcase half.

1. If removed, install the neutral and OD indicator switches (**Figure 261**).

2. If removed, apply a coat of liquid gasket sealer to the threads of the oil pressure switch. Install the switch (**Figure 262**) and tighten to the torque specification listed in **Table 2** or **Table 3**.

3. Install the output gear case as described in this chapter.

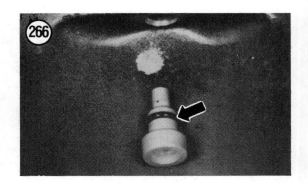

4. Install a new O-ring seal (**Figure 266**) on each oil jet and install an oil jets into each crankcase half (**Figure 266**).

5. If removed, install the locating dowels and O-ring seals (**Figure 267**) into the left-hand crankcase.

6. Refer to Chapter Five and reinstall the transmission shaft assemblies and the internal shift mechanism.

7. Apply a coat of cold grease to the thrust washer and place it on the output gear case final drive bearing in the right-hand crankcase (**Figure 268**).

8. Place the output gear case final drive gear (**Figure 269**) into place in the right-hand crankcase.

9. Align the holes in the gear and washer with the inside diameter of the bearing in the crankcase.

10. Lightly oil the right-hand main bearing and the right-hand end of the crankshaft (primary drive gear splines).

11. Position the crankshaft so the connecting rods are toward the top of the crankcase. Position the front cylinder connecting rod so it fits into the cylinder relief in the crankcase and lower the crankshaft straight into the right-hand crankcase half (**Figure 270**).

12. Hold onto the connecting rods and turn the crankshaft slowly to make sure it spins freely. If not, investigate the reason before proceeding.

13. Install the oil pump assembly into the left-hand crankcase as described in this chapter.

14. Install the alignment dowels (**Figure 271**) into one of the crankcase halves.

15. Spray the sealing surface of both crankcase halves with contact cleaner. This will remove any traces of oil from the surfaces to achieve a better seal.

16. Apply a light even coat of liquid gasket sealer to the sealing surface of one crankcase half.

NOTE
Since the external finish of the engine is black, use a black colored sealer such as Permatex RTV Black Silicone Adhesive Sealer (part No. 16B) or equivalent.

17. Set the left-hand case in place over the right-hand crankcase assembly as follows.

  a. Align the thrust washer and bushing on the output gear final drive gear with the output gear shaft.

  b. Slightly rotate the splines of the output gear case to align the raised cams on the output gear shaft with the depressions in the final drive gear.

  c. Push it down squarely into place until it reaches the crankshaft bearing. There is usually about 0.13 mm (1/2 in.) to go.

18. Lightly tap the case halves together with a plastic or rubber mallet until they seat.

CAUTION
Crankcase halves should fit together without force. If the crankcase halves do not fit together completely, do not attempt to pull them together with the crankcase screws. Separate the crankcase halves and investigate the cause of the interference. If the transmission shafts were disassembled, recheck to make sure that a gear is not installed backwards. Do not risk damage by trying to force the cases together.

19. Rotate the crankshaft and transmission shafts by hand to make sure they rotate freely.

NOTE
*In **Figure 259**, bolt C is used on 1983-1985 models only.*

20. Install and tighten the right-hand crankcase 6 mm and 8 mm bolts (**Figure 259**) in a crisscross pattern in 2-3 steps. Tighten the bolts to the torque specifications listed in **Table 2** or **Table 3**.

NOTE
Note the location of the copper washer
(W, Figure 258).

21. Install and tighten the right-hand crankcase 6 mm and 8 mm bolts (**Figure 259**) in a crisscross pattern in 2-3 steps. Tighten the bolts to the torque specifications listed in **Table 2** or **Table 3**.

NOTE
The crankshaft has so much end float and it is so heavy that it may not want to rotate with the crankcase assembly on its side. Therefore it is necessary for the crankcase to be upright.

22. Install a new O-ring seal on the shift drum holder and install the holder (**Figure 272**) in the left-hand crankcase half. Push the holder all the way in until it bottoms out.

23. After the crankcase halves are completely assembled, turn the crankcase assembly upright. Once again rotate the crankshaft and transmission shafts by hand to make sure they rotate freely and that there is no binding. If any is present, disassemble the crankcase halves and correct the problem.

24. Install all exterior engine assemblies as described in this chapter and other related chapters.

   a. Cylinder head (this chapter)
   b. Cylinder (this chapter)
   c. Piston and piston pin (this chapter)
   d. Alternator (this chapter)
   e. External shift mechanism (Chapter Five)
   f. Water pump (Chapter Eight)
   g. Starter gears (this chapter)
   h. Starter motor (Chapter Seven)

25. See **Figure 253**. Tighten the following bolts, using the same tool set-up used during removal and tighten to the torque specifications listed in **Table 2** or **Table 3**.

   a. *1983-on:* Output gear shaft Allen bolt (A).
   b. *1983-1985:* Countershaft Allen bolt and washer (B).

26. Install the primary drive gear as described in this chapter.

27. Install the clutch as described in Chapter Five.

28. Install the engine as described in this chapter.

29. Fill the engine with the recommended viscosity and quantity of engine oil. Refer to Chapter Three.

Crankshaft Inspection

1. Remove the connecting rods from the crankshaft as described in this chapter.

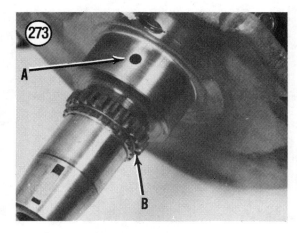

2. Clean crankshaft thoroughly with solvent. Clean oil holes with rifle cleaning brushes. Flush thoroughly with new solvent and dry with compressed air. Lightly oil all bearing journal surfaces immediately to prevent rust.

3. Carefully inspect each journal (A, **Figure 273** and A, **Figure 274**) for scratches, ridges, scoring, nicks, etc. Very small nicks and scratches may be removed with fine emery cloth. More serious damage must be removed by grinding—a job for a machine shop or dealer.

4. If the surface on all journals is satisfactory, take the crankshaft to a dealer or machine shop to be checked for out-of-roundness, taper and wear on the bearing journals. Also check crankshaft runout. The service limit is listed in **Table 1**.

5. Inspect the sprocket teeth (front cylinder) for the cam chain (B, **Figure 273**). If damaged, the crankshaft must be replaced.

6. Inspect the splines (B, **Figure 274**) for the timing sprocket. If damaged, the crankshaft must be replaced.

Crankshaft Main Bearing Selection

1. Check the inside surface of the bearing inserts for wear, bluish tint (burned), flaking, abrasion and scoring. If the bearings are good, they may be reused. If the insert is questionable, replace it.

2. Clean the bearing surfaces of the crankshaft and the main bearing inserts. Measure the main bearing clearance by performing the following steps.

   a. Measure the inside diameter of the bearing insert with an inside micrometer (**Figure 275**).

   b. Measure the outside diameter of the crankshaft main bearing journal with a micrometer.

   c. Subtract the main bearing journal OD from the bearing insert ID. This will give you the clearance between the 2 parts. The service limit dimension is listed in **Table 1**.

3A. *1983-1985:* If the bearing clearance is greater than specified, use the following steps for new bearing selection.

   a. The crankshaft main journals are marked with numbers "1" or "2" (**Figure 276**).

> *NOTE*
> *The number on the left-hand end (end with the cam chain sprocket) relates to the bearing insert in the left-hand side and the number on the right-hand end (primary drive gear splines) relates to the bearing insert in the right-hand crankcase. Remember the left-hand side relates to the engine as it sits in the bike's frame, not as it sits on your workbench.*

   b. If the main journal dimension is within the tolerances stated in **Table 1**, the bearing can be simply selected by colorcode. Select new main bearings by cross-referencing the main journal number (**Figure 276**) in the vertical column of **Table 5** to bearing insert I.D. dimension (**Figure 275**) in the horizontal column. Where the 2 columns intersect, the new bearing color is indicated. **Table 6** gives the bearing insert color and thickness.

   c. If any main bearing journal measurements taken during inspection do not fall within the tolerance range listed in **Table 5**, the serviceability of the crankshaft must be carefully examined. If the main bearing journal in question is not tapered, out-of-round or scored, the crankshaft may be still used, but the bearing selection will have to be made based on the measured diameter of the bearing journal and not by the number code. Honda recommends the crankshaft be replaced whenever a main bearing journal dimension is beyond the specified range of the letter code.

3B. *1986-on:* If the bearing clearance is greater than specified, use the following steps for new bearing selection.

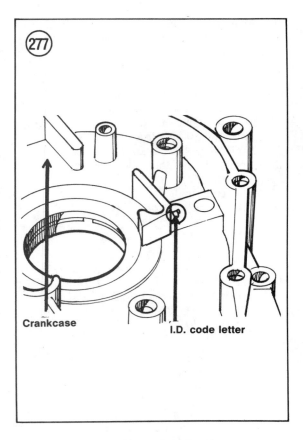

Crankcase

I.D. code letter

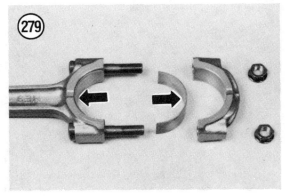

a. The crankshaft main journals are marked with numbers "1" or "2" (**Figure 276**).

NOTE
The number on the left-hand end (end with the cam chain sprocket) relates to the bearing insert in the left-hand side and the number on the right-hand end (primary drive gear splines) relates to the bearing insert in the right-hand crankcase. Remember the left-hand side relates to the engine as it sits in the bike's frame, not as it sits on your workbench.

b. If the main journal dimension is within the tolerances stated in **Table 1**, the bearing can be simply selected by colorcode. Select new main bearings by cross-referencing the main journal number (**Figure 276**) in the vertical column of **Table 7** to the crankcase I.D. letter A or B as shown in **Figure 277**. Where the 2 columns intersect, the new bearing color is indicated. **Table 8** gives the bearing insert color and thickness.

c. If any main bearing journal measurements taken during inspection do not fall within the tolerance range listed in **Table 7**, the serviceability of the crankshaft must be carefully examined. If the main bearing journal in question is not tapered, out-of-round or scored the crankshaft may be still used, but the bearing selection will have to be made based on the measured diameter of the bearing journal and not by the number code. Honda recommends the crankshaft be replaced whenever a main bearing journal dimension is beyond the specified range of the letter code.

4. If the bearings require replacement, refer to *Crankshaft Main Bearing Replacement* in this chapter.

5. After new bearings have been installed, recheck clearance by repeating this procedure.

**Crankshaft Main
Bearing Replacement**

The crankshaft bearings must be removed and installed with a hydraulic press and special tools.

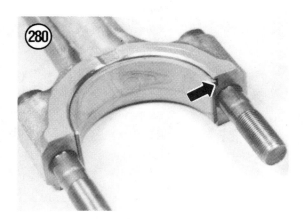

This job is best left to an authorized dealer or machine shop.

> *CAUTION*
> *Do not try to drive out or drive in these bearings. The bearings must be installed and aligned true to the centerline of the crankshaft.*

CONNECTING RODS

Removal/Installation

1. Remove the engine as described in this chapter.
2. Split the crankcases and remove the crankshaft assembly as described under *Crankcase Disassembly* in this chapter.

> *NOTE*
> *Before disassembly, mark the rods and caps. Mark them with an "L" for left-hand end (end with the cam chain sprocket) or "R" for the right-hand end (primary drive gear splines). Remember the left-hand side relates to the engine as it sits in the bike's frame, not as it sits on your workbench.*

3. Measure the connecting rod side clearance as described under *Connecting Rod Inspection* in this chapter.
4. Remove the nuts securing the connecting rod caps and remove the caps (**Figure 278**).
5. Carefully remove the connecting rods from the crankshaft.
6. Remove and mark the back of each bearing insert (**Figure 279**) with the cylinder "R" (right) or "L" (left) location and "U" (upper) or "L" (lower).
7. Install by reversing these removal steps, noting the following.
8. Install the bearing inserts into each connecting rod and cap. Make sure they are locked into place correctly (**Figure 280**).

> *NOTE*
> *If the old bearing inserts are reused, be sure they are installed into their original positions. Refer to Step 6.*

9. Apply molybdenum disulfide grease to the bearing inserts, crankpins and connecting rod bolt threads. Install the connecting rods and rod caps. Tighten the cap nuts evenly in 2-3 steps to the torque specifications listed in **Table 2** or **Table 3**.
10. After all rod caps have been installed, rotate the crankshaft several times and check that the bearings are not too tight. Make sure there is no binding.

Connecting Rod Inspection

1. Before removing the connecting rods from the crankshaft, measure the side clearance as follows.
   a. Insert a flat feeler gauge between the side of the connecting rod and the crankshaft as shown in **Figure 281**.
   b. Refer to the service limit dimension listed in **Table 1**.
   c. Replace the connecting rod(s) if it is worn to the service limit dimension or less.
2. Remove the connecting rods from the crankshaft as described in this chapter.
3. Clean the connecting rods and inserts in solvent and dry with compressed air.
4. Carefully inspect each rod journal on the crankshaft for scratches, ridges, scoring, nicks, etc. Very small nicks and scratches may be removed with fine emery cloth. More serious damage must be removed by grinding—a job for a machine shop or dealer.
5. If the surface on all journals is satisfactory, take the crankshaft to a dealer or machine shop to be checked for out-of-roundness, taper and wear on the rod bearing journals.

**Connecting Rod
Bearing Selection**

1. Check the inside and outside surfaces of the bearing inserts for wear, bluish tint (burned), flaking, abrasion and scoring. If the bearings are good, they may be reused. If any insert is questionable, replace the entire set.

2. Measure the inside diameter of the small end of the connecting rod with an inside dial gauge (**Figure 282**). Check against the dimension listed in **Table 1**. Replace the rod if necessary.

3. Clean the rod bearing surfaces of the crankshaft and the rod bearing inserts. Measure the rod bearing clearance by performing the following steps.

    a. Place a strip of Plastigage over each rod bearing journal parallel to the crankshaft (**Figure 283**). Do not place the Plastigage material over an oil hole in the crankshaft.

*NOTE
Do not rotate connecting rod on the crankshaft while the Plastigage strips are in place.*

    b. Install the rod cap onto one rod and tighten the nuts to the torque specification listed in **Table 2** or **Table 3**.

    c. Remove the rod cap and measure the width of the flattened Plastigage (**Figure 284**) following the manufacturer's instructions. Measure both ends of the Plastigage strip. A difference of 0.025 mm (0.001 in.) or more indicates a tapered journal. Confirm with a micrometer.

    d. New bearing clearance and the service limit are listed in **Table 1**. Remove all of the Plastigage material from the crankshaft journals and the connecting rods.

4. If the rod bearing clearance is greater than specified, use the following steps for new bearing selection.

    a. The crankshaft connecting rod journals are marked with letters "A" or "B" (A, **Figure 285**).

*NOTE
The letter on the counterbalance weight refers to the rod journal to the right of the weight. The left-hand end of the crankshaft is the end with the cam chain sprocket and the right-hand end is the end with the primary drive gear splines. Remember the left-hand side relates to the engine as it sits in the bike's frame, not as it sits on your workbench.*

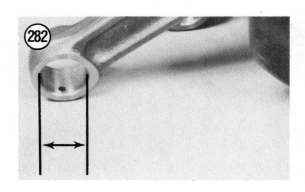

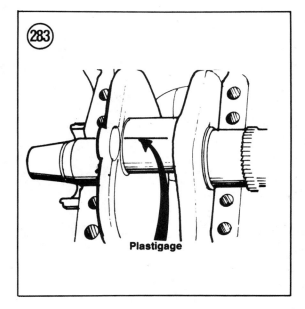

Plastigage

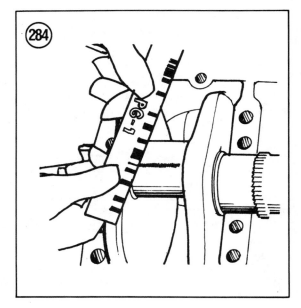

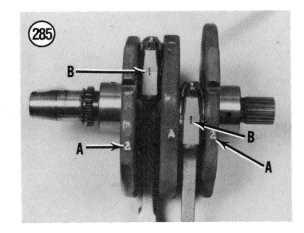

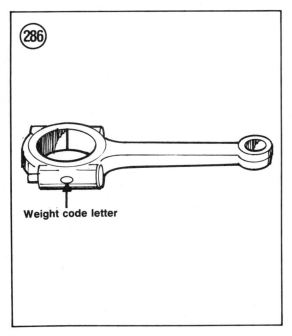

Weight code letter

b. The connecting rod and cap are marked with numbers "1" or "2" (B, **Figure 285**).

c. Measure the rod journal with a micrometer. If the rod journal dimension is within the tolerances stated for each letter code in **Table 9**, the bearing can be simply selected by colorcode.

d. Select new bearings by cross-referencing the rod journal letters (A, **Figure 285**) in the horizontal column of **Table 9** to the rod bearing number (B, **Figure 285**) in the vertical column. Where the 2 columns intersect, the new bearing color is indicated. **Table 10** gives the bearing insert color and thickness.

5. If any rod bearing journal measurements taken during inspection do not fall within the tolerance range for the letter codes, the serviceability of the crankshaft must be carefully examined. If the rod bearing journal in question is not tapered, out-of-round or scored, the crankshaft may be still used, but the bearing selection will have to be made based on the measured diameter of the bearing journal and not by the letter code. Honda recommends the crankshaft be replaced whenever a rod bearing journal dimension is beyond the specified range of the stamped letter code.

6. *1986-on:* When replacing connecting rods on these models, the front and rear rods must be matched to weight. Use the following steps for new connecting rod selection.

a. A weight code is stamped on the connecting rod at the point indicated in **Figure 286**.

b. Cross-reference the front and rear connecting rod codes with the listings in **Table 11**. Where the 2 columns intersect with an "X" mark, the connecting rods are matched and can be used together.

7. After new bearings have been installed, recheck clearance by repeating this procedure.

8. Repeat Steps 1-7 for the other cylinder.

OUTPUT GEAR UNIT

Gear Case
Removal/Installation

1. Remove the engine as described in this chapter.

2. Remove the cap nuts and sealing washers (A, **Figure 287**) securing the output gear case to the left-hand crankcase half.

3. Remove the output gear case.

4. Remove the locating dowel, shim and large O-ring seal. Discard the O-ring seal.

5. Remove the oil control orifice from the crankcase where the oil pickup line is located (B, **Figure 287**).

6. Clean the orifice in solvent and dry with compressed air. Make sure the orifice is clean to ensure maximum oil flow to the output gear assembly.

7. Install by reversing these removal steps, noting the following.

CAUTION
The following shim has an effect on gear backlash and the correct shim thickness must be installed or the output gear unit may be damaged.

8. If the shim requires replacement, replace with a shim of the *same* thickness. There are 5 different shims available from 0.40-0.60 mm (0.016-0.024 in.) in 0.05 mm (0.002 in.) increments. Take the old shim to your dealer and get a replacement shim of the same thickness.

9. Install new O-ring seal on the oil control orifice. Install the oil control orifice in the crankcase.

10. Install a new large O-ring seal next to the cross shaft gear.

11. Install the sealing washers and nuts.

12. Tighten the nuts to the torque specification listed in **Table 2** or **Table 3**.

Output Gear Assembly
Removal/Installation
(1983-1985)

1. Disassemble the crankcase as described in this chapter.

2. Bend down the locking tabs on the set plate (A, **Figure 288**).

3. Remove the nuts (B, **Figure 288**) securing the output gear assembly.

4. Remove the set plate and remove the output gear assembly (C, **Figure 288**) from the crankcase.

5A. On VT750C models, remove the gasket and dowel pin.

5B. On VT700C models, remove the dowel pin.

6. Install by reversing these removal steps, noting the following.

7. On VT750C models, install a new gasket.

8. Install a new set plate and then the nuts. Tighten the nuts to the torque specification listed in **Table 2**.

9. Bend end up the locking tab onto each nut.

Output Gear Assembly
Removal/Installation
(1986-on)

Output gear removal requires a considerable number of special Honda tools. The price of all these tools could be more than the cost of most repairs done by a dealer. Refer removal and installation to a Honda dealer.

Disassembly/Inspection/Assembly

Output gear case disassembly and assembly requires a considerable number of special Honda tools. The price of all of these tools could be more than the cost of most repairs done by a dealer. **Figure 289** (1983-1985) and **Figure 290** (1986-on) show the internal components of the output gear case.

CAUTION
Do not try to disassemble the gear case with makeshift tools. Approximately 13 special tools and a hydraulic press are required to disassemble and assemble the unit. If assembled incorrectly, the gear tooth contact pattern and set-up tolerance will be incorrect and the unit will be damaged.

ALTERNATOR ROTOR, STARTER CLUTCH ASSEMBLY AND GEARS

The alternator rotor, starter clutch assembly and gears can be removed with the engine in the frame. The starter motor can be left in place, if desired.
Refer to **Figure 291** for this procedure.

Removal/Installation

1. Place the bike on the centerstand.
2. Remove both side covers and the seat.
3. Disconnect the battery negative lead.
4. Disconnect the electrical connector (**Figure 292**) going to the alternator stator assembly.
5. Remove the screws securing the left-hand rear crankcase cover and remove the cover.
6. Remove the exhaust system from the rear cylinder as described in Chapter Six.

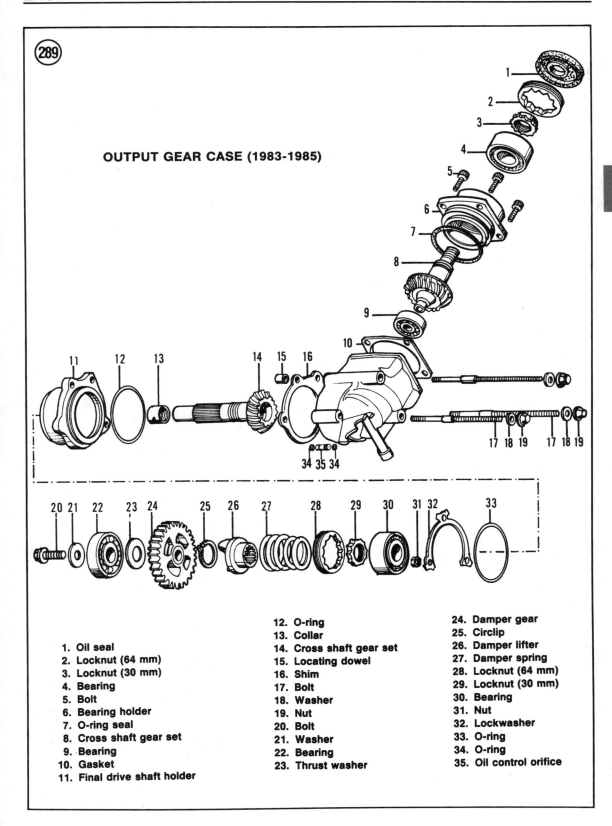

OUTPUT GEAR CASE (1983-1985)

4

1. Oil seal
2. Locknut (64 mm)
3. Locknut (30 mm)
4. Bearing
5. Bolt
6. Bearing holder
7. O-ring seal
8. Cross shaft gear set
9. Bearing
10. Gasket
11. Final drive shaft holder

12. O-ring
13. Collar
14. Cross shaft gear set
15. Locating dowel
16. Shim
17. Bolt
18. Washer
19. Nut
20. Bolt
21. Washer
22. Bearing
23. Thrust washer

24. Damper gear
25. Circlip
26. Damper lifter
27. Damper spring
28. Locknut (64 mm)
29. Locknut (30 mm)
30. Bearing
31. Nut
32. Lockwasher
33. O-ring
34. O-ring
35. Oil control orifice

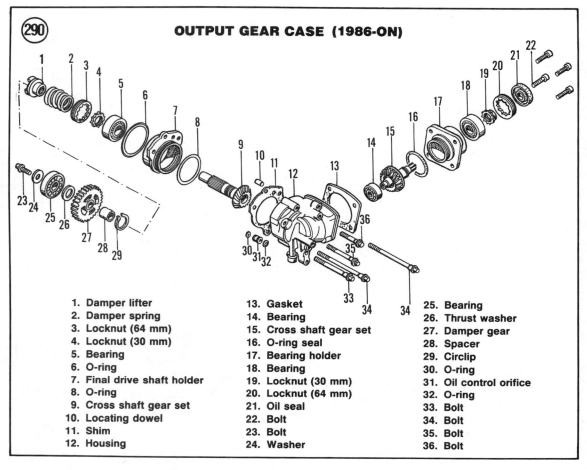

290

OUTPUT GEAR CASE (1986-ON)

1. Damper lifter
2. Damper spring
3. Locknut (64 mm)
4. Locknut (30 mm)
5. Bearing
6. O-ring
7. Final drive shaft holder
8. O-ring
9. Cross shaft gear set
10. Locating dowel
11. Shim
12. Housing
13. Gasket
14. Bearing
15. Cross shaft gear set
16. O-ring seal
17. Bearing holder
18. Bearing
19. Locknut (30 mm)
20. Locknut (64 mm)
21. Oil seal
22. Bolt
23. Bolt
24. Washer
25. Bearing
26. Thrust washer
27. Damper gear
28. Spacer
29. Circlip
30. O-ring
31. Oil control orifice
32. O-ring
33. Bolt
34. Bolt
35. Bolt
36. Bolt

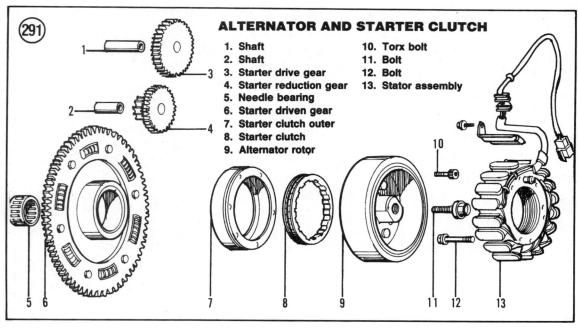

291

ALTERNATOR AND STARTER CLUTCH

1. Shaft
2. Shaft
3. Starter drive gear
4. Starter reduction gear
5. Needle bearing
6. Starter driven gear
7. Starter clutch outer
8. Starter clutch
9. Alternator rotor
10. Torx bolt
11. Bolt
12. Bolt
13. Stator assembly

7. Remove the bolt securing the gearshift pedal and remove the pedal (**Figure 293**).

8. Remove the bolts securing the left-hand front footpeg and remove the footpeg (**Figure 294**).

NOTE
In the following step it is not necessary to disconnect the hydraulic line from the clutch slave cylinder. If the hydraulic lines are disconnected the clutch system must be bled.

9. Remove the bolts (**Figure 295**) securing the clutch slave cylinder and bracket. Remove the bracket and pull the clutch slave cylinder, with the hydraulic line still attached, back and out of the way.

10. Remove the bolts securing the coolant pipe protector (A, **Figure 296**) and remove the protector.

11. Remove the bolts securing the alternator cover (B, **Figure 296**) and remove the cover, gasket and the electrical harness from the frame. Note the path of the wire harness as it must be routed the same during installation.

CAUTION
*The bolt securing the alternator rotor has left-hand threads. The bolt must be turned **clockwise** for removal.*

12. Remove the bolt (**Figure 297**) securing the alternator rotor. Turning a socket *clockwise*, remove the bolt securing the alternator rotor. ·

4

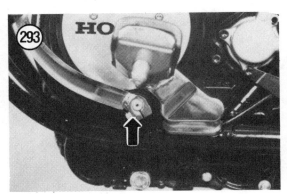

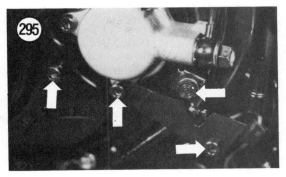

13. To keep the rotor from turning while removing the bolt, use one of the following.

    a. Use a strap wrench (**Figure 298**) on the outer perimeter of the rotor.

    b. Large adjustable wrench on the flats of the alternator rotor inner boss.

    c. Shift the transmission into gear and hold the rear brake on.

14. Screw in the rotor puller (**Figure 299**) until it stops. Use the Honda rotor puller (part No. 07933-3950000), K & N rotor puller (part No. 82-0190) or equivalent.

> *CAUTION*
> *Don't try to remove the rotor without a puller. Any attempt to do so will ultimately lead to some form of damage to the engine and/or rotor. Many aftermarket pullers are available from motorcycle dealers or mail order houses. The cost of one of these pullers is low and it makes an excellent addition to any mechanic's tool box. If you can't buy or borrow one, have the dealer remove the rotor.*

15. Turn the rotor puller with a wrench until the rotor is free.

> *NOTE*
> *If the rotor is difficult to remove, strike the puller with a hammer a few times. This will usually break it loose.*

> *CAUTION*
> *If normal rotor removal attempts fail, do not force the puller as the threads may be stripped out of the rotor causing expensive damage. Take the bike to a dealer and have the rotor removed.*

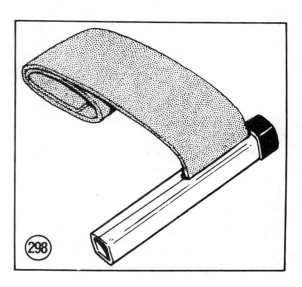

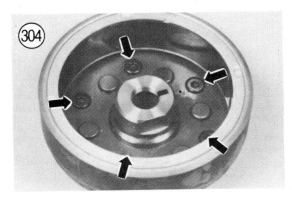

16. Remove the rotor and remove the puller from the rotor.

17. Withdraw the starter drive gear and shaft (**Figure 300**).

18. Withdraw the starter reduction gear and shaft (**Figure 301**).

19. Pull the starter driven gear outward until it stops on the gearshift shaft. Then push the gear back until the edge of the needle bearing is exposed.

20. Remove the needle bearing (**Figure 302**) from the crankshaft.

21. Remove the starter driven gear from the crankshaft (**Figure 303**).

Disassembly/Inspection/Assembly

1. Carefully inspect the inside of the rotor for small bolts, washers or other metal "trash" that may have been picked up by the magnets. These small metal bits can cause severe damage to the alternator stator assembly.

2. Place the alternator rotor with the starter clutch assembly facing down.

3. Remove the Torx screws (**Figure 304**) securing the starter clutch and starter clutch outer.

4. Turn the alternator rotor over and remove the starter clutch (A, **Figure 305**) and starter clutch outer (B, **Figure 305**).

5. Check the rollers (A, **Figure 305**) in the starter clutch for uneven or excessive wear; replace if necessary.

6. Measure the inside diameter of the starter clutch outer. The wear limit is 74.5 mm (2.933 in.). Replace if necessary.

7. Measure the outside diameter of the starter driven gear where the starter clutch rides (**Figure 306**). The wear limit is 57.6 mm (2.268 in.). Replace if necessary.

8. Inspect the teeth on the starter driven gear (A, **Figure 307**). Check for chipped or missing teeth; replace if necessary.

9. Check the needle bearing (B, **Figure 307**) for wear or damage. It must rotate freely; replace if necessary.

10. Inspect the teeth on the starter drive and reduction gears (**Figure 308**). Check for chipped or missing teeth. Look for uneven or excessive wear on the gear faces; replace as a set if necessary.

11. Assemble by reversing these disassembly steps, noting the following.

12. Apply Loctite Lock N' Seal to the threads of the Torx bolts before installing them and tighten to the torque specifications listed in **Table 2** or **Table 3**.

Installation

1. Install the starter driven gear onto the crankshaft (**Figure 303**).

2. Slide the roller bearing (**Figure 302**) onto crankshaft and into the starter driven gear. Slide the bearing all the way in until it stops.

3. Install the starter reduction gear and the shaft (**Figure 301**).

4. Position the starter drive gear with the OUT mark facing toward the outside (**Figure 300**) and install the gear and shaft.

5. Make sure the Woodruff key is in place on the crankshaft.

6. Align the Woodruff key with the slot in the rotor and push the alternator rotor/starter clutch assembly partially into place.

7. With your fingers, rotate the starter driven gear *clockwise* and push the rotor assembly all the way on.

> *CAUTION*
> *Remember, the bolt securing the alternator rotor has left-hand threads. The bolt must be turned **counterclockwise** for installation.*

8. Install the alternator rotor bolt.

9. Use the same tool set-up used for removal and tighten the bolt *counterclockwise* to the torque specification listed in **Table 2** or **Table 3**.

10. Install a new gasket and 2 locating dowels.

11. Install the alternator cover and tighten the .bolts securely.

12. Install the coolant pipe protector and bolts. Tighten the bolts securely.

13. Route the electrical harness through the frame following the same path noted during removal.

14. Connect the stator assembly electrical connector to the harness.

15. Install the left-hand rear crankcase cover.

16. Install the left-hand front footpeg and tighten the bolts securely.

17. Install the gearshift pedal and tighten the bolts securely.

18. Connect the battery negative lead and install the seat and both side covers.

BREAK-IN PROCEDURE

If the rings were replaced, new pistons installed, the cylinders rebored or honed or major lower end work performed, the engine should be broken in just as though it were new. The performance and service life of the engine depends greatly on a careful and sensible break-in.

For the first 800 km (500 miles), no more than one-third throttle should be used and speed should be varied as much as possible within the one-third throttle limit. Prolonged steady running at one speed, no matter how moderate, is to be avoided as well as hard acceleration.

Following the *800 km (500 mile) Service* procedures described in this chapter, more throttle should not be used until the motorcycle has covered at least 1,600 km (1,000 miles) and then it should be limited to short bursts of speed until 2,500 km (1,500 miles) have been logged.

The mono-grade oils recommended for break-in and normal use provide a better bedding pattern for rings and cylinders than do multi-grade oils. As a result, piston ring and cylinder bore life are greatly increased. During this period, oil consumption will be higher than normal. It is therefore important to frequently check and correct oil level. At no time during the break-in or later should the oil level be below the bottom line on the dipstick. If the oil level is low, the oil will become overheated resulting in insufficient lubrication and increased wear.

800 km (500 Mile) Service

It is essential that the oil and filter be changed after the first 800 km (500 miles). In addition, it is a good idea to change the oil and filter at the completion of the break-in (about 2,500 km/1,500 miles) to ensure that all of the particles produced during break-in are removed from the lubrication system. The small added expense may be considered a smart investment that will pay off in increased engine life.

Table 1 ENGINE SPECIFICATIONS

	Specification	Wear limit
General		
Engine type	Water-cooled, 4-stroke, SOHC, V-Twin	
Bore and stroke		
700 cc	76.5×75.5 mm (3.01×2.97 in.)	
750 cc	79.5×75.5 mm (3.13×2.97 in.)	
Displacement		
700 cc	694.5 cc (42.34 cid)	
750 cc	749.5 cc (45.72 cid)	
Compression ratio		
700 cc		
1984-1985	9.6 to 1	
1986-on	9.8 to 1	
750 cc	9.8 to 1	
Valve train	Hi-vo multi-link drive chain, OHC and rocker arms	
Maximum horsepower		
VT700C		
1984-1985	62 BHP @ 7,500 rpm	
1986-on	57 BHP @ 7,000 rpm	
VT750C	66 BHP @ 7,500 rpm	
Maximum torque		
VT700C		
1984-1985	6.3 kg/m (45.8 ft.-lb.) @ 6,000 rpm	
1986-on	6.3 kg/m (45.8 ft.-lb.) @ 5,500 rpm	
VT750C	6.8 kg/m (49.4 ft.-lb.) @ 6,000 rpm	
Lubrication	Wet sump	
Air filtration		
1983-1985	Foam element type	
1986-on	Paper element type	
Engine weight (dry)		
1983-1985	78 kg (171.6 lb.)	
1986-on	80 kg (176 lb.)	
Cylinders		
Bore		
700 cc		
1984-1985	76.500-76.515 mm (3.0118-3.0124)	76.66 mm (3.018 in.)
1986-on	76.500-76.515 (3.0118-3.0124 in.)	76.545 mm (3.0136 in.)
750 cc	79.500-79.515 mm (3.129-3.130 in.)	79.67 mm (3.136 in.)
Out of round	—	0.05 mm (0.002 in.)
Taper	—	0.05 mm (0.002 in.)
Piston/cylinder clearance	0.01-0.045 mm (0.0004-0.0018 in.)	0.32 mm (0.0126 in.)

(continued)

4

Table 1 ENGINE SPECIFICATIONS (continued)

Item	Specification	Wear limit
Pistons		
Diameter		
700 cc		
1984-1985	76.210-76.230 mm (3.0004-3.0012 in.)	76.09 mm (2.996 in.)
1986-on	76.46-76.49 mm (3.0102-3.0114 in.)	76.41 mm (3.0083 in.)
750 cc	79.47-79.49 mm (3.1287-3.1295 in.)	79.35 mm (3.124 in.)
Clearance in bore	0.01-0.045 mm (0.0004-0.0018 in.)	0.32 mm (0.0126 in.)
Piston pin bore		
1983-1985	20.002-20.008 mm (0.7875-0.7877 in.)	20.05 mm (0.789 in.)
1986-on	22.002-22.008 mm (0.8662-0.8665 in.)	22.018 mm (0.8668 in.)
Piston pin outer diameter		
1983-1985	19.994-20.000 mm (0.7872-0.7874 in.)	19.80 mm (0.779 in.)
1986-on	21.994-22.000 mm (0.8659-0.8661 in.)	21.984 mm (0.8655 in.)
Piston rings		
Number per piston		
Compression	2	
Oil control	1	
Ring end gap		
Top and second	0.20-0.35 mm (0.008-0.00138 in.)	0.50 mm (0.002 in.)
Oil (side rail)	0.30-0.90 mm (0.012-0.035 in.)	1.10 mm (0.04 in.)
Ring side clearance		
1983-1985		
Top and second	0.030-0.035 mm (0.0012-0.0014 in.)	0.10 mm (0.004 in.)
Oil (side rail)	0.030-0.035 mm (0.0012-0.0014 in.)	0.1 mm (0.004 in.)
1986-on		
Top and second	0.015-0.045 mm (0.0006-0.0018 in.)	0.25 mm (0.010 in.)
Oil (side rail)	0.030-0.035 mm) (0.0012-0.0014 in.)	0.10 mm (0.004 in.)
Connecting rod		
Small end inner diameter	20.020-20.041 mm (0.7882-0.7890 in.)	20.09 mm (0.7909 in.)
Crankshaft		
Runout	—	0.05 mm (0.002 in.)
Main bearing oil clearance	0.025-0.041 mm (0.0010-0.0016 in.)	0.06 mm (0.002 in.)
Connecting rod oil clearance	0.028-0.052 mm (0.0011-0.0020 in.)	0.07 mm (0.003 in.)

(continued)

Table 1 ENGINE SPECIFICATIONS (continued)

Item	Specification	Wear limit
Connecting rod big end side clearance	0.10-0.25 mm (0.004-0.010 in.)	0.4 mm (0.016 in.)
Camshaft Cam lobe height 1983-1985	36.497 mm (1.4369 in.)	36.28 mm (1.4283 in.)
1986-on	35.843 mm (1.4111 in.)	35.82 mm (1.410 in.)
Runout	0.03 mm (0.0010 in.)	0.05 mm (0.002 in.)
Oil clearance 1983-1985	0.020-0.062 mm (0.0008-0.0024 in.)	0.07 mm (0.0027 in.)
1986-on	0.050-0.111 mm (0.0020-0.0044 in.)	0.130 mm (0.0051 in.)
Rocker arm bore 1983-1985	13.750-13.768 mm (0.5413-0.5420 in.)	13.80 mm (0.5433 in.)
1986-on	13.750-13.768 mm (0.5413-0.5420 in.)	13.78 mm (0.5424 in.)
Rocker arm shaft 1985-on	13.716-13.734 mm (0.5400-0.5406 in.)	13.58 mm (0.5346 in.)
1986-on	13.716-13.734 mm (0.5400-0.5406 in.)	13.71 mm (0.5396 in.)
Tappet assist spring free length 1983-1985	19.46 mm (0.7661 in.)	18.68 mm (0.7354 in.)
1986-on	18.57 mm (0.731 in.)	17.80 mm (0.701 in.)
Tappet compression stroke in kerosene	—	0.20 mm (0.0079 in.)
Valves Valve stem outer diameter Intake	6.570-6.595 mm (0.2587-0.2596 in.)	6.55 mm (0.258 in.)
Exhaust	6.550-6.575 mm (0.2585-0.2587 in.)	6.54 mm (0.258 in.)
Valve guide inner diameter Intake and exhaust 1983-1985	6.600-6.620 mm (0.2589-0.2606 in.)	6.66 mm (0.262 in.)
1986-on	6.600-6.615 mm (0.2598-0.2604 in.)	6.655 mm (0.2620 in.)
Stem to guide clearance 1983-1985 Intake	0.005-0.050 mm (0.0002-0.0020 in.)	0.11 mm (0.004 in.)
Exhaust	0.025-0.070 mm (0.0010-0.0028 in.)	0.12 mm (0.004 in.)
1986-on Intake	0.005-0.045 mm (0.0002-0.0018 in.)	0.075 mm (0.0030 in.)

(continued)

Table 1 ENGINE SPECIFICATIONS (continued)

Item	Specification	Wear limit
Stem to guide clearance (continued)		
1986-on (continued)		
Exhaust	0.025-0.065 mm (0.0010-0.0026 in.)	0.115 mm (0.0045 in.)
Valve seat width		
Intake and	0.9-1.1 mm	1.5 mm (0.059 in.)
exhaust	(0.0354-0.0433 in.)	
Valve springs free length		
Intake		
Outer	45.7 mm (1.79 in.)	43.9 mm (1.73 in.)
Inner	37.9 mm (1.49 in.)	36.40 mm (1.433 in.)
Exhaust		
Outer	43.5 mm (1.71 in.)	41.8 mm (1.64 in.)
Inner	37.9 mm (1.49 in.)	36.40 mm (1.433 in.)
Cylinder head warpage	—	0.10 mm (0.004 in.)
Oil pump		
Inner rotor tip to	0.15 mm	0.20 mm (0.008 in.)
outer clearance	(0.006 in.)	
Outer rotor to	0.15-0.22 mm	0.35 mm (0.014 in.)
body clearance	(0.006-0.009 in.)	
End clearance	0.02-0.07 mm	0.10 mm (0.004 in.)
to body	(0.001-0.003 in.)	
Oil pump pressure (at switch)		
1983-1985	5.4 ±0.7 kg/cm² (62.6 ±9.9 psi)	
1986-on	4.5 kg/cm² (63.99 psi)	
Oil pump delivery		
1983-1985	36 liters/min. @ 6,000 rpm (38.1 U.S. qt./min. @ 6,000 rpm)	
1986-on	NA	

* NA = Information not furnished by Honda.

Table 2 ENGINE TORQUE SPECIFICATIONS (1983-1985)

Item	N·m	ft.-lb.
Engine mounting bolts		
8 mm	20-30	14-22
10 mm	45-60	33-43
12 mm	60-80	43-58
Sub-frame bolts		
Upper	70-80	51-58
Lower	35-45	25-33
Cylinder head cover	20-25	14-18
and cam sprocket cover		
Cam sprocket bolts	16-20	12-14
Camshaft holder bolts and nuts		
8 mm cap nut	20-25	14-18
10 mm cap nut	35-45	25-33
12 mm bolt	20-25	14-18
Spark plug sleeve	10-15	7-11

(continued)

Table 2 ENGINE TORQUE SPECIFICATIONS (continued)

Item	N·m	ft.-lb.
Crankcase bolts		
6 mm	8-12	6-9
8 mm	20-25	14-18
Connecting rod cap nuts	41-45	30-33
Output drive shaft bolt	35-45	25-33
Primary drive gear bolt	80-100	58-72
Oil pipe bolts	10-14	7-10
Alternator rotor bolt	80-100	58-72
Oil pressure switch*	10-14	7-10
Starter clutch Torx bolts**	18-25	13-18

* Apply liquid sealant to threads prior to installation.
** Apply Loctite Lock N' Seal #200 to the threads prior to installation.

Table 3 ENGINE TORQUE SPECIFICATIONS (1986-ON)

Item	N·m	ft.-lb.
Front engine mount bolts	45-60	33-43
Rear lower engine mounts *	60-70	43-51
Rear upper engine mount bolts	45-60	33-43
Front engine mount bracket bolt	30-40	22-29
Front sub-frame bolts *	60-70	43-51
Rear sub-frame bolts	35-45	25-33
Cylinder head cover		
8 mm cap nuts	25-29	18-21
10 mm cap nuts	38-42	27-30
Cam sprocket bolts	16-20	15-18
Oil pipe bolts	10-14	7-10
Oil control bolt	20-25	15-18
Spark plug sleeve **	10-15	7-11
Timing hole **	15-20	11-15
Assist shaft caps	20-24	15-17
Rocker arm shaft caps	35-45	25-33
Crankcase bolts		
6 mm	24-30	17-22
8 mm	25-29	18-21
Connecting rod cap nuts	41-45	30-33
Output drive shaft bolt	45-55	33-40
Bearing set plate		
Bolt ***	8-12	6-9
Screw ***	7-11	5-8
Alternator rotor bolt *	80-100	58-72
Starter clutch bolts ***	21-25	15-18
Oil pressure switch ***	10-14	7-10
Oil pump driven sprocket bolt	15-20	11-14

* Apply oil to threads before installation.
** Apply molybdenum disulfide grease to threads before installation.
*** Apply Loctite Lock N ' Seal #200 to the threads before installation.

Table 4 HYDRAULIC TAPPET SHIM SELECTION

Assist shaft stroke	Number of shims required
0-1.20 mm	0
1.20-1.50 mm	1
1.50-1.80 mm	2
1.80-2.10 mm	3
2.10-2.40 mm	4
2.40-2.70 mm	5

Table 5 MAIN JOURNAL BEARING SELECTION (1983-1985)

Main journal OD size code letter and dimension		
Number 1 49.984- 49.992 mm (1.9679-1.9682 in.)	Number 2 49.992-50.000 mm (1.9682-1.9685 in.)	
Crankcase inside dimension		
54.010-54.020 mm (2.1264-2.1268 in.)	Brown	Black
54.000-54.010 mm (2.1259-2.1264 in.)	Black	Blue

Table 6 MAIN JOURNAL BEARING INSERT THICKNESS (1983-1985)

Color	mm	in.
Brown	1.989-1.999	0.0783-0.0787
Black	1.994-2.004	0.0785-0.0779
Blue	1.999-2.009	0.0787-0.0791

Table 7 MAIN JOURNAL BEARING SELECTION (1986-on)

Main journal OD size code letter and dimension		
Number 1 49.992-50.000 mm (1.9682-1.9685 in.)	Number 2 49.984-49.992 mm (1.9679-1.9682 in.)	
Crankcase inside dimension		
A 54.000-54.010 mm (2.1260-2.1264 in.)	C (Brown)	B (Black)
B 54.010-54.020 mm (2.1264-2.1268 in.)	B (Black)	A (Blue)

Table 8 MAIN JOURNAL BEARING INSERT THICKNESS (1986-ON)

Color	mm	in.
Blue (A)	1.999-2.009	0.0787-0.0791
Black (B)	1.994-2.004	0.0785-0.0779
Brown (C)	1.9849-1.999	0.0781-0.0787

Table 9 CONNECTING ROD BEARING SELECTION

Crankpin journal OD size code letter and dimension		
Letter A 42.982-42.990 mm (1.6922-1.6925 in.	Letter B 42.974-42.982 mm (1.6918-1.6922 in.)	
Connecting rod ID code number and dimension		
Number 1 46.000-46.008 mm (1.8110-1.8113 in.)	Pink (F)	Yellow (E)
Number 2 46.008-46.016 mm (1.8113-1.8116 in.)	Yellow (E)	Green (D)

Table 10 CONNECTING ROD BEARING INSERT THICKNESS

Color	mm	in.
Green (D)	1.495-1.499	0.0589-0.0590
Yellow (E)	1.491-1.495	0.0578-0.0589
Pink (F)	1.487-1.491	0.0585-0.0587

Table 11 CONNECTING ROD WEIGHT SELECTION (1986-ON)

Front rod code marking	Rear rod code marking			
	A	B	C	D
A	X	X		
B	X	X	X	
C	X	X	X	
D	X	X		

CLUTCH AND TRANSMISSION

This chapter describes complete clutch and transmission procedures. **Tables 1-4** are at the end of this chapter.

CLUTCH
(1983-1986)

The clutch is a wet, multiplate type which operates immersed in the engine oil. It is mounted on the right-hand end of the transmission mainshaft. The outside clutch center is splined to the mainshaft. The outer clutch housing can rotate freely on the mainshaft and is geared to the primary driven gear splined to the end of the crankshaft.

A unique feature of this clutch is the "1-way system" that was developed through Honda's Grand Prix racing programs. This system helps prevent rear wheel lock-up when downshifting from fairly rapid speeds. When the rear wheel nears the lock-up point, the one-way clutch allows half of the clutch friction discs to slip just enough to prevent the rear wheel from lockingup or skidding under rapid deceleration.

There are 2 clutch centers. The outside clutch center "B" is controlled by the 1-way clutch and operates 3 clutch friction discs and 3 clutch plates. This clutch center is the one that is allowed to slip in one direction only. The inside clutch center "A" is splined to the transmission mainshaft and operates 3 clutch friction discs and 2 clutch plates.

During acceleration, cruising and normal deceleration the clutch operates the same way as any other clutch assembly.

The clutch release mechanism is hydraulic and requires no routine adjustment. The mechanism consists of a clutch master cylinder on the left-hand handlebar, a slave cylinder on the left-hand side of the engine just behind the alternator and a pushrod that rides within the channel in the transmission mainshaft.

The clutch is activated by hydraulic fluid pressure and is controlled by the clutch master cylinder. The hydraulic pressure generated by the master cylinder activates the clutch slave cylinder that in turn pushes the clutch pushrod. The clutch pushrod pushes on the lifter guide, thus moving the pressure plate which disengages the clutch mechanism.

Removal/Disassembly

Refer to **Figure 1** when performing this procedure.

All clutch components, except for the clutch outer housing, can be removed with the engine in the frame by removing the clutch cover on the right-hand crankcase cover.

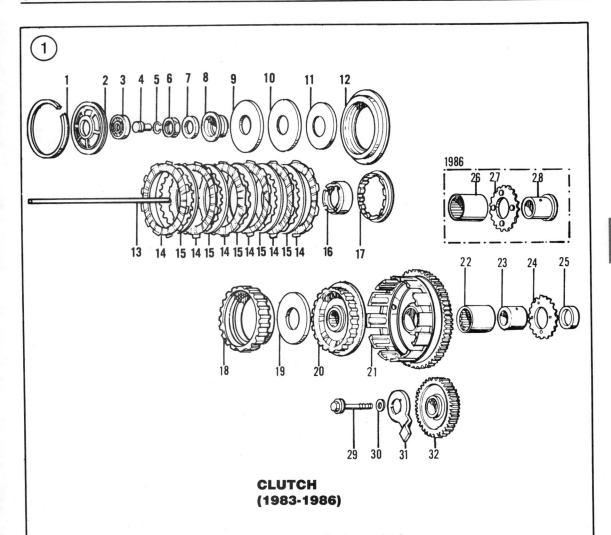

CLUTCH
(1983-1986)

1. Circlip
2. Clutch lifter plate
3. Bearing
4. Clutch lifter
5. Circlip
6. Locknut
7. Washer
8. Spring setting plate
9. Clutch spring (dished)
10. Flat washer (thin)
11. Flat washer (thicker)
12. Pressure plate
13. Clutch pushrod
14. Friction disc
15. Clutch plates
16. 1-way clutch inner race

17. 1-way clutch
18. Clutch center B
19. Washer
20. Clutch center A
21. Clutch outer housing
22. Needle bearing (1983-1985)
23. Clutch outer housing bushing
24. Oil pump drive gear (1983-1985)
25. Collar (1983-1985)
26. Needle bearing (1986)
27. Oil pump drive gear (1986)
28. Clutch outer guide (1986)
29. Bolt
30. Washer
31. Pulse generator plate
32. Primary drive gear

1. Place the bike on the centerstand.

2. Drain the engine oil as described in Chapter Three.

NOTE
Do not operate the clutch lever after the clutch assembly or slave cylinder is removed from the engine. If the lever is applied it will force the slave cylinder piston out of the body and make slave cylinder installation difficult.

3. Place a block of wood between the clutch lever and the hand grip to hold the lever in the released position. Secure the wood with a rubber band or tape. This will prevent the clutch lever from being applied accidentally after the clutch slave cylinder is removed from the crankcase.

4. Remove the exhaust system from the right-hand side as described in Chapter Six.

5A. *1983-1985:* Remove the bolts securing the left-hand front footpeg and brake pedal assembly. Remove both assemblies (**Figure 2**).

5B. *1986:* Perform the following.

    a. Remove the rear brake pivot arm bolt. Then slide the pivot arm off of the pivot shaft.

    b. Remove the right-hand footpeg and brake pedal assembly.

6. Remove the Allen bolts securing the clutch cover (**Figure 3**) and remove the cover and gasket.

7. Remove the snap ring (A, **Figure 4**) securing the clutch lifter plate (B, **Figure 4**) and remove the clutch lifter plate assembly.

8. Remove the clutch nut (**Figure 5**) and the lockwasher (A, **Figure 6**).

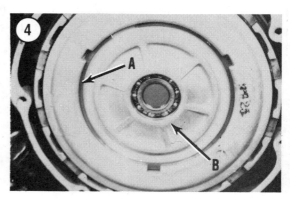

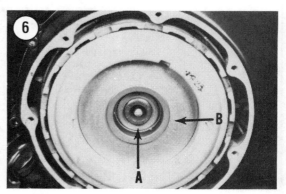

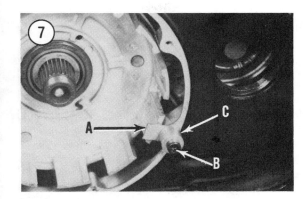

9. Remove the clutch spring setting plate, the clutch spring and the washers (B, **Figure 6**).

NOTE
The following step is shown with most of the clutch parts removed for clarity. Install the clutch holder at this time. If the clutch outer housing comes out of mesh with the pins on the oil pump drive sprocket, the engine will have to be removed from the frame and the right-hand crankcase cover removed to properly mesh these parts again.

10. To prevent the clutch outer housing from coming out of mesh with the pins on the oil pump drive sprocket, make a small holder as follows.

 a. Use a small piece of metal (A, **Figure 7**).
 b. Drill a hole in one end the correct size to accept a clutch cover screw (B, **Figure 7**).
 c. Use a spacer (C, **Figure 7**) or a stack-up of washers long enough so a clutch cover screw can be used.
 d. Bend the end of the piece of metal down so it touches one of the fingers of the clutch outer housing. The end must press against the finger or it will not serve its purpose.

11. Remove the clutch pressure plate (**Figure 8**).
12. Remove the friction discs and the clutch plates.
13. Remove the clutch center "B" (A, **Figure 9**), the 1-way clutch and the 1-way clutch inner race (B, **Figure 9**) as an assembly.
14. Remove the washer (**Figure 10**) and the clutch center "A" (**Figure 11**).
15A. *1983-1985:* To remove the clutch outer housing, perform the following.

 a. Remove the engine from the frame as described in Chapter Four.

b. Remove the screws securing the right-hand crankcase cover (**Figure 12**).

c. Slide the clutch outer housing, needle bearing and bushing (**Figure 13**) off the transmission mainshaft.

15B. *1986:* To remove the clutch outer housing, perform the following.

a. Remove the radiator as described in Chapter Eight.

b. Place a jack underneath the engine. Place wood blocks on top of the jack and raise the jack support so that it just rests against the bottom of the engine.

c. Remove the right-hand subframe (**Figure 14**). Remove the front engine mount bolt and spacer. Then remove the upper and lower Allen bolts and pull the sub-frame away from the engine.

d. Remove the Allen bolts securing the right-hand crankcase cover (**Figure 15**).

e. Remove the 2 dowel pins.

f. Insert a screwdriver into the primary drive gear and align it and the sub-gear teeth (**Figure 16**). Then slide the clutch outer housing (**Figure 16**) off of the transmission mainshaft.

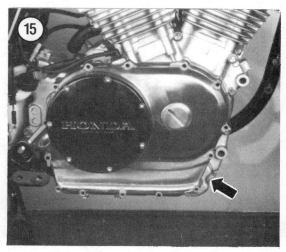

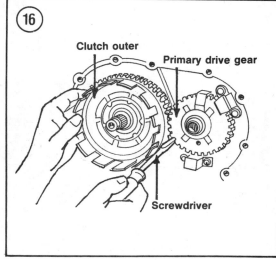

Clutch outer

Primary drive gear

Screwdriver

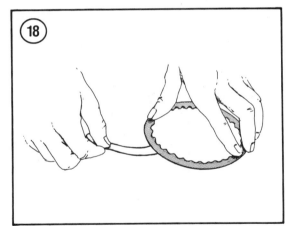

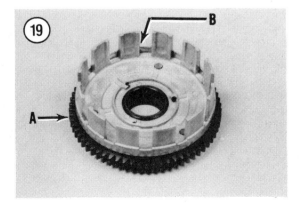

Inspection

1. Clean all clutch parts in petroleum-based solvent such as kerosene and thoroughly dry with compressed air.

2. Measure the thickness of each friction disc at several places around the disc as shown in **Figure 17**. Compare to the specifications listed in **Table 1**. Replace any disc that is worn to the service limit or less. For optimum performance replace all friction discs as a set even if only a few require replacement.

3. Check the clutch plates for warpage on a surface plate such as a piece of plate glass (**Figure 18**). Compare to the specifications listed in **Table 1**. Replace any plate that is warped to the service limit or more. For optimum performance replace all clutch plates as a set even if only a few require replacement.

4. Inspect the teeth of the outer housing (A, **Figure 19**) for damage. Remove any small nicks on the gear teeth with an oilstone. If damage is severe, the housing must be replaced. Also check the teeth and inner splines on the driven gear; it may also need replacing.

5. See **Figure 20** (1983-1985) or **Figure 21** (1986). Inspect the needle bearing for the clutch outer housing. Make sure it rotates smoothly with no signs of wear; replace if necessary.

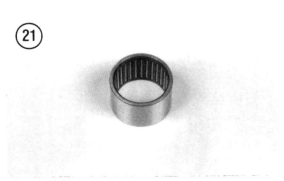

6. Inspect the slots in the clutch outer housing (B, **Figure 19**) for cracks, nicks or galling where they come in contact with the friction disc tabs. If any severe damage is evident, the housing must be replaced.

7. Inspect the inner splines (A, **Figure 22**) of the clutch center "A;" replace if necessary.

8. Inspect the outer grooves (B, **Figure 22**) of clutch center "A;" replace if necessary.

9. Inspect the outer grooves (A, **Figure 23**) of clutch center "B;" replace if necessary.

10. Inspect the inner grooves (**Figure 24**) of the clutch pressure plate; replace if necessary.

11. Inspect the 1-way clutch (**Figure 25**) for smooth operation. Check the rollers for excessive wear, galling, pitting and play by rotating it with your fingers. If any roughness or play can be felt in the 1-way clutch, it must be replaced.

12. Inspect the splines of the 1-way clutch inner race (A, **Figure 26**); replace if necessary.

13. Measure the inside diameter of the clutch center "B" (B, **Figure 23**). If it is worn to the service limit listed in **Table 1**, the clutch center "B" must be replaced.

14. Measure the outside diameter of the 1-way clutch inner race (B, **Figure 26**). If it is worn to the service limit listed in **Table 1**, the 1-way clutch inner race must be replaced.

15. Measure the height of the clutch spring with a vernier caliper as shown in **Figure 27**. Replace the spring if it is worn to the service limit listed in **Table 1**.

16. Measure the inside diameter of the clutch outer housing guide. If it is worn to the service limit listed in **Table 1** the guide must be replaced.

17. Make sure the lifter guide and the bearing rotate smoothly with no signs of wear or damage; replace if necessary.

Assembly/Installation

1A. *1983-1985:* If the clutch outer housing was removed, perform the following.

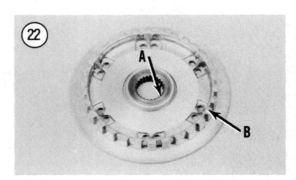

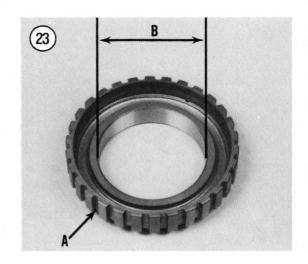

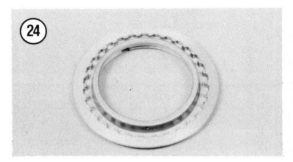

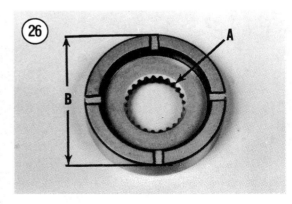

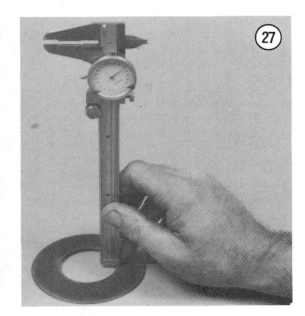

a. Rotate the oil pump drive sprocket so the pins are lined up at the 12, 3, 6 and 9 o'clock positions (A, **Figure 28**).

b. Align the index holes (B, **Figure 28**) in the backside of the clutch outer housing with the sprocket pins and install the clutch outer housing and needle bearing (**Figure 13**) onto the transmission countershaft.

c. Push the housing on all the way and make sure that the pins and holes are indexed properly, then install the clutch outer housing bushing (**Figure 13**).

d. Slowly rotate the oil pump driven gear and drive chain (A, **Figure 29**) until the pins and index holes align properly.

CAUTION
The oil pump sprocket and the clutch outer housing must index properly so that the housing will go on all the way. Otherwise, the clutch will not function properly nor will the oil pump rotate. Severe engine damage will result.

e. Install the locating dowels (B, **Figure 29**) and a new gasket.

f. Install the right-hand crankcase cover and tighten the screws securely.

g. Make sure the holding fixture is still in place on the crankcase cover (**Figure 7**) and is pressing against one of the fingers of the clutch outer housing.

h. The fingers on the clutch outer housing must be *behind* the outer surface (**Figure 30**) of the right-hand crankcase cover where the clutch cover attaches. If the fingers are flush with this surface, chances are that the clutch outer housing has slipped out and may be out of mesh with the pins on the oil pump drive sprocket. Check by rotating the clutch outer housing and look into the crankcase area and see if the oil pump chain is moving. The oil

pump chain must also be moving. If not, repeat this step and correct the problem.

  i. Install the engine into the frame as described in Chapter Four.

1B. *1986:* If the clutch outer housing was removed, perform the following.

  a. Oil the needle bearing pins. Then slide the needle bearing into the clutch outer.

  b. Rotate the oil pump drive sprocket so the pins are lined up at the 12, 3, 6 and 9 o'clock positions (A, **Figure 28**).

  c. Align the index holes (B, **Figure 28**) in the backside of the clutch outer housing with the sprocket pins and install the clutch outer housing partway onto the transmission mainshaft.

  d. Align the primary drive gear with the sub-gear teeth with a screwdriver (**Figure 16**). Then push the housing on all the way and make sure that the pins and holes are indexed properly.

  e. Slowly rotate the oil pump driven gear and drive chain (A, **Figure 29**) until the pins and index holes align properly.

> *CAUTION*
> *The oil pump sprocket and the clutch outer housing must index properly so that the housing will go on all the way. Otherwise, the clutch will not function properly nor will the oil pump rotate. Severe engine damage will result.*

  f. Install a new crankcase gasket and the 2 dowel pins.

  g. Install the right-hand crankcase cover (**Figure 15**). Tighten the bolts.

  h. Install the right-hand sub-frame assembly (**Figure 14**).

  i. Tighten the front engine bracket bolt to 30-40 N•m (22-29 ft.-lb.).

  j. Tighten the front engine mount nut to 45-60 N•m (33-43 ft.-lb.).

  k. Tighten the front sub-frame mount bolt to 60-70 N•m (43-51 ft.-lb.).

  l. Tighten the rear sub-frame mount bolt to 35-45 N•m (25-33 ft.-lb.).

  m. Install the radiator as described in Chapter Eight.

2. Install the clutch center "A" (**Figure 11**) and the washer (**Figure 10**).

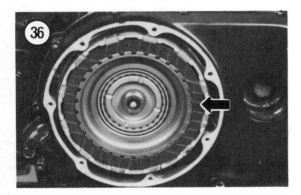

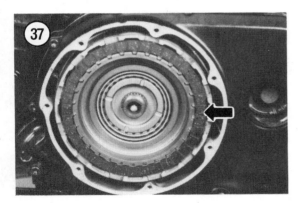

3. Place the clutch center "B" with the grooves facing down (A, **Figure 31**).

4. Install the 1-way clutch into the clutch center "B" with its flange side facing down (B, **Figure 31**).

5. Install the 1-way clutch/clutch center "B" assembly onto this assembly (**Figure 32**) while turning it *clockwise* as viewed from the top. Push it on all the way until it stops.

6. Install the parts assembled in Step 4 and Step 5 onto the transmission mainshaft (**Figure 9**).

CAUTION
*The clutch center "B" must be able to rotate clockwise after it is installed on the 1-way clutch. It must **not** be able to rotate **counterclockwise**. If the clutch center "B" will rotate counterclockwise either the 1-way clutch is installed backwards or is faulty and must be replaced. Remedy the problem before going any further. The clutch will not function properly if the clutch center "B" can rotate freely counterclockwise.*

CAUTION
If either or both friction discs and clutch plates have been replaced with new ones, apply new engine oil to all surfaces to avoid having the clutch lock up when used for the first time.

NOTE
The 2nd and 3rd friction disc from the inside have a different groove pattern. Be sure to install them in their proper sequence.

7. Align the grooves of the clutch centers "A" and "B" (**Figure 33**).

8. Install a friction disc (**Figure 34**) with grooves that radiate out from the center.

9. Install a clutch plate (**Figure 35**) and a friction disc that has 2 sets of grooves that run vertically and 2 sets that run horizontally (**Figure 36**).

10. Install a clutch plate, and the other friction disc that has 2 sets of grooves that run vertically and 2 sets that run horizontally, similar to the one installed in **Figure 36**.

11. Continue to install a clutch plate and then a friction disc. Alternate them until all are installed. The last part installed is a friction disc (**Figure 37**).

12. Install the clutch pressure plate (**Figure 38**).

5

13. Set the clutch spring setting plate upside down (**Figure 39**) and install the following parts.
    a. Install the clutch spring with the dished side facing toward the inside (**Figure 40**).
    b. Install the large diameter thin washer (**Figure 41**) and then the smaller diameter thick washer (**Figure 42**).

14. Install this assembly into the pressure plate (**Figure 43**).

15. Install the lockwasher with the dished side facing toward the inside (A, **Figure 44**).

16. Install the clutch locknut (**Figure 45**) and tighten to the torque specifications listed in **Table 2**.

17. Make sure the clutch lifter rod (**Figure 46**) is installed in the channel in the transmission mainshaft.

18. Make sure the lifter guide and bearing (**Figure 47**) are installed in the clutch lifter plate and install this assembly (**Figure 43**).

19. Because of the slight internal hydraulic pressure within the clutch release mechanism, you must push on the clutch lifter plate with a soft-ended tool while installing the snap ring. Make sure the snap ring is completely seated in the groove in the clutch pressure plate (A, **Figure 48**).

20. Install a new gasket and install the clutch cover. Tighten the bolts securely.

21. Install the exhaust system onto the right-hand side as described in Chapter Six.

22. Install the left-hand front footpeg and brake pedal assemblies.

23. Remove the wood block between the clutch lever and the hand grip.

24. Fill the crankcase with the recommended type and quantity of engine oil. Refer to Chapter Three.

CLUTCH (1987)

The clutch is a wet, multiplate type which operates immersed in the engine oil. It is mounted

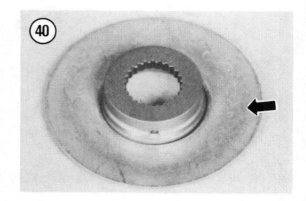

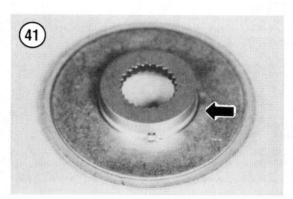

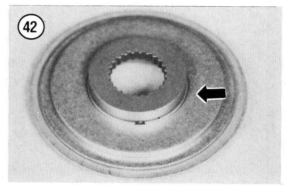

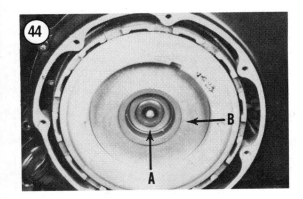

on the right-hand end of the transmission mainshaft. The outside clutch center is splined to the mainshaft. The outer clutch housing can rotate freely on the mainshaft and is geared to the primary driven gear splined to the end of the crankshaft.

The clutch release mechanism is hydraulic and requires no routine adjustment. The mechanism consists of a clutch master cylinder on the left-hand handlebar, a slave cylinder on the left-hand side of the engine just behind the alternator and a pushrod that rides within the channel in the transmission mainshaft.

The clutch is activated by hydraulic fluid pressure and is controlled by the clutch master cylinder. The hydraulic pressure generated by the master cylinder activates the clutch slave cylinder that in turn pushes the clutch pushrod. The clutch pushrod pushes on the lifter guide thus moving the pressure plate which disengages the clutch mechanism.

Removal/Disassembly

Refer to **Figure 49** for the clutch assembly.

All clutch components, except the clutch outer housing, can be serviced by removing the clutch cover (A, **Figure 50**). The clutch outer housing can be serviced by removing the right crankcase cover (B, **Figure 50**). The following procedure describes complete clutch removal and disassembly.

1. Place the bike on the centerstand.
2. Drain the engine oil as described in Chapter Three.

NOTE
Do not operate the clutch lever after the clutch assembly or slave cylinder is removed from the engine. If the lever is applied it will force the slave cylinder piston out of the body and make slave cylinder installation difficult.

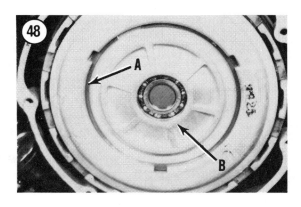

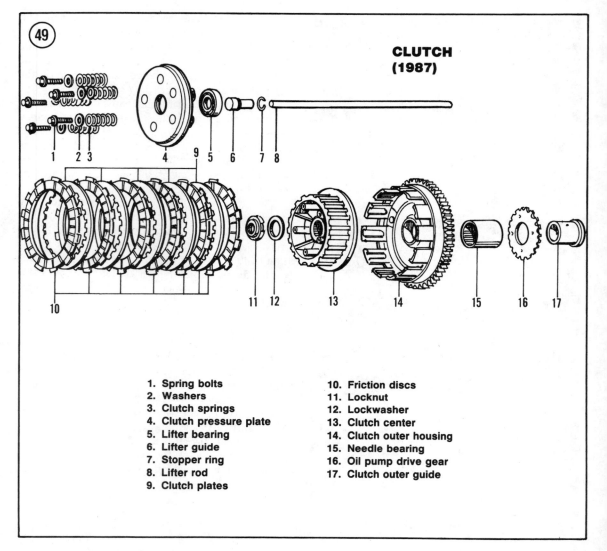

**CLUTCH
(1987)**

1. Spring bolts
2. Washers
3. Clutch springs
4. Clutch pressure plate
5. Lifter bearing
6. Lifter guide
7. Stopper ring
8. Lifter rod
9. Clutch plates

10. Friction discs
11. Locknut
12. Lockwasher
13. Clutch center
14. Clutch outer housing
15. Needle bearing
16. Oil pump drive gear
17. Clutch outer guide

3. Place a block of wood between the clutch lever and the hand grip to hold the lever in the released position. Secure the wood with a rubber band or tape. This will prevent the clutch lever from being applied accidentally after the clutch slave cylinder is removed from the crankcase.

4. Remove the bolt securing the rear brake pivot arm to the pivot shaft (C, **Figure 50**). Then remove the bolts securing the right-hand footpeg and brake pedal assembly (D, **Figure 50**). Remove the brake pedal assembly. If the pivot arm will not slide off of the pivot shaft, insert a screwdriver into the pivot arm slot and pry it open slightly and pull the arm off the shaft.

5A. If removal of the clutch outer housing is not required, remove the clutch cover (A, **Figure 50**) from the right-hand crankcase cover.

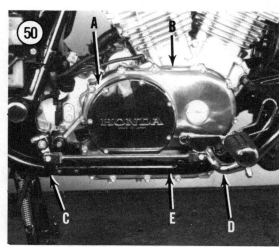

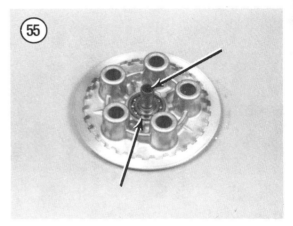

5

5B. If removal of the clutch outer housing is required, perform the following.

    a. Remove the right-hand exhaust pipe as described in Chapter Six.

    b. Remove the radiator as described in Chapter Eight.

    c. Place a jack underneath the engine. Place wood blocks on top of the jack and raise the jack support so that it just rests against the bottom of the engine.

    d. Remove the right-hand subframe (E, **Figure 50**). Remove the front engine mount bolt and spacer. Then remove the upper and lower Allen bolts and pull the sub-frame away from the engine.

    e. Remove the Allen bolts securing the right-hand crankcase cover (**Figure 51**).

6. Remove the 2 dowel pins.

7. Using a crisscross pattern, remove the clutch bolts (**Figure 52**).

8. Remove the clutch springs (**Figure 53**).

9. Remove the pressure plate (**Figure 54**) with the clutch lifter guide and bearing attached. See **Figure 55**.

10. Remove a friction disc (**Figure 56**) and a clutch plate (steel) (**Figure 57**). Continue until all plates are removed. Stack plates in order.

11. Remove the clutch pushrod (**Figure 58**).

> *NOTE*
> *Steps 12-16 describe removal of the clutch center and clutch outer. Removal of these parts require removal of the right-hand crankcase cover. Perform Step 5B, if not previously done.*

> *NOTE*
> *Clutch nut removal requires a special tool available from a Honda dealer (Locknut Wrench part No. 07716-0020203). See **Figure 59**.*

> *NOTE*
> *To keep the clutch inner from turning, use the "Grabbit" special tool available from motorcycle and tool dealers. See **Figure 60**.*

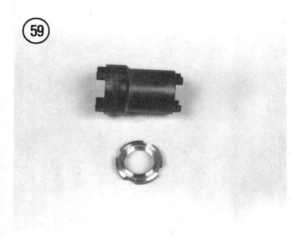

12. Loosen and remove the clutch nut (**Figure 61**).

13. Remove the lockwasher (**Figure 62**).

14. Slide the clutch inner (**Figure 63**) off of the transmission mainshaft.

15. Remove the clutch outer housing. Insert a screwdriver into the primary drive gear and align it and the sub-gear teeth (**Figure 64**). Then slide the clutch outer housing (**Figure 65**) off of the transmission mainshaft.

16. Slide the needle bearing (**Figure 66**) off of the transmission mainshaft.

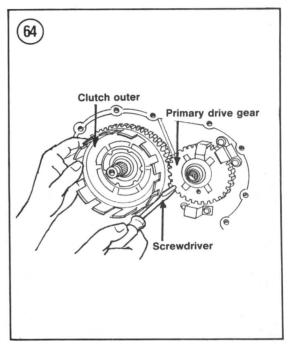

5

Inspection

1. Clean all clutch parts in petroleum-based solvent such as kerosene and thoroughly dry with compressed air.

2. Check the friction discs (**Figure 67**) for tab breakage or cracks. If the discs appear okay, measure the thickness of each friction disc at several places around the disc as shown in **Figure 68**. Compare to the specifications listed in **Table 1**. Replace any disc that is worn to the service limit or less. For optimum performance, replace all frictions discs as a set even if only a few require replacement.

3. Check the clutch plates (**Figure 69**) for heat damage (excessive blue coloration) or cracks. If the clutch plates appear okay, check the clutch plates for warpage on a surface plate such as a piece of plate glass (**Figure 70**). Compare to the specifications listed in **Table 1**. Replace any plate that is warped to the service limit or more. For optimum performance replace all clutch plates as a set even if only a few require replacement.

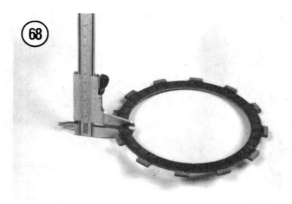

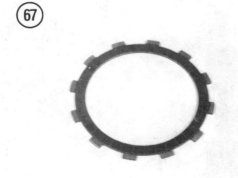

4. Inspect the teeth of the outer housing (**Figure 71**) for damage. Remove any small nicks on the gear teeth with an oilstone. If damage is severe, the housing must be replaced.

5. Inspect the needle bearing (**Figure 72**) for the clutch outer housing. Make sure it rotates smoothly with no signs of wear; replace if necessary.

6. Inspect the slots in the clutch outer housing (**Figure 73**) for cracks, nicks or galling where they come in contact with the friction disc tabs. If any severe damage is evident, the housing must be replaced.

7. Inspect the clutch center inner (**Figure 74**) and outer (A, **Figure 75**) splines. Remove any small nicks with an oilstone.

8. Check the clutch center spring towers (B, **Figure 75**) for cracks or other damage; replace the clutch center if necessary.

9. Measure the free length of each clutch spring as shown in **Figure 76**. Replace any springs that are too short (**Table 1**).

10. Check the pressure plate spring towers (A, **Figure 77**) for cracks or other damage; replace if necessary.

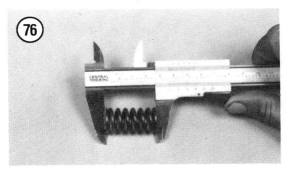

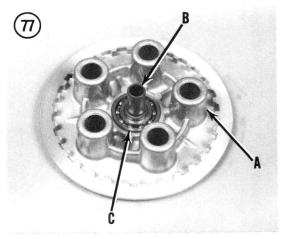

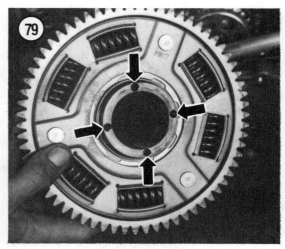

11. Turn the lifter guide (B, **Figure 77**) and check the lifter bearing (C, **Figure 77**) for excessive play or noise. Replace the bearing if necessary. Remove the stopper ring and remove the lifter guide and bearing. Replace the bearing and install the lifter guide. Secure with the stopper ring.

Assembly/Installation

1. If the clutch outer housing was removed, perform the following.

  a. Oil the needle bearing pins. Then slide the needle bearing (**Figure 66**) onto the transmission mainshaft.

  b. Rotate the oil pump drive sprocket so the pins are lined up at the 12, 3, 6 and 9 o'clock positions (**Figure 78**).

  c. Align the index holes (**Figure 79**) in the backside of the clutch outer housing with the

sprocket pins and install the clutch outer housing partway onto the transmission mainshaft.

  d. Align the primary drive gear with the sub-gear teeth with a screwdriver as shown in **Figure 80**. Then push the housing on all the way and make sure that the pins and holes are indexed properly.

  e. Slowly rotate the oil pump driven gear and drive chain (**Figure 81**) until the pins and index holes align properly.

CAUTION
The oil pump sprocket and the clutch outer housing must index properly so that the housing will go on all the way. Otherwise, the clutch will not function properly nor will the oil pump rotate; severe engine damage will result.

f. Install the clutch center (**Figure 82**).

g. Install the lockwasher (**Figure 83**) so that the dished side faces in.

h. Install the locknut so that the side with the shoulder faces out. See **Figure 84**.

i. Using the same tools as during disassembly, hold the clutch inner and tighten the locknut (**Figure 85**) to the torque specifications in **Table 2**.

j. Using a punch as shown in **Figure 86**, tap a portion of the locknut so that it engages the notch in the end of the transmission mainshaft.

2. Insert the clutch pushrod (**Figure 87**) into the transmission mainshaft.

> *CAUTION*
> *If either or both friction discs and clutch plates have been replaced with new ones, apply engine oil to all surfaces to avoid having the clutch lock up when used for the first time.*

3. Install a friction disc (**Figure 88**) and a clutch plate (steel) (**Figure 89**). Continue to install a friction disc and then a clutch plate; alternate them until all are installed. The last part installed is a friction disc.

4. Install the lifter guide and bearing into the pressure plate if removed (**Figure 77**). Secure the lifter guide and bearing with the stopper ring.

5. Install the pressure plate (**Figure 90**).

6. Install the 5 clutch springs and bolts (**Figure 91**).

7. Tighten the clutch bolts in a crisscross pattern in 2 or 3 stages until the bolts are tight.

8A. If the clutch outer was not removed, perform the following.

   a. Install the clutch cover and gasket (**Figure 92**). Tighten the bolts securely.

   b. Install the right-hand footpeg and brake pedal assembly. Tighten the footpeg bolts to 24-30 N•m (17-22 ft.-lb.).

8B. If the clutch inner was removed, perform the following.

   a. Install a new crankcase gasket and the 2 dowel pins (**Figure 93**).

   b. Install the right-hand crankcase cover. Tighten the bolts securely.

   c. Install the right-hand sub-frame assembly.

   d. Tighten the front engine bracket bolt to 30-40 N•m (22-29 ft.-lb.).

   e. Tighten the front engine mount nut to 45-60 N•m (33-43 ft.-lb.).

   f. Tighten the front sub-frame mount bolt to 60-70 N•m (43-51 ft.-lb.).

   g. Tighten the rear sub-frame mount bolt to 35-45 N•m (25-33 ft.-lb.).

   h. Install the radiator as described in Chapter Eight.

   i. Install the right-hand exhaust pipe. Tighten the bolts securely.

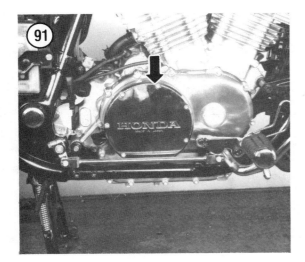

9. Remove the wood block between the clutch lever and the hand grip.

10. Fill the crankcase with the recommended type and quantity of engine oil. Refer to Chapter Three.

CLUTCH HYDRAULIC SYSTEM

The clutch is actuated by hydraulic fluid pressure and is controlled by the hand lever on the clutch master cylinder. As clutch components wear, the fluid level drops in the reservoir and automatically adjusts for wear. There is no routine adjustment necessary or possible.

When working on the clutch hydraulic system, it is necessary that the work area and all tools be absolutely clean. Any tiny particles of foreign matter and grit in the clutch slave cylinder or the clutch master cylinder can damage the components. Also, sharp tools must not be used inside the slave cylinder or on the piston. If there is any doubt about your ability to correctly and safely carry out major service on the clutch hydraulic components, take the job to a dealer.

> *CAUTION*
> *Throughout the text, reference is made to hydraulic fluid. Hydraulic fluid is the same as DOT 3 brake fluid. Use only DOT 3 brake fluid; do **not** use other types of fluids as they are not compatible. Do not intermix silicone based (DOT 5) brake fluid as it can cause clutch component damage leading to clutch system failure.*

CLUTCH MASTER CYLINDER

Removal/Installation

1. Remove the rear view mirror (A, **Figure 94**) from the clutch master cylinder.

> *CAUTION*
> *Cover the fuel tank and instrument cluster with a heavy cloth or plastic tarp to protect them from accidental hydraulic fluid spills. Wash fluid off any painted or plated surfaces immediately, as it will destroy the finish. Use soapy water and rinse completely.*

2. Pull back the rubber boot (A, **Figure 95**) and remove the union bolt securing the clutch hose to the clutch master cylinder. Remove the clutch hose; tie the hose up and cover the end to prevent entry of foreign matter.

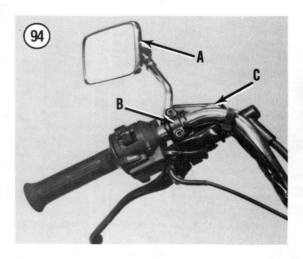

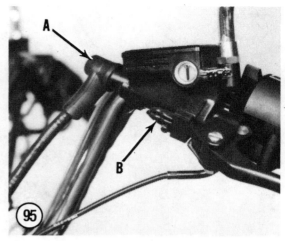

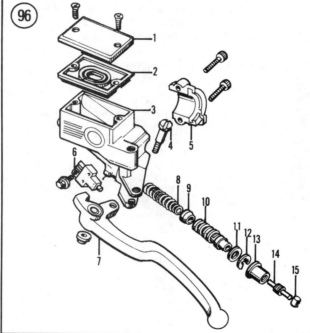

CLUTCH MASTER CYLINDER

1. **Reservoir cover**
2. **Diaphragm**
3. **Reservoir**
4. **Lever pivot bolt**
5. **Clamp**
6. **Clutch switch**
7. **Clutch lever**
8. **Spring**
9. **Primary cup**
10. **Piston and secondary cup**
11. **Washer**
12. **Circlip**
13. **Rubber boot**
14. **Pushrod**
15. **Pushrod end piece**

3. Disconnect the electrical connector to the clutch switch (B, **Figure 95**).

4. Remove the clamping bolts and clamp (B, **Figure 94**) securing the clutch master cylinder to the handlebar and remove the clutch master cylinder (C, **Figure 94**).

5. Install by reversing these removal steps, noting the following.

6. Install the clamp (B, **Figure 94**), aligning the end of the clamp with the punch mark on the handlebar. Tighten the upper bolt first, then the lower. Tighten the bolts securely.

7. Install the clutch hose onto the clutch master cylinder. Be sure to place a sealing washer on each side of the fitting and install the union bolt. Tighten the union bolt to the torque specifications listed in **Table 2**.

8. Attach the electrical connector to the clutch switch.

9. Bleed the clutch as described in this chapter.

Disassembly

Refer to **Figure 96** for this procedure.

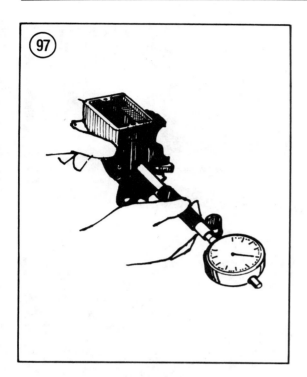

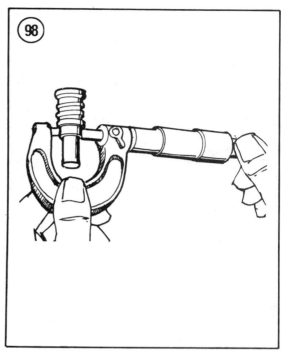

1. Remove the clutch master cylinder as described in this chapter.
2. Remove the pivot bolt and nut securing the. clutch lever and remove the lever.
3. Remove the screws securing the cover and remove the cover and diaphragm; pour out the hydraulic fluid and discard it. *Never* reuse hydraulic fluid.
4. Remove the pushrod and end piece.
5. Remove the rubber boot from the area where the hand lever pushrod actuates the internal piston.
6. Using circlip pliers, remove the internal circlip and washer from the body.
7. Remove the secondary cup and the piston assembly.
8. Remove the primary cup and spring.
9. Remove the clutch switch if necessary.

Inspection

1. Clean all parts in denatured alcohol or fresh hydraulic fluid. Inspect the cylinder bore and piston contact surfaces for signs of wear and damage. If either part is less than perfect, replace it.
2. Check the end of the piston for wear caused by the hand lever pushrod. Replace the piston if necessary.
3. Check both the primary and secondary cup for damage. Replace as necessary. Replace the piston if the secondary cup requires replacement.

4. Check the hand lever pivot bore in the clutch master cylinder. If worn or elongated, the master cylinder must be replaced.
5. Inspect the pivot bore in the hand lever. If worn or elongated it must be replaced.
6. Make sure the passages in the bottom of the fluid reservoir are clear. Check the reservoir cap and diaphragm for damage and deterioration and replace as necessary.
7. Inspect the threads in the bore for the fluid line.
8. Measure the cylinder bore (**Figure 97**). Replace the clutch master cylinder if the bore exceeds the specifications given in **Table 1**.
9. Measure the outside diameter of the piston as shown in **Figure 98** with a micrometer. Replace the piston assembly if it is less than the specifications given in **Table 1**.

Assembly

1. Soak the new cups in fresh hydraulic fluid for at least 15 minutes to make them pliable. Coat the inside of the cylinder with fresh fluid prior to assembly of parts.

> *CAUTION*
> *When installing the piston assembly, do not allow the cups to turn inside out as they will be damaged and allow clutch fluid leakage within the cylinder bore.*

2. Install the spring, primary cup and piston assembly into the cylinder together.

NOTE
Be sure to install the primary cup with the open end in first, toward the spring.

3. Install the washer and the circlip; make sure the circlip seats firmly in the groove.

4. Slide in the rubber boot, the pushrod and the pushrod end piece.

5. Install the diaphragm and cover. Do not tighten the cover screws at this time as fluid will have to be added later.

6. Install the lever onto the master cylinder body.

7. If removed, install the clutch switch.

8. Install the clutch master cylinder and bleed the clutch system as described in this chapter.

Hose Replacement

There is no factory-recommended replacement interval but it is a good idea to replace the clutch hose assembly every four years or when it shows signs of cracking or damage. The hydraulic hose assembly consists of 2 flexible hoses that are permanently attached to each end of the section of metal tubing. The entire hose assembly must be replaced as a unit as it cannot be separated.

CAUTION
Cover the front wheel, fender and frame with a heavy cloth or plastic tarp to protect them from accidental spilling of hydraulic fluid. Wash the fluid off of any painted or plated surface immediately, as it will destroy the finish. Use soapy water and rinse completely.

1. Remove the seat and both side covers.

2. Remove the main fuel tank as described in Chapter Six.

3. Pull back the rubber boot (A, **Figure 95**) and remove the union bolt securing the clutch hose to the clutch master cylinder. Remove the clutch hose; tie the hose up and cover the end to prevent entry of foreign matter.

4. Remove the bolt securing the left-hand rear cranckcase cover and remove the cover.

5. Attach a hose to the bleed valve on the clutch slave cylinder (**Figure 99**).

6. Place the loose end of the hose into a container and open the bleed valve. Operate the clutch lever

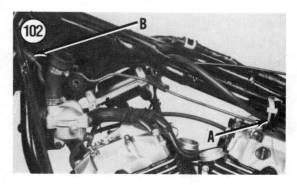

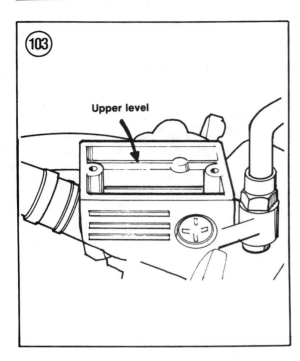

Upper level

CLUTCH SLAVE CYLINDER

1. Insulator
2. Oil seal
3. Piston seal
4. Piston
5. Spring
6. Slave cylinder body

until all fluid is pumped out of the system. Close the bleed valve and remove the hose.

WARNING
Dispose of this fluid—never reuse hydraulic fluid. Contaminated fluid can cause clutch failure.

7. Place a container under the clutch hose at the clutch slave cylinder to catch any remaining fluid. Remove the union bolt and sealing washers (A, **Figure 100**) securing the clutch hose to the clutch slave cylinder. Remove the clutch hose and let any remaining fluid drain out into the container.

8. Remove the radiator filler neck cover (**Figure 101**).

9. Remove the metal clamp bands (A, **Figure 102**) securing the clutch metal hose and other hoses to the frame.

10. Withdraw the flexible clutch hose from between the steering stem and the left-hand fork leg (B, **Figure 102**).

11. Remove the hose assembly from the frame.

CAUTION
After removing the hose assembly, wash any hydraulic fluid off of any painted or plated surface immediately, as it will destroy the finish.

12. Install the hose assembly, sealing washers and union bolts in the reverse order of removal. Be sure to install new sealing washers in the correct position on each side of each union bolt.

13. Tighten all union bolts to torque specifications listed in **Table 2**.

14. Refill the clutch master cylinder to the upper line (**Figure 103**) with fresh hydraulic fluid clearly marked DOT 3 only. Bleed the clutch system as described in this chapter.

15. Install the left-hand rear crankcase cover.

SLAVE CYLINDER

Removal and installation are covered in 2 different ways. The first procedure is for removing the slave cylinder from the crankcase intact when no service procedures are going to be performed. The second procedure is used when the slave cylinder is going to be disassembled, inspected and serviced. Follow the correct procedure for your specific needs.

Refer to **Figure 104** for both procedures.

Removal/Installation (Intact)

This procedure is for removal and installation only—not for disassembly, inspection and service.

1. Place a piece of wood between the clutch lever and the hand grip to hold the lever in the released position. Secure the piece of wood with a rubber band or tape. This will prevent the clutch lever from being applied accidentally after the clutch slave cylinder is removed from the crankcase.

NOTE
Do not operate the clutch lever after the slave cylinder is removed from the crankcase. If the clutch lever is applied it will force the piston out of the slave cylinder body and make installation difficult.

2. Remove the bolts securing the left-hand rear crankcase cover and remove the cover.

3. Remove the bolts (B, **Figure 100**) securing the clutch slave cylinder and bracket to the crankcase and withdraw the unit from the crankcase. Don't lose the thick black insulator between the slave cylinder and the crankcase.

4. Tie the clutch slave cylinder up and out of the way.

NOTE
***Figure 105** is shown with the slave cylinder removed for clarity.*

5. Apply a light coat of high-temperature silicone grease (or hydraulic fluid) to the piston seal and the oil seal (**Figure 105**) prior to installing the assembly.

NOTE
Inspect the piston seal and the oil seal. Replace if their condition is doubtful. If either seal is removed from the piston it must be replaced with a new seal.

6. Make sure the piston seal is still correctly seated in the groove in the piston. If not seated correctly, fluid will leak past the seal and render the clutch useless.

NOTE
Sometimes the piston will move out slightly from the slave cylinder body when the body is withdrawn from the crankcase during removal.

7. Withdraw the clutch pushrod from the transmission main shaft and use it to push the piston as far back in as possible into the slave cylinder body. Reinstall the clutch pushrod into the transmission main shaft.

8. Install the insulator onto the slave cylinder and install the slave cylinder onto the crankcase.

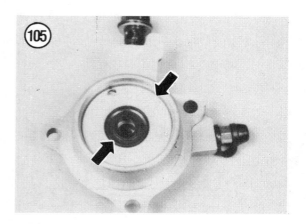

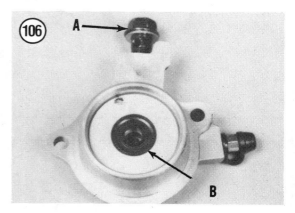

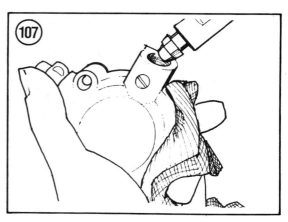

9. Make sure the pushrod is inserted correctly into the receptacle in the slave cylinder piston.

NOTE
After being positioned correctly into the crankcase the slave cylinder assembly may stick out by about 3/8 in. from the mating surface of the crankcase. This is due to the pressure within the hydraulic system.

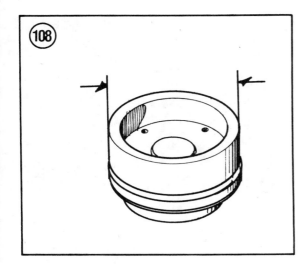

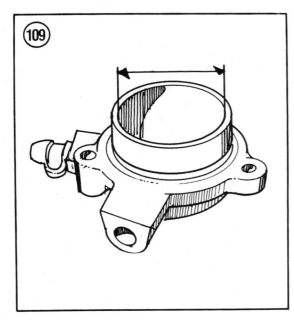

10. Install the bracket and then the bolts securing the slave cylinder. Gradually tighten the bolts in a crisscross pattern. Continue to tighten until the slave cylinder has bottomed out on the mating surface of the crankcase. Tighten the bolts securely.
11. Install the left-hand rear crankcase cover.

Removal

This procedure is for a complete service procedure of removal, disassembly, inspection, assembly and installation of the slave cylinder.
1. Remove the bolts securing the left-hand rear crankcase cover and remove the cover.

2. Attach a hose to the bleed valve on the clutch slave cylinder (**Figure 99**).
3. Place the loose end of the hose into a container and open the bleed valve. Operate the clutch lever until all fluid is pumped out of the system. Close the bleed valve and remove the hose.

WARNING
Dispose of this fluid—never reuse hydraulic fluid. Contaminated fluid can cause clutch failure.

4. Place a container under the clutch hose at the clutch slave cylinder to catch any remaining fluid. Remove the union bolt and sealing washers (A, **Figure 100**) securing the clutch hose to the clutch slave cylinder. Remove the clutch hose and let any remaining fluid drain out into the container.
5. Remove the bolts (B, **Figure 100**) securing the clutch slave cylinder and bracket to the crankcase and withdraw the unit from the crankcase. Don't lose the thick black insulator between the slave cylinder and the crankcase.

Disassembly/Inspection

1. To remove the piston, perform the following:
   a. Remove the union bolt (A, **Figure 106**) from the slave cylinder.
   b. Hold the slave cylinder body in your hand with the piston facing away from you. Place a clean shop cloth behind the piston (B, **Figure 106**).
   c. Carefully apply a *small* amount of compressed air in short spurts into the hole where the union bolt was attached (**Figure 107**). The air pressure will force the piston out of the body.

CAUTION
Be sure to catch the piston when it is pushed out of the body. Failure to do so will result in damage to the piston.

2. Remove the spring from the piston.
3. Check the spring for damage or sagging. Honda does not provide service limit dimensions for this spring. Replace the spring if its condition is doubtful.
4. Remove the oil seal and the piston seal from the piston; discard both seals.
5. Use a vernier caliper and measure the outside diameter of the piston as shown in **Figure 108**. Replace the piston if it is worn to the service limit listed in **Table 1**.
6. Use a vernier caliper and measure the inside diameter of the slave cylinder body as shown in **Figure 109**. Replace the body if it is worn to the service limit listed in **Table 1**.

5

Assembly/Installation

1. Apply a light coat of high-temperature silicone grease (or hydraulic fluid) to the new piston seal and the oil seal prior to installation.

2. Install both seals onto the piston. Make sure the piston seal is correctly seated in the groove in the piston. If not seated correctly, fluid will leak past the seal and render the clutch useless.

NOTE
A new piston seal and oil seal must be installed every time the slave cylinder is removed.

3. Withdraw the clutch pushrod from the transmission main shaft and use it to push the piston all the way into the slave cylinder body. Reinstall the clutch pushrod.

4. Install the insulator onto the slave cylinder and install the slave cylinder onto the crankcase.

5. Install the bracket and then the bolts. Tighten in a crisscross pattern in 2-3 stages. Tighten the bolts securely.

6. Install the union bolt and sealing washers to the slave cylinder. Tighten the union bolts to the torque specification listed in **Table 2**.

7. Clean the top of the clutch master cylinder of all dirt and foreign matter. Remove the cap and diaphragm. Fill the reservoir almost to the top line (**Figure 110**); insert the diaphragm and install the cap loosely.

8. Bleed the clutch as described in this chapter.

BLEEDING THE CLUTCH

This procedure is not necessary unless the clutch feels spongy (air in the line), there has been a leak in the system, a component has been replaced or the hydraulic fluid is being replaced. If the clutch operates correctly when the engine is cold or in cool weather but operates erratically (or not at all) after the engine warms up or in hot weather, there is air in the hydraulic line and the clutch must be bled.

CAUTION
Throughout the text reference is made to hydraulic fluid. Hydraulic fluid is the same as DOT 3 brake fluid. Use only DOT 3 fluid; do not use other fluids as they are not compatible. Do not intermix silicone based (DOT 5) brake fluid as it can cause clutch component damage leading to clutch system failure.

1. Remove the dust cap from the bleed valve on the clutch slave cylinder (**Figure 111**).

2. Connect a length of clear tubing to the bleed valve (**Figure 99**).

3. Place the other end of the tube into a clean container. Fill the container with enough fresh hydraulic fluid to keep the end submerged. The tube should be long enough so that a loop can be made higher than the bleed valve to prevent air from being drawn into the clutch slave cylinder during bleeding.

CAUTION
Cover the clutch slave cylinder and lower frame with a heavy cloth or plastic tarp to protect them from accidental fluid spillings. Wash any fluid off of any painted or plated surface immediately, as it will destroy the finish. Use soapy water and rinse completely.

4. Clean the top of the clutch master cylinder of all dirt and foreign matter. Remove the cap and diaphragm. Fill the reservoir almost to the top line (**Figure 110**), insert the diaphragm and install the cap loosely.

CAUTION
Failure to install the diaphragm on the master cylinder will allow fluid to spurt out when the clutch lever is applied.

CAUTION
Use hydraulic fluid clearly marked DOT 3 only. Others may vaporize and cause clutch failure. Always use the same brand name; do not intermix as many brands are not compatible. Do not intermix silicone based (DOT 5) brake fluid as it can cause clutch component damage leading to clutch system failure.

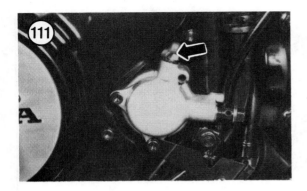

5. Insert a 20 mm (3/4 in.) spacer between the handlebar grip and the clutch lever. This will prevent over-travel of the piston within the clutch master cylinder.

6. Slowly apply the clutch lever several times. Hold the lever in the applied position. Open the bleed valve about one-half turn. Allow the lever to travel to its limit against the installed spacer. When this limit is reached, tighten the bleed valve. Occasionally tap or jiggle the clutch flexible hoses to loosen any trapped air bubbles that won't come out the normal way. As the fluid enters the system, the level will drop in the reservoir. Maintain the level at the top of the reservoir to prevent air from being drawn into the system.

7. Repeat Step 6 until the fluid emerging from the hose is completely free of bubbles.

NOTE
Do not allow the reservoir to empty during the bleeding operation or air will enter the system. If this occurs, the entire procedure must be repeated.

8. Hold the lever in, tighten the bleed valve, remove the bleed tube and install the bleed valve dust cap.

9. If necessary, add fluid to correct the level in the reservoir. It should be to the upper level line.

10. Install the reservoir cap.

11. Test the feel of the clutch lever. It should be firm and should offer the same resistance each time it's operated. If it feels spongy, it is likely that there still is air in the system and it must be bled again. When all air has been bled from the system and the fluid level is correct in the reservoir, double-check for leaks and tighten all the fittings and connections.

EXTERNAL SHIFT MECHANISM

The external shift mechanism is located on the same side of the engine as the clutch assembly and can be removed with the engine in the frame. To remove the shift drum and shift forks it is necessary to remove the engine and split the crankcase. That procedure is covered under *Internal Shift Mechanism* in this chapter.

Refer to **Figure 112** for the following procedures.

Removal

1. Remove the clutch as described in this chapter.

2. Remove the oil pipe (**Figure 113**). Discard the O-rings at each end of the oil pipe. They must be replaced with new ones every time the oil pipe is removed.

3. Remove the bolt and washer (A, **Figure 114**) securing the oil pump driven gear.

4. Remove the oil pump driven gear (B, **Figure 114**), the drive chain (C, **Figure 114**) and the drive sprocket (D, **Figure 114**) all at the same time. It is not necessary to remove the clutch outer housing guide from the transmission main shaft.

5. Remove gearshift spindle assembly B (**Figure 115**) from the crankcase. If the spindle assembly will not come out, shift the transmission to another gear and align the cutout in the gearshift spindle with the ramps on the shift drum cam.

6. Remove the bolt, washer, return spring and shift drum stopper arm (**Figure 116**).

7. Remove the bolt (**Figure 117**) securing the shift drum cam plate and remove the cam plate.

8. Remove the shift drum positive stopper (**Figure 118**) from the shift drum. Don't lose the dowel pin in the end of the shift drum (**Figure 119**).

9. Remove the alternator and starter gears as described in Chapter Four.

10. Remove the shift spindle guide plug (**Figure 120**) from the crankcase. Be careful not to damage the O-ring seal on the plug.

11. Remove the gearshift spindle A (A, **Figure 121**).

Inspection

1. Inspect the spring on the shift spindle plate (**Figure 122**). If broken or weak it must be replaced.

2. Inspect the return spring on the gearshift spindle B (A, **Figure 123**). If broken or weak it must be replaced.

3. Inspect the gearshift spindle A shaft (B, **Figure 123**) and gearshift spindle B (A, **Figure 124**) for bending, wear or other damage; replace if necessary.

4. Inspect the teeth on gearshift spindle A and gearshift spindle B (B, **Figure 124**). If worn or damaged, they must be replaced.

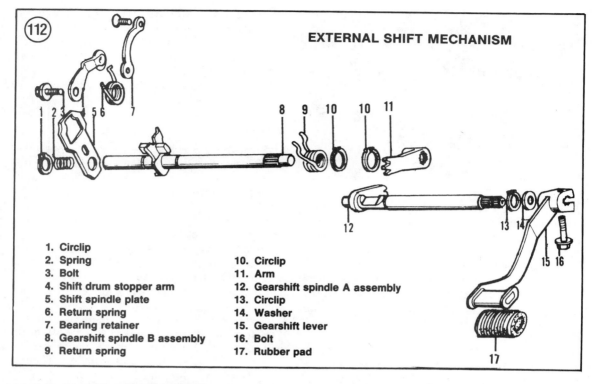

112

EXTERNAL SHIFT MECHANISM

1. Circlip
2. Spring
3. Bolt
4. Shift drum stopper arm
5. Shift spindle plate
6. Return spring
7. Bearing retainer
8. Gearshift spindle B assembly
9. Return spring
10. Circlip
11. Arm
12. Gearshift spindle A assembly
13. Circlip
14. Washer
15. Gearshift lever
16. Bolt
17. Rubber pad

113

115

114

116

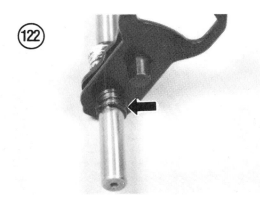

5

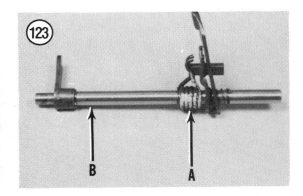

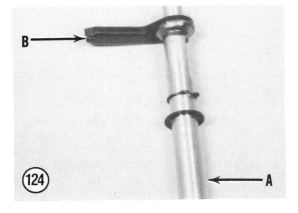

Installation

1. Make sure the dowel pin is installed in the end of the shift drum (**Figure 119**).

2. Align the hole in the gearshift drum positive stopper with the dowel pin in the shift drum and install the positive stopper (**Figure 118**).

3. Align the hole in the backside of the shift drum cam plate with the pin on the shift drum and install the cam plate.

4. Install the bolt (**Figure 117**) securing the cam plate and tighten to the torque specification listed in **Table 2**.

5. Install the shift drum stopper arm, return spring and washer. Index it into the shift drum cam plate. Tighten the bolt to the torque specification listed in **Table 2**.

6. Install the oil pump drive gear and the clutch outer housing guide (if removed) on the transmission main shaft (**Figure 125**).

7. The "IN" mark (**Figure 126**) on the oil pump driven gear must face in toward the engine.

8. Assemble the oil pump driven gear and the drive chain as an assembly. Install this assembly onto the driven gear and the oil pump drive shaft. Mesh the tab on the oil pump drive shaft with the slot in the oil pump driven gear.

9. Install the bolt and washer (A, **Figure 114**) securing the oil pump driven gear.

10. Install the clutch as described in this chapter.

11. Install the engine as described in Chapter Four.

12. From the other side, install the gearshift spindle B (A, **Figure 121**). Align the punch marks (B, **Figure 121**) on the sector gears of both arms and push the gearshift spindle B in all the way.

13. Inspect the O-ring seal (**Figure 127**) on the guide plug and carefully install the gearshift spindle guide plug. Do not damage the O-ring seal during installation.

14. Install the alternator and starter gears as described in Chapter Four.

15. Align the punch marks on the gearshift arm and the gearshift spindle. Install the gearshift arm onto the gearshift spindle assembly. Install and tighten the clamping bolt securely.

TRANSMISSION

The transmission is located within the engine crankcase. To gain access to the transmission and internal shift mechanism it is necessary to remove the engine and disassemble the crankcase. Once the crankcase is split, removal of the transmission main shaft is simple.

Specifications for the transmission components are listed in **Table 3**.

Preliminary Inspection

After the transmission shaft assemblies have been removed from the crankcase halves, clean and inspect the assemblies prior to disassembling them. Place the assembled shaft into a large can or plastic bucket and thoroughly clean with a petroleum based solvent such as kerosene and a stiff brush. Dry with compressed air or let it sit on rags to drip dry. Repeat for the other shaft assembly.

1. After they have been cleaned, visually inspect the components of the assemblies for excessive wear. Any burrs, pitting or roughness on the teeth of a gear will cause wear on the mating gear. Minor roughness can be cleaned up with an oilstone but there's little point in attempting to remove deep scars.

NOTE
Defective gears should be replaced. It's a good idea to replace the mating gear

on the other shaft even though it may not show as much wear or damage.

2. Carefully check the engagement dogs. If any are chipped, worn, rounded or missing, the affected gear must be replaced.

3. Rotate the transmission and shift drum bearings in the crankcases by hand. Refer to **Figure 128.** Check for roughness, noise and radial play. Any bearing that is suspect should be replaced as described in Chapter Four.

4. If the transmission shafts are satisfactory and are not going to be disassembled, apply assembly oil or engine oil to all components and reinstall them in the crankcase as described in this chapter.

NOTE
If disassembling a used, well run-in transmission for the first time by yourself, pay particular attention to any additional shims that may have been added by a previous owner. These may have been added to take up the tolerance of worn components and must be reinstalled in the same position since the shims have developed a wear pattern. If new parts are going to be installed these shims may be eliminated. This is something you will have to determine upon reassembly.

Removal/Installation

1. Disassemble the crankcase as described in Chapter Four.
2. Remove the crankshaft as described in Chapter Four.
3. Remove the main shaft assembly, countershaft assembly and shift forks as an assembly. Inspect them as described below under *Preliminary Inspection.*
4. Remove the bolt and lockwasher securing the center shift fork to the shift fork shaft.

NOTE
Prior to installing any components, coat all bearing surfaces with assembly oil.

5. Mesh the transmission assemblies together and install them into the right-hand crankcase half (**Figure 129**).
6. After both shaft assemblies are installed, tap on the end of both shafts with a plastic or rubber mallet to make sure they are completely seated.
7. Install the center shift fork (**Figure 130**) with its mark facing down toward the right-hand crankcase half.

5

8. Install the shift drum (A, **Figure 131**) and mesh the pin follower of the shift fork into the middle grove of the shift drum (B, **Figure 131**).

9. Install the left and right shift forks (**Figure 132**) with their marks facing down toward the right-hand crankcase half.

10. Mesh the pin followers of the shift forks into the grooves of the shift drum.

11. Position the shift fork shaft with the oil hole (**Figure 133**) facing toward the left-hand crankcase half (**Figure 134**). Install the shift fork shaft (**Figure 135**).

12. Install the shift fork bolt and lockwasher into the center shift fork and tighten the bolt to 16-20 N•m (12-14 ft.-lb.). Bend the tab on the lockwasher up against a flat on the bolt (**Figure 136**).

13. Spin the transmission shafts and shift through the gears using the shift drum. Make sure you can shift into all gears. This is the time to find that something may be installed incorrectly—not after the crankcase is completely assembled.

NOTE

This procedure is best done with the aid of a helper as the assemblies are loose and won't spin very easily. Have the helper spin the transmission shafts while you turn the shift drum through all the gears.

14. Make sure the thrust washers (**Figure 137**) are in place on the transmission shaft assemblies.

15. Install the crankshaft as described in Chapter Four.

16. Assemble the crankcase as described in Chapter Four.

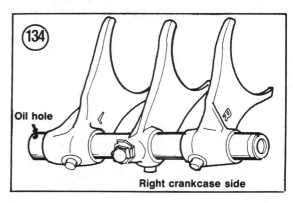

Oil hole

Right crankcase side

A

B

Final Drive Damper
Gear Inspection

Measure the inside diameter of the final drive damper gear (**Figure 138**). Refer to dimensions listed in **Table 4**. If the gear is worn to the service limit, the gear must be replaced.

Measure the inside and outside diameter of the final drive damper gear bushing (**Figure 139**). Refer to dimensions listed in **Table 4**. If the bushing is worn to the service limit, the bushing must be replaced.

Main Shaft Disassembly/
Inspection/Assembly

Refer to **Figure 140** for this procedure.

> *NOTE*
> *A helpful "tool" that should be used for transmission disassembly is a large egg flat (the type restaurants get their eggs in) (**Figure 141**). As you remove a part from the shaft, set it in one of the depressions in the same position from which it was removed. This is an easy way to remember the correct relationship of all parts.*

1. Clean the shaft as described under *Preliminary Inspection* in this chapter.
2. Slide off the thrust washer and the 4th gear.
3. Remove the circlip and slide off the splined washer.
4. Slide off the 6th gear, the 6th gear bushing and the splined washer.
5. Remove the circlip.
6. Slide off the 2nd/3rd combination gear.
7. Remove the circlip and slide off the splined washer.
8. Slide off the 5th gear and the 5th gear bushing.
9. Check each gear for excessive wear, burrs, pitting or chipped or missing teeth. Make sure the gear's dogs are in good condition.

> *NOTE*
> *Defective gears should be replaced. It is a good idea to replace the mating gear on the countershaft even though it may not show as much wear or damage.*

> *NOTE*
> *The 1st gear is part of the main shaft. If the gear is defective, the shaft must be replaced.*

10. Make sure that all gears and bushings slide smoothly on the main shaft splines.

5

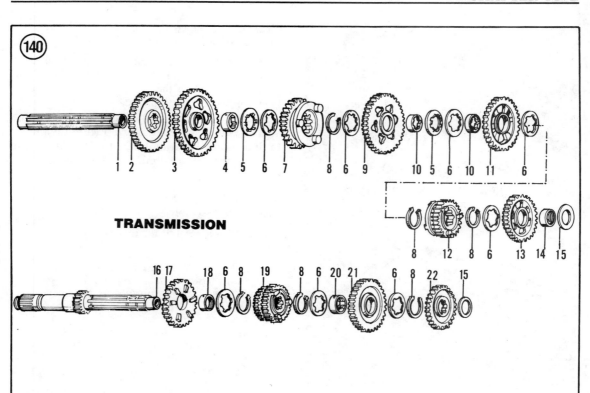

TRANSMISSION

1. Countershaft
2. Final drive gear
3. Countershaft 1st gear
4. Countershaft 1st gear bushing
5. Lockwasher
6. Splined washer
7. Countershaft 5th gear
8. Circlip
9. Countershaft 2nd gear
10. Splined bushing
11. Countershaft 3rd gear

12. Countershaft 6th gear
13. Countershaft 4th gear
14. Countershaft 4th gear bushing
15. Thrust washer
16. Main shaft/1st gear
17. Main shaft 5th gear
18. Main shaft 5th gear bushing
19. Main shaft 2nd/3rd combination gear
20. Main shaft 6th gear bushing
21. Main shaft 6th gear
22. Main shaft 4th gear

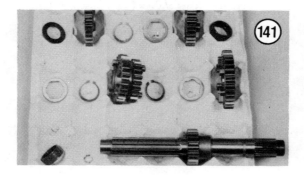

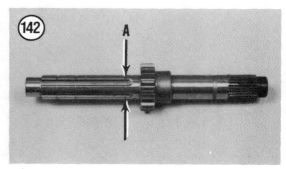

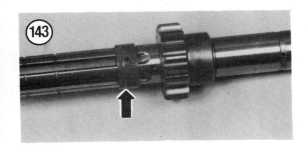

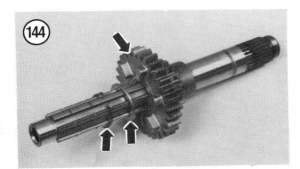

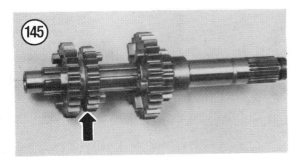

NOTE
The 1st gear is part of the main shaft. If the gear is defective, the shaft must be replaced.

10. Make sure that all gears and bushings slide smoothly on the main shaft splines.

11. Measure the outside diameter of the main shaft at location A as shown in **Figure 142**. Refer to dimensions listed in **Table 3**. If the shaft is worn to the service limit, the shaft must be replaced.

12. Measure the inside diameter of the main shaft 5th and 6th gears. Refer to dimensions listed in **Table 3**. If the gear(s) is worn to the service limit, the gear(s) must be replaced.

13. Measure the inside and outside diameter of the main shaft 5th gear bushing and the outside diameter of the 6th gear bushing. Refer to dimensions listed in **Table 3**. If the bushing(s) is worn to the service limit, the bushing(s) must be replaced.

NOTE
It is a good idea to replace all circlips every other time the transmission shaft is disassembled to ensure proper gear alignment.

14. Slide on the 5th gear bushing (**Figure 143**). There is no oil hole alignment necessary for this bushing.

15. Slide on the 5th gear (flush side on first), splined washer and circlip (**Figure 144**).

16. Position the 2nd/3rd combination gear with the smaller diameter 2nd gear going on first (**Figure 145**). Slide on the 2nd/3rd combination gear and install the circlip and splined washer (**Figure 146**).

17. Align the oil hole in the 6th gear bushing with the oil hole in the main shaft (**Figure 147**) and slide the bushing into place. This alignment is necessary for proper oil flow.

18. Install the 6th gear, splined washer and circlip (**Figure 148**).

19. Install the 4th gear and thrust washer (**Figure 149**).

20. Before installation, double-check the placement of all gears (**Figure 150**). Make sure all circlips are seated in the main shaft grooves.

21. Make sure each gear engages properly with the adjoining gears where applicable.

Countershaft Disassembly/ Inspection/Assembly

Refer to **Figure 140** for this procedure.

NOTE
Use the same large egg flat (used on the main shaft disassembly) during the countershaft disassembly. This is an easy way to remember the correct relationship of all parts.

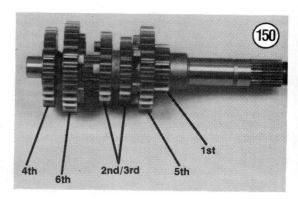

1. Slide off the thrust washer.

2. Slide off the 4th gear, the 4th gear bushing and the splined washer.

3. Remove the circlip and slide off the 6th gear.

4. Remove the circlip and splined washer.

5. Slide off the 3rd gear and 3rd gear bushing.

6. From the other end of the shaft, slide off the final drive gear.

7. Slide off the 1st gear and the 1st gear bushing.

8. Slide off the lockwasher, then rotate the splined washer in either direction so its tangs will clear the transmission spline grooves and slide it off of the shaft.

9. Slide off the 5th gear.

10. Remove the circlip and slide off the splined washer.

11. Slide off the 2nd gear and the 2nd gear bushing.

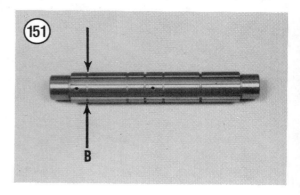

12. Slide off the lockwasher, then rotate the splined washer in either direction so its tangs will clear the transmission spline grooves and slide it off of the shaft.

13. Check each gear for excessive wear, burrs, pitting or chipped or missing teeth. Make sure the lugs are in good condition.

NOTE
Defective gears should be replaced. It is a good idea to replace the mating gear on the main shaft even though it may not show signs of wear or damage.

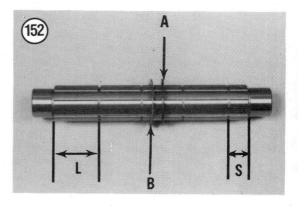

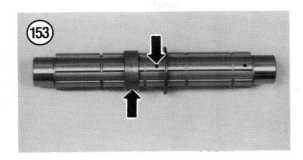

14. Make sure all gears and gear bushings slide smoothly on the countershaft splines.

15. Measure the inside diameter of the 1st, 2nd, 3rd and 4th gears. Compare with the dimensions listed in **Table 3**.

16. Measure the outside diameter of the 1st, 2nd, 3rd and 4th gear bushings and the inside diameter of the 4th gear bushing. Compare with the dimensions listed in **Table 3**.

17. Measure the outside diameter of the shaft at the location B (**Figure 151**). Compare with the dimension listed in **Table 3**.

NOTE
It is a good idea to replace all circlips every other time the shaft is disassembled to ensure proper gear alignment.

CAUTION
*Position the countershaft so the lockwasher groove that is **farthest** from the end (L, **Figure 152**) is to the left-hand side. The first group of gears will be installed onto the shaft from this end—the left-hand end.*

18. Slide on the splined washer and position it in the 3rd groove in the shaft from the left-hand end (A, **Figure 152**). Rotate it in either direction so its tangs are engaged in the 3rd groove from the left in the transmission shaft.

19. Slide on the splined lockwasher (B, **Figure 152**) so that the tangs go into the open areas of the splined washer and lock the washer in place.

20. Align the oil hole in the 2nd gear bushing with the oil hole in the shaft (**Figure 153**) and slide on the bushing. This alignment is necessary for proper oil flow.

21. Slide on the 2nd gear, splined washer (ground surface toward the 2nd gear) and circlip (**Figure 154**).

22. Slide on the 5th gear (A, **Figure 155**).

23. Slide on the splined washer (B, **Figure 155**). Rotate the splined washer in either direction so its tangs are engaged in the groove in the transmission shaft.

24. Slide on the splined lockwasher (C, **Figure 155**) so that the tangs go into the open areas of the splined washer and lock the washer in place.

25. Align the oil hole in the 1st gear bushing with the oil hole in the shaft (**Figure 156**) and slide on the bushing. This alignment is necessary for proper oil flow.

26. Slide on the 1st gear (**Figure 157**).

27. Position the final drive gear with the raised shoulder side on last and slide on the gear (**Figure 158**).

28. Onto the other end of the shaft, align the oil hole in the 3rd gear bushing with the oil hole in the shaft (**Figure 159**) and slide on the bushing. This alignment is necessary for proper oil flow.

29. Slide on the 3rd gear, splined washer and circlip (**Figure 160**).

30. Slide on the 6th gear, splined washer and circlip (**Figure 161**).

31. Slide on 4th gear bushing (**Figure 162**). Oil hole alignment is not necessary with this bushing.

32. Position the 4th gear with the flush side on first. Slide on the 4th gear and thrust washer (**Figure 163**).

33. Before installation, double-check the placement of all gears (**Figure 164**). Make sure all circlips are correctly seated in the countershaft grooves.

34. After both transmission shafts have been assembled, mesh the 2 assemblies together in the correct position (**Figure 165**). Check that all gears meet correctly. This is your last check prior to installing the assemblies into the crankcase; make sure they are correctly assembled.

INTERNAL SHIFT MECHANISM.

The internal shift mechanism is removed during transmission removal as described in this chapter.

Disassembly/Inspection/ Assembly

Refer to **Figure 166** for this procedure.

Refer to **Table 4** for shift fork, shift fork shaft and shift drum specifications.

(158)

(159)

(160)

(157)

(161)

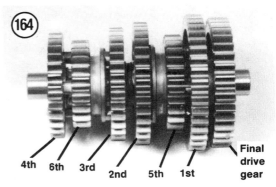

4th   6th   3rd   2nd   5th   1st   Final drive gear

5

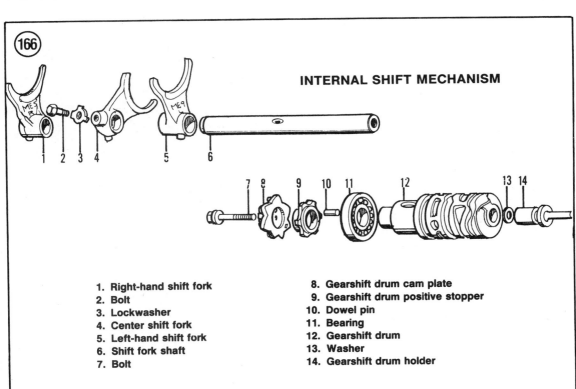

INTERNAL SHIFT MECHANISM

1. Right-hand shift fork
2. Bolt
3. Lockwasher
4. Center shift fork
5. Left-hand shift fork
6. Shift fork shaft
7. Bolt

8. Gearshift drum cam plate
9. Gearshift drum positive stopper
10. Dowel pin
11. Bearing
12. Gearshift drum
13. Washer
14. Gearshift drum holder

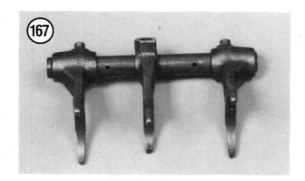

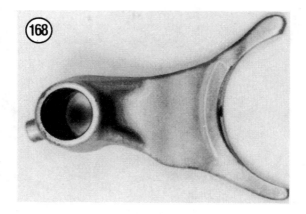

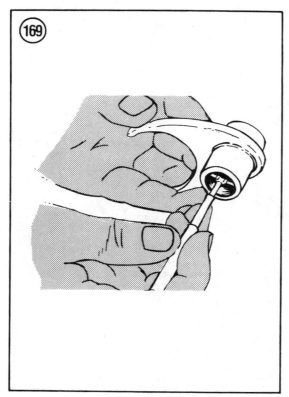

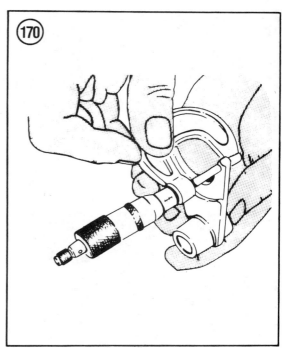

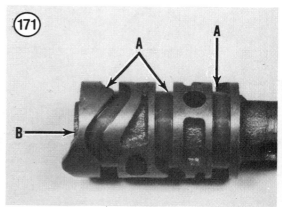

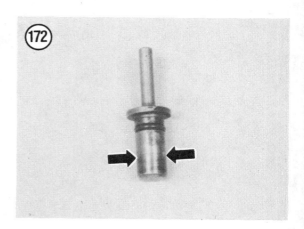

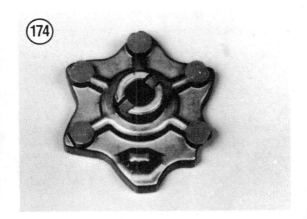

5

NOTE
*Prior to removal or disassembly of any of the components, lay the assembly down on a piece of paper or cardboard and carefully trace around it (**Figure 167**). Write down the identifying numbers and letter next to the item. This will take a little extra time now but it may save some time and prevent frustration later.*

1. Slide the shift forks off the shift fork shaft.
2. Inspect each shift fork for signs of wear or cracking. Check for bending and make sure each fork slides smoothly on the shaft. Replace any worn or damaged forks.
3. Check for any arc-shaped wear or burn marks on the shift forks (**Figure 168**). This indicates that the shift fork has come in contact with the gear. The fork fingers have become excessively worn and the fork must be replaced.
4. Measure the inside diameter of each shift fork with an inside micrometer or snap gauge (**Figure 169**). Replace any that are worn to the service limit listed in **Table 4**.
5. Measure the width of the gearshift fork fingers with a micrometer (**Figure 170**). Replace any that are worn to the service limit listed in **Table 4**.
6. Check the shift drum dowel pin on each shift fork for wear or damage; replace the shift fork as necessary.

7. Roll the shift fork shaft on a flat surface such as a piece of plate glass and check for any bends. If the shaft is bent, it must be replaced.
8. Measure the outside diameter of the shift fork shaft with a micrometer. Replace if worn to the service limit listed in **Table 4**.
9. Check the grooves in the shift drum for wear or roughness (A, **Figure 171**). If any of the groove profiles have excessive wear or damage, replace the shift drum.
10. Measure the inside diameter of the shift drum at the location where the shift drum holder rides (B, **Figure 171**).
11. Measure the outside diameter of the shift drum holder as shown in **Figure 172**.
12. Replace the shift drum or shift drum holder if worn to the service limit dimension listed in **Table 4**.
13. Make sure the oil hole in the shift fork shaft is clear (**Figure 132**). If necessary, clean out the hole with a piece of wire. Thoroughly wash the shaft in solvent and dry with compressed air.
14. Inspect the shift drum bearing (**Figure 173**). It must rotate smoothly with no roughness or noise. If damaged, the bearing must be replaced.
15. Inspect the ramps on the gearshift drum cam plate (**Figure 174**). The ramps must be smooth and free from burrs or nicks.
16. Apply a light coat of oil to the shift fork shafts and the inside bores of the shift forks prior to installation.

Tables are on the following pages.

Table 1 CLUTCH SPECIFICATIONS

Item	Standard	Wear limit
Friction disc thickness	3.72-3.88 mm (0.147-0.153 in.)	3.1 mm (0.12 in.)
Clutch plate warpage	—	0.30 mm (0.012 in.)
Clutch spring height (1983-1985)	3.9 mm (0.15 in.)	3.6 mm (0.14 in.)
Clutch spring free length (1986-on)	35.5 mm (1.40 in.)	35.0 mm (1.38 in.)
Outer guide ID	24.995-25.012 mm (0.9841-0.9847 in.)	25.08 mm (0.987 in.)
Clutch center B ID (1983-1985)	74.414-74.440 mm (2.9296-2.9307 in.)	74.50 mm (2.933 in.)
One-way clutch inner OD (1983-1986)	57.710-57.840 mm (2.2720-2.2772 in.)	57.60 mm (2.268 in.)
Clutch slave cylinder Cylinder ID	38.100-38.162 mm (1.5000-1.5024 in.)	38.18 mm (1.503 in.)
Piston OD	38.036-38.075 mm (1.4975-1.4990 in.)	38.02 mm (1.497 in.)
Clutch master cylinder Cylinder bore ID	14.000-14.043 mm (0.5512-0.5524 in.)	14.06 mm (0.553 in.)
Piston OD	13.957-13.984 mm (0.5495-0.5506 in.)	13.94 mm (0.549 in.)

Table 2 CLUTCH AND GEARSHIFT MECHANISM TORQUE SPECIFICATIONS

Item	N•m	ft.-lb.
Clutch locknut		
1983-1985	45-55	33-40
1986-on	80-100	58-72
Right-hand crankcase cover bolts	8-12	6-9
Sub-frame bolts		
Upper		
1983-1985	70-80	51-58
1986-on	60-70	43-51
Lower	35-45	25-33
Engine front mounting bolt and nut	45-60	33-43
Clutch hose union bolts	25-35	18-25
Clutch master cylinder cover screws	1-2	0.7-0.9
Clutch lever pivot nut	5-7	4-5
Primary drive gear		
1983-1985	80-100	58-72
1986-on	95-105	69-77
Oil pump driven sprocket bolt		
1983-1985	8-12	6-9
1986-on	15-20	11-14

Table 3 TRANSMISSION SPECIFICATIONS

Item	Specification	Wear limit
Gear backlash		
1st	0.089-0.170 mm (0.0035-0.0066 in.)	0.24 mm (0.009 in.)
2nd, 3rd, 4th and 5th	0.068-0.136 mm (0.0027-0.0054 in.)	0.18 mm (0.007 in.)
Gear ID main shaft		
5th, 6th gear	28.000-28.021 mm (1.1023-1.1034 in.)	28.04 mm (1.1039 in.)
Gear ID countershaft		
1st, 2nd, 3rd	28.000-28.021 mm (1.1023-1.1034 in.)	28.04 mm (1.1039 in.)
4th	29.000-29.021 mm (1.1417-1.1426 in.)	29.04 mm (1.1433 in.)
Gear bushing OD		
Main shaft		
5th, 6th	27.959-27.890 mm (1.1007-1.1016 in.)	27.94 mm (1.100 in.)
Countershaft		
1st, 2nd, 3rd		
1983-1985	23.959-23.980 mm (0.9433-0.9441 in.)	23.94 mm (0.9425 in.)
1986-on	27.959-27.980 mm (1.1007-1.1016 in.)	27.94 mm (1.1000 in.)
4th	28.959-28.980 mm (1.1401-1.1410 in.)	28.94 mm (1.1394 in.)
Gear bushing ID		
Main shaft 5th	24.985-24.006 mm (0.9837-0.9845 in.)	25.04 mm (0.986 in.)
Countershaft 4th	24.985-25.006 mm (0.9837-0.9845 in.)	25.04 mm (0.9858 in.)
Main shaft OD		
At 5th gear bushing location (A)	24.959-24.980 mm (0.9826-0.9835 in.)	24.90 mm (0.980 in.)
Countershaft OD		
At 4th gear bushing location	24.959-24.980 mm (0.9826-0.9835 in.)	24.90 mm (0.980 in.)
Damper shaft gear		
Gear ID	24.000-24.001 mm (0.94490.9457 in.)	24.10 mm (0.949 in.)
Bushing OD	23.959-23.980 mm (0.9433-0.9441 in.)	23.70 mm (0.933 in.)
Bushing ID	20.020-20.041 mm (0.7882-0.7890 in.)	20.10 mm (0.791 in.)
Bushing clearance wear limits		
Mainshaft		
5th gear to 5th gear bushing	—	0.10 mm (0.004 in.)
6th gear to 6th gear bushing	—	0.10 mm (0.004 in.)
5th gear bushing to shaft	—	0.060 mm (0.0024 in.)

5

(continued)

Table 3 TRANSMISSION SPECIFICATIONS (continued)

Item	Specification	Wear limit
Bushing clearance wear limits (continued)		
Countershaft		
1st gear to 1st gear bushing	—	0.10 mm (0.004 in.)
2nd gear to 2nd gear bushing	—	0.10 mm (0.004 in.)
3rd gear to 3rd gear bushing	—	0.10 mm (0.004 in.)
4th gear to 4th gear bushing	—	0.10 mm (0.004 in.)
4th gear to 4th gear bushing	—	0.06 mm (0.0024 in.)

Table 4 SHIFT FORK, SHIFT SHAFT AND SHIFT DRUM SPECIFICATIONS

Item	Specification	Wear limit
Shift fork ID (right and left*)	14.000-14.021 mm (0.5512-0.5520 in.)	14.04 mm (0.5528 in.)
Shift fork fingers	6.50-6.57 mm (0.2559-0.2587 in.)	6.20 mm (0.2441 in.)
Shift fork shaft OD	13.996-13.984 mm (0.5498-0.5506 in.)	13.90 mm (0.5472 in.)
Shift drum end ID (shift drum holder)	12.500-12.518 mm (0.4921-0.4928 in.)	12.54 mm (0.5937 in.)
Shift drum holder OD	12.457-12.484 mm (0.4904-0.4915 in.)	12.33 mm (0.4854 in.)

* The center shift fork is bolted to the shift fork shaft so no tolerances are given.

CHAPTER SIX

FUEL, EMISSION CONTROL AND EXHAUST SYSTEMS

The fuel system consists of the fuel tanks, shutoff valve, fuel pump and filter, 2 Keihin constant velocity carburetors and the air filter.

The exhaust system consists of 2 exhaust pipes, a common collector and 2 mufflers.

The air filter must be cleaned frequently. Specific procedures and service intervals are covered in Chapter Three.

This chapter includes service procedures for all parts of the fuel and exhaust systems except the air filter which is covered in Chapter Three. Carburetor specifications are listed in **Table 1**. **Table 1** and **Table 2** are at the end of this chapter.

The carburetors on all U.S. models are engineered to meet stringent EPA (Environmental Protection Agency) regulations. The carburetors are flow tested and preset at the factory for maximum performance and efficiency within EPA regulations. Altering preset carburetor jet needle and pilot screw adjustments is forbidden by law. Failure to comply with EPA regulations may result in heavy fines.

CARBURETOR OPERATION

An understanding of the function of each of the carburetor components and their relation to one another is a valuable aid for pinpointing a source of carburetor trouble.

The carburetor's purpose is to supply and atomize fuel and mix it in correct proportions with air that is drawn in through the air intake. At the primary throttle opening (idle), a small amount of fuel is siphoned through the pilot jet by the incoming air. As the throttle is opened further, the air stream begins to siphon fuel through the main jet and needle jet. The tapered needle increases the effective flow capacity of the needle jet as it is lifted, in that it occupies progressively less of the area of the jet.

At full throttle the carburetor venturi is fully open and the needle is lifted far enough to permit the main jet to flow at full capacity.

The choke circuit is a "bystarter" system in which the choke lever opens a valve rather than closing a butterfly in the venturi area as on many carburetors. In the open position, the slow jet discharges a stream of fuel into the carburetor venturi, to enrich the mixture when the engine is cold.

CARBURETOR SERVICE

Carburetor service (removal and cleaning) should be performed when poor engine performance or hesitation is observed. If, after servicing the carburetors and making the adjustments described in this chapter, the motorcycle does not perform correctly and assuming that other factors affecting performance, such as ignition timing and condition, etc., are correct, the motorcycle should be checked by a dealer or a qualified performance tuning specialist.

Removal/Installation

1. Place the bike on the centerstand and remove the right- and left-hand side covers.
2. Remove the seat and disconnect the battery negative lead.
3. Remove the main fuel tank as described in this chapter.
4A. *1983-1985:* Remove the clamping screws on the air filter connecting tube at the air filter box and at the carburetors (**Figure 1A**). Remove the connecting tube from the frame.
4B. *1986-on:* Remove the air cleaner case. Loosen the clamping screws on the air filter connecting tube at the frame. Remove the air filter mounting bolts and remove the air filter case (**Figure 1B**).
5. Remove the fuel lines (**Figure 2**) to each carburetor. Plug the end of each fuel line with a golf tee to prevent the spillage of fuel.
6. *California models:* Remove the air injection control valve assembly as described in this chapter.
7. Remove the screws (**Figure 3**) securing the throttle linkage cover and remove the cover.
8. At the hand throttle loosen the throttle cable locknut and turn the adjusting barrel (**Figure 4**) all the way in. This provides the necessary slack for ease of cable removal at the carburetor assembly.
9. Pull back the rubber boots at the end of each choke cable.
10. Loosen the choke valve nut on each cable and remove the cable end (choke valve) from each carburetor (A, **Figure 5**).
11. On models so equipped, disconnect the lines (B, **Figure 5**) from the carburetors that go to the PCV valve.
12. Loosen the locknuts (A, **Figure 6**) securing the throttle cables to the cable bracket.

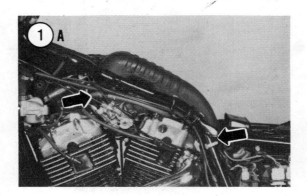

13. Disconnect the throttle cables (B, **Figure 6**) from the throttle wheel. Tie the loose ends of the cables to the frame out of the way.

14. Label and disconnect all hoses at the carburetor.

15. Loosen the clamping bands on the carburetors (**Figure 7**).

16. Pull the carburetors and the rubber intake tubes from the intake parts on the cylinder heads.

17. Slowly and carefully pull the carburetor assembly out toward the left-hand side. Be careful not to damage any of the carburetor components.

18. Remove the carburetor assembly.

19. Install by reversing these removal step, noting the following.

20. Before installing the carburetor assembly, coat the inside surface of both rubber intake tubes with Armor-All or rubber lube. This will make it easier to install the carburetor throats into the intake tubes.

21. Be sure the throttle cables and choke cable are correctly positioned in the frame—not twisted or kinked and without any sharp bends. Tighten the locknuts securely.

22. Attach the "pull" throttle cable into the lower portion of the bracket and into the lower slot (**Figure 8**) in the throttle wheel.

23. Attach the "push" throttle cable into the upper portion of the bracket and into the upper slot (**Figure 9**) in the throttle wheel.

24. *1986-on:* Install the intake tubes so that the arrow on each tube faces "up."

25. Install the rear intake tube hose clamps so that they do not interfere with the throttle wheel.

26. Adjust the throttle cable as described in Chapter Three.

27. Adjust the choke as described in this chapter.

28. *1984-on California models:* Refer to the vacuum hose routing label on the inside of the left- or right-hand side cover and reconnect the vacuum hoses (**Figure 10**).

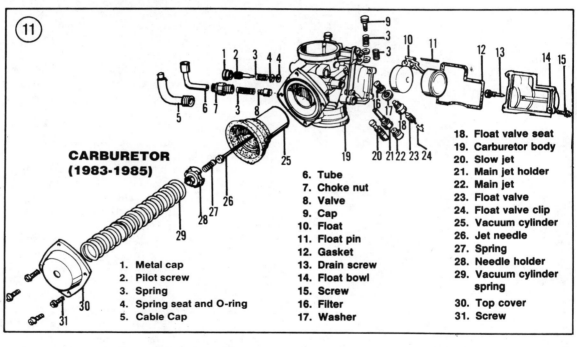

CARBURETOR (1983-1985)

1. Metal cap
2. Pilot screw
3. Spring
4. Spring seat and O-ring
5. Cable Cap

6. Tube
7. Choke nut
8. Valve
9. Cap
10. Float
11. Float pin
12. Gasket
13. Drain screw
14. Float bowl
15. Screw
16. Filter
17. Washer

18. Float valve seat
19. Carburetor body
20. Slow jet
21. Main jet holder
22. Main jet
23. Float valve
24. Float valve clip
25. Vacuum cylinder
26. Jet needle
27. Spring
28. Needle holder
29. Vacuum cylinder spring
30. Top cover
31. Screw

Disassembly/Cleaning/Inspection

Refer to **Figure 11** (1983-1985) or **Figure 12** (1986-on) for this procedure.

It is recommended that only one carburetor be disassembled and cleaned at a time. This will prevent an accidental interchange of parts.

1. Remove the screws securing the carburetor top cover to the main body and remove the cover (**Figure 13**).
2. Remove the vacuum cylinder spring (**Figure 14**).
3. Remove the vacuum cylinder. Carefully work the diaphragm (**Figure 15**) away from the main

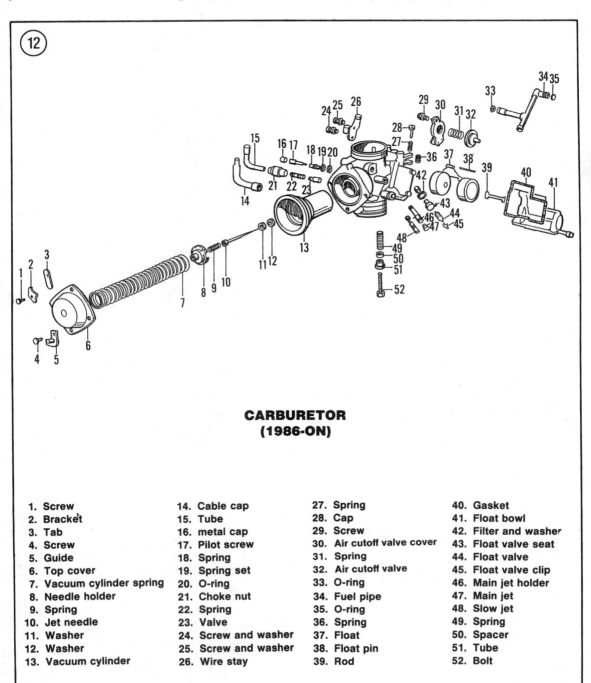

**CARBURETOR
(1986-ON)**

1. Screw	14. Cable cap	27. Spring	40. Gasket
2. Bracket	15. Tube	28. Cap	41. Float bowl
3. Tab	16. metal cap	29. Screw	42. Filter and washer
4. Screw	17. Pilot screw	30. Air cutoff valve cover	43. Float valve seat
5. Guide	18. Spring	31. Spring	44. Float valve
6. Top cover	19. Spring set	32. Air cutoff valve	45. Float valve clip
7. Vacuum cylinder spring	20. O-ring	33. O-ring	46. Main jet holder
8. Needle holder	21. Choke nut	34. Fuel pipe	47. Main jet
9. Spring	22. Spring	35. O-ring	48. Slow jet
10. Jet needle	23. Valve	36. Spring	49. Spring
11. Washer	24. Screw and washer	37. Float	50. Spacer
12. Washer	25. Screw and washer	38. Float pin	51. Tube
13. Vacuum cylinder	26. Wire stay	39. Rod	52. Bolt

body and lift the vacuum cylinder out of the carburetor (**Figure 16**).

4. Remove the jet needle as follows.

    a. Put an 8 mm socket or screwdriver down into the vacuum cylinder cavity (**Figure 17**).

    b. Place the socket or screwdriver on the needle jet holder and turn the holder 60° in either direction to unlock it from the tangs within the vacuum cylinder. Remove the needle jet holder (**Figure 18**).

    c. On 1983-1985 models, remove the jet needle spring and the jet needle (**Figure 19**).

    d. On 1986-on models, remove the jet needle and washer (**Figure 20**).

5. Remove the screws securing the float bowl to the main body and lift the float bowl (**Figure 21**) off.

6. Carefully push out the float pin (**Figure 22**).

7. Lift the float and needle valve (**Figure 23**) out of the main body.

8. Inspect the float valve seat (**Figure 24**) for grooves and nicks. If damaged it must be replaced.

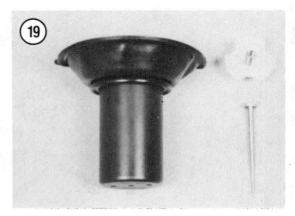

9. Remove the float valve seat and filter (**Figure 25**).

10. Remove the main jet (**Figure 26**).

11. Remove the main jet holder (**Figure 27**).

12. Remove the slow jet (A, **Figure 28**).

13. The starter jet (B, **Figure 28**) is pressed into place and cannot be removed.

14. The needle jet (**Figure 29**) is not removable.

NOTE
*The pilot screws are covered by a metal plug (**Figure 30**) that has to be drilled out in order to remove the screw. If removal is necessary, refer to **Pilot Screw and Plug Removal Installation** in this chapter.*

6

15. *1985-1987:* Remove the air cutoff valve from the main body as described in this chapter.

16. Remove the drain screw (**Figure 31**) on the float bowl. If necessary, clean out the drain tube outlet and reinstall the drain screw.

> *NOTE*
> *Further disassembly is neither necessary nor recommended. If throttle shafts or butterflies are damaged, take the carburetor body to a dealer for replacement.*

17. Clean the carburetor assembly and all parts in solvent.

> *NOTE*
> *If the carburetors are severely gummed with old gas or other contaminants, clean all parts, except rubber or plastic parts in a good grade of carburetor cleaner (**Figure 32**). This solution is available at most automotive supply stores in a resealable tank with a dip basket. If it is tightly sealed when not in use, the solution will last for several cleanings. Follow the manufacturer's instructions for correct soak time—usually about 1/2 hour. Cleaning the carburetors in a carburetor cleaner will require separation of the 2 carburetor main bodies so that they can fit into the tank. Refer to **Separation/Assembly** in this chapter.*

> *NOTE*
> *It is recommended that one carburetor be cleaned at a time to avoid interchanging parts.*

18. Remove the parts from the cleaner and blow dry with compressed air. Blow out the jets (**Figure 33**) with compressed air. Do *not* use a piece of wire

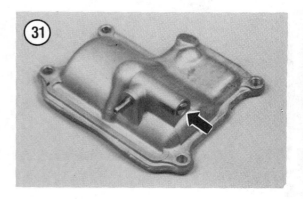

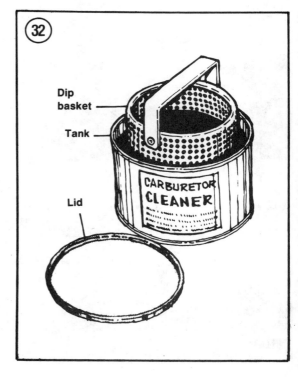

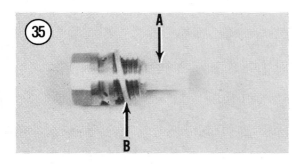

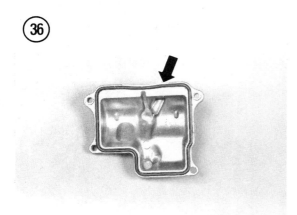

to clean them as minor gouges in a jet can alter flow rate and upset the fuel/air mixture.

WARNING
Wear goggles and a repirator when blowing carburetor cleaner off the parts.

19. Inspect the end of the float valve needle (**Figure 34**) and seat for wear or damage. Replace either or both parts if necessary.

20. Inspect the filter (A, **Figure 35**) on the float valve seat. If damaged, the float valve must be replaced.

21. If removed, inspect the pilot screw for wear or damage that may have occurred during removal. Replace both pilot screws even if only one requires replacement. This is necessary for correct pilot screw adjustment as described in this chapter.

22. Check the float bowl O-ring (**Figure 36**) for flat spots, hardness or other damage; replace if necessary.

23. Repeat Steps 1-22 for the other carburetor.

Assembly

1. If removed, screw the pilot screw into the exact same position (same number of turns) as recorded during disassembly.

NOTE
*If new pilot screws were installed, turn them out the number of turns indicated in **Table 1** from the **lightly** seated position.*

2. To assemble the vacuum cylinder (**Figure 37**), perform the following.

　　a. On 1986-on models, install the washer on the jet needle (**Figure 38**).

b. Insert the jet needle (**Figure 20**) into the vacuum cylinder.

c. Insert the spring in the end of the needle holder (**Figure 39**).

d. Secure the end of the needle jet holder with an 8 mm socket or screwdriver (**Figure 40**) and insert the holder into the vacuum cylinder (**Figure 41**). Turn the needle jet holder 60° in either direction to lock the holder in place within the vacuum holder.

3. Install the vacuum cylinder into the carburetor body. Align the tab on the diaphragm with the hole (**Figure 42**) in the carburetor body.

4. Install the vacuum cylinder compression spring into the vacuum cylinder and index it onto the boss on the top cover (**Figure 43**).

5. Align the hole in the vacuum cylinder with the raised boss on the top cover. Install the top cover and tighten the screws securely.

6. *1985-on California models:* Install the air cutoff valve as described in this chapter.

7. Install the slow jet (**Figure 44**).

8. Install the main jet holder (**Figure 45**) and the main jet (**Figure 46**).

9. Make sure the gasket (B, **Figure 35**) is in place on the float valve and install the float valve seat and filter (**Figure 25**).

10. Install the needle valve onto the float.

11. Install the float and needle valve and install the float pin (**Figure 22**).

12. Inspect the float height and adjust if necessary as described in this chapter.

13. Install the gasket in the float bowl (**Figure 36**).

14. Install the float bowl (**Figure 21**) and tighten the screws securely.

15. After assembly and installation are completed, adjust the carburetors as described in this chapter.

Air Cutoff Valve
Removal/Installation
(1985-1986)

Remove the mounting screws and remove the air cutoff valve (**Figure 47**) from the carburetor housing. If necessary, have the air cutoff valve tested by a Honda dealer as special tools are required. Install by reversing these steps.

Air Cutoff Valve
Removal/Installation
(1987)

1. Remove the carburetors as described in this chapter.

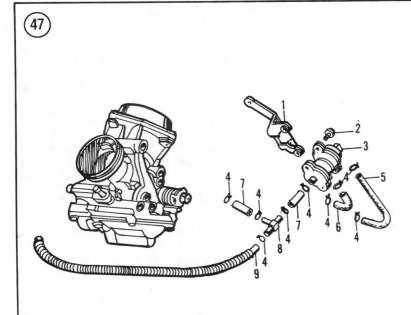

**AIR CUTOFF VALVE
(1985-1986)**

1. Holder
2. Screw
3. Air cutoff valve
4. Spring clamp
5. Hose
6. Hose
7. Hose
8. T-fitting
9. Hose

2. Remove the air cutoff valve cover (**Figure 48A**).

3. See **Figure 48B**. Remove the spring (A), diaphragm (B) and O-ring (C).

4. Check the diaphragm for wear or damage. Also check the diaphragm plunger for wear or damage. Replace the diaphragm if necessary.

5. Check the O-ring (C, **Figure 48B**) for wear or flat spots; replace if necessary.

6. Install by reversing these steps.

Separation/Assembly

1. Remove the carburetor assembly as described in this chapter.

2. Loosen the synchronizing screw (A, **Figure 49**) and remove the spring (B, **Figure 49**).

3. Remove the screw on each side securing the carburetors together. See **Figure 50**.

4. Don't lose the throttle link thrust spring (**Figure 51**) where the carburetors are held together.

5. Carefully pull the carburetors apart.

6. Disconnect the fuel lines and T-fitting.

7. Loosen the throttle adjust screw (A, **Figure 52**).

8. Remove the nut (B, **Figure 52**) securing the throttle drum and remove the throttle drum and return spring.

9. Assemble by reversing these disassembly steps, noting the following.

10. Install new O-ring seals onto the air joint pipe and coat them with oil.

11. Tighten the throttle adjust screw until the throttle valve on the left-hand carburetor aligns with the *small* bypass hole in the venturi (A, **Figure 53**).

12. Turn the synchronizing screw until the throttle valve on the right-hand carburetor aligns with the *small* bypass hole in the venturi (B, **Figure 53**).

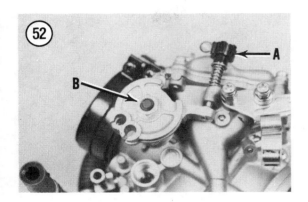

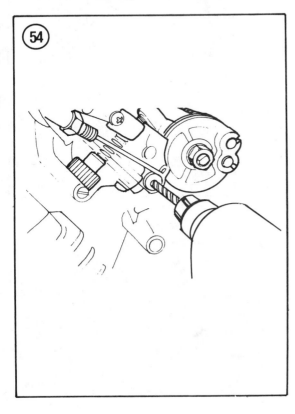

13. Using the throttle linkage, open the throttle a little then release it. The throttle should return smoothly with no drag.

14. If there is drag or the throttle does not move smoothly, recheck all previous steps until the problem is solved.

NOTE
If the carburetors have been assembled correctly and the throttle still does not operate correctly, there may be internal damage to the throttle shafts or butterfly valves. Take the assembly to a dealer for inspection and replacement.

Pilot Screw and Plug
Removal/Installation

The pilot screws are covered by a metal plug (**Figure 30**) that has to be drilled out in order to remove the screw. The screws can be removed with the carburetor assembly either installed on the bike or removed. It is easier to perform this operation with the carburetor assembly installed on the bike. Do not remove these plugs and screws unless you suspect they are not functioning properly.

CAUTION
If the carburetor assembly is removed from the engine, put tape over all openings in the carburetor bodies to keep out metal shavings during the drilling operation.

1. Use a small center punch and hammer to centerpunch the middle of the plug (**Figure 30**) for a drill guide.

CAUTION
Be careful not to drill too far into the plug. You could damage the pilot screw.

2. Drill through the plug (**Figure 54**) with a 4 mm (5/32 in.) drill bit. If available, attach a drill stop to the drill bit 3 mm (1/8 in.) from the end of the drill bit to prevent the accidental drilling of the pilot screw.

NOTE
If you do not have a drill stop, wrap 8-10 layers of masking tape on the drill bit at the prescribed distance from the end. This can be used as a guide for the distance the drill bit has traveled. The tape will not stop the drill from traveling further in—it is only a visual guide.

3. Force a 4 mm self-tapping screw into the drilled hole. Continue to turn the screw until the plug starts to rotate with the screw.

4. Withdraw the plug and screw with a pair of pliers (**Figure 55**) and blow away all metal shavings from the area.

> *NOTE*
> *Before removing the pilot screw, record the number of turns necessary until the screw lightly seats. Record the number of turns for each individual carburetor as the screws must be reinstalled into the exact same setting.*

5. Perform the pilot screw assembly.

6. Perform *Pilot Screw Adjustment and Plug Installation* in this chapter.

CARBURETOR ADJUSTMENTS

Float Adjustment

The carburetor assembly must be removed and partially disassembled for this adjustment.

1. Remove the carburetors as described in this chapter.

2. Remove the screws (**Figure 56**) securing the float bowls to the main bodies and remove them.

3. Hold the carburetor assembly with the carburetor inclined 15-45° from vertical so that the float arm is just touching the float needle. Use a float level gauge (Honda part No. 07401-0010001 or equivalent) and measure the distance from the carburetor body to the float arm (**Figure 57**). The correct height is listed in **Table 1**.

4. Adjust by carefully bending the tang on the float arm (**Figure 58**).

5. If the float level is too high, the result will be a rich fuel/air mixture. If it is too low, the mixture will be too lean.

> *NOTE*
> *The floats on both carburetors must be adjusted at the same height to maintain the same fuel/air mixture to both cylinders.*

6. Reassemble and install the carburetors.

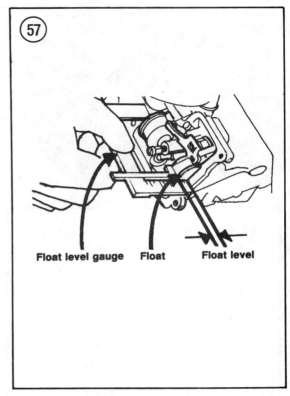

Float level gauge   Float   Float level

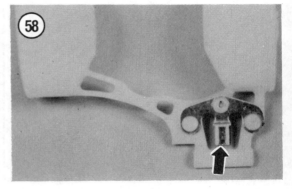

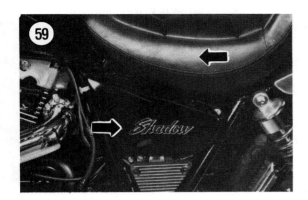

Needle Jet Adjustment

The needle jet is *non-adjustable* on all models.

Choke Adjustment

First make sure the choke operates smoothly with no binding. The choke cable starts out as a single cable at the lever on the handlebar lever and about halfway down it branches out into 2 cables, one cable for each carburetor. If the cable binds, lubricate it as described in Chapter Three. If the cable still does not operate smoothly it must be replaced as described in this chapter.

> *NOTE*
> *The choke circuit is a "bystarter" system in which the choke lever opens a valve rather than closing a butterfly in the venturi area as on many carburetors. In the open position, the slow jet discharges a stream of fuel into the carburetor venturi, to enrich the mixture when the engine is cold.*

1. Remove both side covers and the seat (**Figure 59**).
2. Remove the fuel tank as described in this chapter.
3. Operate the choke lever and check for smooth operation of the cable and choke mechanism.
4. At the carburetor assembly, slide back the rubber boot on the choke cable (**Figure 60**).
5. Unscrew the choke valve nut and remove the choke cable, valve and spring from the carburetor.

6. Move the choke lever all the way *down* to the fully closed position.
7. Using vernier calipers, measure the distance between the end of the threads of the choke valve nut (**Figure 61**) and the choke valve. It should be 10-11 mm (0.39-0.43 in.). Refer to **Figure 62**.
8. To adjust, perform the following.
    a. Loosen the locknut (A, **Figure 63**) on the choke cable at the lever.

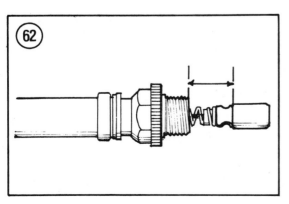

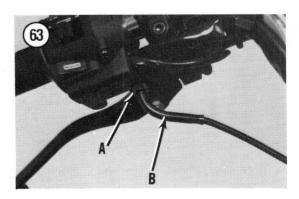

b. Turn the elbow (B, **Figure 63**) in either direction until the dimension at the cable end is correct.

c. Tighten the locknut and recheck the dimension in Step 7.

9. Repeat Steps 4-8 for the other carburetor. The dimension in Step 7 must be the same for both carburetors.

10. Install the choke valve into the carburetor body.

11. Tighten the choke valve nut by hand then turn it an additional 1/4 turn with a 14 mm wrench.

12. Reinstall the fuel tank, seat and side covers.

Pilot Screw Adjustment and Plug Installation

> *NOTE*
> *The pilot screws are pre-set at the factory. Adjustment is not necessary unless the carburetors have been overhauled or someone has misadjusted them.*

The air filter element must be cleaned before starting this procedure or the results will be inaccurate.

The plugs have to be removed from the carburetor bodies as described in this chapter.

1. For the preliminary adjustment, carefully turn the pilot screw on each carburetor in until it *lightly* seats and then back it out the number of turns listed in **Table 1**.

2. Start the engine and let it reach normal operating temperature. Stop-and-go riding for approximately 10-15 minutes is sufficient.

3. Shut the engine off and place the bike on the centerstand.

4. Connect a portable tachometer following the manufacturer's instructions. Use a tachometer that can register a change of 50 rpm. The bike's tachometer is not accurate enough at low rpm.

5. Start the engine and turn the large black plastic idle adjust screw (**Figure 64**) in or out to achieve the idle speed listed in **Table 1**.

6. Turn each pilot screw *out* 1/2 turn from the initial setting in Step 1. If the engine speed increases by 50 rpm or more, turn each pilot screw out by an additional 1/2 turn at a time until engine speed drops by 50 rpm or less.

7. Turn the idle adjust screw in or out again to achieve the idle speed listed in **Table 1**.

8. Turn the pilot screw on the left-hand carburetor *in* 1/2 turn at a time until engine speed drops by 50 rpm.

9. Turn the pilot screw on the left-hand carburetor *out* 1 turn from the position obtained in Step 8.

10. Turn the idle adjust screw in or out again to achieve the desired idle speed listed in **Table 1**.

11. Repeat Steps 8-10 on the right-hand carburetor pilot screw.

12. Turn the engine off and disconnect the portable tachometer.

13. After this adjustment is completed, test ride the bike. Throttle response from idle should be rapid and without any hesitation.

14. Use a suitable size drift and carefully drive a new plug (**Figure 65**) into each pilot screw bore in the carburetor body. The plug is fully seated when it is recessed into the hole by 1 mm.

High Elevation Adjustment

If the bike is going to be ridden for any sustained period of time at high elevation (2,000 m/6,500 ft.), the carburetors must be readjusted to improve performance and decrease exhaust emissions.

1. Remove each pilot screw plug as described in this chapter.

2. Start the engine and let it reach normal operating temperature. Stop-and-go riding for approximately 10 minutes is sufficient. Turn off the engine.

3. Connect a portable tachometer following the manufacturer's instructions. The bike's tachometer is not accurate enough at low rpm.

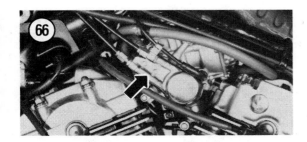

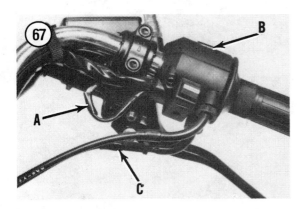

4. Turn each pilot screw clockwise one full turn (1983-1985) or 1/2 turn (1986-on), as viewed from the side of the carburetor.

5. Restart the engine and turn the large idle screw (**Figure 64**) to achieve an idle speed listed in **Table 1**.

6. Turn the engine off and disconnect the portable tachometer.

7. Install new pilot screw plugs as described in this chapter.

8. When the bike is returned to elevations near sea level, the pilot screws must be returned to their original position and the idle speed readjusted to the rpm listed in **Table 1**.

Rejetting The Carburetors

Do not try to solve a poor running engine problem by rejetting the carburetors if all of the following conditions hold true.

    a. The engine has held a good tune in the past with the standard jetting.

    b. The engine has not been modified.

    c. The motorcycle is being operated in the same geographical region under the same general climatic conditions as in the past.

    d. The motorcycle was and is being ridden at average highway speeds.

If those conditions all hold true, the chances are that the problem is due to a malfunction in the carburetor or in another component that needs to be adjusted or repaired. Changing carburetor jet size probably won't solve the problem. Rejetting the carburetors may be necessary if any of the following conditions hold true.

    a. A non-standard type of air filter element is being used.

    b. A non-standard exhaust system is installed on the motorcycle.

    c. Any of the top end components in the engine (pistons, cams, valves, compression ratio, etc.) have been modified.

    d. The motorcycle is in use at considerably higher or lower elevations or in a considerably hotter or colder climate than in the past.

    e. The motorcycle is being operated at considerably higher speeds than before and changing to colder spark plugs does not solve the problem.

    f. Someone has previously changed the carburetor jetting.

    g. The motorcycle has never held a satisfactory engine tune.

If it is necessary to rejet the carburetors, check with a dealer or motorcycle performance tuner for recommendations as to the size of jets to install for your specific situation.

If you do change the jets, do so only one size at a time. After rejetting, test ride the bike and perform a spark plug test. Refer to *Reading Spark Plugs* in Chapter Three.

THROTTLE CABLE REPLACEMENT

1. Place the bike on the centerstand and remove the right- and left-hand side covers.

2. Remove the main fuel tank as described in this chapter.

3. Remove the screws securing the throttle linkage cover and remove the cover (**Figure 66**).

4. Disconnect the front brake light switch electrical connectors (A, **Figure 67**).

5. Remove the screws securing the right-hand switch/throttle housing halves together (B, **Figure 67**).

6. Remove the housing from the handlebar and disengage the throttle cables (C, **Figure 67**) from the throttle grip.

7. At the carburetor assembly, loosen the locknuts (A, **Figure 68**) securing the throttle cables to the cable bracket.

6

8. Disconnect the throttle cables (B, **Figure 68**) from the throttle wheel.

> *NOTE*
> *The string attached in the next step will be used to pull the new throttle cables back through the frame so they will be routed in exactly the same position as the old ones.*

9. Tie a piece of heavy string or cord (approximately 7 ft./2 m long) to the carburetor end of the throttle cables. Wrap this end with masking or duct tape. Do not use an excessive amount of tape as it must be pulled though the frame loop during removal. Tie the other end of the string to the frame or air box.

10. At the throttle grip end of the cables, carefully pull the cables and attached string out through the frame, past the electrical harness and from behind the headlight housing. Make sure the attached string follows the same path as the cable through the frame.

11. Remove the tape and untie the string from the old cables.

12. Lubricate the new cables as described in Chapter Three.

13. Tie the string to the new throttle cables and wrap it with tape.

14. Carefully pull the string back through the frame, routing the new cables through the same path as the old cables.

15. Remove the tape and untie the string from the cables and the frame.

> *CAUTION*
> *The throttle cables are the push/pull type and must be installed as described and shown in Step 16 and Step 17. Do **not** interchange the 2 cables.*

16. Attach the throttle "pull" cable to the bottom portion of the bracket and into the lower hole in the throttle wheel (**Figure 69**). The other end is attached to the front receptacle of the throttle/switch housing.

17. Attach the throttle "push" cable to the upper portion of the bracket and into the upper hole in the throttle wheel (**Figure 70**). The other end is attached to the rear receptacle of the throttle/switch housing.

18. Install the throttle/switch housing and tighten the screws securely.

19. Attach the front brake light switch connectors.

20. Operate the throttle grip and make sure the carburetor throttle linkage is operating correctly with no binding. If operation is incorrect or there is binding carefully check that the cables are attached correctly and there are no tight bends in the cables.

21. Install the carburetor assembly, main fuel tank and seat.

22. Adjust the throttle cables as described in Chapter Three.

23. Test ride the bike slowly at first and make sure the throttle is operating correctly.

CHOKE CABLE REPLACEMENT

The choke cable starts out as a single cable at the lever on the handlebar lever and about half way down the cable it branches out into 2 cables, one for each carburetor.

1. Remove both side covers and the seat.
2. Remove the main fuel tank as described in this chapter.
3. At the carburetor assembly, slide back the rubber boot on the choke cable (**Figure 60**).
4. Unscrew the choke valve nut and remove the choke cable, valve and spring from the carburetor.

5. Repeat Step 3 and Step 4 for the other carburetor.
6. Remove the clutch switch wires at the clutch lever.

CAUTION
Cover the frame and front wheels with a heavy cloth or plastic tarp to protect it from accidental spilling of hydraulic fluid. Wash any spilled hydraulic fluid off any painted or plated surface immediately, as it will destroy the finish. Use soapy water and rinse thoroughly.

7. Remove the bolts (A, **Figure 71**) and clamp securing the clutch master cylinder to the handlebar.
8. Remove the clutch master cylinder and lay it over the front fender. Keep the reservoir in an upright position to minimize loss of hydraulic fluid and to keep air from entering the clutch system.
9. Remove the screw securing the switch assembly together (B, **Figure 71**).
10. Remove the choke cable (C, **Figure 71**) from the switch and choke lever assembly on the handlebar.
11. Remove the plastic trim panels (**Figure 72**) on each side of the steering head.

NOTE
The piece of string attached in the next stop will be used to pull the new choke cable back through the frame so it will be routed in the same position as the old cable.

12. Tie a piece of heavy string or cord (approximately 7 ft./2 m long) to the carburetor end of each choke cable (**Figure 73**). Wrap the end with masking or duct tape. Do not use an excessive amount of tape as it must be pulled through the frame loop during removal. Tie the other end of the strings to the frame or air box.
13. Unhook the choke cable from any clips on the frame (**Figure 74**).
14. At the choke lever end of the cable, carefully pull the cable assembly and attached strings out through the frame and from behind the headlight housing. Make sure the attached strings follow the same path that the cable does through the frame.
15. Remove the tape and untie the strings from the old cable assembly.
16. Lubricate the new cable assembly as described in Chapter Three.
17. Tie the strings to the new choke cable assembly and wrap it with tape.

6

18. Carefully pull the strings back through the frame, routing the new cables through the same path as the old cables.

19. Remove the tape and untie the strings from the cable and the frame.

20. Attach the choke cable onto the choke lever assembly.

21. Install the choke valve onto the carburetor body.

22. Tighten the choke valve nut by hand and then turn it an additional 1/4 turn with a 14 mm wrench.

23. Repeat Steps 20-22 for the other carburetor.

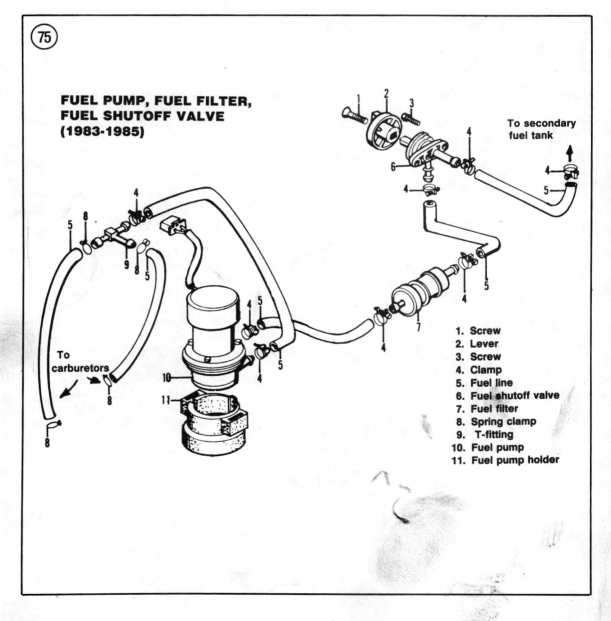

FUEL PUMP, FUEL FILTER, FUEL SHUTOFF VALVE (1983-1985)

To secondary fuel tank

To carburetors

1. Screw
2. Lever
3. Screw
4. Clamp
5. Fuel line
6. Fuel shutoff valve
7. Fuel filter
8. Spring clamp
9. T-fitting
10. Fuel pump
11. Fuel pump holder

24. Install the switch/choke assembly on the handlebar and tighten the screws securely.

25. Install the clutch master cylinder as described in Chapter Five.

26. Attach the clutch switch wires to the clutch lever.

27. Operate the choke lever and make sure the carburetor choke linkage is operating correctly, with no binding. If operation is incorrect or there is binding, carefully check that the cable is attached correctly and there are no tight bends in the cable.

28. Reinstall the main fuel tank, seat and side covers.

29. Adjust the choke cable as described in this chapter.

FUEL SHUTOFF VALVE

The fuel shutoff valve is not equipped with an integral fuel filter. There is a separate fuel filter as described in this chapter.

Refer to **Figure 75** (1983-1985) or **Figure 76** (1986-on) for this procedure.

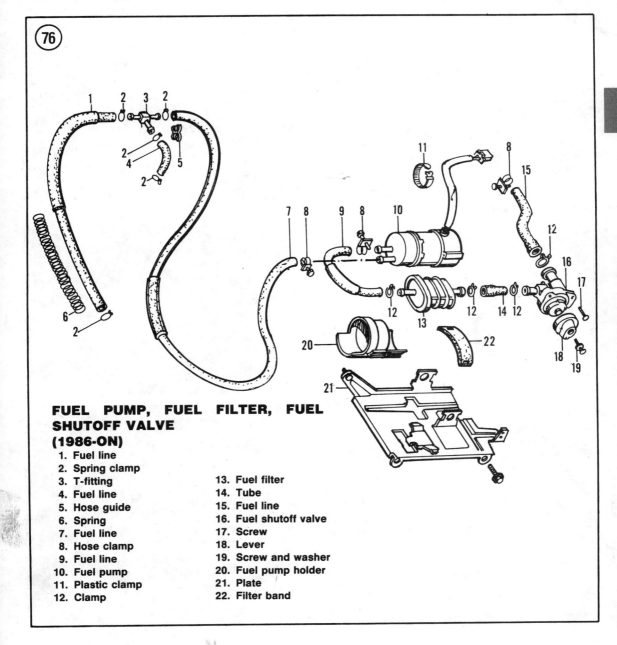

FUEL PUMP, FUEL FILTER, FUEL SHUTOFF VALVE (1986-ON)

1. Fuel line
2. Spring clamp
3. T-fitting
4. Fuel line
5. Hose guide
6. Spring
7. Fuel line
8. Hose clamp
9. Fuel line
10. Fuel pump
11. Plastic clamp
12. Clamp
13. Fuel filter
14. Tube
15. Fuel line
16. Fuel shutoff valve
17. Screw
18. Lever
19. Screw and washer
20. Fuel pump holder
21. Plate
22. Filter band

1A. *1983-1985:* Remove the right-hand side cover and seat.

1B. *1986-on:* Remove the left-hand side cover and seat.

2. Remove the screw (A, **Figure 77**) securing the handle to the fuel shutoff valve and remove the handle.

3. Remove the bolts (B, **Figure 77**) securing the fuel shutoff valve to the frame.

4. Carefully pull the shutoff valve out of the frame and disconnect the fuel lines going to the secondary fuel tank and to the fuel filter. Plug the ends of both lines with golf tees to prevent any fuel drainage.

5. Install by reversing these removal steps. Carefully check for fuel leaks.

FUEL FILTER

These models have a separate fuel filter that cannot be cleaned. If dirty, a new filter must be installed. It should be replaced at the interval indicated in Chapter Three.

Refer to **Figure 75** (1983-1985) or **Figure 76** (1986-on) for this procedure.

Removal/Installation

1A. *1983-1985:* Perform the following.
  a. Remove the right-hand side cover and seat.
  b. Remove the coolant recovery tank cap (A, **Figure 78**).
  c. Carefully pull the fuel filter (B, **Figure 78**) from the frame.

1B. *1986-on:* Perform the following.
  a. Remove the left-hand side cover and seat.
  b. Disconnect the connectors at the spark unit (A, **Figure 79**).
  c. Remove the spark unit base screws and lift the base out of the way (B, **Figure 79**).
  d. Carefully pull the fuel filter (A, **Figure 80**) from the frame.

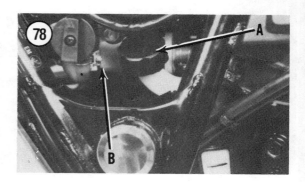

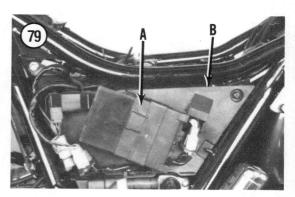

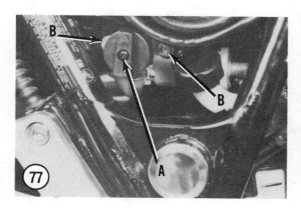

2. Disconnect the flexible fuel lines from the fuel filter and plug the ends of the fuel lines with golf tees.

3. Install a new filter.

4. After installation is complete, thoroughly check for fuel leaks.

5. Complete installation by reversing Step 1.

FUEL PUMP

Fuel pump performance testing is covered in Chapter Seven.

Refer to **Figure 75** (1983-1985) or **Figure 76** (1986-on) for this procedure.

Removal/Installation

1. Turn the fuel shutoff valve to the OFF position.
2A. *1983-1985:* Perform the following.
   a. Remove the seat and the right-hand side covers.
   b. Remove the plastic cover on the fuel pump.
   c. Disconnect the electrical connector to the fuel pump (A, **Figure 81**).
   d. Remove the fuel pump from the rubber mount (B, **Figure 81**) and remove the fuel pump from the frame.

2B. *1986-on:* Perform the following.
   a. Remove the fuel filter as described in this chapter.
   b. Disconnect the electrical connector to the fuel pump.
   c. Remove the fuel pump from the rubber mount (B, **Figure 80**) and remove the fuel pump from the frame.
3. Disconnect the flexible fuel lines from the fuel pump. Plug the ends of the fuel lines with golf tees to prevent fuel leakage.
4. Install by reversing these removal steps.
5. After installation is complete, thoroughly check for fuel leaks.

MAIN FUEL TANK

Removal/Installation

Refer to **Figure 82** (1983-1985) or **Figure 83** (1986-on) for this procedure.
1. Place the bike on the centerstand.
2. Remove the seat and both side covers.
3. Turn the fuel shutoff valve to OFF.

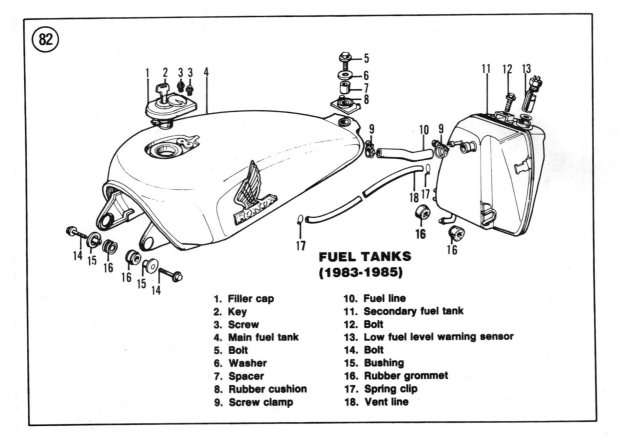

FUEL TANKS (1983-1985)

1. Filler cap
2. Key
3. Screw
4. Main fuel tank
5. Bolt
6. Washer
7. Spacer
8. Rubber cushion
9. Screw clamp
10. Fuel line
11. Secondary fuel tank
12. Bolt
13. Low fuel level warning sensor
14. Bolt
15. Bushing
16. Rubber grommet
17. Spring clip
18. Vent line

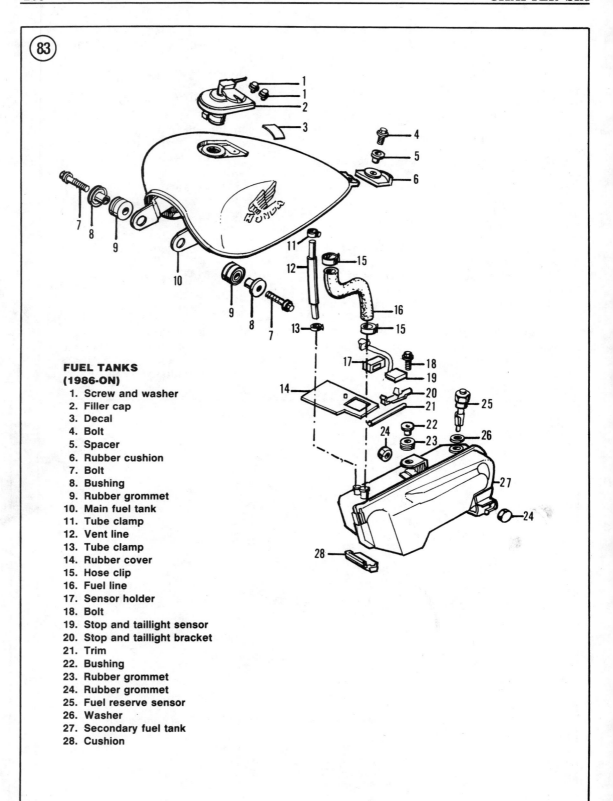

83

**FUEL TANKS
(1986-ON)**
1. Screw and washer
2. Filler cap
3. Decal
4. Bolt
5. Spacer
6. Rubber cushion
7. Bolt
8. Bushing
9. Rubber grommet
10. Main fuel tank
11. Tube clamp
12. Vent line
13. Tube clamp
14. Rubber cover
15. Hose clip
16. Fuel line
17. Sensor holder
18. Bolt
19. Stop and taillight sensor
20. Stop and taillight bracket
21. Trim
22. Bushing
23. Rubber grommet
24. Rubber grommet
25. Fuel reserve sensor
26. Washer
27. Secondary fuel tank
28. Cushion

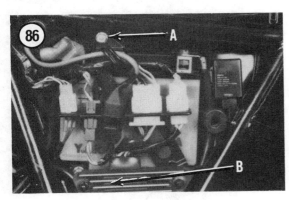

10. Remove the bolt (**Figure 84**) on each side of the front of the main fuel tank.

11. Loosen the clamps on the fuel line and vent line (A, **Figure 85**) and remove both lines from the secondary fuel tank.

12. Remove the bolt and washer securing the rear of the fuel tank (B, **Figure 85**). Don't lose the metal spacer in the rubber cushion.

13A. On models equipped with the evaporative emission control system, perform the following.

  a. Lift up and pull the tank to the rear a short distance.

  b. Lift up the front of the tank and disconnect the vent line going to the PCV valve.

  c. Remove the fuel tank.

13B. On all other models, lift up and pull the tank to the rear and remove it.

14. Install by reversing these removal steps, noting the following.

15. Spray a small amount of WD-40 (or equivalent) onto the inside ends of the fuel and vent lines. This will make installation of the lines a little easier. Make sure they are completely installed onto the fittings on the secondary fuel tank. Tighten the clamps securely.

16. Refill the fuel tanks. Use the drained fuel if it was kept clean.

SECONDARY FUEL TANK

Removal/Installation

Refer to **Figure 82** (1983-1985) or **Figure 83** (1986-on) for this procedure.

1. Place the bike on the centerstand.

2. Remove the seat and both side covers.

3. Remove the main fuel tank as described in this chapter.

4A. *1983-1985:* Remove the bolt (A, **Figure 86**) securing the regulator/rectifier and electrical connector panel (B, **Figure 86**). Move the panel out of the way.

4B. *1986-on:* Disconnect the connectors at the spark unit (A, **Figure 79**). Then remove the spark unit base screws and lift the base out of the way (B, **Figure 79**).

5. Disconnect the battery negative and positive leads in that order. Remove the battery vent tube from the battery. Slide the battery out of the frame.

6. Remove the rear wheel as described in Chapter Ten.

7. Remove the rear fender as described in Chapter Twelve.

4. Disconnect the fuel line that goes to the fuel filter from the base of the shutoff valve. See **Figure 75** or **Figure 76**.

5. Attach a piece of fuel line to the fitting on the fuel shutoff valve and place the loose end in a clean sealable metal container.

6. Turn the fuel shutoff valve to the ON position.

7. Drain both the main and secondary fuel tanks. If the fuel is kept clean it can be reused.

8. Open the fuel filler cap. This will speed up the flow of fuel.

9. Reinstall the fuel line onto the fuel shutoff valve after both tanks are drained.

8. Disconnect the electrical connectors from the low fuel level warning sensor. See A, **Figure 87** (1983-1985) or A, **Figure 88** (1986-on).

9. Remove the mounting bolt and washer securing the secondary fuel tank to the frame. See B, **Figure 87** (1983-1985) or B, **Figure 88** (1986-on).

10. Remove the secondary fuel tank from the frame. See C, **Figure 87** (1983-1985) or C, **Figure 88** (1986-on).

11. Install the secondary fuel tank by reversing these removal steps, noting the following.

12. Make sure all fuel lines are correctly connected and are tight.

13. Test ride the bike and check for fuel leaks.

CRANKCASE BREATHER SYSTEM (1983-1985 U.S. ONLY)

To comply with air pollution standards, the 1983-1985 Honda V-twins are equipped with a crankcase breather system. This system draws blow-by gases from the crankcase and recirculates them into the fuel/air mixture and thus into the engine to be burned.

Inspection/Cleaning

Make sure all hose clamps are tight. Check all hoses for deterioration and replace as necessary.

Slide the drain tube out of the bracket on the battery holder. Remove the drain plug (**Figure 89**) from the drain hose and drain out all residue. This cleaning procedure should be done more frequently if a considerable amount of riding is done at full throttle or in the rain.

Install the drain plug and clamp.

EVAPORATIVE EMISSION CONTROL SYSTEM (1984-ON CALIFORNIA MODELS ONLY)

Fuel vapor from the fuel tank is routed into a charcoal canister (**Figure 90** or **Figure 91**). This vapor is stored when the engine is not running. When the engine is running, these vapors are drawn through a purge control valve and into the carburetor to be burned. Make sure all hose clamps are tight. Check all hoses for deterioration and replace as necessary. See **Figure 90** or **Figure 91**.

Refer to the vacuum hose routing label (**Figure 92**) mounted on the backside of one of the side covers for correct hose routing for your model.

Testing

If the engine becomes difficult to start after it is warm or hot, have the purge control valve (PCV) tested by a Honda dealer.

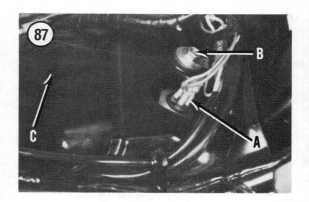

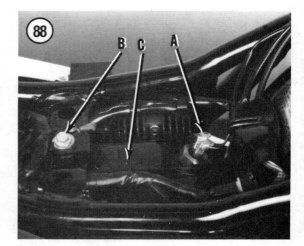

Charcoal Canister Removal/Installation

When removing the hoses on any emission control component, mark the hose and the fitting with a piece of masking tape and identify where the hose goes. There are so many vacuum hoses on these models that reconnection can be very confusing.

1. Remove both side covers and the seat.

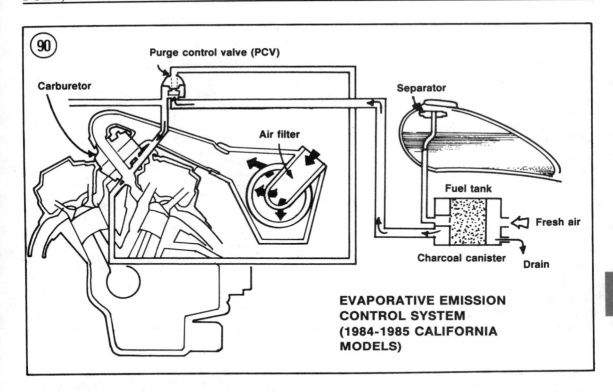

EVAPORATIVE EMISSION CONTROL SYSTEM (1984-1985 CALIFORNIA MODELS)

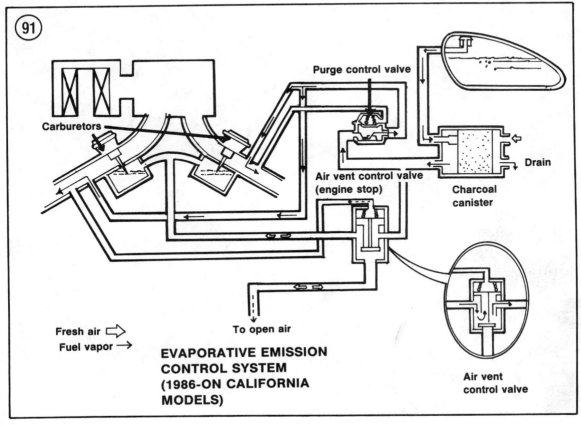

EVAPORATIVE EMISSION CONTROL SYSTEM (1986-ON CALIFORNIA MODELS)

2. Remove the main fuel tank as described in this chapter.

3. Remove the radiator trim panel (**Figure 93**).

4. Disconnect the hoses going to the charcoal canister from the PCV valve.

5. Remove the hoses from the clip alongside the radiator.

6. Remove the bolts (**Figure 94**) securing the charcoal canister to the frame and remove the canister assembly.

7. Check the canister (**Figure 95**) for damage; replace if necessary.

8. Install by reversing these removal steps. Be sure to install the hoses to their correct place on the PCV.

Purge Control Valve (PCV)
Removal/Installation

The PCV on 1984 and 1985 models is located in front of the front cylinder. On 1986 and later models, the PCV is located behind the horn. See **Figure 96** (typical). Label all hoses with masking tape and identify where the hose goes.

Air Vent Control Valve (AVCV)
Removal/Installation (1986-on)

1. Remove the air cleaner case. Loosen the clamping screws on the air filter connecting tube at the frame. Remove the air filter mounting bolts and remove the air filter case (**Figure 97**).

2. See **Figure 98**. Label all AVCV hoses with masking tape and identify where the hoses go.

3. Remove the AVCV mounting bolt and remove the AVCV (**Figure 98**) unit from the frame.

4. Install by reversing these steps.

SECONDARY AIR SUPPLY SYSTEM (1986-ON CALIFORNIA MODELS ONLY)

The secondary air supply system improves emission performance by routing filtered fresh air into the exhaust port (**Figure 99**).

Removal/Installation

1. Remove the air injection control valve cover (**Figure 100**).

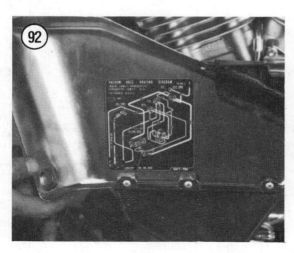

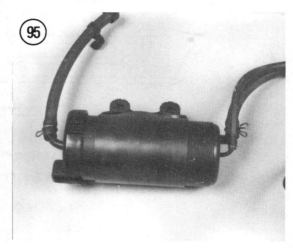

6

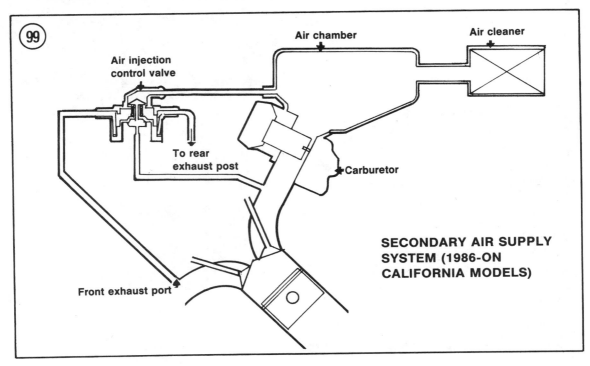

Air chamber

Air cleaner

Air injection
control valve

To rear
exhaust post

Carburetor

Front exhaust port

**SECONDARY AIR SUPPLY
SYSTEM (1986-ON
CALIFORNIA MODELS)**

2. Refer to **Figure 101**. Disconnect the following hoses at the air injection control valve.

   a. Air supply hoses (A)

   b. Vacuum hose (B)

   c. Air intake hose (C)

3. Remove the air injection control valve mounting bolts and remove the valve (D, **Figure 101**).

4. If necessary, disconnect the air supply hoses at the cylinder head pipe and remove the hoses. See A, **Figure 102** (left hose) or **Figure 103** (right hose).

> *NOTE*
> *The small hose pipes (B, **Figure 102**) that connect the air supply hoses to the cylinder head can only be removed when the engine is removed from the frame. If the pipes are damaged, refer to Chapter Four.*

5. Install by reversing these steps.

Testing

Testing of the secondary air supply system should be referred to a Honda dealer as special tools and procedures are required.

Inspection

1. Check the air tank (A, **Figure 104**) for cracks or damage. Replace the air tank if necessary.

2. Check the hoses (B, **Figure 104**) for soft spots or damage; replace hoses as necessary.

3. Check air suction valve cover (C, **Figure 104**) for looseness or damage.

4. Check the diaphragm as follows.

   a. Remove the diaphragm cover screws and remove the cover (**Figure 105**).

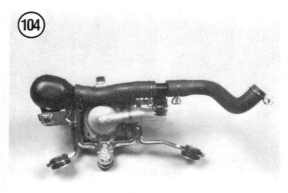

b. Check the diaphragm (A, **Figure 106**) for tears or cracks. Replace the air suction valve housing (B, **Figure 106**) if the diaphragm is damaged.

c. Reverse to install the diaphragm cover.

5. Inspect the reed valve as follows.

a. Remove the reed valve cover screws and remove the cover (**Figure 107**).

b. Lift the reed valve (**Figure 108**) out of the housing.

c. Inspect the reed valve (**Figure 109**) for fatigue or cracks. Then check that there is no clearance between the reed valve and seat. If there is clearance, check for debris that may be holding the valve open. If there is no debris, replace the reed valve assembly. Also check the reed valve rubber seat for cracks or damage. If any wear or damage is identified, replace the reed valve as an assembly. Do not attempt replacement of the reed only.

d. Install the reed valve by reversing these steps.

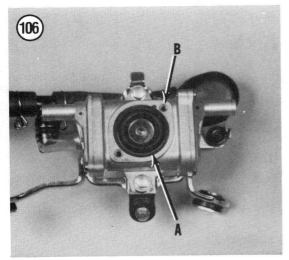

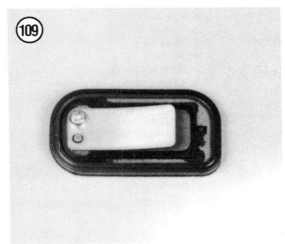

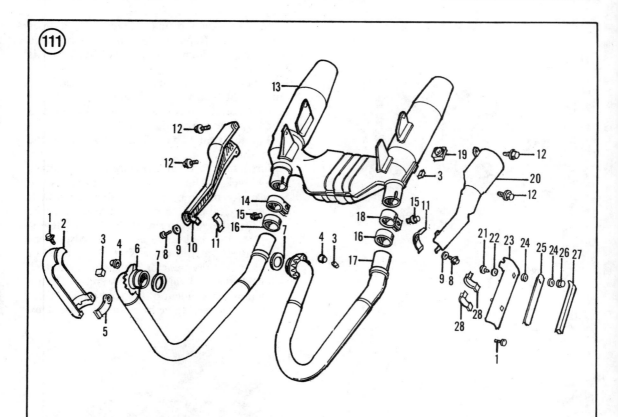

**EXHAUST SYSTEM
(1986-ON)**

1. Bolt
2. Protector
3. Packing
4. Nut
5. Clamp
6. Exhaust pipe (rear cylinder)
7. Gasket
8. Bolt
9. Washer
10. Protector
11. Protector band
12. Bolt
13. Muffler/power chamber assembly
14. Clamp

15. Screw
16. Gasket
17. Exhaust pipe (front cylinder)
18. Clamp
19. Rubber stopper
20. Protector
21. Screw
22. Washer
23. Protector
24. Washer
25. Protector
26. Nut
27. Protector
28. Clamp

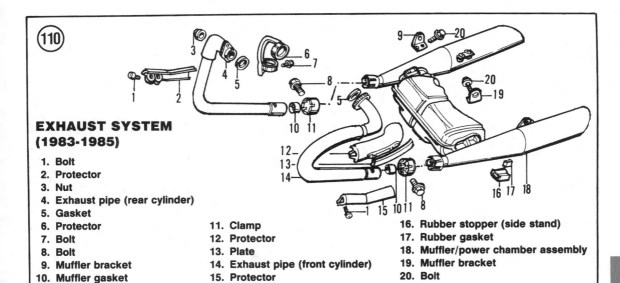

**EXHAUST SYSTEM
(1983-1985)**

1. Bolt
2. Protector
3. Nut
4. Exhaust pipe (rear cylinder)
5. Gasket
6. Protector
7. Bolt
8. Bolt
9. Muffler bracket
10. Muffler gasket
11. Clamp
12. Protector
13. Plate
14. Exhaust pipe (front cylinder)
15. Protector
16. Rubber stopper (side stand)
17. Rubber gasket
18. Muffler/power chamber assembly
19. Muffler bracket
20. Bolt

6

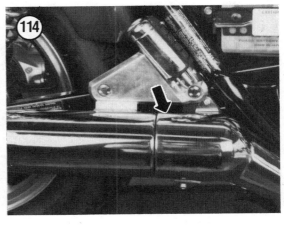

EXHAUST SYSTEM

The exhaust system consists of 2 exhaust pipes, a common collector and 2 mufflers.

Removal/Installation

Refer to **Figure 110** (1983-1985) or **Figure 111** (1986-on) for this procedure.

1. Place the bike on the centerstand.
2. To remove the exhaust pipe from the front cylinder, perform the following.
   a. Remove the upper protector (**Figure 112**).
   b. Remove the nuts (**Figure 113**) securing the right-hand exhaust pipe flange to the cylinder head.
   c. Slide the flange down.
   d. On 1986-on models, remove the lower protector (**Figure 114**).

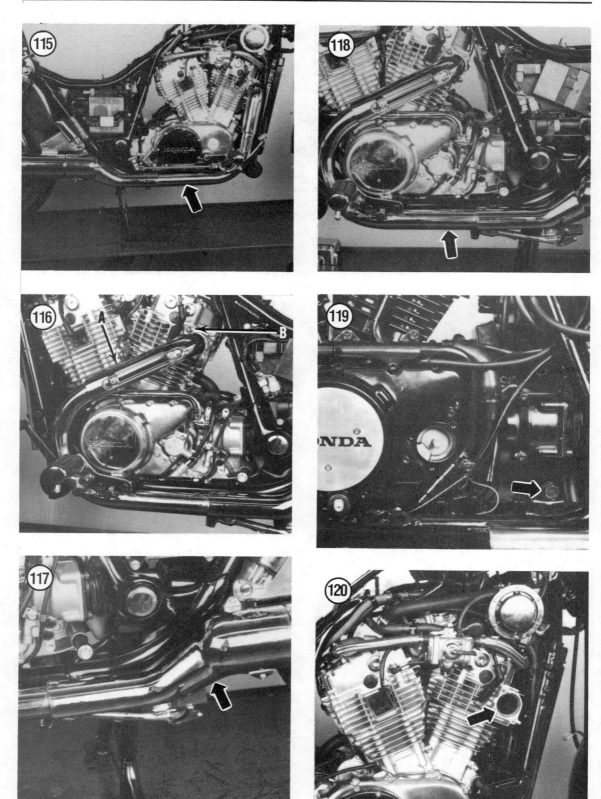

e. Loosen the clamping bolt securing the exhaust pipe to the power chamber.

f. Remove the right-hand exhaust pipe (**Figure 115**).

3. To remove the exhaust pipe from the rear cylinder, perform the following.

    a. Remove the upper protector (A, **Figure 116**).

    b. Remove the nuts (B, **Figure 116**) securing the left-hand exhaust pipe flange to the cylinder head.

    c. Slide the flange down.

    d. Remove the lower cover (**Figure 117**).

    e. Remove the left-hand exhaust pipe (**Figure 118**).

4. Remove the bolt (**Figure 119**) on each side securing the power chamber/muffler assembly to the frame. Move the assembly down and out from the frame.

5. Inspect the gaskets at all joints; replace as necessary.

6. Be sure to install a new gasket in each exhaust port in both cylinder heads (**Figure 120**).

7. Apply a light coat of multipurpose grease to the inside surface of the gaskets in the power chamber. This will make insertion of the exhaust pipes into the power chamber easier.

8. Install the assembly into position and install all bolts and nuts only finger-tight until the exhaust flange nuts and washers are installed and securely tightened. This will minimize an exhaust leak at the cylinder heads.

9. Tighten all bolts and nuts to the torque specifications listed in **Table 2**.

10. After installation is complete, make sure there are no exhaust leaks.

6

Tables are on the following page.

Table 1 CARBURETOR SPECIFICATIONS

	1983 VT750C	1984 VT700C
Carburetor model No.	VD7AA	VD7CA
		VD7BA (Calif.)
Main jet number		
Front cylinder	115	120
Rear cylinder	115	120
Slow jet	40	40
Jet needle clip setting	Non-adjustable	Non-adjustable
Float level	7.5 mm (0.30 in.)	7.5 mm (0.30 in.)
Idle speed	900 ±100 rpm	1,000 ±100 rpm
Pilot screw initial setting		
Front cylinder	2 3/4 turns out	2 1/2 turns out
Rear cylinder	2 3/4 turns out	2 1/2 turns out
	1985 VT700C	**1986 VT700C**
Carburetor model No.	VD7CB	VD7CC
	VD7BB (Calif.)	VD7BC (Calif.)
Main jet number		
Front cylinder	120	112
Rear cylinder	120	112
Slow jet	40	40
Jet needle clip setting	Non-adjustable	Non-adjustable
Float level	7.5 mm (0.30 in.)	9.0 mm (0.35 in.)
Idle speed	1,000 ±100 rpm	1,000 ±100 rpm
	1,100 ±100 rpm (Calif.)	
Pilot screw initial setting		
Front cylinder	3 turns out	2 turns out
Rear cylinder	3 turns out	2 turns out
	1987 VT700C	
Carburetor model No.	VDGCA	
	VDGDA (Calif.)	
Main jet number		
Front cylinder	112	
Rear cylinder	112	
Slow jet	38	
Jet needle clip setting	Non-adjustable	
Float level	8.0 mm (0.31 in.)	
Idle speed	1,000 ±100 rpm	
	1,100 ±100 rpm (Calif.)	
Pilot screw initial setting		
Front cylinder	2 turns out	
Rear cylinder	2 turns out	

Table 2 EXHAUST SYSTEM TORQUE SPECIFICATIONS

Item	N•m	ft.-lb.
Exhaust pipe joint nut	8-14	6-10
Muffler clamp bolt	18-28	18-20

CHAPTER SEVEN

ELECTRICAL SYSTEM

The electrical system consists of the following.
a. Charging system
b. Ignition system
c. Lighting system
d. Directional signal system
e. Switches
f. Electrical components

Tables 1-4 are located at the end of this chapter. Wiring diagrams are at the end of the book.

For complete spark plug and battery information, refer to Chapter Three.

CHARGING SYSTEM

The charging system consists of the battery, alternator and a voltage regulator/rectifier. See **Figure 1** (1983-1985) or **Figure 2** (1986-on).

Alternating current generated by the alternator is rectified to direct current. The voltage regulator maintains the voltage to the battery and additional electrical loads (lights, ignition, etc.) at a constant voltage regardless of variations in engine speed and load.

Output Test (1983-1985)

Whenever a charging system trouble is suspected, make sure the battery is fully charged and in good condition before going any further. Clean and test the battery as described in Chapter Three.

Before starting this test, start the bike and let it reach normal operating temperature. Shut off the engine.

1. Remove the left-hand side cover and the seat.

2. Remove the headlight and disconnect the electrical wires going to the bulb.

3. Disconnect the regulator/rectifier 5-pin connector (**Figure 3**). Use a narrow blade screwdriver and carefully push the male end of the black wire out of the connector. Reconnect the connector with the black wire left out in the open, not connected.

NOTE
Do not disconnect either the positive or negative battery cables. They are to remain in the circuit.

4. Connect a 0-10 DC ammeter in line with the main fuse connectors (fusible link) as follows.
   a. Remove the rubber cover (**Figure 4**) on the fusible link.
   b. Loosen the screws securing the fusible link and remove the fusible link.
   c. Install an inline fuse/fuse holder (available at most auto supply or electronic supply stores) along with the ammeter as shown in **Figure 5**.

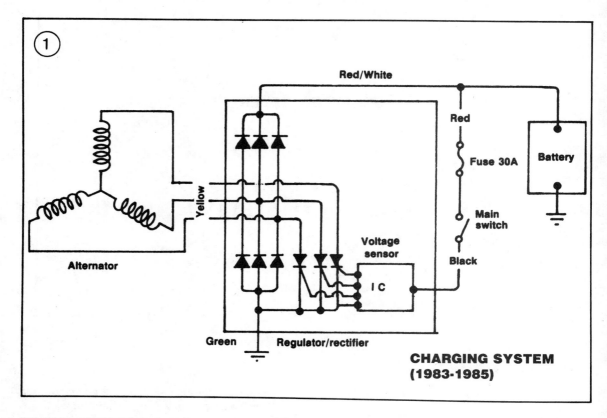

**CHARGING SYSTEM
(1983-1985)**

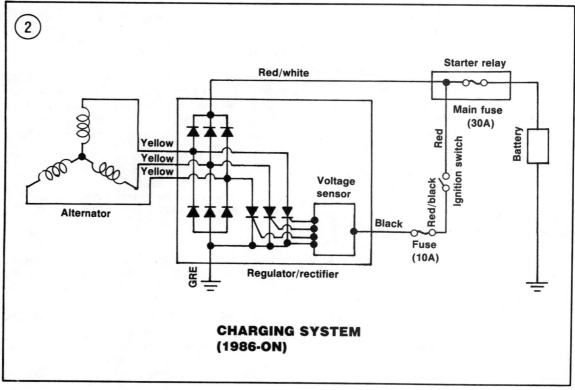

**CHARGING SYSTEM
(1986-ON)**

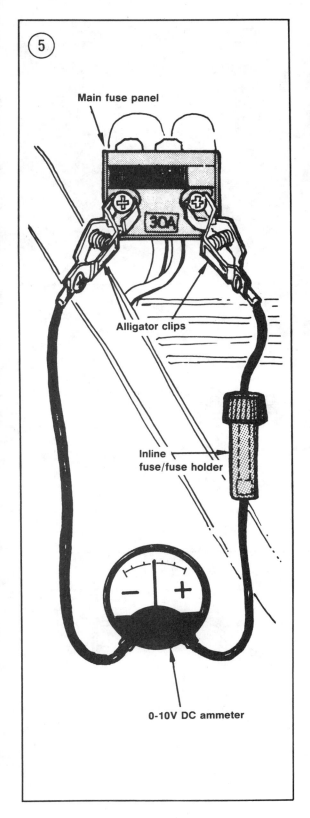

⑤

Main fuse panel

30A

Alligator clips

Inline fuse/fuse holder

0-10V DC ammeter

③

④

7

d. Use alligator clips on the test leads for a good electrical connection.

CAUTION
In order to protect the ammeter, always run the test with the inline fuse in the circuit. Do not try to test the charging system by connecting an ammeter between the positive battery terminal and the starter cable. The ammeter will burn out when the electric starter is operated.

NOTE
During the test, if the needle of the ammeter reads in the opposite direction on the scale, reverse the polarity of the test leads.

5. Start the engine and gradually increase engine speed. Charging amperage should start at 1,000 rpm and should be a minimum of 11.8 amperes. At 5,000 rpm it should be a minimum of 25.6 amperes. If the charging amperage is not within specifications, first check the alternator stator and

then the voltage regulator/rectifier as described in this chapter.

6. Disconnect the ammeter and reinstall the fusible link.

7. Reinstall the headlight and reconnect the black wire to the voltage regulator/rectifier connector.

Output Test (1986-on)

Whenever a charging system trouble is suspected, make sure the battery is fully charged and in good condition before going any further. Clean and test the battery as described in Chapter Three.

1. Before making the output test on these models, check the battery for voltage leakage as follows.

   a. Remove the right-hand side cover.

   b. Turn the ignition switch to OFF.

   c. Remove the negative battery cable (**Figure 6**).

   d. Connect a 0-15 volt DC voltmeter between the negative battery terminal and the negative battery cable (**Figure 7**).

   e. The voltmeter should read 0 volts. If any other volt reading is obtained, replace the battery.

   f. Reconnect the negative battery cable at the negative battery terminal.

2. If the battery tested correctly in Step 1 or if the battery was replaced, perform the following.

3. Start the engine and let it reach normal operating temperature. Turn the engine off.

4. Leave the battery wires connected to the battery and connect a 0-15 volt DC voltmeter between the battery terminals (**Figure 8**).

> *CAUTION*
> *Make sure the positive voltmeter cable does not touch any component on the frame.*

5. Start the engine and let it idle. Gradually increase engine speed to 5,000 rpm. At 5,000 rpm, the voltmeter should read 13-16 volts. If the output voltage is not within specifications, first check the alternator-to-battery wire harness for loose or damaged connectors. If the wire harness connectors are correct, check the alternator stator and then the voltage regulator/rectifier as described in this chapter.

6. Disconnect the voltmeter and reinstall the right-hand side cover.

ALTERNATOR

An alternator is a form of electrical generator in which a magnetized field called a rotor revolves within a set of stationary coils called a stator. As the rotor revolves, alternating current is induced in

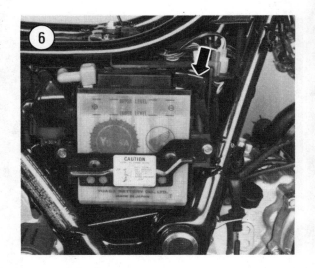

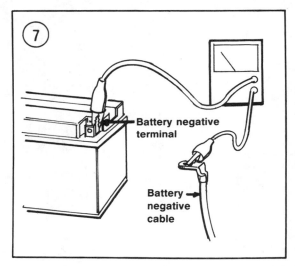

Battery negative terminal

Battery negative cable

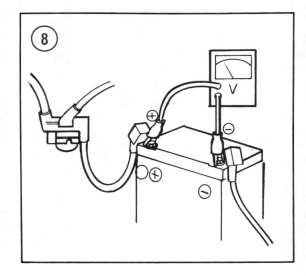

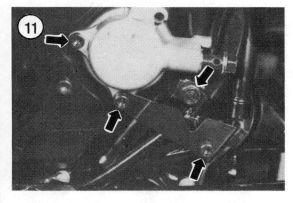

the stator. The current is then rectified to direct current and used to operate the electrical accessories on the motorcycle and to charge the battery. The rotor is permanently magnetized.

Rotor removal and installation procedures are covered in Chapter Four.

Rotor Testing

The rotor is permanently magnetized and cannot be tested except by replacement with a rotor known to be good. A rotor can lose magnetism from old age or a sharp blow. If defective, the rotor must be replaced. It cannot be remagnetized.

Stator Removal/Installation

1. Place the bike on the centerstand.
2. Remove both side covers and the seat.
3. Disconnect the battery negative lead.
4A. *1983-1985:* Disconnect the electrical connector (**Figure 9**) going to the alternator stator assembly.
4B. *1986-on:* Remove the fuel pump stay. Then disconnect the electrical connector (**Figure 10**) going to the alternator stator assembly.
5. Remove the screws securing the left-hand rear crankcase cover and remove the cover.
6. Remove the exhaust system from the rear cylinder as described in Chapter Six.
7. Remove the bolt securing the gearshift pedal and remove the pedal.
8. Remove the bolts securing the left-hand front footpeg and remove the footpeg.

> *NOTE*
> *In the following step it is not necessary to disconnect the hydraulic line from the clutch slave cylinder. If the hydraulic line is disconnected the clutch system must be bled.*

9. Remove the bolts (**Figure 11**) securing the clutch slave cylinder and bracket. Remove the bracket and pull the clutch slave cylinder, with the hydraulic line still attached, back and out of the way.
10. Remove the bolts securing the coolant pipe protector (A, **Figure 12**) and remove the protector.
11. Remove the bolts securing the alternator cover (B, **Figure 12**) and remove the cover, gasket and the electrical harness from the frame. Note the path of the wire harness as it must be routed the same during installation.
12. Remove the electrical harness from the clips on the frame.

13. Remove the bolt and wire clamp (A, **Figure 13**) securing the wire to the housing.

14. Remove the bolts (**Figure 14**) securing the alternator stator to the alternator cover.

15. Carefully pull the rubber grommet (B, **Figure 13**) and electrical wire harness from the alternator cover.

16. Install by reversing these removal steps, noting the following.

17. Be sure to install the wire clamp. If the clamp is left off the rotor may rub against the wires, wear off the insulation and cause a short in the circuit.

Stator Testing
(1983-1985)

1. Remove both side covers and the seat.

2. Disconnect the 3-pin alternator electrical connector (**Figure 9**).

3. Use an ohmmeter set on R×1 and check continuity between each yellow terminal. Replace the stator if any yellow terminal shows no continuity to any other. This would indicate an open in the winding.

4. Use an ohmmeter and check for continuity between each yellow terminal and ground. Replace the stator if any of the terminals show continuity to ground. This would indicate a short within a winding.

> *NOTE*
> *Before replacing the stator with a new one, check the electrical wires to and within the terminal connector for any opens or poor connections.*

Stator Testing
(1986-on)

1. Remove the fuel pump stay. Then disconnect the electrical connector (**Figure 10**) going to the alternator stator assembly.

> *NOTE*
> *The following tests should be made when the stator is at an approximate temperature of 68° F (20° C).*

2. Use an ohmmeter set at R×1 and check resistance between each yellow terminal. The correct resistance reading is 0.3-0.5 ohms. Replace the stator if the resistance reading for any yellow terminal tested incorrectly.

3. Use an ohmmeter and check for continuity between each yellow terminal and ground. Replace the stator if any of the terminals show continuity to

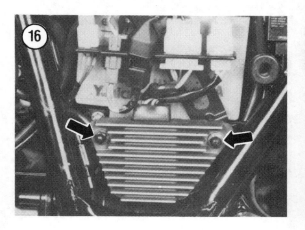

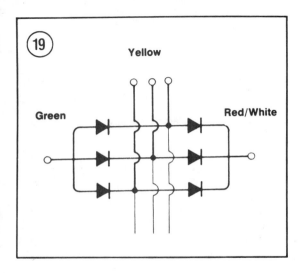

Yellow

Green

Red/White

ground. This would indicate a short within a winding.

NOTE
Before replacing the stator with a new one, check the electrical wires to and within the terminal connector for any opens or poor connections.

VOLTAGE REGULATOR/RECTIFIER

**Removal/Installation
(1983-1985)**

1. Remove both side covers and the seat.
2. Disconnect the battery negative lead.
3. Disconnect the 2 electrical connectors. One connector contains 5 wires and the other contains 3 wires (**Figure 15**).
4. Remove the bolts securing the voltage regulator/rectifier to the battery holder and remove the voltage regulator/rectifier (**Figure 16**).
5. Carefully pull the voltage regulator/rectifier and the 2 electrical connectors and wires out from the frame.
6. Install by reversing these removal steps. Make sure all electrical connections are tight.

**Removal/Installation
(1986-on)**

1. Remove the left-hand side cover.
2. Remove the battery as described in Chapter Three.
3. Disconnect the group of connectors shown in **Figure 17**.
4. Disconnect the starter motor cable and the main fuse connector at the starter relay switch (**Figure 18**).
5. Remove the battery case from the frame.
6. Remove the voltage regulator/rectifier and the 2 electrical wires from the battery case.
7. Install by reversing these steps. Make sure all electrical connections are tight.

Testing

To test the voltage regulator/rectifier, disconnect the 2 electrical connectors from the harness. One connector contains 5 wires and the other contains 3 wires. See **Figure 15** (1983-1985) or **Figure 17** (1986-on).

Make the following measurements using an ohmmeter and referring to **Figure 19**. These are the only measurements Honda specifies.

NOTE
The following tests are set up for a positive ground ohmmeter. If a negative ground ohmmeter is used, the test results will be the opposite.

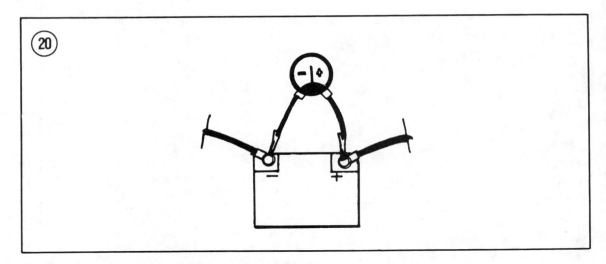

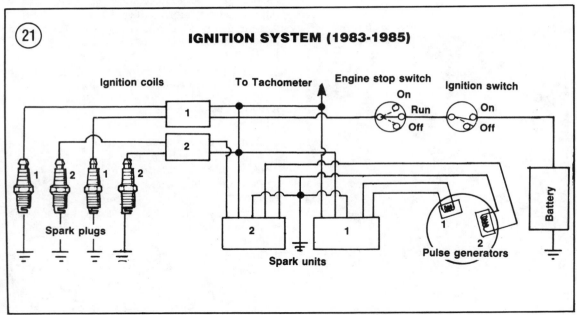

IGNITION SYSTEM (1983-1985)

Ignition coils

To Tachometer

Engine stop switch
On
Run
Off

Ignition switch
On
Off

Spark plugs

Spark units

Pulse generators

Battery

1. Connect the positive (+) ohmmeter lead to the yellow lead and the negative (–) ohmmeter lead to the green lead. There should be continuity (low resistance).

2. Reverse the ohmmeter leads and repeat Step 1. This time there should be no continuity (infinite resistance).

3. Connect the positive (+) ohmmeter lead to the red/white lead and the negative (–) ohmmeter lead to the yellow lead. There should be continuity (low resistance).

4. Reverse the ohmmeter leads and repeat Step 3. This time there should be no continuity (infinite resistance).

5. If the voltage regulator/rectifier fails to pass any of these tests, the unit is defective and must be replaced.

Voltage Regulator Performance Test (1983-1985)

Connect a voltmeter to the battery negative and positive terminals (**Figure 20**). Leave the battery cables attached. Start the engine and let it idle. Increase engine speed until the voltage going to the battery reaches 14.0-15.0 volts. At this point, the voltage regulator/rectifier should prevent any further increase in voltage. If this does not happen and voltage increases above specifications, the

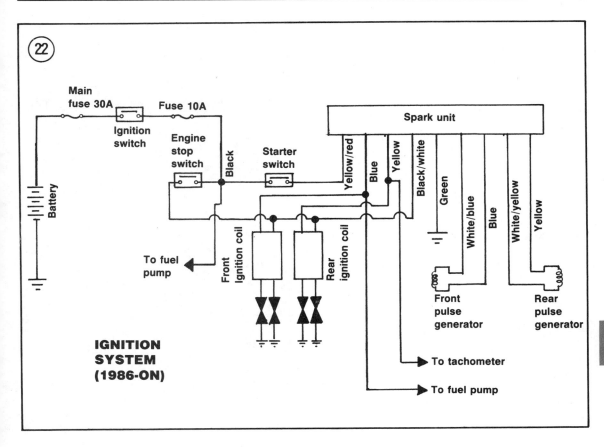

IGNITION
SYSTEM
(1986-ON)

voltage regulator/rectifier is faulty and must be replaced.

IGNITION SYSTEM

The ignition system consists of 2 ignition coils, 2 spark units, 2 ignition pulse generators and 4 spark plugs, (2 spark plugs per cylinder). Refer to **Figure 21** (1983-1985) or **Figure 22** (1986-on) for a diagram of the ignition circuit.

The V-twins are equipped with a solid state capacitor discharge ignition (CDI) system that uses no breaker points. This system provides a longer life for components and delivers a more efficient spark throughout the entire speed range of the engine. Ignition timing is fixed with no means of adjustment. If ignition timing is incorrect it is due to a faulty unit within the ignition system.

Direct current charges the capacitor. As the piston approaches the firing position, a pulse from the pulse generator coil triggers the silicone controlled rectifier. The rectifier in turn allows the capacitor to discharge quickly into the primary circuit of the ignition coil, where the voltage is stepped up in the secondary circuit to a value sufficient to fire the spark plugs. Both spark plugs

in the same cylinder will fire at the same time. The distribution of the pulses from the pulse generators is controlled by the rotation of the pulse generator plate that is attached to the primary drive gear.

CDI Precautions

Certain measures must be taken to protect the capacitor discharge system. Instantaneous damage to the semiconductors in the system will occur if the following precautions are not observed.

1. Never connect the battery backwards. If the connected battery polarity is wrong, damage will occur to the voltage regulator/rectifier, the alternator and the spark units.

2. Do not disconnect the battery when the engine is running. A voltage surge will occur which will damage the voltage regulator/rectifier and possibly burn out the lights.

3. Keep all connections between the various units clean and tight. Be sure the wiring connections are pushed together firmly to help keep out moisture.

4. Do not substitute another type of ignition coil.

5. Each component is mounted within a rubber vibration isolator. Always be sure that the isolator is in place when installing any units in the system.

CDI Troubleshooting

Problems with the capacitor discharge system usually result in a weak spark or no spark at all.

1. Check all connections to make sure they are tight and free of corrosion.

2. Check the ignition coils as described in this chapter.

3A. *1983-1985:* Check the ignition pulse generator coils with an ohmmeter.

   a. Remove the seat, both side covers and the fuel tank.

   b. Disconnect the 4-pin ignition pulse generator electrical connector (**Figure 23**).

   c. Connect the ohmmeter leads between the white and the yellow leads (rear cylinder) and then between the white and the blue leads (front cylinder).

   d. The resistance for each coil should be 432-528 ohms at 68° F (20° C). If the pulse generator coils do not meet these specifications, the ignition pulse generator assembly must be replaced as described in this chapter. It cannot be serviced.

3B. *1986-on:* Check the ignition pulse generator coils with an ohmmeter.

   a. Remove the left-hand side cover.

   b. Disconnect the 4-pin ignition pulse generator electrical connector (**Figure 17**). The connector housing is white and contains 4 wires.

   c. Connect the ohmmeter leads between the white/yellow and yellow leads (rear cylinder) and then between the white/blue and the blue leads (front cylinder).

   d. The resistance for each coil should be 450-550 ohms at 68° F (20° C). If the pulse generator coils do not meet these specifications the ignition pulse generator assembly must be replaced as described in this chapter. It cannot be serviced.

4. If the ignition coils and ignition pulse generator assembly check out okay, the spark units are at fault and must be replaced.

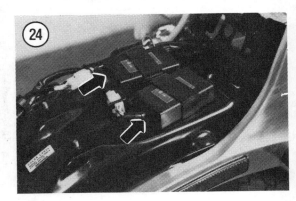

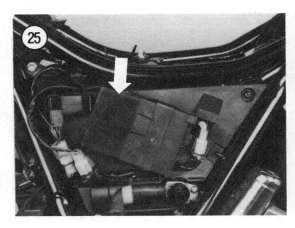

SPARK UNIT

Replacement (1983-1985)

1. Remove the seat and both side covers.

2. Disconnect the electrical connectors going to the spark units.

3. Unhook the rubber straps securing the spark units.

4. Remove the spark units (**Figure 24**) from the rear fender.

5. Install by reversing these removal steps. Make sure all electrical connections are tight and free of corrosion.

Replacement (1986-on)

1. Remove the left-hand side cover.

2. Disconnect the electrical connectors at the spark unit and remove the spark unit (**Figure 25**).

3. Install by reversing these removal steps. Make sure all electrical connections are tight and free of corrosion.

3. Disconnect the spark plug leads (**Figure 26**).
4. Remove the plastic trim panels on the right- and left-hand side of the steering head.
5. Disconnect the primary wire connectors for both coils. The front cylinder's wires are blue and black/white; the rear cylinder's wires are yellow and black/white.
6. Remove the bolts securing the ignition coils and bracket (**Figure 27**) to the frame and remove both coils.
7. Install by reversing these removal steps. Note the following.
8. Make sure all electrical connections are tight and free of corrosion.
9. Route the spark plug wires to the correct cylinder. Each stock spark plug wire is numbered adjacent to the spark plug rubber boot.

Dynamic Test

Disconnect the high voltage lead from one of the spark plugs. Remove the spark plug from the cylinder head. Connect a new or known good spark plug to the high voltage lead and place the spark plug base on a good ground like the engine cylinder head. Position the spark plug so you can see the electrodes.

> *WARNING*
> *If it is necessary to hold the high voltage lead, do so with an insulated pair of pliers. The high voltage generated could produce serious or fatal shocks.*

Push the starter button to turn the engine over a couple of times. If a fat blue spark occurs the coil is in good condition; if not, it must be replaced. Make sure that you are using a known good spark plug for this test. If the spark plug used is defective the test results will be incorrect.

Reinstall the spark plug in the cylinder head.

Continuity Test

1. Use an ohmmeter set at $R \times 10$ and measure between the 2 primary connector lugs on the coil. The specified resistance is:
   a. 1983-1985: 2.0 ohms
   b. 1986-on: 2.0-2.2 ohms
2. Use an ohmmeter set at $R \times 1,000$ and measure between the 2 secondary leads (spark plug leads) with the spark plug caps in place. The specified resistance is:
   a. 1983-1985: 29,000-40,000 ohms
   b. 1986-on: 27,000-37,000 ohms
3. Use an ohmmeter set at $R \times 10$ and measure between the 2 secondary leads (spark plug leads)

Testing

Honda does not provide test procedures or specifications for the spark units. If the ignition coils, the pulse generator assembly and the wiring harness are good and the ignition timing is not within specifications, replace the spark units with known good units.

IGNITION COIL

There are 2 ignition coils; one fires the plugs for the front cylinder and the other fires the plugs for the rear cylinder.

The ignition coil is a form of transformer which develops the high voltage required to jump the spark plug gap. The only maintenance required is that of keeping the electrical connections clean and tight and occasionally checking to see that the coils are mounted securely.

Removal/Installation

1. Remove both side covers, seat and fuel tank.
2. Disconnect the battery negative lead.

7

with the spark plugs removed. The specified resistance is:

    a. 1983-1985: 20,600-27,400 ohms

    b. 1986-on: 19,000-25,000 ohms

4. If the coil(s) pass the test in Step 3 but failed Step 2, the spark plug caps may be faulty. Disconnect the spark plug leads from the ignition coil. Use an ohmmeter and check for continuity through the spark plug cap. There should be continuity, although resistance should be high. If there is no continuity, the spark plug cap is faulty and must be replaced.

5. If the coil(s) fail to pass any of these tests the coil should be replaced.

PULSE GENERATOR

Removal/Installation

1. Drain the engine oil as described in Chapter Three.

2. Remove the seat and both side covers.

3. Remove the main fuel tank as described in Chapter Six.

4. Remove the clutch as described under *Clutch Removal/Installation* in Chapter Five.

5. Disconnect the 4-pin ignition pulse generator electrical connector.

6. Remove the bolts securing each pulse generator (A, **Figure 28**) to the crankcase.

7. Remove the bolt (B, **Figure 28**) securing the wiring harness clip and remove the clip.

8. Carefully remove the rubber grommet (C, **Figure 28**) and electrical wires from the crankcase and remove the assembly from the frame.

9. Install by reversing these removal steps, noting the following.

10. *1986-on:* Turn the crankshaft clockwise and align the pulse generator magnet (A, **Figure 29**) with the pulse generator rotor tip (B, **Figure 29**). Measure the distance (air gap) as shown in **Figure 30** with a feeler gauge. The correct air gap is 0.3-0.7 mm (0.012-0.028 in.). If necessary, loosen the mounting bolts and reposition the pulse generator. Tighten the bolts securely.

11. Make sure the bolts securing the pulse generators are tight and that the wires are routed correctly in the frame.

12. Install the clutch as described in Chapter Five.

13. Refill the engine with the recommended viscosity and quantity of engine oil as described in Chapter Three.

STARTING SYSTEM

The starting system consists of the starter motor, starter gears, solenoid and the starter button.

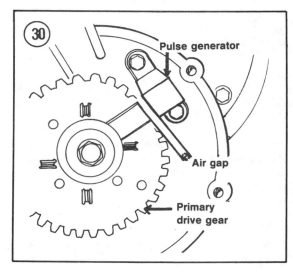

Pulse generator

Air gap

Primary drive gear

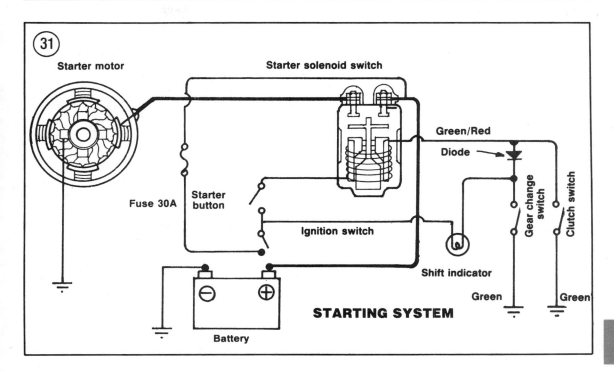

STARTING SYSTEM

7

The layout of the starting system is shown in **Figure 31**. When the starter button is pressed, it allows current flow through the solenoid coil. The coil contacts close, allowing electricity to flow from the battery to the starter motor.

> *CAUTION*
> *Do not operate the starter for more than 5 seconds at a time. Let it rest approximately 10 seconds, then use it again.*

The starter gears and starter clutch assembly are covered in Chapter Four.

Table 1, at the end of the chapter, lists possible starter problems, probable causes and most common remedies.

STARTER

Removal/Installation

1. Place the bike on the centerstand.
2. Remove the seat and both side covers.
3. Disconnect the battery negative lead.
4. On 1984-1985 700 cc models, slide the taillight sensor (A, **Figure 32**) out of the rubber mount just behind the starter motor.
5. Disconnect the electric starter cable from the starter (B, **Figure 32**).
6. Remove the bolts (**Figure 33**) securing the starter to the crankcase.

NOTE
*Figure 33 is shown with the engine
removed and partially disassembled for
clarity.*

7. Pull the starter to the right and remove the
starter from the crankcase.
8. Install by reversing these removal steps. Make
sure the electrical wire connections is tight and free
of corrosion.

Disassembly/Inspection/Assembly

The overhaul of a starter motor is best left to an
expert. This procedure shows how to detect a
defective starter.
1. Remove the case screws and separate the case
and covers.

NOTE
*Write down the number of shims used
on the shaft next to the commutator. Be
sure to install the same number when
reassembling the starter.*

2. Clean all grease, dirt and carbon from the
armature, case and end covers.

CAUTION
*Do not immerse brushes or the wire
windings in solvent as the insulation
may be damaged. Wipe the windings
with a cloth lightly moistened with
solvent and dry thoroughly.*

3. Measure the length of each brush (**Figure 34**)
with a vernier caliper. If the length is 6.5 mm (0.26
in.) or less for any one of the brushes, the brush
holder assembly and cable terminal and brush
assembly must be replaced. The brushes cannot be
replaced individually.
4. To replace the brushes, perform the following.

NOTE
*Before removing the nuts and washers,
write down their description and order.
They must be reinstalled in the same
order to insulate this set of brushes
from the case.*

a. Remove the nuts, washers and O-ring (A,
Figure 35) securing the cable terminal and
brush assembly.
b. Slide the armature and brush holder
assemblies partially out of the case.
c. Remove the old brush holders and install new
brush holders.
d. Slide the armature and brush holder
assemblies back into the case.

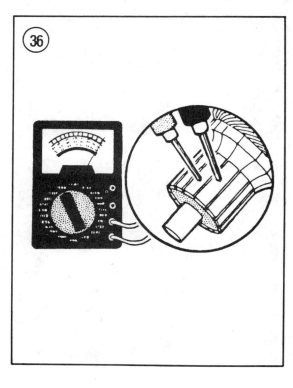

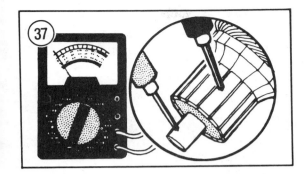

e. Install the nuts and washers in the original order to secure the cable terminal and brush assembly.

5. Inspect the commutator. The mica in a good commutator is below the surface of the copper bars. On a worn commutator the mica and copper bars may be worn to the same level. If necessary, have the commutator serviced by a dealer or electrical repair shop.

6. Inspect the commutator copper bars for discoloration. If a pair of bars are discolored, grounded armature coils are indicated.

7. Use an ohmmeter and check for continuity between the commutator bars (**Figure 36**). There should be continuity between pairs of bars. Also check for continuity between the commutator bars and the shaft (**Figure 37**). There should be no continuity. If the unit fails either of these tests the armature is faulty and must be replaced.

8. Use an ohmmeter and check for continuity between the starter cable terminal and the starter case. There should be no continuity (infinite resistance). Also check for continuity between the starter cable terminal and each brush wire terminal. There should be continuity (low resistance). If the unit fails either of these tests the case/field coil assembly must be replaced.

9. Assemble the case as follows.

   a. Align the pin in the brush holder with the notch in the case (**Figure 38**).

   b. Align the slot in the rear cover (B, **Figure 35**) with the pin on the brush holder (C, **Figure 35**).

   c. Align the marks on the case and end covers (**Figure 39**) and install the case screws.

10. Inspect the gear and O-ring seal (**Figure 40**). If the gear is chipped or worn, the armature must be replaced. Replace the O-ring if it has hardened or is starting to deteriorate.

STARTER SOLENOID

Removal/Installation

1. Remove the seat and both side covers.

2. Disconnect the negative battery lead.

3. Slide off the rubber protective boots and disconnect the electrical wires from the top solenoid terminals.

4. Remove the solenoid from the rubber mounting receptacle on the frame. See **Figure 41** (1983-1985) or **Figure 42** (1986-on).

5. Install by reversing these removal steps, noting the following.

6. If installing a new solenoid, transfer the fuse holder from the old solenoid to the new solenoid.

CLUTCH DIODE

Testing

1. Remove the seat and right-hand side cover.
2. Disconnect the clutch diode from the wire harness.
3. Use an ohmmeter and check for continuity between the 2 terminals on the clutch diode. There should be continuity (low resistance) in the normal direction and no continuity (infinite resistance) in the reverse direction. Replace the diode if it fails this test.

LIGHTING SYSTEM

The lighting system consists of a headlight, taillight/brake light combination, turn signals, indicator lights and meter illumination lights. **Table 2** lists replacement bulbs for these components.

Always use the correct wattage bulb as indicated in this section. The use of a larger wattage bulb will give a dim light and a smaller wattage bulb will burn out prematurely.

Headlight Replacement

The headlight is equipped with a quartz halogen bulb. Special handling of the quartz halogen bulb is required as specified in this procedure.

Refer to **Figure 43** (1983-1985) or **Figure 44** (1986-on) for this procedure.

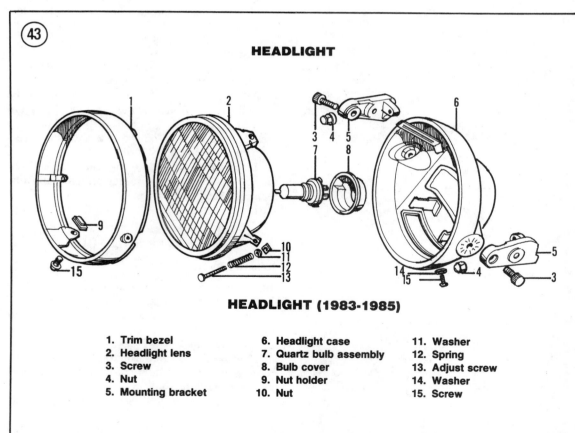

HEADLIGHT

HEADLIGHT (1983-1985)

1. Trim bezel
2. Headlight lens
3. Screw
4. Nut
5. Mounting bracket
6. Headlight case
7. Quartz bulb assembly
8. Bulb cover
9. Nut holder
10. Nut
11. Washer
12. Spring
13. Adjust screw
14. Washer
15. Screw

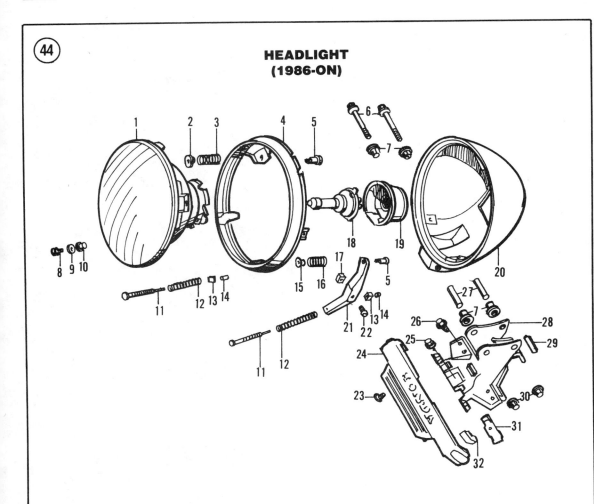

**HEADLIGHT
(1986-ON)**

1. Headlight lens	17. Nut
2. Nut	18. Quartz bulb assembly
3. Spring	19. Bulb holder
4. Trim bezel	20. Headlight case
5. Screw	21. Headlight stay
6. Bolt	22. Screw
7. Nut	23. Screw
8. Screw	24. Cover
9. Washer	25. Nut
10. Spacer	26. Bolt
11. Beam adjusting screw	27. Bushing
12. Spring	28. Headlight stay
13. Nut	29. Grommet
14. Cover	30. Nut
15. Nut	31. Guide
16. Spring	32. Guide

7

1. Remove the screw (**Figure 45**) on each side of the bottom of the trim bezel securing the headlight assembly.

2. Pull out on the bottom of the headlight assembly and disengage it from the locating tab on top of the headlight housing.

3. Disconnect the electrical connector from the headlight lens unit.

> *CAUTION*
> *Carefully read all instructions shipped with the replacement quartz halogen bulb. Do not touch the bulb glass with your fingers. Any traces of oil on the glass will drastically reduce the life of the bulb. Clean any traces of oil from the bulb with a cloth moistened in alcohol or lacquer thinner.*

4. Remove the bulb cover (**Figure 46**).

5. Remove the set spring and the bulb (**Figure 47**).

6. Replace with a new bulb assembly. Do not touch the bulb with your fingers. Assemble by reversing this sequence.

7. Install by reversing these removal steps.

8. Adjust the headlight as described in this chapter.

**Headlight Housing
Removal/Installation
(1983-1985)**

Refer to **Figure 43** for this procedure.

1. Remove the headlight (A, **Figure 48**) as described in this chapter.

2. Disconnect all electrical connectors within the headlight housing.

3. Carefully withdraw the electrical connectors through the headlight housing.

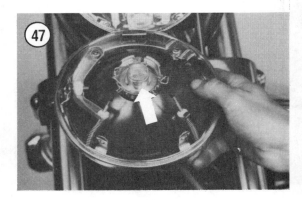

4. Remove the Allen bolts and nuts (B, **Figure 48**) on each side securing the headlight case assembly to the case mounting brackets on the forks. Remove the housing.

5. To remove the assembly mounting brackets, disconnect all electrical connectors to the front turn signals. Remove the cap nut securing each headlight bracket/turn signal assembly and remove each assembly from the upper fork bridge.

6. Install by reversing these removal steps, noting the following.

7. Install the headlight bracket/turn signal bracket and align the index mark on the bracket with the index mark on the upper fork bridge.

8. Before installing the headlight lens assembly, check out the operation of the following items controlled by the electrical connections in the headlight housing.

a. Headlight

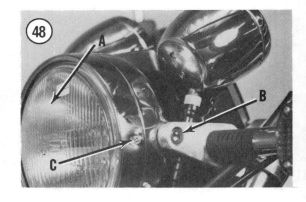

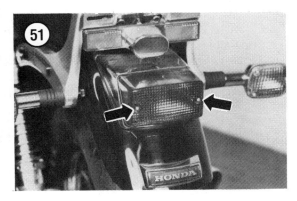

b. Right and left turn signals

9. For a preliminary adjustment, locate the headlight case so the index marks on the case and the bracket align.

10. Adjust the headlight as described in this chapter.

Headlight Housing Removal/Installation (1986-on)

Refer to **Figure 44** for this procedure.

1. Remove the headlight as described in this chapter.

2. Disconnect and remove all wiring and connectors from the headlight housing.

3. Remove the 2 headlight housing bolts at the bottom of the headlight housing.

4. Remove the headlight housing.

5. Install by reversing these steps.

6. Adjust the headlight as described in this chapter.

Headlight Adjustment

Adjust the headlight horizontally and vertically according to Department of Motor Vehicles regulations in your state.

1. *Horizontal adjustment:* Turn the screw on the left-hand side of the headlight trim bezel. See C, **Figure 48** (1983-1985) or **Figure 49** (1986-on). Turn the screw as required for adjustment.

2. *Vertical adjustment:* Perform the following.

    a. 1983-1985: Loosen the Allen bolts (B, **Figure 48**) on each side of the headlight assembly. Position the headlight correctly. Retighten the Allen bolts.

    b. 1986-on: Turn the screw on the right-hand side of the headlight trim bezel (**Figure 50**) as required for adjustment.

Taillight/Brake Light Replacement

1. Remove the screws securing the lens and remove the lens (**Figure 51**).

2. Wash the inside and outside of the lens with a mild detergent and wipe dry. Wipe off the reflective base surrounding the bulbs with a soft cloth.

3. Inspect the lens gasket and replace if it is damaged or deteriorated.

4. Replace the bulb and install the lens. Do not overtighten the screws as the lens may crack.

Turn Signal Light Replacement

1. Remove the screws securing the lens and remove the lens (**Figure 52**).

7

2. Wash the inside and outside of the lens with a mild detergent and wipe dry. Wipe off the reflective base surrounding the bulbs with a soft cloth.

3. Inspect the lens gasket and replace if it is damaged or deteriorated.

4. Replace the bulb and install the lens. Do not overtighten the screws as the lens may crack.

Indicator Light Replacement

1. Remove the screw (**Figure 53**) on each side of the indicator panel and remove the panel.

2. Remove the defective bulb(s) (**Figure 54**) and replace with new ones.

3. Install the indicator panel and screws.

Meter Illumination
Light Replacement

1. Remove the instrument cluster as described in this chapter.

2. Remove the screws securing the indicator panel and remove the indicator panel.

> *CAUTION*
> *In the next step do not allow the instruments to remain upside-down any longer than necessary as the needle damping fluid will leak out onto the instrument face and lens.*

3. Turn the instrument cluster upside down on the workbench.

4. Remove the screws securing the fuse holder to the instrument bracket and remove the fuse holder.

5. Remove the Allen bolts securing each instrument to the bracket and remove both instruments.

6. Remove the Phillips screws securing the instrument cover to the instrument. Remove the cover.

7. Carefully pull the socket/bulb assembly out of the backside of the housing.

8. Replace the defective bulb(s).

9. Assemble and install by reversing these disassembly steps.

SWITCHES

Ignition Switch
Removal/Installation
(1983-1985)

1. Remove the left-hand side cover and the seat.

2. Disconnect the battery negative lead.

3. Remove the headlight and case as described in this chapter.

4. Remove the bolt securing the right-hand horn and remove the horn.

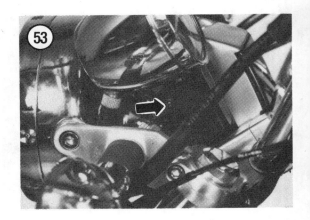

5. Carefully pull the rubber cover from the base of the ignition switch.

6. Remove the screws securing the lower cover on the instrument and remove the lower cover.

7. Remove the screws securing the junction box cover and remove the cover.

8. Disconnect the 2 ignition switch electrical connectors from the junction box.

9. Remove the bolts securing the ignition switch to the upper fork bridge.

10. Install by reversing these removal steps.

Ignition Switch
Removal/Installation
(1986-on)

1. Remove the upper fork bridge as described in Chapter Nine.

2. Remove the ignition switch mounting bolts and remove the switch from the upper fork bridge.

3. Install by reversing these removal steps.

Ignition Switch
Disassembly/Assembly

1. Open the wire clamp on the wire harness at the base of the switch. On 1986-on models, remove the 3 screws.

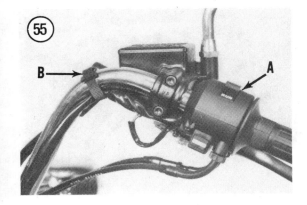

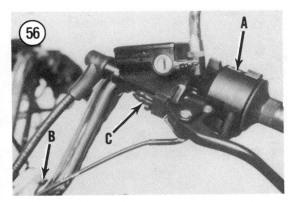

2. Insert the ignition key and turn the tumbler on between the ON and OFF positions. The key must be between the detents.

3. Push in on the lugs of the electrical switch portion, depressing them enough to clear the slots in the mechanical portion of the switch assembly.

4. Withdraw the electrical switch from the mechanical portion of the ignition switch.

5. Replace the defective component.

6. Assemble by reversing these disassembly steps.

Engine Stop Switch and Starter Button
Removal/Installation

The engine stop switch and starter button are an integral part of the right-hand switch assembly. If either of these switches are faulty the entire switch assembly must be replaced.

1. Remove the headlight and headlight case as described in this chapter.

2. Remove the screws securing the junction box cover and remove the cover.

3. Disconnect the 11-pin electrical connector (going to the right-hand switch assembly) from the junction box panel.

4. Remove the screws clamping the right-hand switch assembly together (A, **Figure 55**).

5. Unhook any straps (B, **Figure 55**) securing the electrical wires to the handlebar.

6. Remove the right-hand switch assembly and electrical wires from the frame.

7. Install a new switch by reversing these removal steps. Make sure all electrical connections are tight and free of corrosion.

Headlight Dimmer Switch,
Horn Button and Turn Signal Switch
Removal/Installation

The headlight dimmer switch, horn button and turn signal switch are an integral part of the left-hand switch assembly. If any are faulty, the entire switch assembly must be replaced.

1. Remove the headlight and headlight case as described in this chapter.

2. Remove the screws securing the junction box cover and remove the cover.

3. Disconnect the 11-pin electrical connector (going to the right-hand switch assembly) from the junction box panel.

4. Remove the screws clamping the left-hand switch assembly together (A, **Figure 56**).

5. Unhook any straps (B, **Figure 56**) securing the electrical wires to the handlebar.

6. Remove the left-hand switch assembly and electrical wires from the frame.

7. Install a new switch by reversing these removal steps. Make sure all electrical connections are tight and free of corrosion.

Clutch Switch
Testing/Replacement

1. Disconnect the electrical wires (C, **Figure 56**) from the clutch switch.

2. Use an ohmmeter and check for continuity between the 2 terminals on the clutch switch. There should be no continuity (infinite resistance) with the clutch lever released. With the clutch lever applied there should be continuity (low resistance). If the switch fails either of these tests, the switch must be replaced.

3. Remove the screw securing the clutch switch and remove the clutch switch from the clutch master cylinder.

4. Install a new switch by reversing these removal steps. Make sure all electrical connections are tight and free of corrosion.

Oil Pressure Switch
Testing/Replacement

The oil pressure switch is located on the lower left-hand side of the crankcase just in front of the oil filter.

7

1. Drain the engine oil as described in Chapter Three.

2. Pull back the rubber boot and remove the screw securing the electrical connector to the switch.

3. Unscrew the switch (**Figure 57**) from the upper crankcase.

4. Use an ohmmeter and check for continuity between the electrical connector and the base of the switch. There should be no continuity (infinite resistance) with no pressure applied. With 0.2-0.4 kg/cm2 (2.8-5.6 psi) (1983-1985) or 0.1-0.2 kg/cm2 (1.4-2.8 psi) (1986-on) of air pressure applied to the bottom of the switch there should be continuity (low resistance). If the switch fails either of these tests, the switch must be replaced.

5. Apply a non-hardening gasket sealer to the switch threads. Install the switch and screw it in until there are 2 threads exposed. Then tighten to 15-20 N•m (11-14 ft.-lb.).

6. Attach the electrical wire. Make sure the connection is tight and free from oil.

7. Slide the rubber boot back into position.

8. Refill the engine with the correct type and quantity of engine oil. Refer to Chapter Three.

Thermostatic Switch
Testing/Replacement

The thermostatic switch controls the radiator according to engine coolant temperature.

> *NOTE*
> *If the cooling fan is not operating correctly, make sure that one of the fuses has not blown before starting this test. There is no specific fuse for the fan, so check all fuses. Also clean off any rust or corrosion from the electrical terminals on the thermostatic switch.*

> *NOTE*
> *Use a cooking type thermometer designed for high temperatures. Do not use a medical type thermometer as it is rated for much lower temperatures.*

Thermostatic Switch
Testing/Replacement
(1983-1985)

1. Place the bike on the centerstand.

2. Remove the radiator filler cap and put a thermometer into the coolant.

3. Start the engine and let it idle. When the coolant temperature reaches 80-102° C (176-216° F), the cooling fan should start running. When the coolant temperature cools down to 83-97° C (200-207° F), the fan should stop running.

4. If the fan does not run at the specified temperature, shut the engine off.

5. Disconnect the electrical wires from the back of the thermostatic switch located on the lower left-hand side of the radiator.

6. Place a jumper wire between the black and green electrical wires.

7. Turn the ignition switch to ON. The cooling fan should start running.

8. If the fan now runs, the thermostatic switch is defective and must be replaced.

9. If the fan does not run under any circumstances, either the fan or the wiring to the fan is faulty. Replace the fan if the wiring checks out okay.

10. Turn the ignition switch to OFF.

11. Drain the cooling system as described in Chapter Three.

12. Pull back the rubber boot (**Figure 58**) and carefully unscrew the switch from the radiator.

> *NOTE*
> ***Figure 58*** *is shown with the radiator removed for clarity. It is easier but not necessary to remove the radiator in order to remove the thermostatic switch.*

13. Install a new O-ring seal on the switch and install the switch into the radiator.

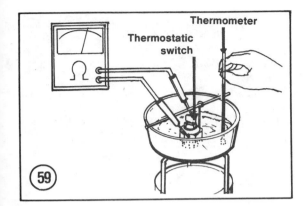

3. Place a jumper wire between the black/blue wire and ground.

4. Turn the ignition switch to ON. The cooling fan should start running.

5. If the fan now runs, perform Step 6. If the fan does not run, check for a blown fuse, loose connectors or an open circuit.

6. Check the thermostatic switch as follows.

   a. Drain the cooling system as described in Chapter Three.

   b. Remove the thermostatic switch from the radiator.

   c. Place the thermostatic switch in a pan filled with a 50/50 mixture of antifreeze and water. Suspend the switch with a rod as shown in **Figure 59** so that the coolant is below the switch threads.

   d. Place a thermometer in the pan (use a cooking thermometer that is rated higher than the test temperature). Check switch continuity with an ohmmeter as shown in **Figure 59**. With the coolant mixture at room temperature, the switch should have no continuity (infinity).

   e. Heat the coolant to 199-207° F (93-97° C). The switch should show continuity. Continue to heat the coolant for 3 minutes to make sure the continuity reading is maintained.

   f. Replace the thermostatic switch if it failed either of the previous test(s).

7. Install the thermostatic switch if removed.

8. Install all items removed.

9. Refill the cooling system with the recommended type and quantity of coolant. Refer to Chapter Three.

Temperature Sensor
Testing/Replacement
(1983-1985)

The engine must be cold for this test, preferably not operated for 12 hours.

1. Remove the seat and side covers.

2. Remove the main fuel tank as described in Chapter Six.

3. Remove the radiator filler cap cover (**Figure 60**) from the side of the steering head.

4. Disconnect the green/blue electrical wire from the temperature sensor located on the thermostat housing (**Figure 61**).

14. Install all items removed.

15. Refill the cooling system with the recommended type and quantity of coolant. Refer to Chapter Three.

Thermostatic Switch
Testing/Replacement
(1986-on)

If the fan does not run, perform the following.

1. Place the bike on the centerstand.

2. Disconnect the electrical wires from the back of the thermostatic switch located on the lower left-hand side of the radiator.

NOTE
Use a cooking type thermometer designed for high temperatures. Do not use a medical type thermometer as it is rated for much lower temperatures.

5. Remove the radiator filler cap and put a thermometer into the coolant.

6. Check the temperature of the coolant.

7. Start the engine and let it idle. Use an ohmmeter and check resistance between the terminal on the temperature sensor and ground. As the coolant temperature increases, compare to the temperature and resistance values listed in **Table 3**.

8. If the resistance values do not match those listed in **Table 3**, the sensor must be replaced.

9. If faulty, remove the temperature sensor from the thermostat housing.

10. Apply a non-hardening sealer to the threads and install the temperature sensor.

11. Connect the electrical wires to the temperature sensor.

12. Install all items removed.

Temperature Sensor Testing/Replacement (1986-on)

The engine must be cold for this test, preferably not operated for 12 hours.

1. Remove the seat and side covers.

2. Remove the main fuel tank as described in Chapter Six.

3. Using an ohmmeter check for continuity between the sensor body (**Figure 62**) and ground. There should be continuity. If not, check the thermostat housing for looseness. Retighten the housing and recheck.

> *WARNING*
> *Antifreeze is poisonous. Do not use a cooking pan for this procedure.*

4. Test the temperature sensor as follows.

   a. Remove the horn.

   b. Remove the temperature sensor from the thermostat housing.

   c. Place the temperature sensor in a pan filled with a 50/50 mixture of antifreeze and water. Suspend the switch with a rod as shown in **Figure 59**.

   d. Place a thermometer in the pan (use a cooking thermometer that is rated higher than the test temperature).

   e. Heat the coolant and check resistance between the terminal on the temperature sensor and ground. As the coolant temperature increases, compare to the temperature and resistance values listed in **Table 4**.

   f. If the resistance values do not match those listed in **Table 4**, the sensor must be replaced.

   g. Apply a non-hardening sealer to the threads and install the temperature sensor.

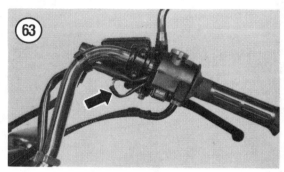

   h. Connect the electrical wires to the temperature sensor.

   i. Install all items removed.

Front Brake Light Switch Testing/Replacement

1. Disconnect the electrical wires to the brake light switch (**Figure 63**).

2. Use an ohmmeter and check for continuity between the 2 terminals on the brake light switch. There should be no continuity (infinite resistance) with brake lever released. With the brake lever applied there should be continuity (low resistance). If the switch fails either of these tests the switch must be replaced.

3. Remove the screw securing the brake switch and remove the brake switch from the brake master cylinder.

4. Install a new switch by reversing these removal steps. Make sure all electrical connections are tight and free of corrosion.

Rear Brake Light Switch
Testing/Replacement

1. Disconnect the electrical wires (A, **Figure 64**) to the rear brake light switch.

2. Use an ohmmeter and check for continuity between the 2 terminals on the brake light switch. There should be no continuity (infinite resistance) with the brake pedal released. With the brake pedal down or applied there should be continuity (low resistance). If the switch fails either of these tests, the switch must be replaced.

3. Unhook the return spring and unscrew the locknut securing the rear brake light switch to the frame. Remove the switch from the frame.

4. Install a new switch by reversing these removal steps, noting the following.

5. Make sure all electrical connections are tight and free of corrosion.

6. Adjust the switch as described in this chapter.

Rear Brake Light
Switch Adjustment

1. Turn the ignition switch to ON.

2. Depress the brake pedal. The light should come on just as the brake light begins to work.

3. To make the light come on earlier, hold the switch body and turn the adjusting nut (B, **Figure 64**) *clockwise* as viewed from the top. Turn *counterclockwise* to delay the light from coming on.

> *NOTE*
> *Some riders prefer the light to come on a little early. This way, they can tap the pedal without braking to warn drivers who are following too closely.*

ELECTRICAL COMPONENTS

This section contains information on electrical components other than switches.

Turn Signal Relay Replacement
(1983-1985)

1. Remove the seat and the left-hand side cover.

2. Pull the turn signal relay (**Figure 65**) out of the rubber mount.

3. Transfer the electrical wires to the new relay and install the relay in the rubber mount. Install all parts removed.

Pilot Lamp Checker
Testing/Replacement (1986-on)

1. Remove the left-hand side cover.

2. Disconnect the electrical connector at the pilot lamp checker (A, **Figure 66**).

3. Connect a voltmeter across the black/brown and green pilot lamp checker terminals on the wire harness side. Turn the ignition switch to ON. There should be battery voltage present. If there is no voltage, check the wire harness and the connectors for damage.

4. If necessary, transfer the electrical wires to the new pilot lamp checker and install the checker. Install all parts removed.

Brake/Taillight Sensor
Testing/Replacement (1986)

A brake/taillight sensor is located underneath the fuel tank.

1. Remove the seat.

2. Connect a voltmeter across the black/brown and green sensor wires. Turn the ignition switch to

7

ON. There should be battery voltage. Interpret results as follows.

   a. Battery voltage: If battery voltage was recorded and the warning lights do not work, replace the brake/taillight sensor.

   b. No battery voltage: Check the wire harness and the connectors for damage.

3. If necessary, transfer the electrical wires to the new brake/taillight sensor and install the sensor.

4. Install the seat.

Instrument Cluster
Removal/Installation

1. Remove the left-hand side cover and the seat.

2. Disconnect the battery negative lead.

3. Remove the headlight and case as described in this chapter.

4. Remove the screws securing the lower cover on the instrument cluster and remove the lower cover.

5. Remove the screws securing the junction box cover and remove the cover.

6. Disconnect all electrical connectors going to the instrument cluster from the junction box.

7. Disconnect the speedometer cable from the meter.

8. Remove the bolts securing the headlight bracket/turn signal assemblies and the instrument cluster.

9. Remove the headlight/turn signal assemblies and place them over the front fender.

> *CAUTION*
> *After the instrument cluster has been removed, set the cluster down with the meter face and needles facing upward. If the cluster is set face-down the needle damping fluid will leak out onto the instrument face and lens.*

10. Remove the instrument cluster.

11. Install by reversing these removal steps.

Horn Removal/Installation
(1983-1985)

> *CAUTION*
> *The fork cover panel is plastic and has two mounting post(s) in the middle. This part can easily be broken if not removed carefully.*

1. Carefully pull on the center of the fork cover panel (A, **Figure 67**) and remove it from the rubber grommets on the lower fork bridge.

2. Disconnect the electrical connections from the horns (B, **Figure 67**).

3. Remove the nuts and washers securing each horn to the mounting bracket and remove the horns.

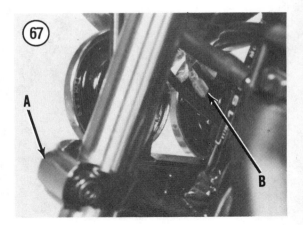

4. Install by reversing these removal steps. Make sure the electrical connections are tight and free of corrosion.

Horn Removal/Installation
(1986-on)

1. Disconnect the electrical connections from the horn (**Figure 68**).

2. Remove the bolt and remove the horn and its mounting bracket.

3. Install by reversing these removal steps. Make sure the electrical connections are tight and free of corrosion.

Horn Testing

Remove the horn as described in this chapter. Connect a 12-volt battery to the horn. If the horn is good, it will sound. If not, replace it.

Fuel Pump Flow Test

The electromagnetic fuel pump pumps fuel from the secondary fuel tank.

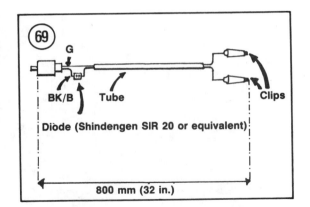

G

BK/B   Tube   Clips

Diode (Shindengen SIR 20 or equivalent)

800 mm (32 in.)

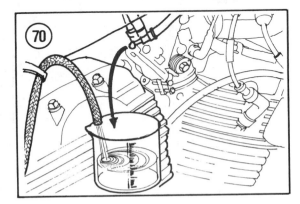

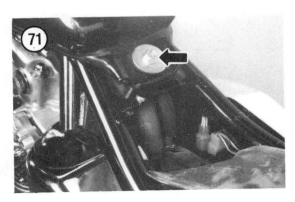

When the ignition switch is turned to the ON position the electromagnet is energized, pulling the armature and the diaphragm up. This causes a vacuum and pulls fuel through the inlet check valve. As the armature reaches the limit of its upward travel, the contact points are opened in the switch and the circuit is broken. The electromagnet is pushed down by the return spring which in turn pushes the fuel through the outlet check valve and to the carburetors. This continuing up-and-down movement moves or pumps the fuel from the secondary fuel tank into the carburetors.

Fuel pump removal and installation is covered in Chapter Six.

1983-1985

1. Fabricate a test wire as shown in **Figure 69**.
2. Disconnect the electrical connector from the fuel pump.
3. Connect the test wire to the fuel pump and to the battery.
4. Disconnect the fuel line going to the carburetors.
5. Place the loose end of the fuel line into a graduated beaker (**Figure 70**).
6. Turn the ignition switch to ON and allow the fuel to run out of the fuel line (into the graduated beaker) for 5 seconds.
7. Turn the ignition switch to OFF.
8. Multiply the amount of fuel in the beaker by 12 ($12 \times 5 = 60$ seconds). This will give the fuel pump flow capacity for one minute.
9. The fuel pump flow capacity for one minute should be 614 cc (22 oz.) ± 10 per cent per minute.
10. If the fuel pump does not flow to the specified capacity it must be replaced. Refer to Chapter Six.
11. Reconnect the fuel line to the carburetors and the electrical connector to the fuel pump.

1986-on

1. Turn the ignition switch to the OFF position.
2. Remove the left-hand side cover.
3. Disconnect the fuel pump wire connector (the connector is green). See B. **Figure 66**.
4. Connect a voltmeter between the black and green terminals. Turn the ignition switch to ON. There should be battery voltage at the terminals. If there is no voltage, check the wire harness for damage.
5. Turn the ignition switch to OFF.
6. Connect a jumper wire between the black/yellow and black terminals.
7. Remove the rear fuel tank mounting bolt (**Figure 71**) and raise the rear of the tank slightly. Support the tank with a block of wood.
8. Disconnect the fuel hose from the T-joint (**Figure 72**).
9. Place the loose end of the fuel line into a graduated beaker (**Figure 70**).
10. Turn the ignition switch to ON and allow the fuel to run out of the fuel line into the graduated beaker for 5 seconds.
11. Turn the ignition switch to OFF.
12. Multiply the amount of fuel in the beaker by 12 ($12 \times 5 = 60$ seconds). This will give the fuel pump flow capacity for one minute.
13. The fuel pump flow capacity for one minute should be 700 cc (25 oz.) per minute.

7

14. If the fuel pump does not flow to the specified capacity it must be replaced. Refer to Chapter Six.
15. Reconnect the fuel line to the carburetors and the electrical connector to the fuel pump.

Temperature Gauge Testing

1. Remove the seat and both side covers.
2. Remove the main fuel tank as described in Chapter Seven.
3. Remove the covers on both sides of the steering head.
4. Disconnect the electrical wire going to the temperature sensor on the thermostat housing. See **Figure 61** (1983-1985) or **Figure 62** (1986-on).
5. Turn the ignition switch to ON.

> *CAUTION*
> *Do not short the temperature sensor wire to ground for longer than a few seconds or the temperature gauge will be damaged.*

6. Run a jumper wire from the electrical connector and short the other end to ground.
7. When the wire is grounded the gauge needle should move all the way to the right to the "H" position on the gauge face.
8. If the gauge fails the test, the gauge must be replaced.
9. Remove the jumper wire and reconnect the temperature sensor wire to the sensor.

Low Fuel Warning Light and Sensor Testing (1983-1985)

> *NOTE*
> *The fuel tank must contain less than 1.7 liters (0.45 U.S. gal.) of fuel in order to perform this test.*

1. Place the bike on the centerstand on level ground.
2. Turn the ignition switch to ON.
3. The low fuel warning light will not come on immediately after the ignition switch is turned to ON. The light must come on within 60 seconds after the ignition has been turned to ON when there is the specified minimum amount of fuel (or less) in the tank.
4. If the light fails to come on, check the following.
   a. Blown fuse
   b. Blown indicator bulb
   c. Broken wire in the circuit
5. If the items in Step 4 check out okay then the sensor is faulty and must be replaced as described in this chapter.

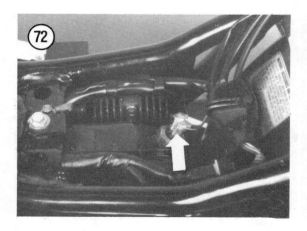

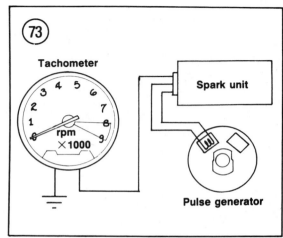

6. After a new sensor is installed, add additional fuel to the tank to bring the total amount to above 6.5 liters (1.72 U.S. gal.).
7. Turn the ignition switch to ON.
8. The low fuel warning light should not come on. If the light comes on, check for a short in the circuit or in the electrical connector.

Fuel Sensor Testing (1986-on)

1. Perform the pilot lamp checker test in this chapter.
2. Place the bike on the centerstand on level ground.
3. Remove the seats.
4. Disconnect the fuel sensor wire connectors **(Figure 72)**.
5. Connect a voltmeter between the gray/black and green fuel sensor wires. Turn the ignition switch to ON. There should be battery voltage. If there is no voltage, check the wire harness for damage.

NOTE
If there is battery voltage and the fuel warning light does not come on and the bulb is okay, replace the fuel sensor.

Fuel Sensor Replacement (All Models)

1. Remove the fuel tank as described in Chapter Six.
2. Disconnect the electrical connector from the sensor (**Figure 72**).
3. Carefully unscrew the sensor from the secondary fuel tank.
4. Apply a light coat of non-hardening gasket sealer to the threads of the new sensor. Install the sensor and O-ring into the secondary fuel tank. Tighten the sensor securely.

Tachometer Testing (1983-1985)

The electronic tachometer receives signals from the rear cylinder's pulse generator (**Figure 73**). If the tachometer is not operating at all or operating erratically, perform this test.

1. Remove the main fuel tank as described in Chapter Six.
2. Test the rear cylinder's pulse generator as described in this chapter.
3. If the pulse generator tests okay, use an ohmmeter and check the continuity from the yellow wire terminal at the tachometer end of the wire harness to the yellow wire terminal of the rear cylinder's ignition coil (left-hand coil).
4. There should be continuity (indicated low resistance). If there is no continuity, there is an open in the circuit.
5. If the tachometer still is not operating correctly after the wiring is repaired, replace the tachometer.

Fuses

Whenever a fuse blows, find out why before replacing the fuse. Usually the trouble is a short circuit in the wiring. This may be caused by worn-through insulation or a disconnected wire shorted to ground.

CAUTION
Never substitute aluminum foil or wire for a fuse. Never use a higher amperage fuse than specified. An overload could cause a fire and complete loss of the motorcycle.

NOTE
These fuses are not the typical glass tube with metal ends. Carry extra fuses in your tool box as this type fuse may not be available everywhere.

1983-1985

There are 6 fuses. The main fuse (fusible link) is located above the voltage regulator/rectifier. The cooling fan has an inline fuse and the remaining 4 are located in the fuse panel between the speedometer and tachometer.

CAUTION
When replacing a fuse, make sure the ignition switch is in the OFF position. This will lessen the chance of a short circuit.

If the main fusible link blows, remove the cover (**Figure 74**) and remove the Phillips screws securing the fusible link and replace it. There is a spare link inside the cover.

The remaining fuses are located in the fuse panel between the speedometer and tachometer. Remove the screw (**Figure 75**) on each side of the indicator and fuse panel. Move the cover up and forward and remove the cover.

7

1986-on

There are 8 fuses. The main fuse is located near the battery next to the starter solenoid (A, **Figure 76**). The 7 inline fuses are located in the fuse panel behind the headlight housing on the left-hand side (**Figure 77**).

> *CAUTION*
> *When replacing a fuse, make sure the ignition switch is OFF. This will lessen the chance of a short circuit.*

If the main fuse blows, remove the right-hand side cover. Then disconnect the wiring connector and remove the fuse. There is a spare fuse (B, **Figure 76**) located underneath the starter solenoid.

To replace an inline fuse, remove the fuse box cover (**Figure 77**). Pull the blown fuse out of the fuse box with the plastic fuse remover. There are 2 spare fuses inside the fuse box cover.

Table 1 STARTER TROUBLESHOOTING

Symptom	Probable Cause	Remedy
Starter does not work	Low battery	Recharge battery
	Worn brushes	Replace battery
	Defective relay	Repair or replace
	Defective switch	Repair or replace
	Defective wiring connection	Repair wire or clean connection
	Internal short circuit	Repair or replace defective component
Starter action is weak	Low battery	Recharge battery
	Pitted relay contacts	Clean or replace
	Worn brushes	Replace brushes
	Defective connection	Clean and tighten
	Short circuit in commutator	Replace armature
Starter runs continuously	Stuck relay	Replace relay
Starter turns; does not turn engine	Defective starter clutch	Replace starter clutch

Table 2 REPLACEMENT BULBS

Item	Wattage	Number
Headlight (quartz bulb)	12V 60/55	H4
Tail/brakelight		
1983-1985	12V 8/27W	SAE No. 1157
1986	12V 2/32	SAE No. 1157
1987	12V 2/32×2	—
Turn signals		
Front	12V 23/8W	SAE No. 1034
Rear	12V 23 W	SAE No. 1073
Instrument lights	12V 3W	—
Indicator lights	12V 3W	—
High beam indicator	12V 3W	—
Neutral indicator	12V 3W	—
Oil pressure warning	12V 3W	—
Gear position light	12V 8W	SAE No. 1034

Table 3 TEMPERATURE SENSOR READINGS (1983-1985)

Temperature	Resistance (ohms)
140° F (60° C)	104.0
185° F (85° C)	43.9
230° F (110° C)	20.3
248° F (120° C)	16.1

7

Table 4 TEMPERATURE SENSOR READINGS (1986-ON)

Temperature	Resistance (ohms)
122° F (50° C)	130-180
212° F (100° C)	25-30

CHAPTER EIGHT

COOLING SYSTEM

The pressurized cooling system consists of the radiator, water pump, radiator cap, thermostat, electric cooling fan and a coolant reservoir tank.

The water pump requires no routine maintenance and is replaced as a complete unit if defective.

It is important to keep the coolant level to the FULL mark on the coolant reservoir tank. See **Figure 1** (1983-1985) or **Figure 2** (1986-on). Always add coolant to the reservoir tank, not to the radiator.

> *CAUTION*
> *Drain and flush the cooling system at least every 2 years. Refill with a mixture of ethylene glycol antifreeze (formulated for aluminum engines) and distilled water. Do not reuse the old coolant as it deteriorates with use. Do **not** operate the cooling system with only distilled water even in climates where antifreeze protection is not required. This is important because the engine is all aluminum. It will not rust, but it will oxidize internally and have to be replaced. Refer to **Coolant Change** in Chapter Three.*

This chapter describes repair and replacement of cooling system components. **Table 1** at the end of the chapter lists all of the cooling system specifications. For routine maintenance of the system, refer to *Cooling System Inspection* in Chapter Three.

> *WARNING*
> *Do not remove the radiator filler cap (**Figure 3**) when the engine is hot. The coolant is very hot and is under pressure. Severe scalding could result if the coolant comes in contact with your skin.*

The cooling system must be cooled before removing any component of the system.

There are 3 different types of hose clamps used on the coolant hoses. Always install the same type of clamp to its original position, as in some cases the clearance is so minimal there is only room for one type of clamp. Throughout the text there is mention of loosening the clamping screws. In some cases a spring type clamp may be used.

Major components of the cooling system are shown in **Figure 4** (1983-1985) and **Figure 5** (1986-on).

COOLING SYSTEM CHECK

The following checks should be made before disassembly if a cooling system fault is suspected.

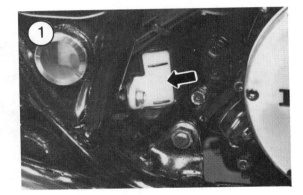

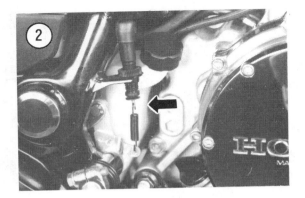

1. Run the engine until it reaches normal operating temperature. While the engine is running a pressure surge should be felt when the upper radiator hose is squeezed.

2. If a substantial coolant loss is noted, one of the head gaskets may be blown. In extreme cases sufficient coolant will leak into a cylinder(s) when the bike is left standing for several hours so the engine cannot be turned over with the starter. White smoke (steam) might also be observed at the muffler(s) when the engine is running. Coolant may also find its way into the oil. Unscrew the dipstick and look at the oil residue on it. If the oil looks like a "green chocolate malt" or is light-colored and foamy there is coolant in the oil system. If so, correct the problem immediately.

CAUTION
*After the problem is corrected, drain and thoroughly flush out the engine oil system to eliminate all coolant residue. Refill with fresh engine oil. Refer to **Engine Oil and Filter Change** in Chapter Three.*

3. Check the radiator for clogged or damaged fins. If more than 15 percent of the radiator fin area is damaged, repair or replace the radiator.

4. Check all coolant hoses for cracks or damage. Replace all questionable parts. Make sure the hose clamps are tight, but not so tight that they cut the hoses.

5. Pressure test the cooling system as described under *Cooling System Inspection* in Chapter Three.

8

RADIATOR

Removal/Installation

The radiator and fan are removed as an assembly.

1. Remove the seat and both side covers.

2. Drain the cooling system as described in Chapter Three.

3. Disconnect the overflow tube from the radiator filler neck.

4. Remove the main fuel tank as described in Chapter Six.

5. Remove the plastic trim panel from each side of the steering head. See **Figure 6** (1983-1985) or **Figure 7** (1986-on).

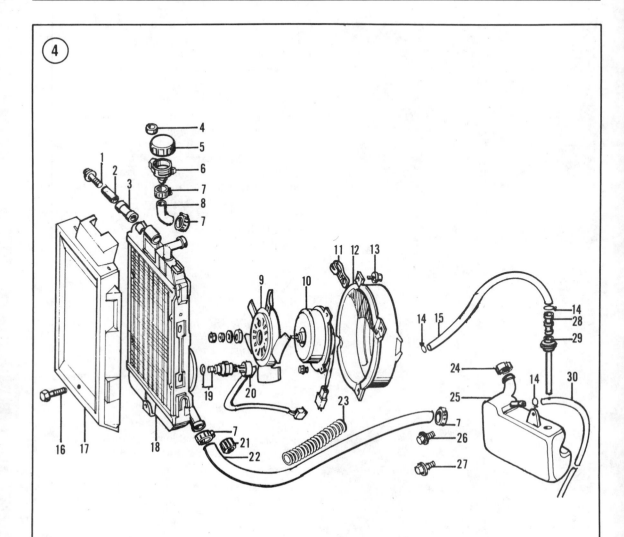

COOLING SYSTEM (1983-1985)

1. Bolt
2. Collar
3. Rubber mounting grommet
4. Rubber stopper
5. Filler neck cap
6. Filler neck
7. Hose clamp
8. Hose
9. Cooling fan
10. Fan motor

11. Clip
12. Fan shroud
13. Bolt
14. Spring clamp
15. Breather hose
16. Bolt
17. Radiator cover
18. Radiator
19. Thermostat switch
20. Electrical connector

21. Rubber mount
22. Hose
23. Hose protector spring
24. Reserve tank cap
25. Reserve tank
26. Bolt
27. Bolt
28. Joint
29. Level tube
30. Reserve tank tube

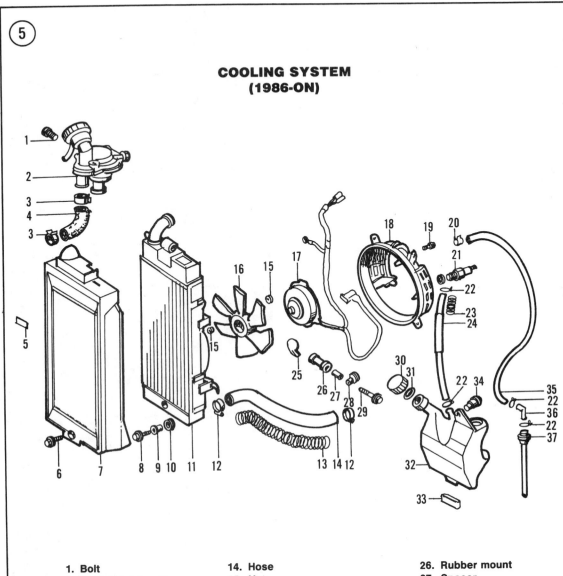

**COOLING SYSTEM
(1986-ON)**

1. Bolt
2. Themostat housing
3. Hose clamp
4. Hose
5. Decal
6. Bolt
7. Radiator cover
8. Bolt
9. Bushing
10. Grommet
11. Radiator
12. Hose clamp
13. Hose protector spring

14. Hose
15. Nut
16. Cooling fan
17. Fan motor
18. Fan shroud
19. Bolt
20. Hose clip
21. Thermoswitch and washer
22. Spring clamp
23. Spring
24. Reserve tank tube
25. Rubber tube

26. Rubber mount
27. Spacer
28. Harness clip
29. Bolt
30. Reserve tank cap
31. Washer
32. Reserve tank
33. Grommet
34. Bolt
35. Breather hose
36. Joint
37. Level tube

6. On models so equipped, remove the charcoal canister assembly (A, **Figure 8**) and hoses from the area below the radiator. Refer to Chapter Six.

7. Remove the screws securing the black radiator cover (B, **Figure 8**) and remove the radiator cover.

8. Disconnect the cooling fan 2-pin electrical connector.

9. Pull back the rubber boot and disconnect the electrical wires from the thermostatic switch coupler.

10. Loosen the clamping screws on the upper (**Figure 9**) and lower (**Figure 10**) radiator hose bands.

> *NOTE*
> *Figure 10 does not actually show the hose. The arrow is pointing to the area where the hose is located behind the radiator core.*

11. Remove the radiator upper mounting bolt (**Figure 11**).

12. *1986-on:* Remove the 2 radiator lower mounting bolts (**Figure 12**).

13. Pull the radiator (**Figure 13**) slightly forward while working both radiator hoses loose from the radiator. Pull the radiator forward, up and out of the lower receptacles on the frame.

14. Install by reversing these removal steps, noting the following.

15. Replace both radiator hoses if either is starting to deteriorate or is damaged.

16. *1986-on:* The upper radiator hose (**Figure 14**) on these models is a tight fit through the frame. Make sure to slide the hose clamp on the upper radiator hose before installing the radiator.

17. Refill the cooling system with the recommended type and quantity of coolant as described in Chapter Three.

Inspection

1. Flush off the exterior of the radiator with a garden hose on low pressure. Spray both the front and the back to remove all road dirt and bugs. Carefully use a whisk broom or stiff paint brush to remove any stubborn dirt.

> *CAUTION*
> *Do not press too hard or the cooling fins and tubes may be damaged causing a leak.*

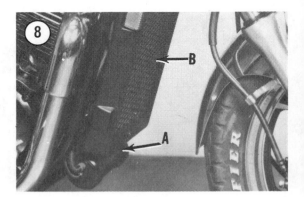

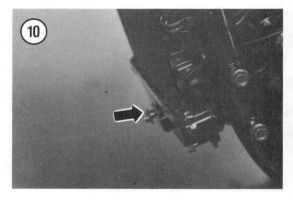

2. Carefully straighten out any bent cooling fins with a broad tipped screwdriver.

3. Check for cracks or leakage (usually a moss-green colored residue) at the filler neck, the inlet and outlet hoses fittings and the upper and lower tank seams. See **Figure 15**.

4. Inspect the radiator cap top and bottom seals for deterioration or damage. Check the spring for damage. Pressure test the radiator cap as described under *Cooling System Inspection* in Chapter Three. Replace the radiator cap if necessary.

5. If the condition of the radiator is doubtful, have it pressure-checked as described in Chapter Three. The radiator can be pressure-checked while removed or while installed on the bike.

COOLING FAN

Removal/Installation

Refer to **Figure 4** (1983-1985) or **Figure 5** (1986-on) for this procedure.

1. Remove the radiator as described in this chapter.

2. Remove the bolts securing the fan shroud and fan assembly and remove the assembly from the radiator.

3. To remove the fan blade from the motor, remove the nut and washers securing the fan blade to the motor and remove the fan blade.

4. To remove the fan motor, remove the screws securing the fan assembly to the fan shroud and remove the fan motor.

5. Install by reversing these removal steps, noting the following.

6. Apply Loctite Lock N' Seal to the threads on the fan motor shaft before installing the fan blade nut. Install the washer, lockwasher and nut and tighten the nut securely.

7. Refill the cooling system with the recommended type and quantity of coolant as described in Chapter Three.

8

THERMOSTAT

Removal/Installation

1. Remove the seat and both side covers.

2. Remove the main fuel tank as described in Chapter Six.

3. Drain the cooling system as described in Chapter Three.

4A. *1983-1985:* Perform the following.

    a. Remove the bolts securing the black radiator cover and remove the cover.

    b. Loosen the clamping screws on the radiator upper hose at the radiator.

    c. Remove the overflow tube (A, **Figure 16**).

    d. Remove the bolt (B, **Figure 16**) securing the thermostat housing to the frame.

    e. Disconnect the electrical connector to the temperature sensor (C, **Figure 16**).

    f. Pull the upper hose and thermostat housing back away from the radiator.

    g. Remove the bolts securing the thermostat housing cover (D, **Figure 16**).

    h. Remove the thermostat housing cover and O-ring seal.

    i. Remove the thermostat from the housing.

4B. *1986-on:* Perform the following.

    a. Remove the right-hand plastic trim panel (**Figure 7**).

    b. Remove the bolt (**Figure 17**) securing the thermostat housing to the frame.

    c. Remove the 4 bolts securing the thermostat housing cover (**Figure 18**) and remove the cover.

    d. Remove the O-ring (A, **Figure 19**) and thermostat (B, **Figure 19**) from the housing.

5. Install by reversing these removal steps, noting the following.

6. Make sure the O-ring seal in the thermostat housing cover is in good condition. If it is starting to deteriorate or has become brittle with age, it should be replaced as it will no longer seal properly.

7. *1986-on:* Install the thermostat by aligning the rib in the thermostat with the slot in the housing (**Figure 19**).

8. Refill the cooling system with the recommended type and quantity of coolant as described in Chapter Three.

Inspection

Test the thermostat to ensure proper operation. The thermostat should be replaced if it remains

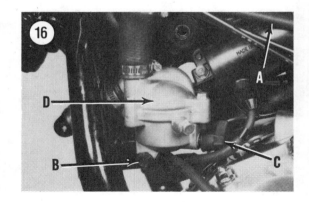

open at normal room temperature or stays closed after the specified temperature has been reached during the test procedure.

Place the thermostat on a small piece of wood in a pan of water (**Figure 20**). Place a thermometer in the pan of water (use a cooking or candy thermometer that is rated higher than the test temperature). Gradually heat the water and continue to gently stir the water until it reaches 176-183° F (80-84° C). At this temperature the thermostat should open.

NOTE
Valve operation is sometimes sluggish. It usually takes 3-5 minutes for the valve to operate properly.

If the valve fails to open, the thermostat should be replaced. It cannot be serviced. Be sure to replace it with one of the same temperature rating.

WATER PUMP

Mechanical Seal Inspection

1. Remove the bolts securing the left-hand rear crankcase cover and remove the cover.
2. Check the lower area of the water pump (**Figure 21**) for signs of coolant leakage—usually a moss-green colored residue.
3. If the mechanical seal is leaking, the coolant will drip out of the weep hole (A, **Figure 22**) in the bottom of the water pump. If the seal is leaking, the water pump assembly must be replaced. It cannot be serviced.

Removal

Refer to **Figure 23** for this procedure.
1. Remove the engine as described in Chapter Four.
2. Disconnect the electrical connector from the oil pressure switch.
3. Remove the bolts securing the water pump cover and remove the cover and the hose (**Figure 24**). Don't lose the locating dowels.
4. Withdraw the water pump from the crankcase (**Figure 25**).

Inspection

1. Inspect the water pump assembly for wear or damage.
2. Rotate the impeller to make sure the bearings are not worn or damaged. If the bearings are damaged, the assembly must be replaced as it cannot be serviced.

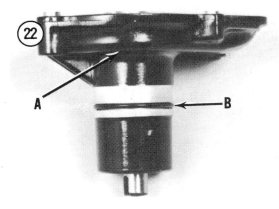

8

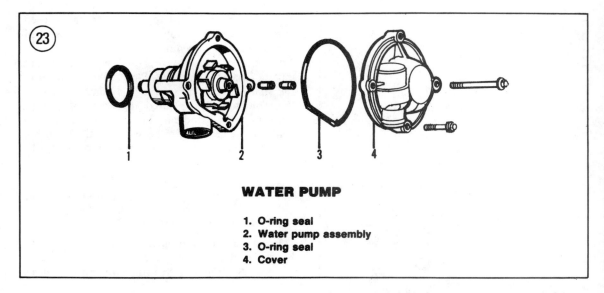

WATER PUMP

1. O-ring seal
2. Water pump assembly
3. O-ring seal
4. Cover

3. Check the impeller blades (A, **Figure 26**) for wear or damage.

4. Remove the O-ring seal (**Figure 27**) in the water pump assembly. Replace O-ring seal with a new one.

5. Inspect the cover and inlet and outlet pipes for cracks or damage (**Figure 28**). If damaged, the assembly must be replaced. It cannot be serviced.

6. If removed, install the locating dowels (B, **Figure 26**) into the water pump assembly.

Installation

1. Within the crankcase, rotate the oil pump shaft so the tab on the end of the shaft is vertical.

2. Apply a coat of clean engine oil to the new O-ring seal (B, **Figure 22**) on the water pump housing.

3. Position the groove on the water pump shaft vertically so it will align with the tab on the oil pump shaft.

4. Install the water pump into the crankcase and slightly wiggle the water pump impeller to assure proper alignment of the tab and groove. Push the water pump assembly all the way on until it is properly seated against the crankcase. The assembly should fit snugly without using any force. If it will not fit properly, withdraw the assembly and realign the tab of the oil pump shaft and the groove on the water pump.

CAUTION
Do not install the cover or any bolts until the assembly is completely seated against the crankcase. Do not try to force the assembly into place with the mounting screws.

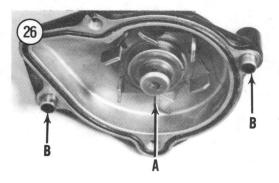

5. Make sure the dowel pins are installed in the water pump assembly.

6. Make sure the O-ring seal is installed in the water pump assembly.

7. Install the water pump cover and the bolts and tighten the bolts securely.

8. Connect the electrical connector onto the oil pressure switch.

9. Install the engine into the frame as described in Chapter Four.

10. Refill the cooling system with the recommended type and quantity of coolant as described in Chapter Three.

11. Start the bike and check for leaks.

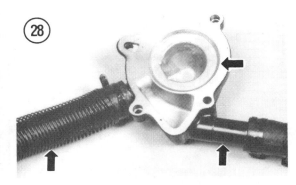

COOLANT PIPES

Removal/Installation

Refer to **Figure 29** (1983-1985) or **Figure 30** (1986-on) for this procedure.

1. Remove the seat and both side covers.

2. Remove the main fuel tank as described in Chapter Six.

8

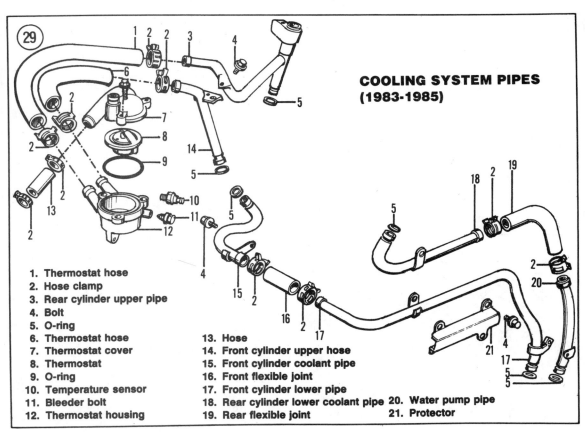

COOLING SYSTEM PIPES (1983-1985)

1. Thermostat hose
2. Hose clamp
3. Rear cylinder upper pipe
4. Bolt
5. O-ring
6. Thermostat hose
7. Thermostat cover
8. Thermostat
9. O-ring
10. Temperature sensor
11. Bleeder bolt
12. Thermostat housing
13. Hose
14. Front cylinder upper hose
15. Front cylinder coolant pipe
16. Front flexible joint
17. Front cylinder lower pipe
18. Rear cylinder lower coolant pipe
19. Rear flexible joint
20. Water pump pipe
21. Protector

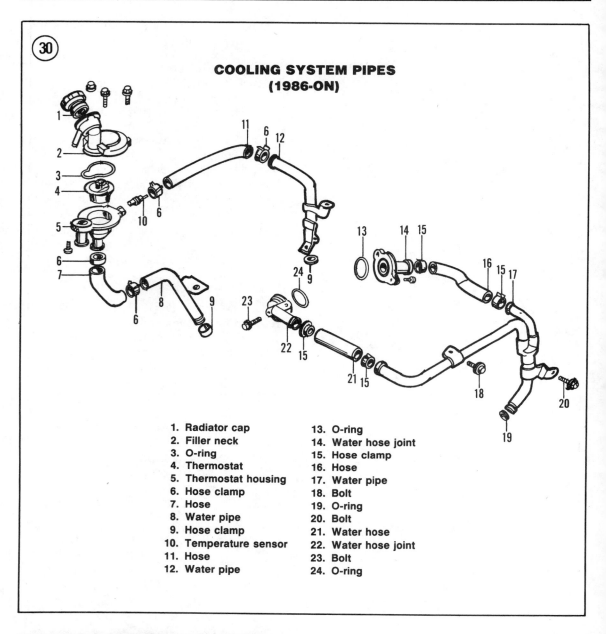

**COOLING SYSTEM PIPES
(1986-ON)**

1. Radiator cap
2. Filler neck
3. O-ring
4. Thermostat
5. Thermostat housing
6. Hose clamp
7. Hose
8. Water pipe
9. Hose clamp
10. Temperature sensor
11. Hose
12. Water pipe
13. O-ring
14. Water hose joint
15. Hose clamp
16. Hose
17. Water pipe
18. Bolt
19. O-ring
20. Bolt
21. Water hose
22. Water hose joint
23. Bolt
24. O-ring

3. Drain the cooling system as described in Chapter Three.

4. Remove the hydraulic clutch slave cylinder as described in Chapter Five.

5. Remove the bolts securing the lower coolant pipe for the front cylinder (**Figure 31**).

6. Remove the hose clamps on the front flexible joint and disconnect the front flexible joint from the front cylinder coolant pipe.

7. Disconnect the front cylinder lower coolant pipe from the water pump and remove the lower coolant pipe from the engine.

8. Remove the hose clamp on the rear flexible joint where it attaches to the rear cylinder coolant pipe.

9. Remove the water pump coolant pipe and the rear flexible joint from the engine.

10. Remove the rear cylinder lower coolant pipe from the rear cylinder.

11. Remove the front cylinder lower coolant pipe from the front cylinder.

12. Remove the bolts securing the black radiator cover and remove the cover.

13. Loosen the clamping screws on the radiator upper hose at the radiator.

14. Remove the overflow tube.

15. Remove the bolt securing the thermostat housing to the frame.

16. Disconnect the electrical connector to the temperature sensor.

17. Pull the upper hose and thermostat housing back away from the radiator.

18. If the thermostat is going to be removed, loosen the bolts on the top cover.

19. Remove the bolts securing the front and rear cylinder's upper coolant pipes and remove both pipes and thermostat housing.

20. Install by reversing these removal steps, noting the following.

21. Install new O-ring seals on all coolant pipes.

22. Refill the cooling system with the recommended type and quantity of coolant as described in Chapter Three.

HOSES

Hoses deteriorate with age and should be replaced periodically or whenever they show signs of cracking or leakage. To be safe, replace the hoses every 2 years. The spray of hot coolant from a cracked hose can injure the rider and passenger. Loss of coolant can also cause the engine to overheat, causing damage.

Whenever any component of the cooling system is removed, inspect the hoses(s) and determine if replacement is necessary.

Inspection

1. With the engine cool, check the cooling hoses for brittleness or hardness. A hose in this condition will usually show cracks and must be replaced.

2. With the engine hot, examine the hoses for swelling along the entire hose length. Eventually a hose will rupture at this point.

3. Check area around hose clamps. Signs of rust around clamps indicate possible hose leakage.

Replacement

Hose replacement should be performed when the engine is cool.

1. Drain the cooling system as described under *Coolant Change* in Chapter Three.

2. Loosen the hose clamps from the hose to be replaced. Slide the clamps along the hose and out of the way.

3. Twist the hose end to break the seal and remove from the connecting joint. If the hose has been on for some time, it may have become fused to the joint. If so, cut the hose parallel to the joint connections with a knife or razor. The hose then can be carefully pried loose with a screwdriver.

CAUTION
Excessive force applied to the hose during removal could damage the connecting joint.

4. Examine the connecting joint for cracks or other damage. Repair or replace parts as required. If the joint is okay, clean it of any rust with sandpaper.

5. Inspect hose clamps and replace as necessary.

6. Slide hose clamps over outside of hose and install hose to inlet and outlet connecting joint. Make sure hose clears all obstructions and is routed properly.

NOTE
If it is difficult to install a hose on a joint, soak the end of the hose in hot water for approximately 2 minutes. This will soften the hose and ease installation.

7. With the hose positioned correctly on joint, position clamps back away from end of hose slightly. Tighten clamps securely, but not so much that hose is damaged.

8. Refill cooling system as described under *Coolant Change* in Chapter Three. Start the engine and check for leaks. Retighten hose clamps as necessary.

Table is on the following page.

Table 1 COOLING SYSTEM SPECIFICATIONS

Coolant capacity	
1983-1985	
Total system	2.1 liters (2.22 qt.)
Radiator and engine	1.7 liters (1.8 qt.)
Reserve tank	0.4 liters (0.42 qt.)
1986-on	
Total	1.83 liters (1.92 qt.)
Radiator and engine	1.56 liters (1.64 qt.)
Reserve tank	0.27 liters (0.28 qt.)
Radiator cap	0.75-1.05 kg/cm² (10.7-14.9 psi)
relief pressure	
Thermostat	
Begins to open	80-84° C (176-183° F)
Valve lift	Minimum of 8 mm @ 95° C (203° F)
Boiling point (50/50 mixture)	
Unpressurized	107.7° C (226° F)
Pressurized (cap on)	125.6° C (258° F)
Freezing point (hydrometer test)	
Water/antifreeze ratio	
55/45 water/antifreeze ratio	-32° C (-25° F)
50/50 water/antifreeze ratio	-37° C (-34° F)
45/55 water/antifreeze ratio	-45° C (-48° F)

CHAPTER NINE

FRONT SUSPENSION
AND STEERING

This chapter describes repair and maintenance procedures for the front wheel, forks and steering components.

Front suspension torque specifications are covered in **Table 1**. **Tables 1-4** are at the end of this chapter.

FRONT WHEEL

Removal (1983-1985)

1. Place the bike on the centerstand or place wood blocks under the engine or frame to support it securely with the front wheel off the ground.

2. Remove the speedometer cable set screw. Pull the speedometer cable (**Figure 1**) free from the speedometer gear box.

3. Remove the bolts (**Figure 2**) securing both brake caliper assemblies to the front fork and tie them up to the front fork.

> *NOTE*
> *Insert a piece of vinyl tubing or wood in the calipers in place of the brake discs. That way if the brake lever is inadvertently squeezed, the pistons will not be forced out of the cylinder. If this does happen, the caliper may have to be disassembled to reseat the pistons and*

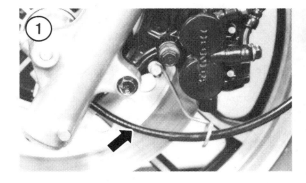

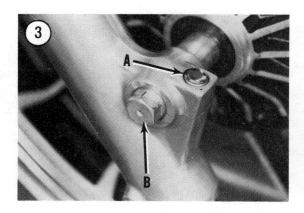

the system will have to be bled. By using the wood, bleeding the brake is not necessary when installing the wheel.

4. Remove the chrome cap (A, **Figure 3**) from the axle pinch bolt and remove the axle pinch bolt.
5. Unscrew and withdraw the front axle (B, **Figure 3**).
6. Pull the wheel down and forward and remove it.

CAUTION
*Do not set the wheel down on the disc surface as it may get scratched or warped. Set the sidewalls on 2 wood blocks (**Figure 4**).*

Installation (1983-1985)

1. Make sure the axle bearing surfaces of the fork slider and axle are free from burrs and nicks.
2. Remove the vinyl tubing or pieces of wood from the brake calipers.
3. Position the wheel into place.
4. Position the speedometer housing tang *behind* the raised boss on the left-hand fork (**Figure 5**).
5. Insert the front axle from the right-hand side and screw it into the left-hand fork leg.

6. Tighten the front axle to the torque specification listed in **Table 1**.
7. Install the pinch bolt and nut and tighten it to the torque specification listed in **Table 1**. Install the chrome cap into the pinch bolt.
8. Install the calipers, being careful not to damage the brake pads.
9. Tighten the caliper mounting bolts to the torque specification listed in **Table 1**.
10. Slowly rotate the wheel and install the speedometer cable into the speedometer housing. Install the cable set screw.
11. After the wheel is completely installed, rotate it several times and apply the brakes a couple of times to make sure that it rotates freely and that the brake pads are against the discs correctly.

Removal (1986-on)

1. Place the bike on the centerstand with the front wheel touching the ground.
2. Remove the speedometer cable set screw. Pull the speedometer cable (**Figure 6**) free from the speedometer gear box.

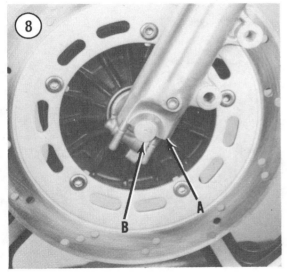

NOTE
Insert a piece of vinyl tubing or wood in the calipers in place of the brake discs. That way if the brake lever is inadvertently squeezed, the pistons will not be forced out of the cylinder. If this does happen, the caliper may have to be disassembled to reseat the pistons and the system will have to be bled. By using the wood, bleeding the brake is not necessary when installing the wheel.

3. Remove the left- and right-hand axle holders. See **Figure 7**.
4. Jack up the engine until the front forks (A, **Figure 8**) clear the front axle (B, **Figure 8**) and roll the front wheel away from the fork tubes. See **Figure 9**.

CAUTION
*Do not set the wheel down on the disc surface as it may get scratched or warped. Set the sidewalls on 2 wood blocks (**Figure 4**).*

**Installation
(1986-on)**

1. Make sure the front axle and the axle holder bearing surfaces are free from burrs and nicks.
2. Remove the vinyl tubing or pieces of wood from the brake calipers.
3. Make sure the axle and axle nut (**Figure 10**) are installed on the wheel. Refer to *Front Hub Disassembly* in this chapter.

4. Place the front wheel between the front forks so that the brake disc is on the left-hand side. Lower the engine so that the front forks rest on the front axle as shown in **Figure 8** (left-hand side) or **Figure 11** (right-hand side).

5. Position the speedometer housing tang *behind* the raised boss on the left-hand fork (**Figure 12**).

6. Install the axle holders so that the arrow (**Figure 13**) on the bottom of the holders faces to the front.

7. Install the axle holder nuts (**Figure 14**). Tighten the front nut and then the rear nut to the torque specifications in **Table 1**.

8. Support the bike so that the front wheel clears the ground.

9. Slowly rotate the wheel and install the speedometer cable into the speedometer housing. Install the cable set screw.

10. After the front wheel is completely installed, rotate it several times and apply the brake a couple of times to make sure that it rotates freely and that the brake pads are against the discs correctly.

Inspection

Measure the axial and radial runout of the wheel with a dial indicator as shown in **Figure 15**. The maximum axial and radial runout is 2.0 mm (0.08 in.). If the runout exceeds this dimension, check the wheel bearing condition.

If the wheel bearings are okay, the alloy wheel will have to be replaced as it cannot be serviced. Inspect the wheel for signs of cracks, fractures, dents or bends. If it is damaged in any way, it must be replaced.

> *WARNING*
> *Do not try to repair any damage to an alloy wheel as it will result in an unsafe riding condition.*

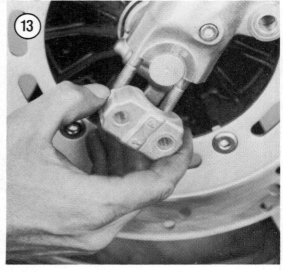

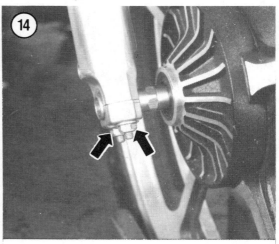

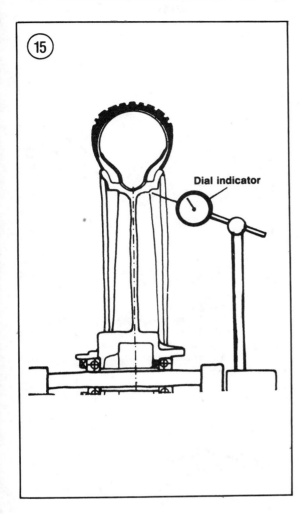

Check axle runout as described under *Front Hub Inspection* in this chapter.

FRONT HUB

Inspection

Inspect each wheel bearing prior to removing it from the wheel hub.

> *CAUTION*
> *Do not remove the wheel bearings for inspection as they will be damaged during removal. Remove wheel bearings only if they are to be replaced.*

1. Perform Steps 1-3 of *Disassembly* in this chapter.
2. Turn each bearing by hand (**Figure 16**). Make sure bearings turn smoothly.
3. On non-sealed bearings, check the balls for evidence of wear, pitting or excessive heat (bluish tint). Replace the bearings if necessary; always replace as a complete set. When replacing the bearings, be sure to take your old bearings along to ensure a perfect matchup.

> *NOTE*
> *Fully sealed bearings are available from many bearing specialty shops. Fully sealed bearings provide better protection from dirt and moisture that may get into the hub.*

4. Check the axle for wear and straightness. Use V-blocks and a dial indicator as shown in **Figure 17**. If the runout is 0.2 mm (0.01 in.) or greater, the axle should be replaced.

9

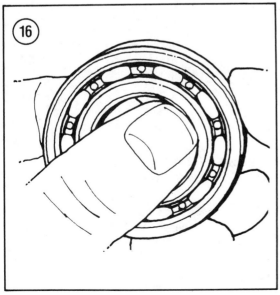

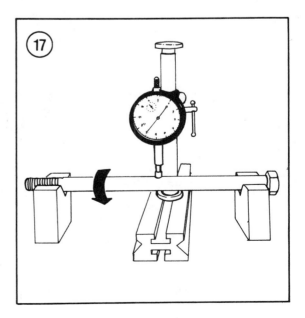

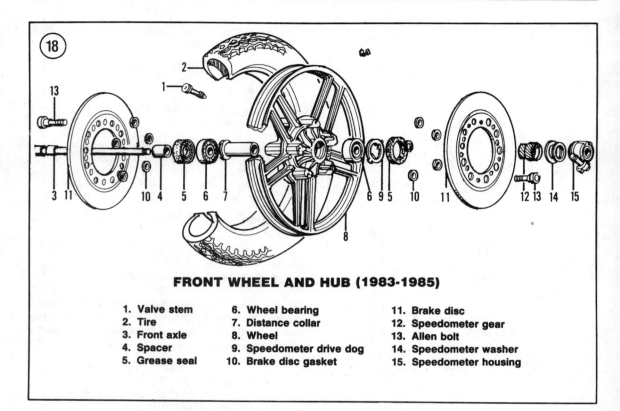

FRONT WHEEL AND HUB (1983-1985)

1. Valve stem
2. Tire
3. Front axle
4. Spacer
5. Grease seal
6. Wheel bearing
7. Distance collar
8. Wheel
9. Speedometer drive dog
10. Brake disc gasket
11. Brake disc
12. Speedometer gear
13. Allen bolt
14. Speedometer washer
15. Speedometer housing

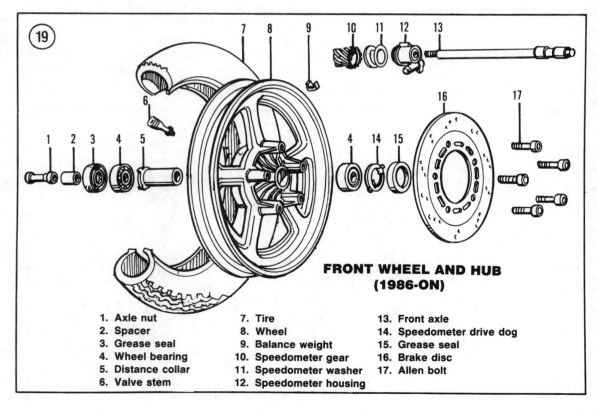

FRONT WHEEL AND HUB (1986-ON)

1. Axle nut
2. Spacer
3. Grease seal
4. Wheel bearing
5. Distance collar
6. Valve stem
7. Tire
8. Wheel
9. Balance weight
10. Speedometer gear
11. Speedometer washer
12. Speedometer housing
13. Front axle
14. Speedometer drive dog
15. Grease seal
16. Brake disc
17. Allen bolt

Disassembly

Refer to **Figure 18** (1983-1985) or **Figure 19** (1986-on) for this procedure.

1. Remove the front wheel as described in this chapter.

2A. *1983-1985:* Perform the following.

  a. Remove the spacer (**Figure 20**) from the right-hand side.

  b. Remove the speedometer housing (**Figure 21**) from the left-hand side.

2B. *1986-on:* Perform the following.

  a. Hold the left side of the axle (**Figure 22**) with a wrench.

  b. Loosen and remove the right-hand axle nut (**Figure 23**).

  c. Remove the axle from the left-hand side.

  d. Remove the speedometer gear box (**Figure 21**) from the left-hand side.

  e. Remove the spacer (**Figure 20**) from the right-hand side.

3. Remove the grease seal from the right-hand side.

4. Remove the grease seal and speedometer drive dog from the left-hand side. See **Figure 24**.

5. Before proceeding further, inspect the wheel bearings as described in this chapter. If they must be replaced, proceed as follows.

6. Remove the bolts (**Figure 25**) securing the brake discs. Remove the discs and the individual gaskets

located between the disc and the hub at each bolt hole.

7A. A special Honda tool set-up can be used to remove the wheel bearings as follows:

    a. Install the 15 mm bearing remover (Honda part No. 07746-0050400) into the right-hand bearing.

    b. Turn the wheel over (left-hand side up) on the workbench so the bearing remover is touching the workbench surface.

    c. From the left-hand side of the hub, install the bearing remover expander (Honda part No. 07746-050100) into the bearing remover. Using a hammer, tap the expander into the bearing remover with a hammer.

    d. Stand the wheel up to a vertical position.

    e. Tap on the end of the expander (**Figure 26**) and drive the right bearing out of the hub. Remove the bearing and the distance collar.

    f. Repeat for the left bearing.

7B. If special tools are not available, perform the following:

    a. To remove the right- and left-hand bearings and distance collar, insert a soft aluminum or brass drift into one side of the hub.

    b. Push the distance collar over to one side and place the drift on the inner race of the lower bearing.

    c. Tap the bearing out of the hub with a hammer, working around the perimeter of the inner race.

    d. Repeat for the other bearing.

8. Clean the inside and the outside of the hub with solvent. Dry with compressed air.

Assembly

1. On non-sealed bearings, pack the bearings with a good quality bearing grease. Work the grease in between the balls thoroughly; turn the bearing by hand a couple of times to make sure the grease is distributed evenly inside the bearing.

2. Blow any dirt or foreign matter out of the hub prior to installing the bearings.

> *CAUTION*
> *Install non-sealed bearings with the single sealed side facing outward. Tap the bearings squarely into place and tap on the outer race only. Use a socket (**Figure 27**) that matches the outer race diameter. Do not tap on the inner race or the bearing might be damaged. Be sure that the bearings are completely seated.*

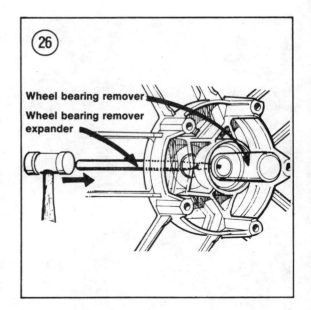

Wheel bearing remover

Wheel bearing remover expander

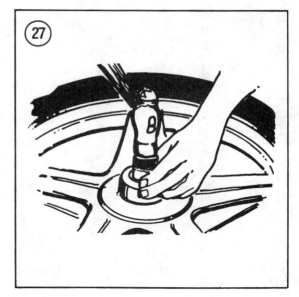

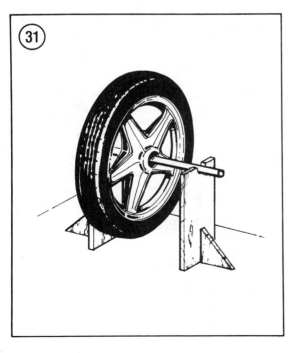

3. Install the right-hand bearing and press the distance collar into place.

4. Install the left-hand bearing.

5. Install the individual gaskets onto the hub and then install the brake disc. Install the bolts and tighten to the torque specification listed in **Table 1**. Repeat for the other disc.

6. Install the grease seal (**Figure 28**) on the right-hand side.

7. Align the tangs of the speedometer drive gear (**Figure 29**) with the drive dog in the hub and install the speedometer gear box.

8. Install the spacer (**Figure 20**) on the right-hand side.

9. *1986-on:* Perform the following.

   a. Insert the axle from the left-hand side (**Figure 30**).

   b. Install the axle nut (**Figure 23**) and tighten it to the torque specifications in **Table 1**.

10. Install the front wheel as described in this chapter.

WHEEL BALANCE

An unbalanced wheel is unsafe. Depending on the degree of unbalance and the speed of the motorcycle, the rider may experience anything from a mild vibration to a violent shimmy which may even result in loss of control.

On alloy wheels, weights are attached to the rim. A kit of Tape-A-Weight or equivalent may be purchased from most motorcycle supply stores. This kit contains test weights and strips of adhesive-backed weights that can be cut to the desired weight and attached directly to the rim.

Before you attempt to balance the wheel, check to be sure that the wheel bearings are in good condition and properly lubricated and that the brakes do not drag. The wheel must rotate freely.

1. Remove the wheel as described in this chapter or Chapter Ten.

2. Mount the wheel on a fixture such as the one shown in **Figure 31** so it can rotate freely.

3. Give the wheel a spin and let it coast to a stop. Mark the tire at the lowest point.

4. Spin the wheel several more times. If the wheel keeps coming to rest at the same point, it is out of balance.

5. Tape a test weight to the upper (or light) side of the wheel.

6. Experiment with different weights until the wheel, when spun, comes to a rest at a different position each time.

7. Remove the test weight and install the correct size adhesive-backed or clamp-on weight (**Figure 32**).

TIRE CHANGING

The rim of the alloy wheel is aluminum and the exterior appearance can easily be damaged. Special care must be taken with tire irons when changing a tire to avoid scratches and gouges to the outer rim surface. Insert scraps of leather between the tire iron and the rim to protect the rim from gouges. Honda offers rim protectors (part No. 07772-0020200) for this purpose that are very handy to use. All models are factory-equipped with tubeless tires and wheels designed specifically for use with tubeless tires.

> *WARNING*
> *Do not install tubeless tires on wheels designed for use only with tube-type tires. Personal injury and tire failure may result from rapid tire deflation while riding. Wheels for use with tubeless tires are so marked (**Figure 33**).*

Removal

1. Remove the valve core to deflate the tire.
2. Press the entire bead on both sides of the tire into the center of the rim. Lubricate the beads with soapy water.
3. Insert the tire iron under the bead next to the valve (**Figure 34**). Force the bead on the opposite side of the tire into the center of the rim and pry the bead over the rim with the tire iron.
4. Insert a second tire iron next to the first to hold the bead over the rim. Then work around the tire with the first tire iron, prying the bead over the rim (**Figure 35**).
5. Stand the tire upright. Insert the tire iron between the second bead and the side of the rim that the first bead was pried over (**Figure 36**). Force

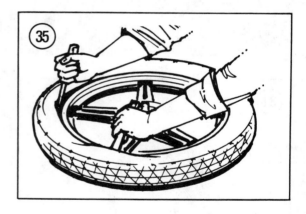

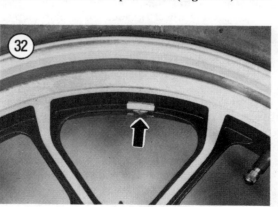

the bead on the opposite side from the tire iron into the center of the rim. Pry the second bead off the rim, working around as with the first.

6. Honda recommends that the tire valve stem be replaced whenever the tire is removed from the wheel.

Installation

1. Carefully inspect the tire for any damage, especially inside.

2. A new tire may have balancing rubbers inside. These are not patches and should not be disturbed. A colored spot near the bead indicates a lighter point on the tire. This spot (**Figure 37**) should be placed next to the valve stem.

3. Lubricate both beads of the tire with soapy water.

4. Place the backside of the tire into the center of the rim. The lower bead should go into the center of the rim and the upper bead outside. Work around the tire in both directions (**Figure 38**). Use a tire iron for the last few inches of bead (**Figure 39**).

5. Press the upper bead into the rim opposite the valve (**Figure 40**). Pry the bead into the rim on both sides of the initial point with a tire iron, working around the rim to the valve (**Figure 41**).

6. Check the bead on both sides of the tire for even fit around the rim.

7. Bounce the wheel several times, rotating it each time. This will force the tire beads against the rim

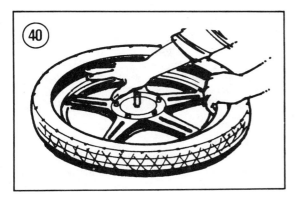

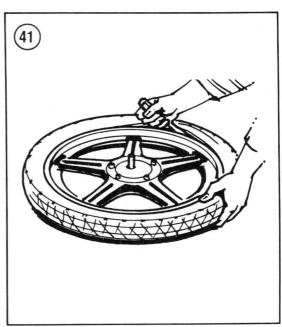

9

flanges. After the tire beads are in contact with the rim evenly, inflate the tire to seat the beads.

NOTE
If you are unable to get an airtight seal this way, install an inflatable band around the circumference of the tire. Slowly inflate the band until the beads are seated against the rim flanges, then inflate the tire. If you still encounter trouble, deflate the inflation band and the tire. Apply additional lubricant to the beads and repeat the inflation procedure. Also try rolling the tire back and forth while inflating it.

8. Inflate the tire to more than the recommended inflation pressure for the initial seating of the rim flanges. Once the beads are seated correctly, deflate the tire to the correct pressure. Refer to **Table 2**.

WARNING
Never exceed 4.0 kg/cm² (56 psi) inflation pressure as the tire could burst causing severe injury. Never stand directly over the tire while inflating it.

TIRE REPAIRS

Patching a tubeless tire on the road is very difficult. If both beads are still in place against the rim, a can of pressurized tire sealant may inflate the tire and seal the hole. The beads must be against the wheel for this method to work. Another solution is to carry a spare inner tube that could be temporarily installed and inflated. This will enable you to get to a service station where the tire can be correctly repaired. Be sure that the tube is designed for use with a tubeless tire.

Honda (and the tire industry) recommends that the tubeless tire be patched from the inside. Therefore, do not patch the tire with an external type plug. If you find an external patch on a tire, it is recommended that it be patch-reinforced from the inside.

Due to the variations of material supplied with different tubeless tire repair kits, follow the instructions and recommendations supplied with the repair kit.

Honda recommends that the valve stem be replaced each time the tire is removed from the wheel.

HANDLEBAR

Removal

1. Remove the left-hand side cover.
2. Disconnect the battery negative lead.

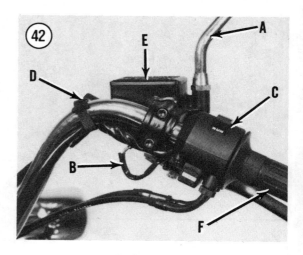

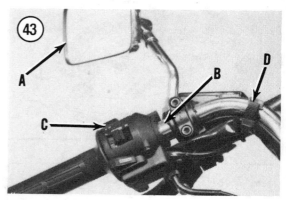

3. Remove the main fuel tank as described in Chapter Seven.
4. Remove the right-hand rear view mirror (A, **Figure 42**).
5. Disconnect the brake light switch electrical connector (B, **Figure 42**).
6. Remove the screws securing the right handlebar switch assembly (C, **Figure 42**) and remove the electrical wires from the clips (D, **Figure 42**) on the handlebar.

CAUTION
Cover the frame with a heavy cloth or plastic tarp to protect it from accidental spilling of brake fluid. Wash any spilled brake fluid off any painted or plated surface immediately, as it will destroy the finish. Use soapy water and rinse thoroughly.

7. Remove the 2 bolts securing the brake master cylinder (E, **Figure 42**) and lay it over the frame. Keep the reservoir in the upright position to minimize loss of brake fluid and to keep air from

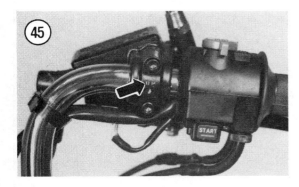

section of the handlebar with a wire brush. It should be kept rough so it will be held securely by the holders. The handlebar holder and the holders on the upper fork bridge should also be kept clean and free of any metal that may have been gouged loose by handlebar slippage.

Installation

1. Position the handlebar on the upper fork bridge so the punch mark on the handlebar is aligned with the top surface of the raised portion of the upper fork bridge.

2. Install the handlebar holder and install the Allen bolts. Tighten the forward bolts first and then the rear bolts. Tighten all bolts to the torque specification listed in **Table 1**. Install the plastic plugs.

3. After installation is complete, recheck the alignment of the handlebar punch mark.

4. Apply a light coat of multipurpose grease to the throttle grip area on the handlebar prior to installing the throttle grip assembly.

NOTE
When installing all assemblies, align the punch mark on the handlebar with the slit on the mounting bracket.

5. Install the throttle grip assembly and right-hand switch assembly.

6. Install the brake master cylinder onto the handlebar. Install the clamp with the punch mark facing down or with the "UP" arrow (**Figure 45**) facing up and align the clamp mating surface with the punch mark on the handlebar. Tighten the upper bolt first and then the lower bolt.

WARNING
After installation is completed, make sure the brake lever does not come in contact with the throttle grip assembly when it is pulled on fully. If it does the brake fluid may be low in the reservoir; refill as necessary. Refer to Chapter Eleven.

7. Install the clutch master cylinder onto the handlebar. Install the clamp and tighten the upper bolt first and then the lower bolt.

WARNING
*After installation is completed, make sure the clutch lever does not come in contact with the hand grip assembly when it is pulled on fully. If it does the hydraulic fluid may be low in the reservoir; refill as necessary. Refer to **Clutch Master Cylinder** in Chapter Five.*

entering into the brake system. It is not necessary to remove the hydraulic brake line.

8. Remove the throttle assembly (F, **Figure 42**) and carefully lay the throttle assembly and cables over the fender or back over the frame. Be careful that the cables do not get crimped or damaged.

9. Remove the left-hand rear view mirror (A, **Figure 43**).

10. Disconnect the clutch switch wires.

11. Remove the 2 bolts (B, **Figure 43**) securing the clutch master cylinder and lay it over the frame. Keep the reservoir in the upright position to minimize loss of hydraulic fluid and to keep air from entering the clutch system. It is not necessary to remove the hydraulic line.

12. Disconnect the choke cable from the choke lever.

13. Remove the screws securing the left-hand handlebar switch assembly (C, **Figure 43**) and remove the electrical wires from the clips on the handlebar (D, **Figure 43**).

14. Remove the plastic plugs (**Figure 44**) and remove the Allen bolts securing the handlebar upper holder in place.

15. Remove the handlebar upper holder then remove the handlebar.

16. To maintain a good grip on the handlebar and to prevent it from slipping down, clean the knurled

9

8. Connect the choke cable to the choke lever.

9. Install the left-hand handlebar switch assembly and tighten the bolts securely.

10. Install the clips onto the electrical wires on the handlebar.

11. Connect the battery negative lead to the battery.

12. Install the main fuel tank, seat and rear view mirrors.

13. Adjust the throttle operation as described in Chapter Three.

STEERING HEAD AND STEM

Disassembly

Refer to **Figure 46** (1983-1985) or **Figure 47** (1986-on) for this procedure.

1. Remove the front wheel as described in this chapter.

2. Remove the handlebar (A, **Figure 48**) as described in this chapter.

3. Remove the instrument cluster (B, **Figure 48**) as described in Chapter Seven.

4. Remove the headlight assembly as described in Chapter Seven.

5. Remove the ignition switch as described in Chapter Seven.

6. Loosen the upper fork bridge bolts.

7A. *1983-1985:* Remove the steering stem nut and washer (C, **Figure 48**).

7B. *1986-on:* Remove the steering stem nut.

8. Remove the front forks (D, **Figure 48**) as described in this chapter.

9. Remove the upper fork bridge (E, **Figure 48**).

10. Disconnect the electrical connector from the horns and remove the horns.

11. Remove the hydraulic brake 3-way hose connector assembly from the lower portion of the steering stem assembly. It is not necessary to disconnect any of the hydraulic lines. If any of the lines are disconnected or loosened, the brake system will have to be bled as described in Chapter Eleven.

> *NOTE*
> *When removing the steering stem adjusting nut in Step 12, loosen the nut with a large drift and hammer or use the easily improvised tool as shown in* **Figure 49**.

12A. *1983-1985:* Perform the following.

   a. Remove the steering stem adjusting nut.

   b. Have an assistant hold a large pan under the steering stem to catch the loose ball bearings and carefully lower the steering stem assembly down and out of the steering head.

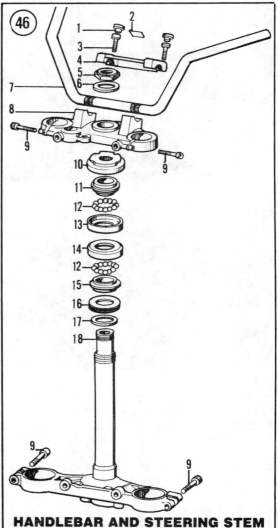

HANDLEBAR AND STEERING STEM (1983-1985)

1. Cap
2. Label
3. Allen bolt
4. Cover
5. Steering stem locknut
6. Washer
7. Handlebar
8. Upper fork bridge
9. Bolt
10. Adjusting nut
11. Top bearing inner race
12. Steel balls #8 (1/4 in. dia.)
    Quantity—18 top, 19 lower
13. Top bearing outer race
14. Lower bearing outer race
15. Lower bearing inner race
16. Dust seal
17. Washer
18. Steering stem

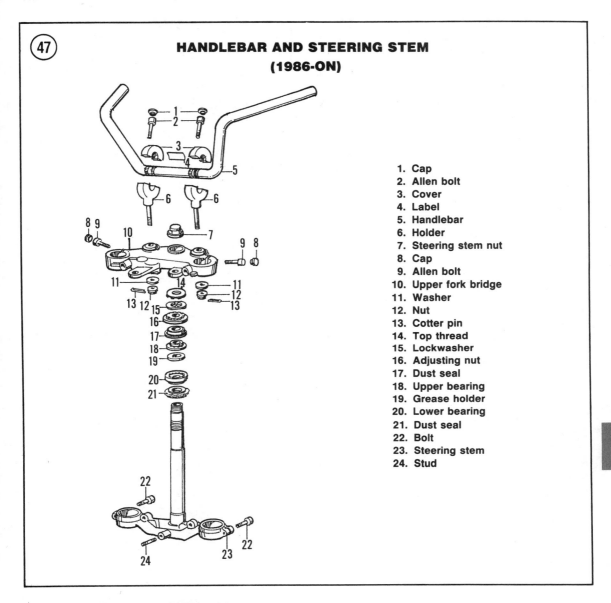

HANDLEBAR AND STEERING STEM
(1986-ON)

1. Cap
2. Allen bolt
3. Cover
4. Label
5. Handlebar
6. Holder
7. Steering stem nut
8. Cap
9. Allen bolt
10. Upper fork bridge
11. Washer
12. Nut
13. Cotter pin
14. Top thread
15. Lockwasher
16. Adjusting nut
17. Dust seal
18. Upper bearing
19. Grease holder
20. Lower bearing
21. Dust seal
22. Bolt
23. Steering stem
24. Stud

9

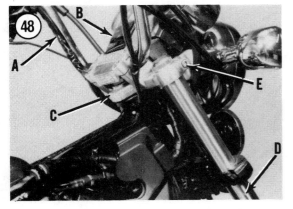

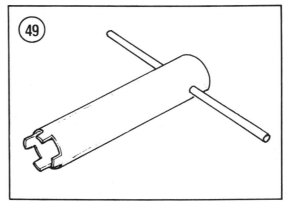

NOTE
There are 37 balls total—18 on the top and 19 on the bottom. These balls are the same size.

12B. *1986-on:* Perform the following.
  a. Pry the lockwasher tab away from the steering stem locknut (**Figure 50**).
  b. Lift the steering stem locknut and lockwasher (**Figure 50**) off of the steering stem.
  c. Remove the bearing adjusting nut (**Figure 51**) and the upper bearing inner race (**Figure 52**).
  d. Lower the steering stem assembly down and out of the steering head.

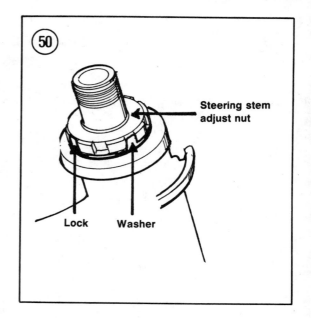

Inspection

1. Clean the bearing races in the steering head and the bearings with solvent.
2. Check the welds around the steering head for cracks and fractures. If any are found, have them repaired by a competent frame shop or welding service.
3. Check the bearings for pitting, scratches or discoloration indicating wear or corrosion.
4. On 1986-on models, turn the bearings by hand and check for excessive noise, looseness or roughness. After cleaning the bearings, dip them in clean engine oil and cover them with a clean rag to prevent contamination.
5. Check the races for pitting, galling and corrosion. If any of these conditions exist, replace the races as described in this chapter.
6. Check the steering stem for cracks and check its races for damage or wear; replace if necessary.

Assembly

Refer to **Figure 46** or **Figure 47** for this procedure.
1. Make sure both steering head bearing outer races are properly seated in the steering head tube.
2A. *1983-1985:* Perform the following.
  a. Apply a coat of cold grease to the top bearing race cone and fit 18 balls into it (**Figure 53**).
  b. Apply a coat of cold grease to the bottom bearing race cone and fit 19 balls into it (**Figure 54**).
  c. Install the steering stem into the steering head tube and hold it firmly in place.
  d. Install the top bearing inner race.
  e. Install the steering stem adjusting nut and tighten it until it is snug against the top race, then back it off 1/8 turn.

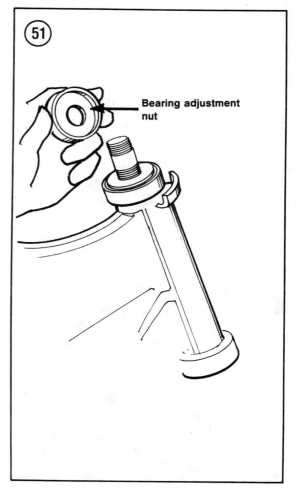

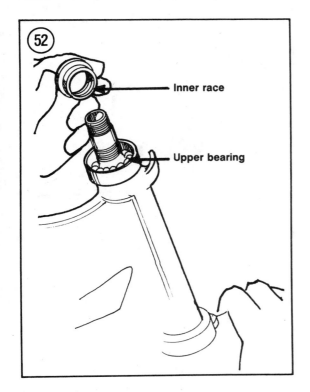

Inner race

Upper bearing

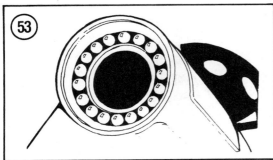

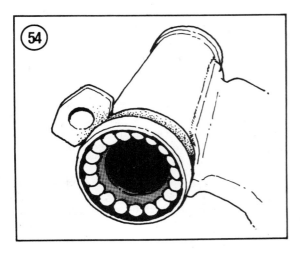

9

NOTE
The steering stem adjusting nut should be just tight enough to remove play, both vertical and horizontal, yet loose enough so that the assembly will turn to both lock positions under its own weight after a light push.

f. Install the upper fork bridge, washer and the steering stem nut. Tighten the nut only finger-tight at this time.

2B. *1986-on:* Perform the following.

a. Apply a coat of cold grease to the upper bearing outer race and to the upper bearing.

b. Install the upper bearing into the upper bearing outer race.

c. Apply a coat of cold grease to the lower bearing inner race and to the lower bearing.

d. Install the lower bearing over the steering stem and onto the lower bearing inner race.

e. Install the steering stem into the steering head tube and hold it firmly in place.

f. Install the top bearing inner race (**Figure 52**).

g. Install the bearing adjustment nut (**Figure 51**) and tighten to 23-27 N•m (17-20 ft.-lb.). Then turn the steering stem back and forth a few times to seat the bearings.

h. Retighten the bearing adjustment nut to the torque specification in sub-step "g".

i. Install a new bearing adjustment nut lockwasher. Bend two of the lockwasher tabs (opposite from each other) into the bearing adjustment nut grooves.

NOTE
Step 3 and Step 4 must be performed in this order to assure proper upper and lower fork bridge to fork alignment.

3. Install the fork tubes in the lower fork bridge and continue to slide the fork tubes into position. Align the top of each fork tube so it is flush with the top surface of the upper fork bridge.

4. Tighten these items in the following order.

a. Lower fork bridge bolts.

b. Stem nut.

c. Upper fork bridge bolts.

Tighten all items to the torque specifications listed in **Table 1**.

5. *1986-on:* Check steering head bearing preload as follows.

a. Install the front wheel.

b. Support the motorcycle so that the front wheel clears the ground.

c. Position the steering so that the front wheel faces straight ahead.

d. Attach a spring scale onto the right-hand fork tube as shown in **Figure 55**.

e. Pull the right-hand fork tube to the left and note the reading on the spring scale.

f. Repeat sub-steps "d" and "e" for the left-hand fork tube.

g. The spring scale should show a bearing preload of 1.1-1.6 kg (2.4-3.5 lb.). If the bearing preload is incorrect, remove the fork tubes and the upper fork bridge and retighten or loosen the bearing adjustment nut.

6. Install the hydraulic brake 3-way hose connector onto the lower portion of the steering stem assembly.

7. Install the horn and connect the electrical connector to the horn.

8. Install the ignition switch, headlight assembly and the instrument cluster as described in Chapter Seven.

9. Install the handlebar as described in this chapter.

10. Complete the installation of the front forks as described in this chapter.

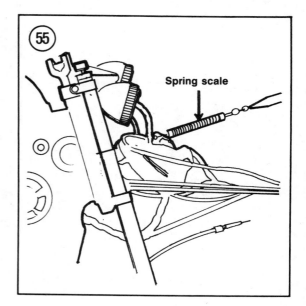

Spring scale

STEERING HEAD BEARING RACES

The headset and steering stem bearing races are pressed into place. Because they are easily bent, do not remove them unless they are worn and require replacement.

The top and bottom bearing races are not the same size. The bottom race is the slightly larger of the two. Be sure that you install them in the proper ends of the frame steering head tube.

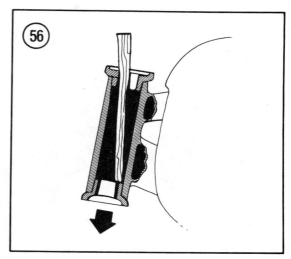

Steering Head Bearing Outer Race Replacement

To remove the headset race, insert a hardwood stick or soft punch into the head tube (**Figure 56**) and carefully tap the race out from the inside. After it is started, tap around the race so that neither the race nor the steering head tube are damaged. To install the steering head bearing race, tap it in slowly with a block of wood, a suitable size socket or piece of pipe (**Figure 57**). Make sure that the race is squarely seated in the steering head race bore before tapping it into place. Tap the race in until it is flush with the steering head surface.

Steering Stem Lower Bearing and Race and Grease Seal Removal/Installation

NOTE
Do not remove the steering stem lower bearing race unless it is going to be replaced with a new bearing race. Do not reinstall a bearing race that has been removed as it is no longer true to alignment.

1. To remove the steering stem lower bearing inner race, try twisting and pulling it up by hand. If it will not come off, carefully pry it up from the base of the steering stem with a screwdriver; work around in a circle, prying a little at a time. Remove

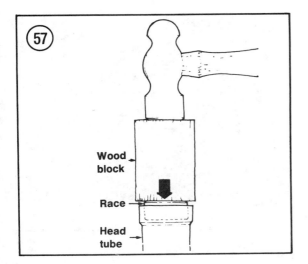

Wood
block

Race

Head
tube

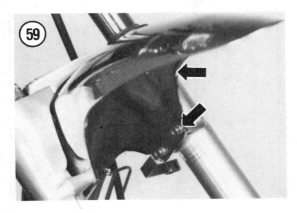

the bearing inner race, dust seal and dust seal washer.

2. Slide on a new dust seal washer and dust seal over the steering stem.

3. Slide the lower bearing inner race over the steering stem.

4. Tap the race down with a long piece of metal pipe that fits the inner race diameter or use a piece

of hardwood; work around in a circle so the bearing and inner race will not be bent. Make sure it is seated squarely and is all the way down.

FRONT FORKS

The front suspension uses spring controlled, hydraulically damped, telescopic forks with air assist.

Before suspecting major trouble, drain the front fork oil and refill with the proper type and quantity; refer to Chapter Three. If you still have trouble, such as poor damping, a tendency to bottom or top out or leakage around the rubber seals, follow the service procedures in this section.

To simplify fork service and to prevent the mixing of parts, the legs should be removed, serviced and installed individually.

Removal

1. Remove the front wheel and brake caliper assemblies as described in this chapter.

> *NOTE*
> *The Allen bolt at the base of the slider has been secured with Loctite. It is often very difficult to remove because the damper rod will turn inside the slider. It sometimes can be removed with an air impact driver. If you are unable to remove it, take the fork tubes to a dealer and have the screws removed.*

2. If the fork assembly is going to be disassembled, perform the following:
   a. Have an assistant hold the front brake on, compress the front fork and hold it in that position.
   b. Using a 6 mm Allen wrench, slightly loosen the Allen bolt at the base of the slider. If the bolt is loosened too much, fork oil may start to drain out of the slider.

3. Remove the air valve cap (**Figure 58**) and bleed off *all* air pressure by depressing the valve stem.

> *WARNING*
> *Always bleed off all air pressure; failure to do so may cause personal injury when disassembling the fork assembly.*

> *NOTE*
> *Release the air pressure gradually. If released too fast, fork oil will spurt out with the air. Protect your eyes and clothing accordingly.*

4. Remove the bolts securing the front fender (**Figure 59**) and remove the fender.

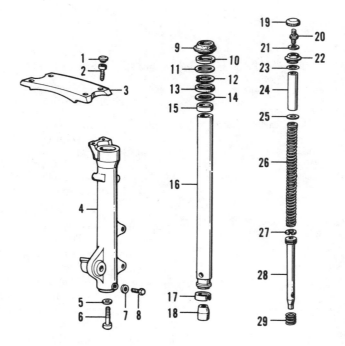

FRONT FORK

1. Chrome cap (1983-1985)
2. Bolt (1983-1985)
3. Fork brace (1983-1985)
4. Fork slider
5. Washer
6. Allen bolt
7. Washer
8. Drain bolt
9. Dust seal
10. Sponge seal (discard)
11. Plastic washer (discard)
12. Circlip (1983-1985)
     Stopper ring (1986-on)
13. Oil seal
14. Backup ring
15. Slider bushing
16. Fork tube
17. Fork tube bushing
18. Oil lock piece
19. Top cap
20. Air valve
21. O-ring
22. Fork top cap bolt
23. O-ring
24. Fork tube spreader
25. Spring seat
26. Spring
27. Damper rod seal
28. Damper rod
29. Rebound spring

5A. *1983-1985:* Remove the chrome cover caps. Remove the Allen bolts securing the fork brace (**Figure 60**) and remove the fork brace.

5B. *1986-on:* Remove the steering stem cover bolts and remove the cover from the lower steering stem.

6. Loosen, but do not remove, the fork top cap bolts.

7. Loosen the upper and lower fork bridge bolts (**Figure 61**).

8. Remove the fork tubes. It may be necessary to slightly rotate the fork tubes while pulling them down and out.

Installation

1. Insert the fork tubes up through the lower and upper fork bridges.

2. Align the top of the fork tube with the top surface of the upper fork bridge.

3. Tighten the upper and lower fork bridge bolts loosely at this time—just enough to hold them in place.

4. Tighten the upper and lower fork bridge bolts to the torque specifications in **Table 1**.

5A. *1983-1985:* Install the fork brace and tighten the Allen bolts to the torque specifications listed in **Table 1**. Install the trim caps into the bolt heads.

5B. *1986-on:* Install the steering stem cover and tighten the bolts securely.

> *NOTE*
> *The steering stem adjusting nut should be just tight enough to remove play, both vertical and horizontal, yet loose enough so that the assembly will turn to both lock positions under its own weight after a light push.*

6. Install the front fender and tighten the bolts securely.

7. Install the front wheel and brake caliper assemblies as described in this chapter.

8. Make sure the front wheel is off the ground and inflate the forks to 0-0.4 kg/cm^2 (0-6 psi). Do not use compressed air, only use a small hand-operated air pump.

> *WARNING*
> *Never use any type of compressed gas as an explosion may be lethal. Never heat the fork assembly with a torch or place it near an open flame or extreme heat, as this will also result in an explosion.*

> *CAUTION*
> *Never exceed an air pressure of 3.0 kg/cm^2 (43 psi) as damage may occur to internal components of the fork assembly.*

9. Take the bike off of the centerstand, apply the front brake and pump the forks several times. Recheck the air pressure and readjust if necessary.

Disassembly

Refer to **Figure 62** during the disassembly and assembly procedures.

1. Clamp the slider in a vise with soft jaws.

2. If not loosened during the fork removal sequence, loosen the Allen bolt and gasket from the base of the slider.

> *NOTE*
> *This bolt has been secured with thread sealant and is often very difficult to remove because the damper rod will turn inside the slider. It sometimes can be removed with an air impact driver. If you are unable to remove it, take the fork tubes to a dealer and have the screws removed.*

3. Remove the Allen bolt (**Figure 63**) at the base of the slider.

4. Hold the upper fork tube in a vise with soft jaws and loosen the fork top cap bolt (if it was not loosened during the fork removal sequence).

> *WARNING*
> *Be careful when removing the fork top cap bolt as the spring is under pressure. Protect your eyes accordingly.*

5. Remove the fork top cap bolt from the fork.

6. Remove the fork tube spacer, the spring seat and the fork spring.

7. Remove the fork from the vise, pour the fork oil out and discard it. Pump the fork several times by hand to expel most of the remaining oil.

8. Remove the dust seal, sponge washer and the plastic washer. Discard the sponge seal and plastic

9

washei as they are not to be reinstalled. These 2 parts were installed on the 1983 models and the early 1984 production run of these models and then were eliminated on later 1984 production bikes. **Figure 62** shows these 2 parts and indicates that they should be discarded.

9A. *1983-1985:* Using circlip pliers, remove the circlip from the slider.

9B. *1986-on:* Using a screwdriver, carefully pry the stopper ring from the slider.

10. Install the fork slider in a vise with soft jaws.

> *NOTE*
> *On this type of fork, force is needed to remove the fork tube from the slider.*

11. There is an interference fit between the bushing in the fork slider and the bushing on the fork tube. In order to remove the fork tube from the slider, pull hard on the fork tube using quick in and out strokes. Doing this will withdraw the bushing, backup ring and oil seal from the slider.

> *NOTE*
> *It may be necessary to slightly heat the area on the slider around the oil seal prior to removal. Use a rag soaked in hot water; do not apply a flame directly to the fork slider.*

12. Withdraw the fork tube from the slider.

> *NOTE*
> *Do not remove the fork tube bushing unless it is going to be replaced. Inspect it as described in this chapter.*

13. Turn the fork tube upside down and slide off the oil seal, backup ring and slider bushing from the fork tube (**Figure 64**).

> *NOTE*
> *Do not discard the slider bushing at this time. It will be used during the installation procedure.*

14. Remove the oil lock piece, the damper rod and rebound spring.

15. Inspect the components as described in this chapter.

Inspection

1. Thoroughly clean all parts in solvent and dry them. Check the fork tube for signs of wear or scratches.

2. Check the damper rod for straightness. **Figure 65** shows one method. The rod should be replaced if the runout is 0.2 mm (0.008 in.) or greater.

3. Carefully check the damper rod and piston ring for wear or damage (**Figure 66**).

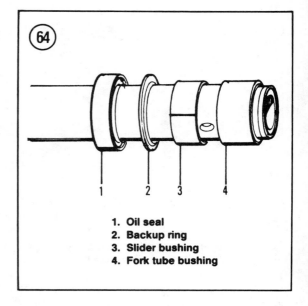

64

1. **Oil seal**
2. **Backup ring**
3. **Slider bushing**
4. **Fork tube bushing**

65

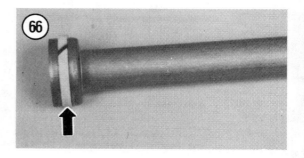

66

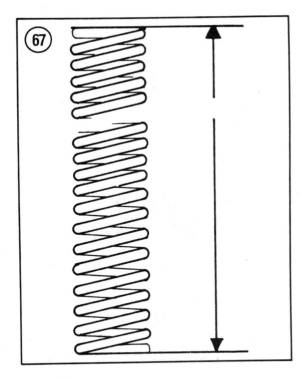

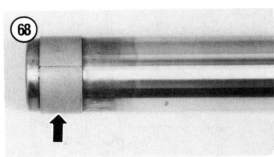

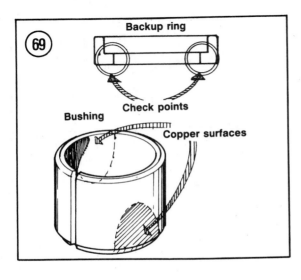

4. Check the upper fork tube for straightness. If bent or severely scratched, it should be replaced.

5. Check the lower slider for dents or exterior damage that may cause the upper fork tube to hang up during riding. Replace if necessary.

6. Measure the uncompressed length of the fork spring (not rebound spring) as shown in **Figure 67**. If the spring has sagged to the service limit dimensions listed in **Table 3** the spring must be replaced.

7. Inspect the slider and fork tube bushings (**Figure 68**). If either is scratched or scored they must be replaced. If the Teflon coating is worn off so that the copper base material is showing on approximately 3/4 of the total surface, the bushing must be replaced. Also check for distortion on the check points of the backup ring; replace as necessary. Refer to **Figure 69**.

8. Any parts that are worn or damaged should be replaced. Simply cleaning and reinstalling unserviceable components will not improve performance of the front suspension.

Assembly

1. Coat all parts with fresh DEXRON automatic transmission fluid or fork oil prior to installation.

2. If removed, install a new fork tube bushing (**Figure 68**).

3. Install the rebound spring onto the damper rod and insert this assembly into the fork tube (**Figure 70**).

9

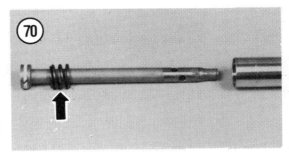

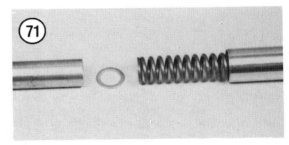

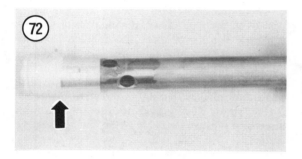

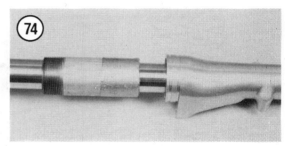

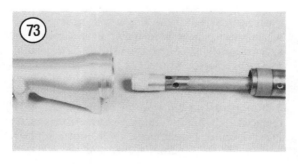

4. Temporarily install the fork spring, spring seat, spacer (**Figure 71**) and fork top cap bolt. This will help hold the damper rod in place.

5. Install the oil lock piece onto the damper rod (**Figure 72**).

6. Install the upper fork assembly into the slider (**Figure 73**).

7. Slide the fork slider bushing down the fork tube and rest it on the slider.

8. Slide the fork slider backup ring (flange side up) down the fork tube and rest it on top of the fork slider bushing.

9. Place the old fork slider bushing on top of the backup ring. Drive the bushing into the fork slider with Honda special tool Fork Seal Driver (part No. 07947-4630100). Drive the bushing into place until it seats completely in the recess in the slider. Remove the installation tool and the old fork slider bushing.

> *NOTE*
> *A piece of 2 in. galvanized pipe can also work as a tool. If both ends are threaded (a close nipple pipe fitting), wrap one end with duct tape (**Figure 74**) to prevent the threads from damaging the interior of the slider.*

10. Coat the new seal with DEXRON automatic transmission fluid. Position the seal with the marking facing upward (**Figure 75**) and slide it down onto the fork tube. Drive the seal into the slider with Honda special tool Fork Seal Driver (part No. 07947-4630100); refer to **Figure 76**.

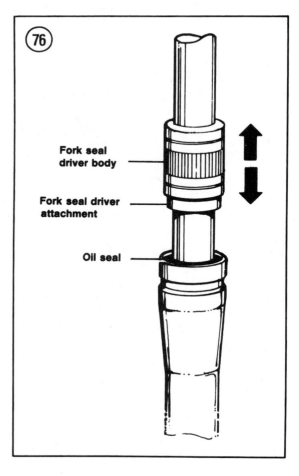

Fork seal driver body

Fork seal driver attachment

Oil seal

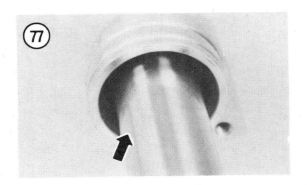

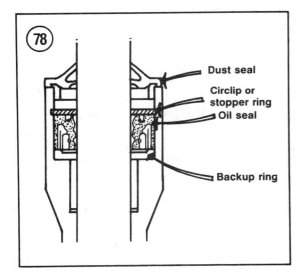

Dust seal

Circlip or
stopper ring

Oil seal

Backup ring

Drive the oil seal in until the groove in the slider can be seen above the top surface of the oil seal.

NOTE
The slider seal can be driven in with a homemade tool as described in the NOTE following Step 9.

11A. *1983-1985:* Install the circlip with the sharp side facing up. Make sure the circlip is completely seated in the groove in the fork slider (**Figure 77**).
11B. *1986-on:* Install the stopper ring in the slider. Make sure the ring is seated in the slider groove completely.

NOTE
***Figure 78** shows the correct placement of all components installed in Step 12.*

12. Install the plastic seal washer (**Figure 79**). Remember, do *not* install the plastic washer and the sponge seal. Discard them if they are included in a new seal kit you have purchased. Refer to the Note regarding these items in the Disassembly procedure.
13. Make sure the gasket is on the Allen bolt (**Figure 80**).
14. Apply Loctite Lock N' Seal to the threads of the Allen bolt prior to installation. Install it in the fork slider (**Figure 63**) and tighten to the torque specification listed in **Table 1**. If you are unable to tighten the bolt to the correct torque specification, finish tightening the bolt after the fork tube is reinstalled in the bike's frame.
15. Remove the fork top cap bolt, the fork tube spacer, the spring seat and the fork spring.
16. Fill the fork tube with the correct quantity of DEXRON automatic transmission fluid or fork oil as listed in **Table 4**.
17. Install the fork spring with the closer wound coils toward the top end of the fork.
18. Install the fork seat and the fork tube spacer (**Figure 71**).
19. Inspect the O-ring seal (**Figure 81**) on the fork top cap bolt; replace if necessary.

20. Install the fork top cap bolt (**Figure 82**) while pushing down on the spring. Start the bolt slowly, don't cross-thread it.

21. Place the slider in a vise with soft jaws and tighten the top fork cap bolt to the torque specification listed in **Table 1**.

22. Repeat for the other fork assembly.

23. Install the fork assemblies as described in this chapter.

Table 1 FRONT SUSPENSION TORQUE SPECIFICATIONS

Item	N•m	ft.-lb.
Front axle	55-65	40-47
Front axle		
Pinch bolt (1983-1985)	18-28	13-20
Holder nut (1986-on)	27-33	20-24
Caliper mounting bolts	30-40	22-29
Brake system union bolts	25-35	18-25
Brake disc bolts		
1983-1985	35-40	25-29
1986-on	37-43	27-31
Handlebar holder bolts	20-30	14-22
Fork bridge bolts		
Upper	9-13	7-9
Lower	45-55	33-40
Fork cap bolt	15-30	11-22
Fork brace Allen bolts		
(1983-1985)	15-25	11-18
Fork slide Allen bolt	15-25	11-18
Steering stem nut		
1983-1985	80-120	58-87
1986-on	90-120	65-87

Table 2 TIRE INFLATION PRESSURE (COLD)

	Air pressure	
	Normal	Maximum load limit*
Front		
110/90-19	32 psi (2.25 kg/cm²)	32 psi (2.25 kg/cm²)
Rear		
140/90-15	32 psi (2.25 kg/cm²)	40 psi (2.80 kg/cm²)
* Maximum load limit includes total weight of motorcycle with accessories, rider(s) and luggage.		

Table 3 FRONT FORK SPRING LENGTH

	Standard	Service limit
1983-1985	465.6 mm (18.33 in.)	456.3 mm (18.0 in.)
1986-on	426.2 mm (16.78 in.)	417.7 mm (16.44 in.)

Table 4 FORK OIL CAPACITY *

1983-1985	467.5-472.5 cc (15.82-15.99 oz.)
1986-on	442.5-447.5 cc (14.99-15.16 oz.)

* Capacity for each fork leg.

9

CHAPTER TEN

REAR SUSPENSION AND FINAL DRIVE

This chapter includes repair and replacement procedures for the rear wheel, rear suspension components and the final drive unit.

Power from the engine is transmitted to the rear wheel by a drive shaft and the final drive unit.

Tire changing and wheel balancing is covered in Chapter Nine.

Refer to **Table 1** for rear suspension torque specifications. **Table 1** and **Table 2** are located at the end of this chapter.

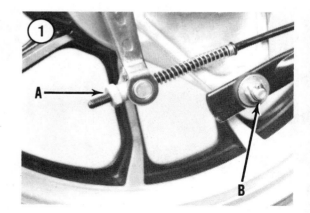

REAR WHEEL

Removal/Installation

1. Place the bike on the centerstand or block up the engine so that the rear wheel clears the ground.
2. Completely unscrew the rear brake adjusting nut (A, **Figure 1**).
3. Depress the brake pedal and remove the brake rod from the pivot joint in the brake arm. Remove the pivot joint from the brake arm and install the pivot joint and the adjusting nut onto the brake rod to avoid misplacing them.
4. To remove the brake torque link from the brake panel, perform the following:

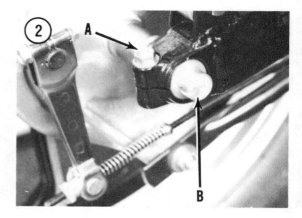

a. Remove the cotter pin from the bolt (B, **Figure 1**).

b. Remove the bolt, nut and washer.

c. Swing the brake arm down and out of the way.

5. Loosen the axle pinch bolt (A, **Figure 2**).

6. Remove the rear axle self-locking nut (**Figure 3**).

7. Insert a drift or screwdriver into the hole in the end of the rear axle and withdraw the axle (B, **Figure 2**) from the right-hand side.

8. Slide the wheel to the right to disengage it from the hub drive splines and remove the wheel.

9. Don't lose the spacer on the right-hand side between the brake and the swing arm.

Inspection

Measure the axial and radial runout of the wheel with a dial indicator as shown in **Figure 4**. The maximum axial and radial runout is 2.0 mm (0.08 in.). If the runout exceeds this dimension, check the wheel bearing condition.

If the wheel bearings are okay, the wheel will have to be replaced, as it cannot be serviced. Inspect the wheel for signs of cracks, fractures, dents or bends. If it is damaged in any way, it must be replaced.

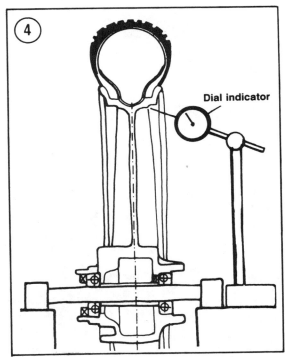

Dial indicator

WARNING
Do not try to repair any damage to an alloy wheel as it will result in an unsafe riding condition.

Check axial runout as described under *Rear Hub Inspection* in this chapter.

Installation

1. The distance collar within the final drive unit may move out during axle and wheel removal. If so, push it back into place. If the distance collar falls out, reinstall it into the hub with the narrow end in first (**Figure 5**).

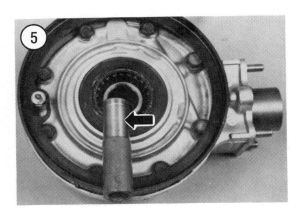

NOTE
Figure 5 is shown with the final drive unit removed for clarity.

2. Apply a light coat of grease (lithium based NLGI No. 2 grease with molybdenum disulfide) to

10

the final driven flange spline and to the rear wheel ring gear (**Figure 6**).

3. Loosen the final drive case nuts (**Figure 7**).

4. Position the rear wheel so that the splines of the final driven flange and the final drive align. Slowly move the wheel back and forth and push the wheel to the left until it completely seats.

5. Position the spacer (**Figure 8**) on the right-hand side between the brake and the swing arm.

6. Install the rear axle from the right-hand side and install the axle nut only finger-tight.

7. To install the brake torque link, perform the following:

    a. Swing the brake arm up and into position.

    b. Install the bolt from the backside and install the washer and nut. Tighten the bolt and nut to the torque specification listed in **Table 1**.

    c. Install a new cotter pin and bend the ends over completely.

8. Insert a drift into the hole in the axle to keep the axle from turning.

9. Tighten the rear axle nut to the torque specifications listed in **Table 1**.

10. Tighten the final drive gear case nuts, then the axle pinch bolt to the torque specifications listed in **Table 1**.

11. After the wheel is installed, completely rotate it and apply the brake several times to make sure it rotates freely and that the brakes work properly.

12. Adjust the rear brake free play as described in Chapter Three.

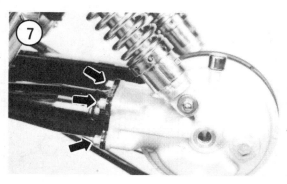

REAR HUB

Inspection

Inspect each wheel bearing prior to removing it from the wheel hub.

> *CAUTION*
> *Do not remove the wheel bearings for inspection as they will be damaged during removal. Remove wheel bearings only if they are to be replaced.*

1. Perform Step 1 and Step 2 of *Disassembly* in this chapter.

2. Turn each bearing by hand (**Figure 9**). Make sure the bearings turn smoothly.

3. On non-sealed bearings, check the balls for evidence of wear, pitting or excessive heat (bluish tint). Replace the bearings if necessary; always replace as a complete set. When replacing the bearings, be sure to take your old bearings along to ensure a perfect matchup.

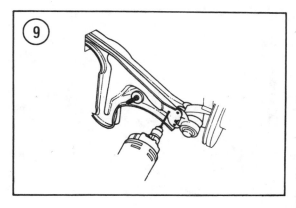

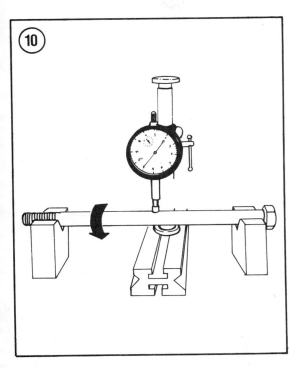

NOTE
Fully sealed bearings are available from many bearing specialty shops. Fully sealed bearings provide better protection from dirt and moisture that may get into the hub.

4. Check the axle for wear and straightness. Use V-blocks and a dial indicator as shown in **Figure 10**. If the runout is 0.2 mm (0.01 in.) or greater, the axle should be replaced.

5. Inspect the splines of the final driven flange. If any are damaged the flange must be replaced.

Disassembly

Refer to **Figure 11** for this procedure.

1. Remove the rear wheel as described in this chapter.

2. Remove the bolts securing the final driven flange and remove the flange (**Figure 6**).

3. Before proceeding further, inspect the wheel bearings as described in this chapter. If they must be replaced, proceed as follows.

4A. A special Honda tool set-up can be used to remove the wheel bearings as follows:

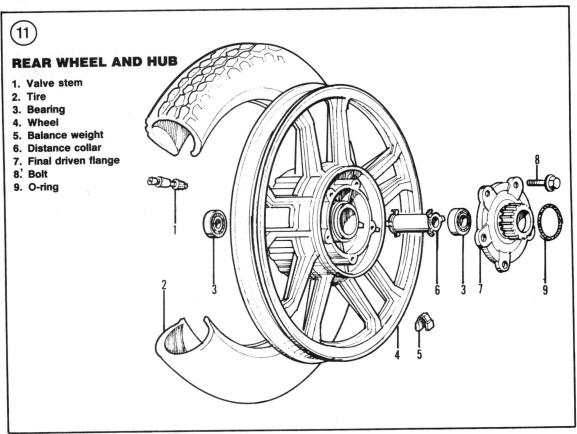

REAR WHEEL AND HUB

1. Valve stem
2. Tire
3. Bearing
4. Wheel
5. Balance weight
6. Distance collar
7. Final driven flange
8. Bolt
9. O-ring

a. Install the 15 mm bearing remover (Honda part No. 07746-0050400) into the right-hand bearing.

b. Turn the wheel over (left-hand side up) on the workbench so the bearing remover is touching the workbench surface.

c. From the left-hand side of the hub, install the bearing remover expander (Honda part No. 07746-050100) into the bearing remover. Using a hammer, tap the expander into the bearing remover.

d. Stand the wheel up to a vertical position.

e. Tap on the end of the expander (**Figure 12**) and drive the right-hand bearing out of the hub. Remove the bearing and the distance collar.

f. Repeat for the left-hand bearing.

4B. If special tools are not available, perform the following:

a. To remove the right- and left-hand bearings and distance collar, insert a soft aluminum or brass drift into one side of the hub.

b. Push the distance collar over to one side and place the drift on the inner race of the lower bearing.

c. Tap the bearing out of the hub with a hammer, working around the perimeter of the inner race.

d. Repeat for the other bearing.

5. Clean the inside and the outside of the hub with solvent. Dry with compressed air.

6. Clean the inside and the outside of the final driven flange with solvent. Remove and discard the O-ring seal at the base of the splines. Dry with compressed air.

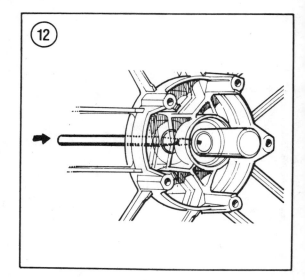

Assembly

1. On non-sealed bearings, pack the bearings with a good quality bearing grease. Work the grease in between the balls thoroughly; turn the bearing by hand a couple of times to make sure the grease is distributed evenly inside the bearing.

2. Blow any dirt or foreign matter out of the hub prior to installing the bearings.

> *CAUTION*
> *Install non-sealed bearings with the single sealed side facing outward.*

3. Pack the hub with multipurpose grease.

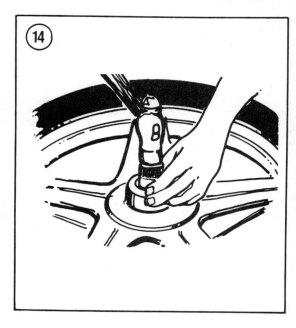

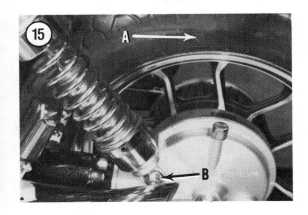

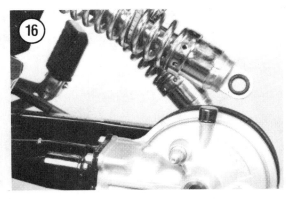

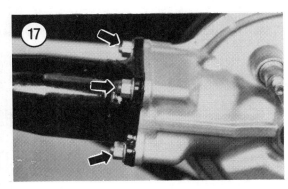

4. Press the distance collar into the hub from the left-hand side.

CAUTION
*Install the standard bearings (they are sealed on one side only) with the sealed side facing out (**Figure 13**). Tap the bearings squarely into place and tap on the outer race only. Use a socket (**Figure 14**) that matches the outer race diameter. Do not tap on the inner race or the bearing might be damaged. Be sure that the bearings are completely seated.*

5. Install the right-hand bearing into the hub.
6. Install the left-hand bearing into the hub.
7. Install the final driven flange and bolts. Tighten the bolts to the torque specifications listed in **Table 1**.
8. Install a new O-ring seal onto the base of the splines on the final driven flange.
9. Install the rear wheel as described in this chapter.

FINAL DRIVE UNIT AND DRIVE SHAFT

Removal

1. Remove the rear wheel (A, **Figure 15**) as described in this chapter.
2. Drain the final drive unit oil as described in Chapter Three.
3. Remove the lower nut and washer (B, **Figure 15**) securing the left-hand shock absorber to the final drive unit. Pivot the shock absorber up and out of the way and secure it to the frame with a Bungee cord (**Figure 16**).
4. Remove the nuts and washers (**Figure 17**) securing the final drive unit to the swing arm.
5. Pull the final drive unit and drive shaft straight back until it is disengaged from the splines on the universal joint.

Disassembly/Inspection/ Assembly

The final drive unit requires a considerable number of special Honda tools for disassembly and assembly. The price of all of these tools could be more than the cost of most repairs or seal replacement by a dealer.

Figure 18 shows all of the internal components of the final drive unit.

1. Using a circular motion, carefully pull the drive shaft from the final drive unit.
2. Check that the dust cover flange bolt (**Figure 19**) is in place and is tight.

10

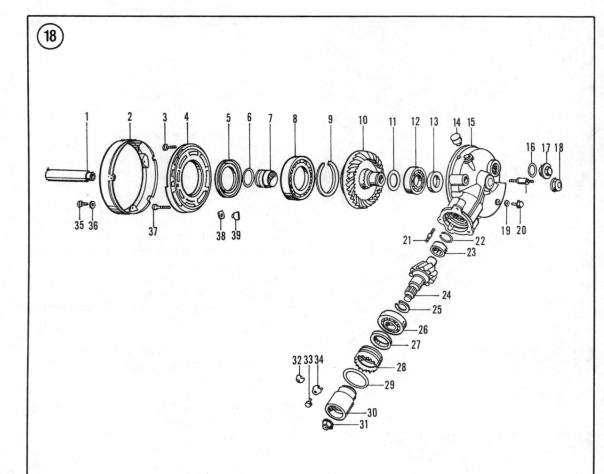

FINAL DRIVE UNIT

1. Distance collar
2. Dust guard plate
3. Bolt
4. Gear case cover
5. Oil seal
6. O-ring seal
7. O-ring seal holder
8. Bearing
9. Spacer
10. Gear set (part of No. 24)
11. Wave washer
12. Bearing
13. Oil seal
14. Breather cap
15. Case
16. O-ring seal
17. Cap
18. Nut
19. Washer
20. Drain bolt
21. Threaded pin
22. Clip
23. Needle bearing
24. Gear set (part of No. 10)
25. Shim
26. Bearing
27. Oil seal
28. Bearing retainer
29. O-ring seal
30. Primary joint
31. Nut
32. Bearing adjust lock
33. Bolt
34. Bearing adjust lock
35. Bolt
36. Nut
37. Bolt
38. Nut
39. Pin

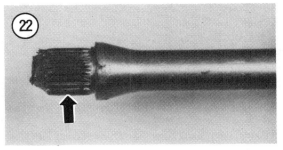

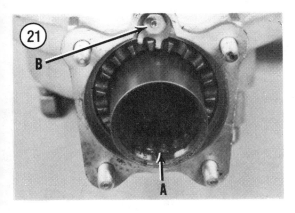

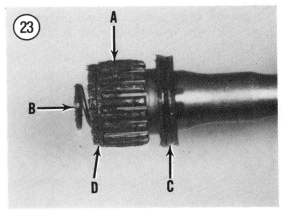

3. Inspect the splines on the final driven ring gear (**Figure 20**). If they are damaged or worn the ring gear must be replaced.

NOTE
If these splines are damaged, also inspect the splines on the rear wheel final driven flange; it may also need to be replaced.

4. Inspect the splines on the final driven primary joint (A, **Figure 21**). If they are damaged or worn the primary joint must be replaced. If these splines are damaged, also inspect the splines on the drive shaft; it may also need to be replaced.
5. Make sure the bearing retainer adjust lock and bolt (B, **Figure 21**) are in place and tight.
6. Inspect the splines on the universal joint end of drive shaft (**Figure 22**). If they are damaged or worn, the drive shaft must be replaced. If these splines are damaged, also inspect the splines on the universal joint; it may also need to be replaced.
7. Inspect the splines on the final drive unit end of drive shaft (A, **Figure 23**). If they are damaged or worn, the drive shaft must be replaced. If these splines are damaged, also inspect the splines in the final drive unit; it may also need to be replaced.
8. Check the damper spring (B, **Figure 23**); replace if necessary.

9. Replace the oil seal (C, **Figure 23**) on the drive shaft. The oil seal must be replaced every time it is removed from the drive shaft.
10. Remove the stopper ring (D, **Figure 23**) from the groove in the end of the drive shaft splines. Discard the stopper ring.
11. Check that gear oil has not been leaking from either side of the unit (ring gear side or pinion joint side). If there are traces of oil leakage, take the unit to a dealer for oil seal replacement.
12. Make sure the damper spring (B, **Figure 23**) is installed in the end of the drive shaft.
13. Install a new stopper ring into the groove in the end of the drive shaft splines. Make sure it is correctly seated in the groove.

Installation

1. Apply a light coat of molybdenum disulfide grease (NGLI No. 2) to the splines of the drive shaft and install the drive shaft into the final drive unit. Using a soft-faced mallet, tap on the end of the drive shaft to make sure the drive shaft is completely seated into the final drive unit splines.
2. Apply a light coat of molybdenum disulfide grease (NGLI No. 2) to the final driven spline.
3. Install the final drive unit and drive shaft into the swing arm. It may be necessary to slightly rotate the final driven spline back and forth to align

10

the splines of the drive shaft and the universal joint.

4. Install the final drive unit's washers and nuts only finger-tight at this time. Do not tighten the nuts until the rear wheel and rear axle are in place.

5. Install the rear wheel as described in this chapter.

6. Tighten the final drive unit nuts to the specifications listed in **Table 1**.

7. Install the shock absorber lower washer and nut and tighten to the torque specifications listed in **Table 1**.

8. Refill the final drive unit with the correct amount and type of gear oil. Refer to Chapter Three.

UNIVERSAL JOINT

Removal/Inspection/ Installation

1. Remove the swing arm as described in this chapter.

2. Remove the universal joint from the engine output shaft.

3. Clean the universal joint in solvent and thoroughly dry with compressed air.

4. Inspect the universal joint pivot points for play (**Figure 24**). Rotate the joint in both directions. If there is noticeable side play the universal joint must be replaced.

5. Inspect the splines at each end of the universal joint (**Figure 25**). If they are damaged or worn, the universal joint must be replaced.

> *NOTE*
> *If these splines are damaged, also inspect the splines in the final drive unit and the engine output shaft; they may also need to be replaced.*

6. Apply a light coat of molybdenum disulfide grease (NGLI No. 2) to both splined ends.

7. Install the universal joint onto the engine output shaft.

8. Install the swing arm as described in this chapter.

SWING ARM

In time, the roller bearings will wear and will have to be replaced. The condition of the bearings can greatly affect handling performance and if worn parts are not replaced they can produce erratic and dangerous handling. Common

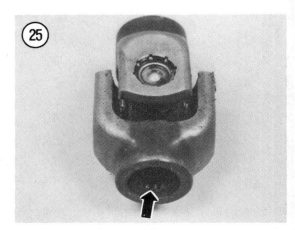

symptoms are wheel hop, pulling to one side during acceleration and pulling to the other side during braking.

A Honda special tool is required for loosening and tightening of the pivot adjusting bolt locknut. The tool is the Swing Arm Pivot Locknut Wrench (Honda part No. 07908-ME90000). This tool is required for proper and safe installation of the swing arm. If this locknut is not tightened to the correct torque specification it may allow the adjusting bolt to work loose. This could result in the swing arm working free from the right-hand side of the frame causing a serious accident.

Refer to **Figure 26** (1983-1985) or **Figure 27** (1986-on) for these procedures.

Removal

1. Place the bike on the centerstand and remove the seat.

2. Remove the exhaust system as described in Chapter Six.

3. Remove the rear wheel as described in this chapter.

4. Remove the final drive unit and drive shaft as described in this chapter.

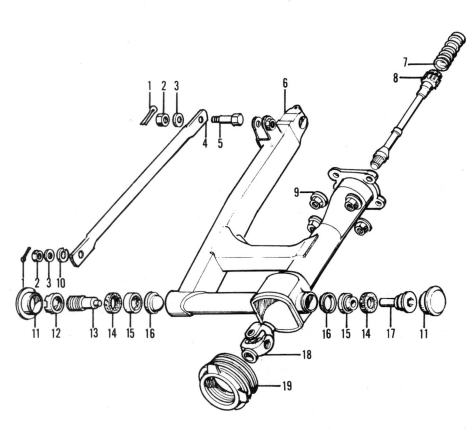

SWING ARM/DRIVE SHAFT
(1983-1985)

1. Cotter pin
2. Nut
3. Washer
4. Brake torque link
5. Bolt
6. Swing arm
7. Damper spring
8. Drive shaft
9. Nut
10. Lockwasher

11. Cap
12. Pivot bolt locknut
13. Right-hand pivot bolt
14. Dust seal
15. Bearing
16. Grease retainer plate
17. Left-hand pivot bolt
18. Universal joint
19. Rubber boot

10

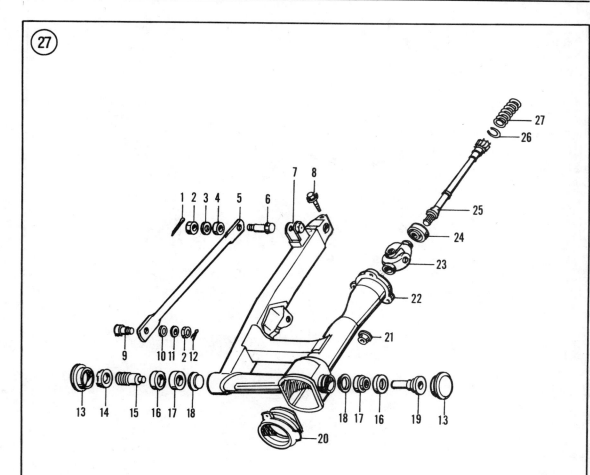

SWING ARM/DRIVE SHAFT
(1986-ON)

1. Cotter pin
2. Nut
3. Washer
4. Spacer
5. Brake torque link
6. Bolt
7. Swing arm
8. Bolt
9. Bolt
10. Spacer
11. Washer
12. Cotter pin
13. Cap
14. Pivot bolt locknut

15. Right-hand pivot bolt
16. Dust seal
17. Bearing
18. Grease retainer plate
19. Left-hand pivot bolt
20. Rubber boot
21. Nut
22. Drive shaft opening
23. Universal joint
24. Bearing
25. Drive shaft
26. Clip
27. Damper spring

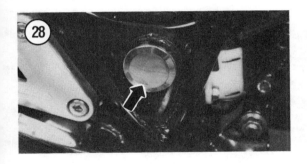

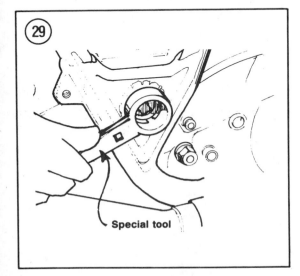

Special tool

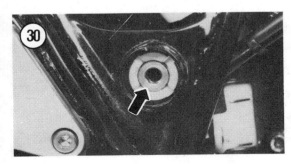

5. Remove the lower mounting bolt and nut securing the right-hand shock absorber.

NOTE
It is not necessary to remove the shock absorber unit, just pivot the unit up and out of the way with a Bungee cord.

6. Grasp the rear end of the swing arm and try to move it from side to side in a horizontal arc. There should be no noticeable side play. If play is evident and the pivot adjusting bolt is tightened correctly, the bearings should be replaced.

7. Remove the cap on both pivot bolts (**Figure 28**).

8. Use the special tool, Swing Arm Pivot Locknut Wrench (Honda part No. 07908-ME90000), and loosen the right-hand pivot bolt locknut (**Figure 29**).

9. Use a 10 mm Allen wrench and remove the right-hand adjusting bolt (**Figure 30**).

10. Remove the left-hand pivot bolt.

11. Pull back on the swing arm, free it from the frame and remove it from the frame.

12. Leave the universal joint on the engine output shaft.

Installation

1. Make sure the universal joint is installed on the engine output shaft.

2. If removed, install the rubber boot on the drive shaft side of the swing arm with the "UP" mark facing up.

3. Position the swing arm into the mounting area of the frame. Align the holes in the swing arm with the holes in the frame.

4. Apply a light coat of grease to the inner end of both the right- and left-hand pivot bolts. Install the right- and left-hand pivot bolts.

5. Make sure the swing arm is properly located in the frame and then tighten the left-hand pivot bolt to the torque specifications listed in **Table 1**.

6A. *1983-1985:* Tighten the right-hand pivot bolt to 20 N•m (14 ft.-lb.), then loosen it and retighten it to the torque specification listed in **Table 1**.

6B. *1986-on:* Tighten the right-hand pivot bolt to 12 N•m (9 ft.-lb.), then loosen it and retighten it to the torque specification listed in **Table 1**.

7. Move the swing arm up and down several times to make sure all components are properly seated.

8. Retighten the right-hand pivot bolt to the correct torque specification.

9. On the left-hand side, perform the following:
   a. Hold onto the right-hand pivot bolt with a 10 mm Allen wrench to make sure the pivot bolt does not move while tightening the locknut.
   b. Use special tool, Swing Arm Pivot Locknut Wrench (Honda part No. 07908-ME90000) (**Figure 31**), and tighten the locknut to the torque specification listed in **Table 1**.

10. Install the final drive unit and drive shaft assembly as described in this chapter.

11. Install the rubber boot onto the rear of the engine. Make sure it is correctly installed on both the engine and swing arm. This is necessary to keep out dirt and water.

12. Install the rear shock absorbers as described in this chapter.

10

13. Install the rear wheel as described in this chapter.

14. Install the exhaust system as described in Chapter Six.

Bearing Replacement

The swing arm is equipped with a roller bearing at each end. The inner race and roller bearing will come right out. No force should be needed. After the grease seal is removed. The bearing outer race is pressed in place and has to be removed, so don't remove it unless the bearing is going to be replaced.

The bearing outer race must be removed and installed with special tools that are available from a Honda dealer. The special tools are as follows.

a. Bearing remover (1983-1985): Honda part No. 07936-3710200

b. Slide hammer weight (1983-1985): Honda part No. 07936-3710100

c. Slide hammer weight (1983-1985): Honda part No. 07936-3710200

d. Driver handle: Honda part No. 07749-00100000

e. Outer bearing driver (1983-1985): Honda part No. 07746-0010200

f. Outer bearing driver (1986-on): Honda part No. 07746-0010100

g. 1986-on: A 1/4 in. steel rod approximately 16 in. long

1. Remove the swing arm as described in this chapter.

2. Remove the dust seal and bearing assembly from each side of the swing arm.

3. Secure the swing arm in a vise with soft jaws.

> *NOTE*
> *The special tools used on 1983-1985 models grab the outer race and then withdraw it from the swing arm with the use of a tool similar to a body shop slide hammer.*

4A. *1983-1985:* Remove the right-hand bearing race first (**Figure 32**) as follows.

a. Remove the attachment from the end of the bearing remover.

b. Slide the bearing remover shaft through the hole in the bearing race and install a 29 mm OD washer or equivalent attachment onto the end of the shaft.

c. Slide the weight on the hammer upward several times and remove the bearing race.

d. Remove the grease retainer plate and discard it.

e. Repeat for the left-hand bearing.

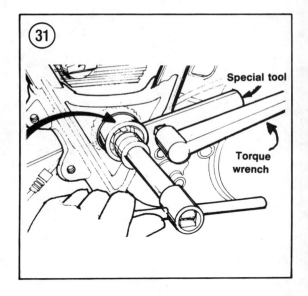

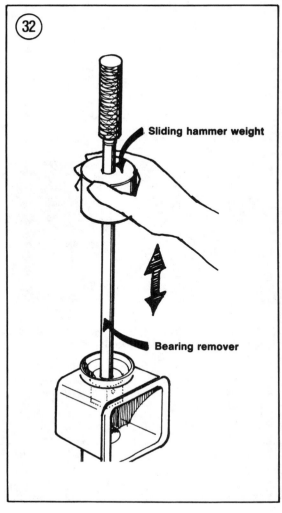

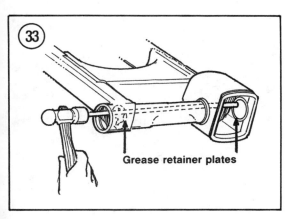

Grease retainer plates

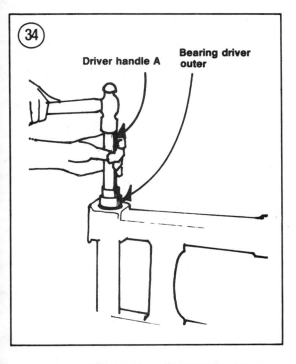

Driver handle A   Bearing driver outer

4B. *1986-on:* Remove the grease retainer plates and bearing races as follows.

    a. Drill a 3/8 in. hole through the right-hand grease retainer plate.

    b. Insert the 1/4 in. steel rod through the hole in the right-hand retainer plate and knock the left-hand outer race and grease retainer plate out of the swing arm. See **Figure 33**.

    c. Repeat for the right-hand grease retainer plate and bearing race.

5. Thoroughly clean out the inside of the swing arm with solvent and dry with compressed air.

6. Apply a light coat of waterproof grease to all parts before installation.

7. Install new grease retainer plate(s) into the bearing receptacle.

NOTE
Either the right- or left-hand bearing race can be installed first.

8. To install the new roller bearing outer race, place the outer bearing driver over the bearing race and drive the race into place with the driver handle and a hammer (**Figure 34**). Drive the race into place slowly and squarely. Make sure it is properly seated.

CAUTION
Never reinstall a bearing outer race that has been removed. During removal it becomes slightly damaged and is no longer true to alignment. If installed, it will damage the roller bearing assembly and create an unsafe riding condition.

9. Repeat Step 8 for the other bearing race.

10. Install a new roller bearing and dust seal on each end of the swing arm.

11. Install the swing arm as described in this chapter.

SHOCK ABSORBERS

The shock absorbers are spring controlled and hydraulically dampened. Spring preload can be adjusted by rotating the spring lower seat at the base of the spring (**Figure 35**) *clockwise to increase* preload and *counterclockwise to decrease* it.

NOTE
Use the wrench furnished in the factory tool kit.

Both cams must be indexed on the same detent. The shocks are sealed and cannot be rebuilt. Service is limited to removal and replacement of the hydraulic unit or the spring.

10

Removal/Installation

Removal and installation of the rear shocks is easier if done separately. The remaining unit will support the rear of the bike and maintain the correct relationship between the top and bottom shock mounts.

1. Place the bike on the centerstand and remove the seat.

NOTE
It is not necessary to remove the seat but it will protect the cover from the accidental slippage of a tool during removal and installation of the upper Allen bolt.

2. Adjust both shocks to their softest setting, completely counterclockwise.
3. On the left-hand side, remove the lower nut and washer and the upper Allen bolt (**Figure 36**).
4. On the right-hand side, remove the lower bolt and washer and the upper Allen bolt.
5. Pull the unit straight off the upper bolt and remove it.
6. Install by reversing these removal steps. Tighten the upper mounting nut and lower mounting bolt or nut to the torque specifications listed in **Table 1**.
7. Repeat for the other side.

Disassembly/Inspection/Assembly

Refer to **Figure 37** (1983-1985) or **Figure 38** (1986-on) for this procedure.

The shock is spring-controlled and hydraulically damped. The shock damper unit is sealed and cannot be serviced. Service is limited to removal and replacement of the damper unit and the spring.

The shock must be disassembled with the use of special tools that are available from a Honda dealer. They are described in this procedure.

WARNING
Without the proper tool, this procedure can be dangerous. The spring can fly loose, causing injury. For a small bench fee, a dealer can do the job for you.

1. Install the shock absorber in a compression tool (Honda part No. 07959-3290001) as shown in **Figure 39**.

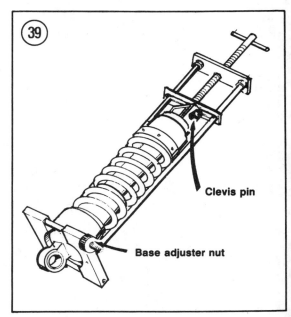

Clevis pin

Base adjuster nut

NOTE
The shock compressor tool must be modified to safely accomodate this particular shock absorber. Two additional components have to be added to the basic compressor tool. Replace the base and guide of the compressor tool with a set of attachments (Honda part No. 07959-MB-1000). Also place a collar (Honda part No. 52486-463-0000) in the shock absorber's lower joint prior to installing the shock absorber into the compressor tool.

2. Compress the spring just enough (approximately 30 mm) to gain access to the locknut under the upper joint.

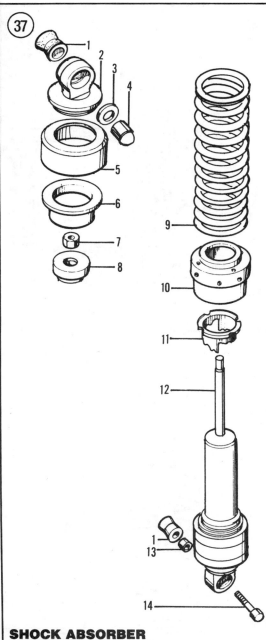

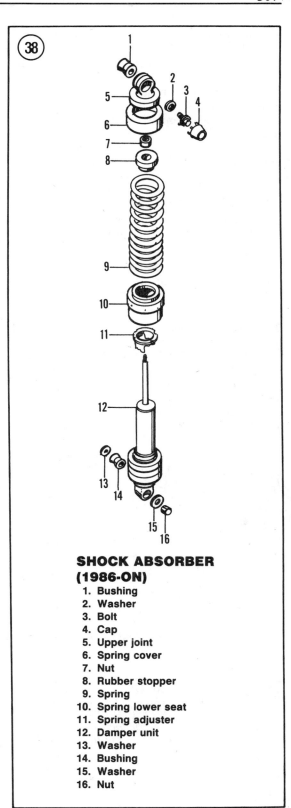

SHOCK ABSORBER
(1983-1985)

1. Bushing
2. Upper joint
3. Washer
4. Cap nut
5. Spring cover
6. Spring guide

7. Locknut
8. Rubber stopper
9. Spring
10. Spring lower seat
11. Spring adjuster
12. Damper unit
13. Bushing
14. Bolt

SHOCK ABSORBER
(1986-ON)

1. Bushing
2. Washer
3. Bolt
4. Cap
5. Upper joint
6. Spring cover
7. Nut
8. Rubber stopper
9. Spring
10. Spring lower seat
11. Spring adjuster
12. Damper unit
13. Washer
14. Bushing
15. Washer
16. Nut

10

3. Place the upper joint in a vise with soft jaws and loosen the locknut (**Figure 40**).

4. Completely unscrew the upper joint. This part may be difficult to break loose as Loctite Lock N' Seal was applied during assembly.

5. Release the spring tension and remove the shock from the compression tool.

6. Remove the spring cover, spring guide, spring, spring lower seat and spring adjuster from the damper unit.

7. Measure the spring free length (**Figure 41**). The spring must be replaced if it has sagged to the service limit listed in **Table 2** or less.

8. Check the damper unit for leakage and make sure the damper rod is straight.

NOTE
The damper unit cannot be rebuilt; it must be replaced as a unit.

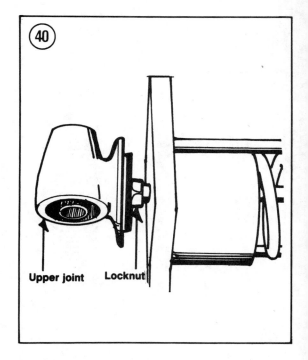

Upper joint   **Locknut**

9. Inspect the rubber bushings in the upper and lower joints. Replace if necessary.

10. Inspect the rubber stopper. If it is worn or deteriorated, remove the locknut and slide off the rubber stopper. Replace with a new one.

11. Assembly is the reverse of these disassembly steps, noting the following.

12. If the locknut was removed, apply Loctite Lock N' Seal to the threads of the damper rod prior to installing the locknut. Screw the locknut all the way down to the end of the threads.

13. Apply Loctite Lock N' Seal to the threads of the damper rod prior to installing the upper joint. Screw the upper joint on all the way. Secure the upper joint in a vise with soft jaws and tighten the locknut along with the damper rod against the upper joint.

NOTE
The damper rod should rotate with the locknut when the locknut is tightened against the bottom surface of the upper joint.

NOTE
After the locknut is tightened completely the locknut must be against the bottom surface of the upper joint and against the end of the threads on the damper rod.

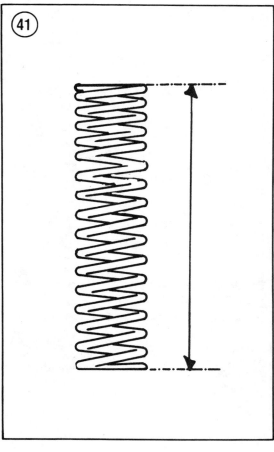

14. Align the upper spring seat with the upper joint when releasing the spring compressor tool.

Table 1 REAR SUSPENSION TORQUE SPECIFICATIONS

Item	N·m	ft.-lb.
Rear axle nut		
1983-1985	60-80	43-58
1986-on	80-100	58-72
Rear axle pinch bolt		
1983-1985	20-30	14-22
1986-on	24-30	17-22
Shock absorber nut and bolt		
1983-1985	30-40	22-29
1986-on		
Upper	24-30	17-22
Lower	30-40	22-29
Brake torque link bolt		
1983-1985	15-25	11-18
1986-on	24-30	17-22
Final drive unit nuts	50-60	36-43
Swing arm		
1983-1985		
Left-hand pivot bolt	100-130	72-94
Right-hand pivot bolt	10-14	7-10
1986-on		
Left-hand pivot bolt	80-120	58-87
Right-hand pivot bolt	8-12 6-9	
Pivot locknut		
1983-1985	100-130	72-94
1986-on	80-120	58-87

Table 2 REAR SHOCK ABSORBER SPRING FREE LENGTH

	Standard	Service limit
1983-1985	223.8 mm (8.81 mm)	211 mm (8.3 in.)
1986-on	240.1 mm (9.45 in.)	235.3 mm (9.26 in.)

10

CHAPTER ELEVEN

BRAKES

The brake system consists of disc brake(s) on the front wheel and a drum brake on the rear.

Refer to **Table 1** for brake specifications and **Table 2** for torque specifications. **Table 1** and **Table 2** are located at the end of this chapter.

FRONT DISC BRAKES

The front disc brakes are actuated by hydraulic fluid and are controlled by a hand lever on the master cylinder. As the brake pads wear, the brake fluid level drops in the reservoir and automatically adjusts for wear.

When working on hydraulic brake systems, it is necessary that the work area and all tools be absolutely clean. Any tiny particles of foreign matter and grit in the caliper assembly or the master cylinder can damage the components. Also, sharp tools must not be used inside the caliper or on the piston. If there is any doubt about your ability to correctly and safely carry out major service on the brake components, take the job to a dealer or brake specialist.

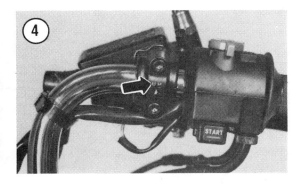

FRONT MASTER CYLINDER

Removal/Installation

1. Remove the rear view mirror (A, **Figure 1**) from the master cylinder.

> *CAUTION*
> *Cover the fuel tank and instrument cluster with a heavy cloth or plastic tarp to protect them from accidental brake fluid spills. Wash brake fluid off any painted or plated surfaces immediately, as it will destroy the finish. Use soapy water and rinse completely.*

2. Pull back the rubber boot (B, **Figure 1**) and remove the union bolt (**Figure 2**) securing the brake hose to the master cylinder. Remove the brake hose. Tie the brake hose up and cover the end to prevent the entry of foreign matter.

3. Remove the clamping bolts (**Figure 3**) and clamp securing the master cylinder to the handlebar and remove the master cylinder.

4. Install by reversing these removal steps, noting the following.

5. Install the clamp with the "UP" arrow (**Figure 4**) facing up. Align the face of the clamp with the punch mark on the handlebar (**Figure 5**). Tighten the upper bolt first, then the lower to the torque specification listed in **Table 2**.

6. Install the brake hose onto the master cylinder. Be sure to place a sealing washer on each side of the fitting and install the union bolt. Tighten the union bolt to the torque specification listed in **Table 2**.

7. Bleed the brake as described in this chapter.

Disassembly

Refer to **Figure 6** for this procedure.

11

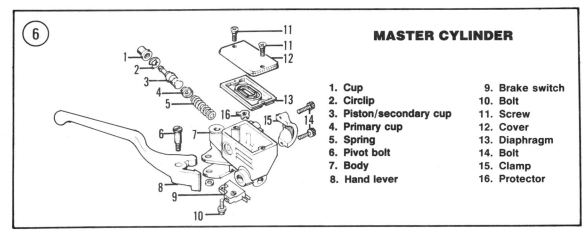

MASTER CYLINDER

1. Cup
2. Circlip
3. Piston/secondary cup
4. Primary cup
5. Spring
6. Pivot bolt
7. Body
8. Hand lever

9. Brake switch
10. Bolt
11. Screw
12. Cover
13. Diaphragm
14. Bolt
15. Clamp
16. Protector

1. Remove the master cylinder as described in this chapter.

2. Remove the bolt and nut securing the brake lever and remove the lever.

3. Remove the screws securing the cover and remove the cover and diaphragm; pour out the brake fluid and discard it. *Never* reuse brake fluid.

4. Remove the rubber boot from the area where the hand lever actuates the internal piston.

5. Using circlip pliers, remove the internal circlip from the body.

6. Remove the secondary cup and the piston assembly.

7. Remove the primary cup and spring.

8. Remove the brake light switch if necessary.

Inspection

1. Clean all parts in denatured alcohol or fresh brake fluid. Inspect the cylinder bore and piston contact surfaces for signs of wear and damage. If either part is less than perfect, replace it.

2. Check the end of the piston for wear caused by the hand lever. Replace if worn.

3. Replace the piston if the secondary cup requires replacement.

4. Inspect the pivot hole in the hand lever. If worn or elongated it must be replaced.

5. Make sure the passages in the bottom of the brake fluid reservoir are clear. Check the reservoir cap and diaphragm for damage and deterioration and replace as necessary.

6. Inspect the threads in the bore for the brake line.

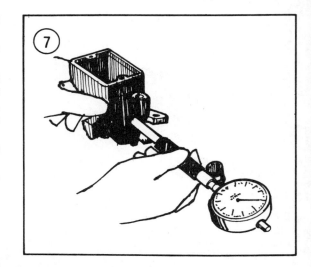

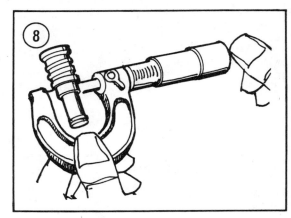

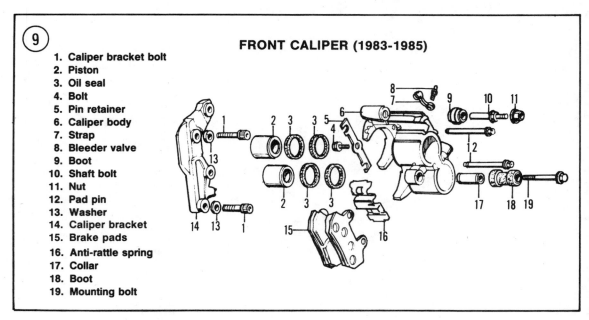

FRONT CALIPER (1983-1985)

1. Caliper bracket bolt
2. Piston
3. Oil seal
4. Bolt
5. Pin retainer
6. Caliper body
7. Strap
8. Bleeder valve
9. Boot
10. Shaft bolt
11. Nut
12. Pad pin
13. Washer
14. Caliper bracket
15. Brake pads
16. Anti-rattle spring
17. Collar
18. Boot
19. Mounting bolt

7. Check the hand lever pivot lugs on the master cylinder body for cracks.

8. Measure the cylinder bore (**Figure 7**). Replace the master cylinder if the bore exceeds the specifications given in **Table 1**.

9. Measure the outside diameter of the piston as shown in **Figure 8** with a micrometer. Replace the piston assembly if it is less than the specifications given in **Table 1**.

Assembly

1. Soak the new cups in fresh brake fluid for at least 15 minutes to make them pliable. Coat the inside of the cylinder with fresh brake fluid prior to the assembly of parts.

> *CAUTION*
> *When installing the piston assembly, do not allow the cups to turn inside out as they will be damaged and allow brake fluid leakage within the cylinder bore.*

2. Install the spring, primary cup and piston assembly into the cylinder together. Install the spring with the tapered end facing toward the primary cup.

> *NOTE*
> *Be sure to install the primary cup with the open end in first, toward the spring.*

3. Install the circlip and slide in the rubber boot.

4. Install the diaphragm and cover. Do not tighten the cover screws at this time as fluid will have to be added later when the system is bled.

5. Install the brake lever onto the master cylinder body.

6. If removed, install the brake light switch.

7. Install the master cylinder as described in this chapter.

FRONT BRAKE
PAD REPLACEMENT

There is no recommended mileage interval for changing the friction pads in the disc brake. Pad wear depends greatly on riding habits and conditions. The pads should be checked for wear every 6,400 km (4,000 miles) and replaced when the wear indicator reaches the edge of the brake disc. To maintain an even brake pressure on the disc always replace both pads in each caliper at the same time.

> *CAUTION*
> *Check the pads more frequently when the wear line approaches the disc. On some pads the wear line is very close to the metal backing plate. If pad wear happens to be uneven for some reason the backing plate may come in contact with the disc and cause damage.*

1983-1985

Refer to **Figure 9** for this procedure.

1. Remove the mounting bolt (A, **Figure 10**) and the caliper shaft bolt (B, **Figure 10**) securing the caliper assembly to the caliper bracket.

2. Pivot the caliper assembly up and off the disc and remove the caliper assembly.

3. Remove the bolt (A, **Figure 11**) securing the pad pin retainer to the caliper assembly and remove the pad pin retainer (B, **Figure 11**).

4. Remove both pad pins and both brake pads.

5. Clean the pad recess and the end of the pistons with a soft brush. Do not use solvent, a wire brush or any hard tool which would damage the cylinders or pistons.

6. Carefully remove any rust or corrosion from the disc.

7. Lightly coat the end of the pistons and the backs of the new pads (*not* the friction material) with disc brake lubricant.

> *NOTE*
> *When purchasing new pads, check with your dealer to make sure the friction compound of the new pad is compatible*

11

with the disc material. Remove any roughness from the backs of the new pads with a fine-cut file; blow them clean with compressed air.

8. When new pads are installed in the caliper the master cylinder brake fluid level will rise as the caliper pistons are repositioned. Perform the following:

a. Clean the top of the master cylinder of all dirt and foreign matter.

b. Remove the cap and diaphragm from the master cylinder and slowly push the caliper pistons into the caliper. Constantly check the reservoir to make sure brake fluid does not overflow. Remove fluid, if necessary, prior to it overflowing.

c. The pistons should move freely. If they don't and there is evidence of them sticking in the cylinder, the caliper should be removed and serviced as described in this chapter.

9. Push the caliper pistons in all the way (**Figure 12**) to allow room for the new pads.

10. Install the anti-rattle spring as shown in **Figure 13**.

11. Install the outboard pad (**Figure 14**) and partially install the pins through that pad.

12. Install the inboard pad (**Figure 15**).

13. Push the pins (**Figure 16**) all the way through.

14. Install the pad pin retainer onto the ends of the pins. Push the pin retainer down and make sure it seats completely on the groove in each pin.

15. Install the pad pin retaining bolt (A, **Figure 11**).

16. Carefully install the caliper assembly onto the disc. Be careful not to damage the leading edge of the pads during installation.

17. Lubricate the caliper upper pivot bolt and pivot boot on the caliper bracket with silicone grease.

18. Install the caliper mounting bolt and caliper shaft bolt. Tighten both bolts to torque specifications listed in **Table 2**.

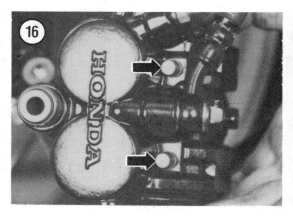

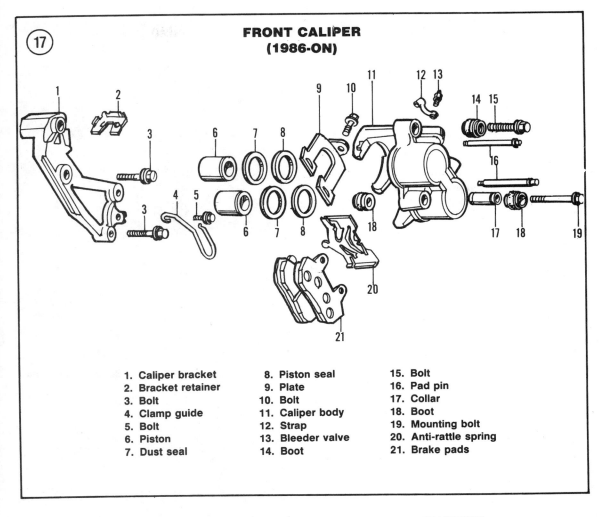

**FRONT CALIPER
(1986-ON)**

1. Caliper bracket	8. Piston seal	15. Bolt
2. Bracket retainer	9. Plate	16. Pad pin
3. Bolt	10. Bolt	17. Collar
4. Clamp guide	11. Caliper body	18. Boot
5. Bolt	12. Strap	19. Mounting bolt
6. Piston	13. Bleeder valve	20. Anti-rattle spring
7. Dust seal	14. Boot	21. Brake pads

19. Place wood blocks under the engine or frame so that the front wheel is off the ground. Spin the front wheel and activate the brake lever as many times as it takes to refill the cylinder in the caliper and correctly locate the pads.

20. Repeat Steps 1-19 for the other caliper assembly.

21. Refill the master cylinder reservoir, if necessary, to maintain the correct fluid level. Install the diaphragm and top cap.

WARNING
Use brake fluid from a sealed container clearly marked DOT 3 . Other types may vaporize and cause brake failure. Always use the same brand name; do not intermix as many brands are not compatible. Do not intermix silicone-based (DOT 5) brake fluid as it can cause brake component damage leading to brake system failure.

WARNING
Do not ride the motorcycle until you are sure the brakes are operating correctly with full hydraulic advantage. If necessary, bleed the brake as described in this chapter.

22. Bed the pads in gradually for the first 80 km (50 miles) by using only light pressure as much as possible. Immediate hard application will glaze the new friction pads and greatly reduce the effectiveness of the brake.

1986-on

Refer to **Figure 17** for this procedure.

1. Remove the caliper mounting bolt (**Figure 18**) securing the caliper assembly to the caliper bracket.

11

2. Pivot the caliper assembly up (**Figure 19**) and slide it off of the brake disc. Then slide the caliper assembly off of the caliper bracket (A, **Figure 20**).
3. Remove the pad pin retainer bolt (**Figure 21**).
4. Lift the pad pin retainer (**Figure 22**) off of the caliper assembly.
5. Pull the 2 pad pins (B, **Figure 20**) out of the caliper.
6. Lift the inboard (**Figure 23**) and outboard (**Figure 24**) brake pads out of the caliper.
7. Remove the pad spring (**Figure 25**).
8. Clean the pad recess and the end of the pistons with a soft brush. Do not use solvent, a wire brush or any hard tool which would damage the cylinders or pistons.
9. Carefully remove any rust or corrosion from the disc.
10. Lightly coat the ends of the pistons and the backs of the new pads (*not* the friction material) with disc brake lubricant.

NOTE
When purchasing new pads, check with your dealer to make sure the friction compound of the new pad is compatible with the disc material. Remove any roughness from the backs of the new pads with a fine-cut file.

11. When new pads are installed in the caliper, the master cylinder brake fluid will rise as the caliper pistons are repositioned. Perform the following.
   a. Clean the top of the master cylinder of all dirt and foreign matter.
   b. Remove the cap and diaphragm from the master cylinder and slowly push the caliper pistons into the caliper. Constantly check the

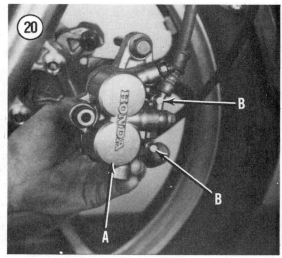

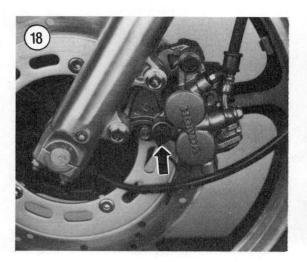

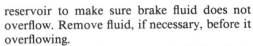

reservoir to make sure brake fluid does not overflow. Remove fluid, if necessary, before it overflowing.

   c. The pistons should move freely. If they don't and there is evidence of them sticking in the cylinder, the caliper should be removed and serviced as described in this chapter.

12. Push the caliper pistons in all the way to allow room for the new pads.

13. Install the anti-rattle spring as shown in **Figure 25**.

14. Insert the outboard pad (**Figure 24**) into the caliper.

15. Install the inboard pad (**Figure 23**) into the caliper.

16. Align the pins (A, **Figure 20**) with the caliper and pad pin bore and push the pins all the way through the caliper (**Figure 26**). Make sure the pins engage both brake pads.

11

17. Align the pad pin retainer with the pad pins. Push the pin retainer down and make sure it engages completely with each pin (**Figure 22**).

18. Install and tighten the pad pin retaining bolt (**Figure 21**) to the torque specifications in **Table 2**.

19. Make sure the retainer clip is positioned on the caliper bracket (**Figure 17**).

20. Lubricate the caliper upper pivot bolt and pivot boot on the caliper bracket with silicone grease.

21. Insert the upper caliper pivot pin into the caliper bracket (**Figure 19**). Then swing the caliper assembly down and onto the brake disc. Be careful not to damage the leading edge of the pads during installation.

22. Install the caliper mounting bolt and tighten to the torque specifications in **Table 2**.

23. Place wood blocks under the engine or frame so that the front wheel is off the ground. Spin the front wheel and activate the brake lever as many times as it takes to refill the cylinder in the caliper and correctly locate the pads.

24. Refill the master cylinder reservoir, if necessary, to maintain the correct fluid level. Install the diaphragm and top cap.

> *WARNING*
> *Use brake fluid from a sealed container clearly marked DOT 3. Other types may vaporize and cause brake failure. Always use the same brand name. Do not intermix as many brands are not compatible. Do not intermix silicone based (DOT 5) brake fluid as it can cause brake component damage leading to brake system failure.*

25. Bed the pads in gradually for the first 80 km (50 miles) by using only light pressure as much as possible. Immediate hard application will glaze the new friction pads and greatly reduce the effectiveness of the brake.

FRONT CALIPER

Removal/Installation

Refer to **Figure 9** (1983-1985) or **Figure 17** (1986-on) for this procedure.

> *CAUTION*
> *Do not spill any brake fluid on the painted portion of the front wheel. Wash off any spilled brake fluid immediately, as it will destroy the finish. Use soapy water and rinse completely.*

1. Place a container under the brake line at the caliper. Remove the union bolt and sealing washers (A, **Figure 27**) securing the brake line to the caliper assembly. Remove the brake line and let the brake fluid drain out into the container. Dispose of this brake fluid—never reuse brake fluid. To prevent the entry of moisture and dirt, cap the end of the brake line and tie the loose end up to the forks.

2. Loosen the caliper mounting bolt (B, **Figure 27**) and caliper shaft bolt (C, **Figure 27**) gradually in several steps. Push on the caliper while loosening the bolts to push the pistons back into the caliper.

3. Remove the caliper mounting bolt (B, **Figure 27**) and caliper shaft bolt (C, **Figure 27**). Pivot the caliper assembly up and off the disc and remove the caliper assembly.

4. Repeat Steps 1-3 for the other caliper assembly.

5. Lubricate the caliper upper pivot bolt and pivot boot with silicone grease.

6. Install by reversing these removal steps, noting the following.

7. Carefully install the caliper assembly onto the disc. Be careful not to damage the leading edge of the pads during installation.

8. Tighten the caliper mounting bolt and caliper shaft bolt to the torque specifications listed in **Table 2**.

9. Install the brake hose, with a sealing washer on each side of the fitting, onto the caliper. Install the union bolt and tighten to the torque specifications listed in **Table 2**.

10. Bleed the brake as described in this chapter.

> *WARNING*
> *Do not ride the motorcycle until you are sure that the brakes are operating properly.*

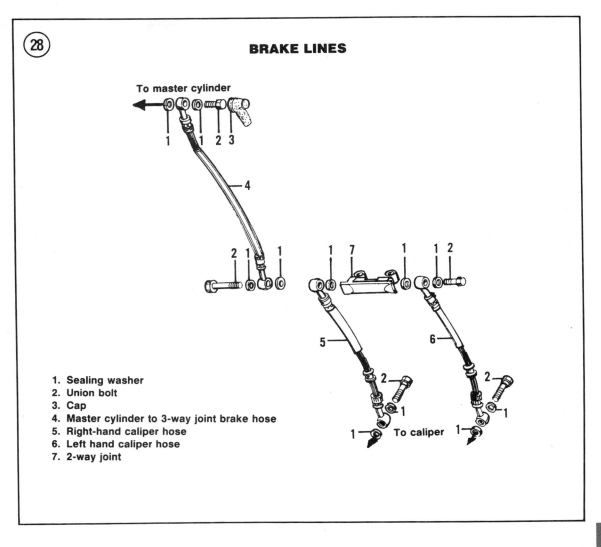

㉘ **BRAKE LINES**

To master cylinder

1. Sealing washer
2. Union bolt
3. Cap
4. Master cylinder to 3-way joint brake hose
5. Right-hand caliper hose
6. Left hand caliper hose
7. 2-way joint

To caliper

11

Rebuilding

If the caliper leaks, the caliper should be rebuilt. If the pistons stick in the cylinders, indicating severe wear or galling, the entire unit should be replaced. Rebuilding a leaky caliper requires special tools and experience.

Caliper service should be entrusted to a dealer, motorcycle repair shop or brake specialist. Considerable money can be saved by removing the caliper yourself and taking it in for repair.

Refer to **Figure 28** (1983-1985) or **Figure 29** (1986-on) for this procedure.

FRONT BRAKE HOSE REPLACEMENT

There is no factory-recommended replacement interval but it is a good idea to replace all brake hoses every four years or when they show signs of cracking or damage.

CAUTION
Cover the front wheel, fender and fuel tank with a heavy cloth or plastic tarp to protect it from accidental spilling of brake fluid. Wash brake fluid off of any painted or plated surface immediately, as it will destroy the finish. Use soapy water and rinse completely.

1. Place a container under the brake hose at the caliper. Remove the union bolt and sealing washers (A, **Figure 27**) securing the brake hose fitting to the caliper assembly.
2. Remove the brake hose from the clip on the fork leg. Remove the brake hose and let the brake fluid drain out into the container. To prevent the

entry of moisture and dirt, plug the brake hose inlet in the caliper.

> *WARNING*
> *Dispose of this brake fluid—never reuse brake fluid. Contaminated brake fluid can cause brake failure.*

3. *1983-1985:* Repeat for the other caliper.

4. Remove the union bolt and sealing washers (**Figure 30**) securing the brake hose to the master cylinder and remove the hose and sealing washers.

5. *1983-1985:* Perform the following.

   a. Remove the union bolt and sealing washers (A, **Figure 31**) securing the left-hand brake hose to the 2-way joint.

   b. Remove the union bolt and sealing washers (B, **Figure 31**) securing the upper hose and the right-hand lower hose to the 2-way joint and remove them and the sealing washers.

6. Install new hoses, sealing washers and union bolts in the reverse order of removal. Be sure to install new sealing washers in the correct positions. Refer to **Figure 28** (1983-1985) or **Figure 29** (1986-on).

7. Tighten all union bolts to torque specifications listed in **Table 2**.

8. Refill the master cylinder with fresh brake fluid clearly marked DOT 3 only. Bleed the brake as described in this chapter.

> *WARNING*
> *Use brake fluid from a sealed container clearly marked DOT 3. Other types may vaporize and cause brake failure. Always use the same brand name. Do not intermix, as many brands are not compatible. Do not intermix silicone-based (DOT 5) brake fluid as it can cause brake component damage leading to brake system failure.*

> *WARNING*
> *Do not ride the motorcycle until you are sure that the brakes are operating properly.*

FRONT BRAKE DISC

Removal/Installation

1. Remove the front wheel as described in Chapter Nine.

> *NOTE*
> *Place a piece of wood or vinyl tube in the calipers in place of the disc. This way, if the brake lever is inadvertently squeezed the pistons will not be forced out of the cylinders. If this does happen,*

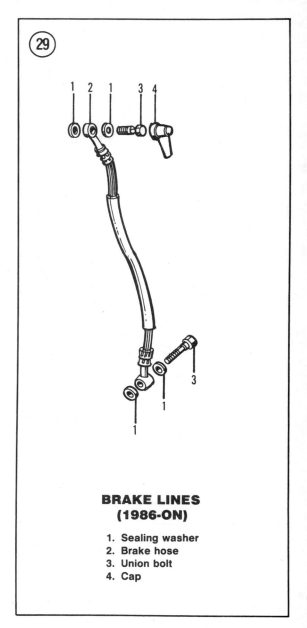

BRAKE LINES (1986-ON)

1. Sealing washer
2. Brake hose
3. Union bolt
4. Cap

the caliper might have to be disassembled to reseat the pistons and the system will have to be bled. By using the wood or vinyl tube, bleeding the system is not necessary when installing the wheel.

CAUTION
*Do not set the wheel down on the disc surface, as it may get scratched or warped. Set the wheel on 2 blocks of wood (**Figure 32**).*

2. Remove the speedometer housing from the left-hand side and the spacer from the right-hand side.

3. If the discs are going to be reinstalled (not replaced with new discs), mark them so they will be installed onto the same side of the wheel from where they were removed. Mark them with either an "R" (right-hand side) or "L" (left-hand side). Be sure to install the disc on the correct side during installation.

4. Remove the Allen bolts (**Figure 33**) securing the brake disc to the hub and remove the disc.

5. Remove the individual gaskets at each bolt hole on the disc.

6. If necessary, repeat Step 4 and Step 5 for the disc on the other side of the wheel.

7. Install by reversing these removal steps, noting the following.

8. Install the individual gaskets to each bolt hole on the disc.

9. Tighten the disc mounting Allen bolts to the torque specifications listed in **Table 2**.

Inspection

It is not necessary to remove the disc from the wheel to inspect it. Small marks on the disc are not important, but radial scratches deep enough to snag a fingernail reduce braking effectiveness and increase brake pad wear. If these grooves are found, the disc should be replaced.

1. Measure the thickness of the disc at several locations around the disc with a micrometer or vernier caliper (**Figure 34**). The disc must be replaced if the thickness in any area is less than that specified in **Table 1**.

2. Make sure the disc bolts are tight prior to running this check. Check the disc runout with a

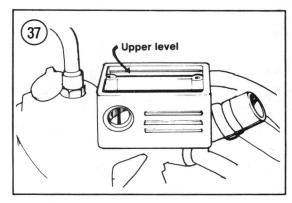

Upper level

dial indicator as shown in **Figure 35**. Slowly rotate the wheel and watch the dial indicator. If the runout exceeds that listed in **Table 1** the disc(s) must be replaced.

3. Clean the disc of any rust or corrosion and wipe clean with lacquer thinner. Never use an oil-based solvent that may leave an oil residue on the disc.

BLEEDING THE SYSTEM

This procedure is not necessary unless the brakes feel spongy, there has been a leak in the system, a component has been replaced or the brake fluid has been replaced. When bleeding the front system do one caliper at a time.

1. Remove the dust cap from the brake bleed valve.

2. Connect a length of clear tubing to the bleed valve on the caliper (**Figure 36**).

3. Place the other end of the tube into a clean container.

4. Fill the container with enough fresh brake fluid to keep the end submerged. The tube should be long enough so that a loop can be made higher than the bleed valve to prevent air from being drawn into the caliper during bleeding.

> *CAUTION*
> *Cover the fuel tank and instrument cluster with a heavy cloth or plastic tarp to protect it from the accidental spilling of brake fluid. Wash brake fluid off of any painted or plated surface immediately, as it will destroy the finish. Use soapy water and rinse completely.*

5. Clean the cover of the master cylinder of all dirt and foreign matter. Remove the screws securing the top cover and remove the cover and diaphragm. Fill the reservoir almost to the top lip; insert the diaphragm and the cover loosely. Leave the cover in place during this procedure to prevent the entry of dirt.

> *WARNING*
> *Use brake fluid from a sealed container clearly marked DOT 3 . Other types may vaporize and cause brake failure. Always use the same brand name; do not intermix as many brands are not compatible. Do not intermix silicone based (DOT 5) brake fluid as it can cause brake component damage leading to brake system failure.*

6. Insert a 20 mm (3/4 in.) spacer between the handlebar grip and the brake lever. This will prevent over-travel of the piston within the master cylinder.

7. Slowly apply the brake lever (or pedal) several times. Hold the lever in the applied position.

8. Open the bleed valve about one-half turn. Allow the lever to travel to its limit against the installed spacer. When this limit is reached, tighten the bleed screw.

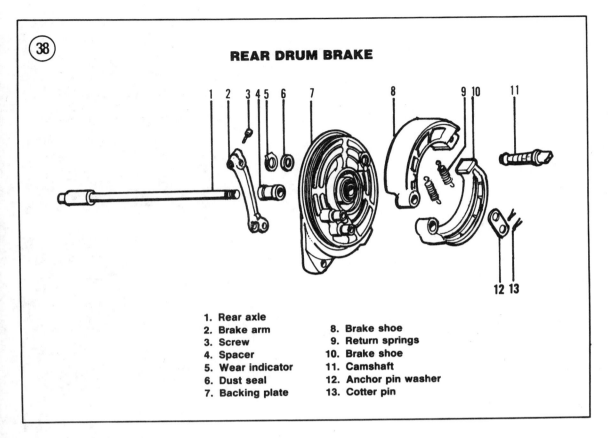

REAR DRUM BRAKE

1. Rear axle
2. Brake arm
3. Screw
4. Spacer
5. Wear indicator
6. Dust seal
7. Backing plate
8. Brake shoe
9. Return springs
10. Brake shoe
11. Camshaft
12. Anchor pin washer
13. Cotter pin

9. As the fluid enters the system, the level will drop in the reservoir. Maintain the level at about 3/8 inch from the top of the reservoir to prevent air from being drawn into the system.

10. Continue to pump the lever and fill the reservoir until the fluid emerging from the hose is completely free of bubbles.

NOTE
Do not allow the reservoir to empty during the bleeding operation or more air will enter the system. If this occurs, the entire procedure must be repeated.

11. Hold the lever in, tighten the bleed valve, remove the bleed tube and install the bleed valve dust cap.

12. If necessary, add fluid to correct the level in the reservoir. It should be to the upper level line (**Figure 37**).

13. Install the reservoir cover and tighten the screws.

14. Remove the spacer from the brake lever (installed in Step 6). Test the feel of the brake lever. It should be firm and should offer the same resistance each time it's operated. If it feels spongy,

it is likely that there still is air in the system and it must be bled again. When all air has been bled from the system and the fluid level is correct in the reservoir, double-check for leaks and tighten all the fittings and connections.

WARNING
Before riding the motorcycle, make certain that the brakes are operating correctly by operating the lever several times.

REAR DRUM BRAKE

Pushing down on the brake foot pedal pulls the rod which in turn rotates the camshaft. This forces the brake shoes out into contact with the brake drum.

Pedal free play must be maintained to minimize brake drag and premature brake wear and maximize braking effectiveness. Refer to Chapter Three for complete adjustment procedure.

Disassembly

Refer to **Figure 38** for this procedure.

1. Remove the rear wheel as described in Chapter Ten.

11

2. Pull the brake assembly straight up and out of the brake drum.

3. Remove the cotter pin and washer from the brake backing plate (**Figure 39**).

4. Remove the bolt and nut (A, **Figure 40**) securing the brake arm and remove the brake arm, wear indicator and dust seal. Withdraw the camshaft from the backing plate.

5. Using needlenose pliers remove the return spring (next to the camshaft) from the brake linings. Remove the other return spring in the same manner.

Inspection

1. Thoroughly clean and dry all parts except the brake linings.

2. Check the contact surface of the drum (**Figure 41**) for scoring. If there are grooves deep enough to snag your fingernail the drum should be reground.

3. Measure the inside diameter of the brake drum with vernier calipers (**Figure 42**). If the measurement is greater than the service limit listed in **Table 1** the rear wheel must be replaced (the brake drum is an integral part of the wheel).

4. If the drum can be turned and still stay within the maximum service limit diameter, the linings will have to be replaced and the new ones arced to conform to the new drum contour.

5. Measure the brake linings with a vernier caliper (**Figure 43**). They should be replaced if the lining portion is worn to the service limit dimension or less. Refer to specifications listed in **Table 1**.

6. Inspect the linings for imbedded foreign material. Dirt can be removed with a stiff wire brush. Check for any traces of oil or grease; if they are contaminated they must be replaced.

7. Inspect the cam lobe and pivot pin area of the backing plate (**Figure 44**) for wear or corrosion. Minor roughness can be removed with fine emery cloth.

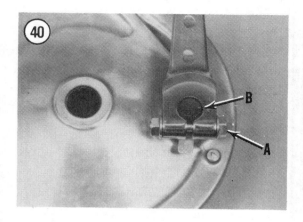

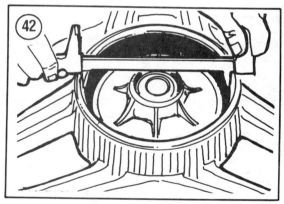

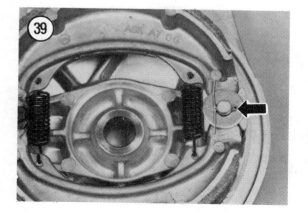

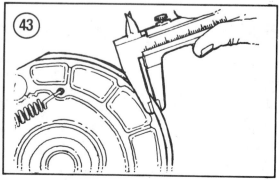

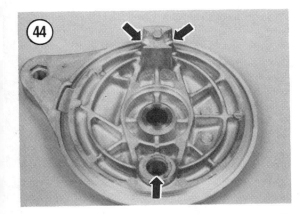

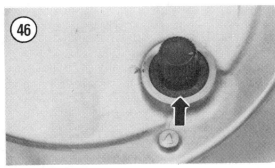

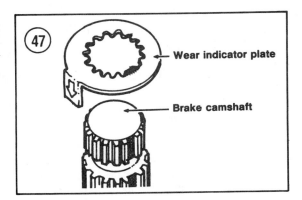

Wear indicator plate

Brake camshaft

8. Inspect the brake shoe return springs for wear. If they are stretched, they will not fully retract the brake shoes. Replace as necessary.

Assembly

1. Grease the camshaft with a light coat of molybdenum disulfide grease. Install the cam into the backing plate from the backside (**Figure 45**).

2. From the outside of the backing plate install the dust seal (**Figure 46**).

3. Align the wear indicator to the camshaft as shown in **Figure 47** and push it down all the way to the backing plate (**Figure 48**).

4. When installing the brake arm onto the camshaft, be sure to align the dimples on the two parts (B, **Figure 40**). Tighten the bolt and nut to the torque specification listed in **Table 2**.

5. Grease the camshaft and pivot post with a light coat of molybdenum disulfide grease; avoid getting any grease on the brake backing plate where the brake linings may come in contact with it.

6. Hold the brake shoes in a "V" formation with the return springs attached and snap them into place on the brake backing plate. Make sure they are firmly seated on it (**Figure 49**). Install the double lockwasher and new cotter pins. Bend the ends over completely.

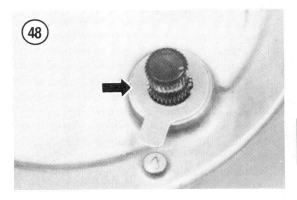

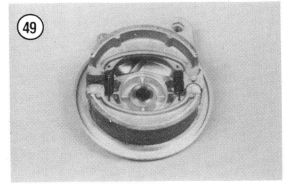

11

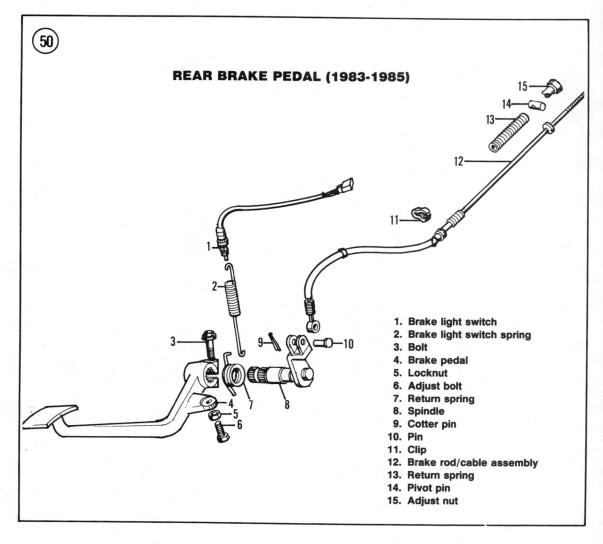

REAR BRAKE PEDAL (1983-1985)

1. Brake light switch
2. Brake light switch spring
3. Bolt
4. Brake pedal
5. Locknut
6. Adjust bolt
7. Return spring
8. Spindle
9. Cotter pin
10. Pin
11. Clip
12. Brake rod/cable assembly
13. Return spring
14. Pivot pin
15. Adjust nut

7. Install the brake panel assembly into the brake drum.

8. Install the rear wheel as described in Chapter Ten.

9. Adjust the rear brake as described in Chapter Three.

REAR BRAKE PEDAL

Removal/Installation

Refer to **Figure 50** (1983-1985) or **Figure 51** (1986-on) for this procedure.

1. Completely unscrew the adjustment nut (**Figure 52**) on the brake rod.

2. Push down on the brake pedal and remove the brake rod from the pivot joint in the brake arm. Install the pivot joint onto the brake rod and reinstall the adjustment nut to avoid losing any small parts.

3. Disconnect the brake light switch return spring and the brake pedal return spring from the brake lever.

4. Remove the bolt and nut securing the brake lever/foot peg assembly to the frame (**Figure 53**). Remove the brake pedal.

5. Remove the cotter pin and pivot pin securing the brake cable/rod assembly to the pivot shaft arm.

6. Disconnect the return spring from the pivot shaft arm.

7. Remove the pivot arm shaft from the frame.

8. Install by reversing these removal steps, noting the following.

9. Apply a light coat of multipurpose grease to all pivot areas prior to installing any components.

10. Install the brake pedal. Align the punch marks on the brake pedal and the brake pivot shaft.

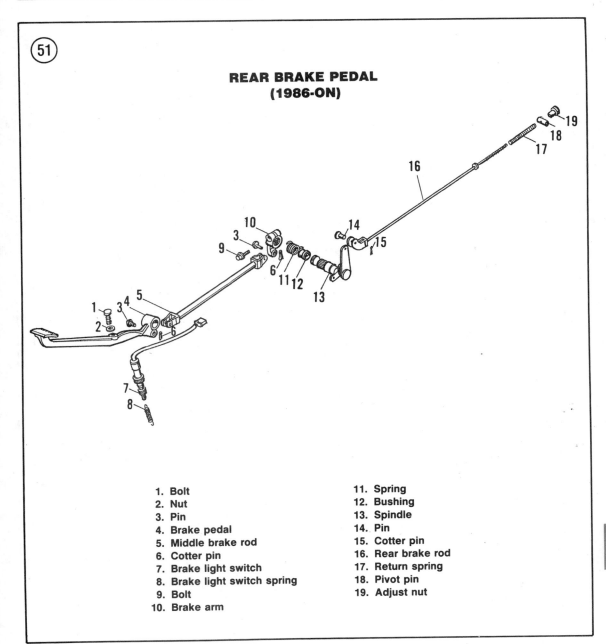

**REAR BRAKE PEDAL
(1986-ON)**

1. Bolt	11. Spring
2. Nut	12. Bushing
3. Pin	13. Spindle
4. Brake pedal	14. Pin
5. Middle brake rod	15. Cotter pin
6. Cotter pin	16. Rear brake rod
7. Brake light switch	17. Return spring
8. Brake light switch spring	18. Pivot pin
9. Bolt	19. Adjust nut
10. Brake arm	

11

Table 1 BRAKE SPECIFICATIONS

Item	Specification	Wear limit
Master cylinder		
Cylinder bore ID		
1983-1985	15.870-15.913 mm (0.6248-0.6265 in.)	15.93 mm (0.627 in.)
1986-on	14.000-14.043 mm (0.5512-0.5529 in.)	14.055 mm (0.5533 in.)
Piston OD		
1983-1985	15.827-15.854 mm (0.6231-0.6242 in.)	15.82 mm (0.623 in.)
1986-on	13.957-13.984 mm (0.5495-0.5506 in.)	13.945 mm (0.5490 in.)
Front caliper		
Front caliper		
Cylinder bore ID		
1983-1985	30.148-30.280 mm (1.1901-1.1921 in.)	30.290 mm (1.1925 in.)
1986-on	32.030-32.080 mm (1.2610-1.2630 in.)	32.090 mm (1.2634 in.)
Piston OD		
1983-1985	30.230-30.280 mm (1.1902-1.1913 in.)	30.10 mm (1.187 in.)
1986-on	31.948-31.998 mm (1.2578-1.2598 in.)	31.940 mm (1.2575)
Front brake disc thickness		
1983-1985	4.8-5.2 mm (0.19-0.20 in.)	4.0 mm (0.16 in.)
1986-on	4.5-5.2 mm (0.18-0.20 in.)	4.0 mm (0.16 in.)
Disc runout	—	0.3 mm (0.12 in.)
Rear brake drum ID		
1983-1985	160.0-160.3 mm (6.30-6.31 in.)	161 mm (6.34 in.)
1986-on	180 mm (7.09 in.)	181.0 mm (7.13 in.)
Rear brake shoe thickness		
1983-1985	4.9-5.0 mm (0.19-0.20 in.)	2.0 mm (0.08 in.)
1986-on	5.0 mm (0.20 in.)	2.0 mm (0.08 in.)

Table 2 BRAKE TORQUE SPECIFICATIONS

Item	N·m	ft.-lb.
Brake hose union bolts	25-35	18-25
Front master cylinder cover screws	1-2	0.7-0.9
Brake caliper		
1983-1985		
Bracket bolt	30-40	22-29
Caliper bolt	18-23	13-17
Pivot bolt	30-36	22-26
1986-on		
Bracket bolt	20-25	14-18
Caliper mounting bolt	30-40	22-29
Pin bolt	25-30	18-25
Pad pin retainer bolt	8-13	6-9
Brake disc mounting bolts		
1983-1985	35-40	25-29
1986-on	37-43	27-31
Rear brake arm bolt	24-30	17-22

CHAPTER TWELVE

FRAME AND REPAINTING

This chapter includes replacement procedures for miscellaneous components attached to the frame.

This chapter also describes procedures for completely stripping the frame. Recommendations are provided for repainting the stripped frame.

KICKSTAND (SIDESTAND)

Removal/Installation

1. Place a wood block(s) under the frame to support the bike securely.
2. Raise the kickstand and disconnect the return spring (A, **Figure 1**) from the pin on the frame with Vise Grips.
3. From under the frame, remove the bolt and nut (B, **Figure 1**) and remove the kickstand from the frame.
4. Install by reversing these removal steps. Apply a light coat of multipurpose grease to the pivot surfaces of the frame tab and the kickstand yoke prior to installation.

CENTERSTAND

Removal/Installation

1. Place a wood block(s) under the frame to hold the bike securely in place.
2. Raise the centerstand and use Vise Grips to unhook the return spring (A, **Figure 2**) for the centerstand.

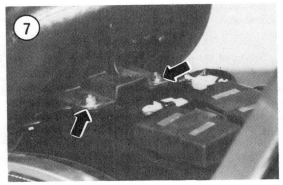

3. Unscrew the bolt (B, **Figure 2**) on each side securing the centerstand to the frame.

4. Remove the centerstand from the frame.

5. Remove the pivot collar from each pivot area on the centerstand.

6. Install by reversing these removal steps, noting the following.

7. Apply multipurpose grease to the pivot collar and to the pivot area of the centerstand where the pivot collar rides.

FOOTPEGS

Replacement

Remove the cotter pin and washer securing the footpeg to the bracket on the frame. Remove the pivot pin (**Figure 3**) and footpeg.

Make sure the spring is in good condition and not broken. Replace as necessary.

Lubricate the pivot point and pivot pin prior to installation. Install a new cotter pin and bend the ends over completely.

To remove the entire footpeg assembly, remove the bolts securing the assembly to the crankcase and remove the assembly.

SEATS

Removal/Installation
(1983-1985)

1. Using the ignition key, unlock the tool box (**Figure 4**).

2. Hinge the tool box back (**Figure 5**) and withdraw it from the assist bar area.

3. Remove the nuts (**Figure 6**) securing the rear seat.

4. Pull up on the rear of the rear seat and unhook it from the retainer on the front seat.

5. Remove the nuts (**Figure 7**) securing the front seat to the rear fender.

6. Pull the rear seat toward the rear and remove it.

7. Install by reversing these removal steps.

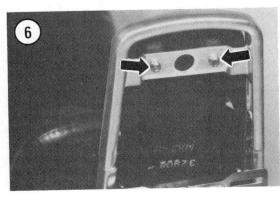

12

Removal/Installation
(1986-on)

1. Remove the rear seat as follows.
   a. Insert the ignition key into the helmet holder.
   b. Turn the key counterclockwise.
   c. Pull the rear seat backwards and remove it.
2. Remove the front seat as follows.
   a. Remove the nuts securing the rear seat.
   b. Pull the front seat backwards and remove it.
3. Install by reversing these removal steps.

REAR FENDER

Removal/Installation

1. Using the ignition key, unlock the tool box (**Figure 4**).
2. Hinge the tool box back (**Figure 5**) and withdraw it from the assist bar area.
3. Remove both side covers and the seats.
4. Remove the bolts (**Figure 8**) securing the tool box holder and remove the tool box holder.
5. Remove the bolts securing the upper portion of the grab rail (**Figure 9**) and remove the grab rail.
6. Disconnect the electrical connectors to both rear turn signals, the taillight/brake light, the spark units and the taillight sensor (A, **Figure 10**).
7. Carefully remove both reflex reflectors (B, **Figure 10**) from the lower portion of the grab rail.
8. Remove the bolts securing the lower portion of the grab rail (C, **Figure 10**) on each side and remove both grab rails.
9. Remove the front and rear sections of the fender from the frame.
10. Install by reversing these removal steps.

FRAME

The frame does not require routine maintenance. However, it should be inspected immediately after any accident or spill.

Component Removal/Installation

1. Remove the seat, side cover panels and fuel tank.
2. Remove the engine as described in Chapter Four.
3. Remove the front wheel, steering head and front forks as described in Chapter Nine.
4. Remove the rear wheel, shock absorber and swing arm as described in Chapter Ten.
5. Remove the battery as described in Chapter Three.
6. Remove the wiring harness.

7. Remove the kickstand and footpegs as described in this chapter.
8. Remove the centerstand as described in this chapter.
9. Remove the steering head races from the steering head tube as described in Chapter Nine.
10. Inspect the frame for bends, cracks or other damage, especially around welded joints and areas that are rusted.
11. Assemble by reversing these removal steps.

Stripping and Painting

Remove all components from the frame. Thoroughly strip off all old paint. The best way is to have it sandblasted down to bare metal. If this is not possible, you can use a liquid paint remover and steel wool and a fine, hard wire brush.

CAUTION
Some of the fenders, side covers, frame covers and air box are molded plastic. If you wish to change the color of these parts, consult an automotive paint supplier for the proper procedure. Do not use any liquid paint remover on these components as it will damage the surface. The color is an integral part of some of these components and cannot be removed.

When the frame is down to bare metal, have it inspected for hairline and internal cracks. Magnaflux is the most common and complete process.

Make sure that the primer is compatible with the type of paint you are going to use for the finish color. Spray on one or two coats of primer as smoothly as possible. Let it dry thoroughly and use a fine grade of wet sandpaper (400-600 grit) to remove any flaws. Carefully wipe the surface clean and then spray a couple of coats of the final color. Use either lacquer or enamel base paint and follow the manufacturer's instructions.

A shop specializing in painting will probably do the best job. However, you can do a surprisingly good job with a good grade of spray paint. Spend a few extra dollars and get a good grade of paint as it will make a difference in how good it looks and how long it will stand up. It's a good idea to shake the can and make sure the ball inside the can is loose when you purchase the can of paint. Shake the can as long as is stated on the can. Then immerse the can *upright* in a pot or bucket of *warm* water (not hot—not over 120° F).

WARNING
*Higher temperatures could cause the can to burst. Do **not** place the can in direct contact with any flame or heat source.*

Leave the can in the water for several minutes. When thoroughly warmed, shake the can again and spray the frame. Be sure to get into all the crevices where there may be rust problems. Several light mist coats are better than one heavy coat. Spray painting is best done in temperatures of 70-80° F (21-26° C); any temperature above or below this will cause problems.

After the final coat has dried completely, at least 48 hours, any overspray or orange peel may be removed with a *light* application of Dupont rubbing compound (red color) and finished with Dupont polishing compound (white color). Be careful not to rub too hard or you will go through the finish.

Finish off with a couple coats of good wax prior to reassembling all the components.

It's a good idea to keep the frame touched up with fresh paint if any minor rust spots or scratches appear.

12

INDEX

WIRING DIAGRAMS

1983 VT750C Shadow

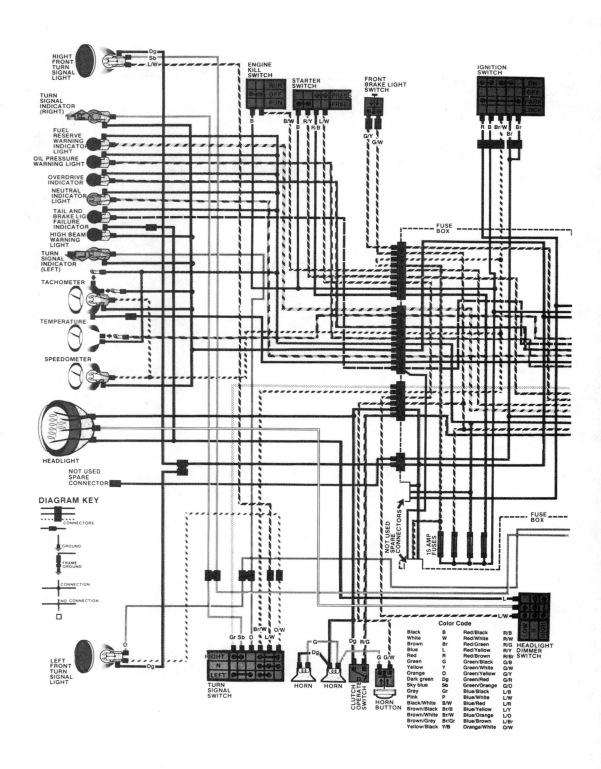

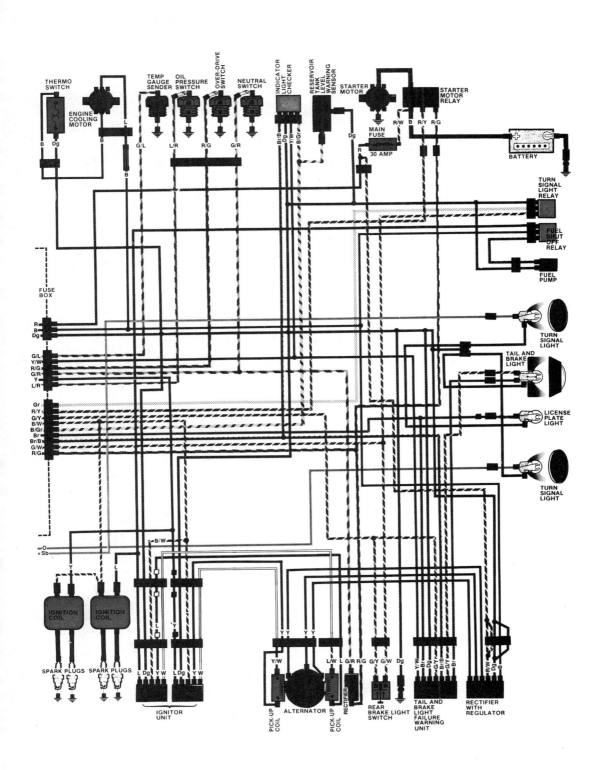

1984 VT700C Shadow

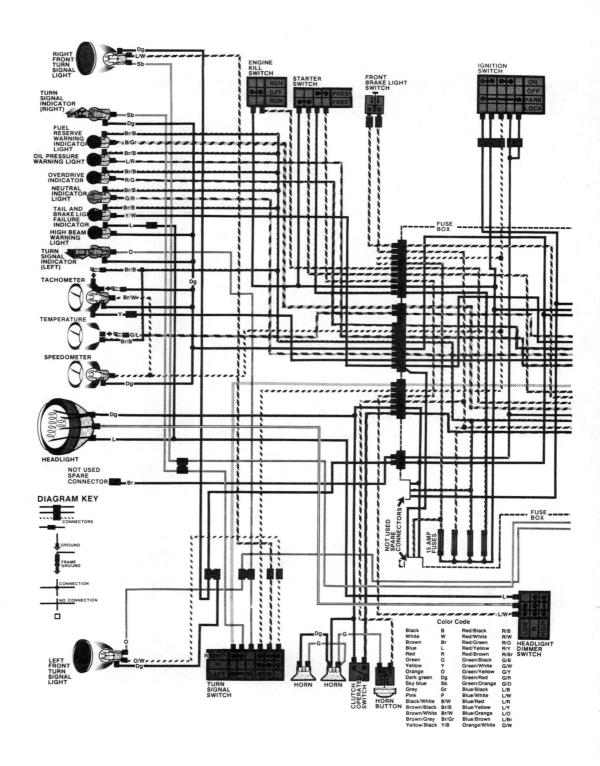

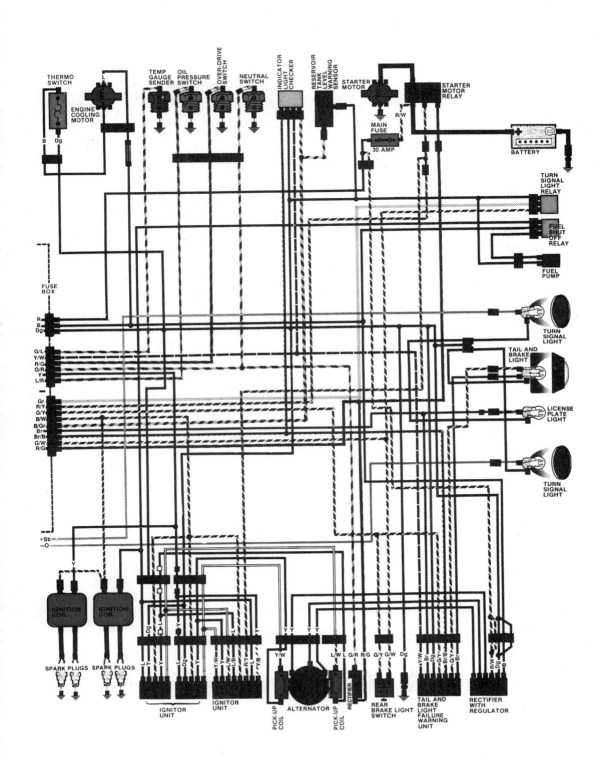

1985 HONDA VT700C SHADOW

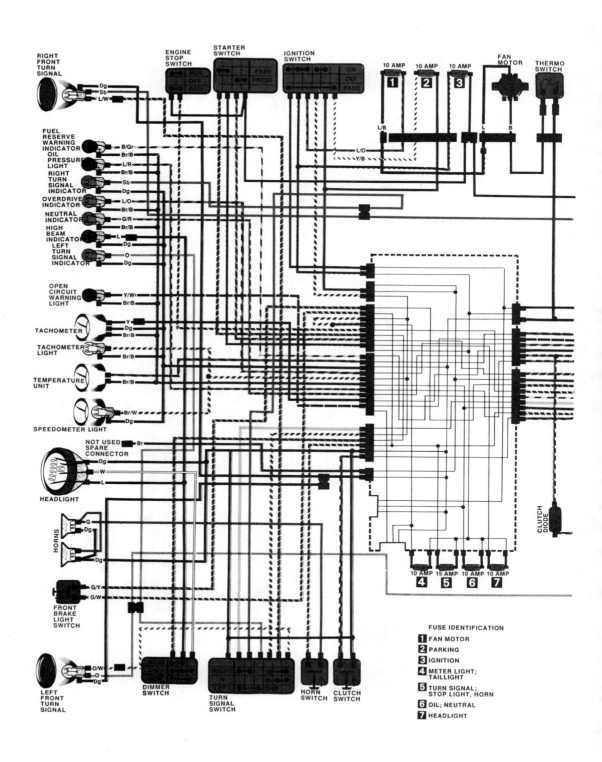

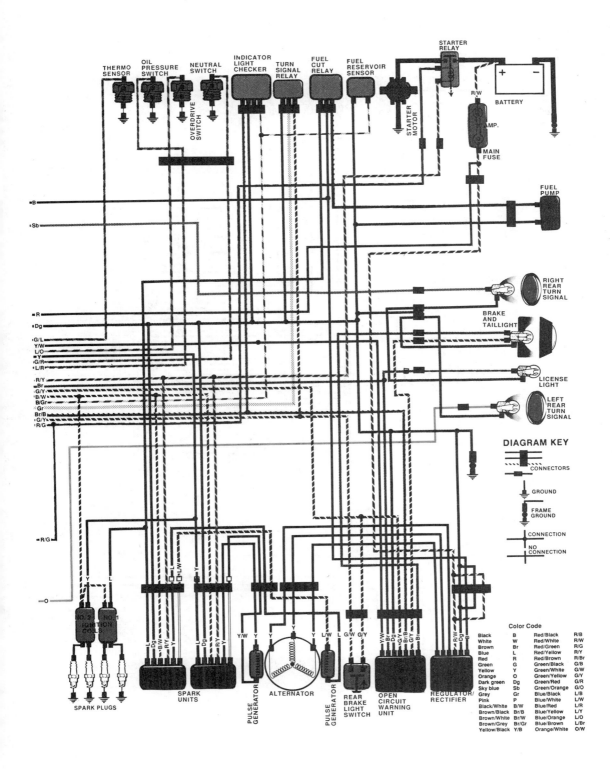

1986 HONDA VT700C SHADOW

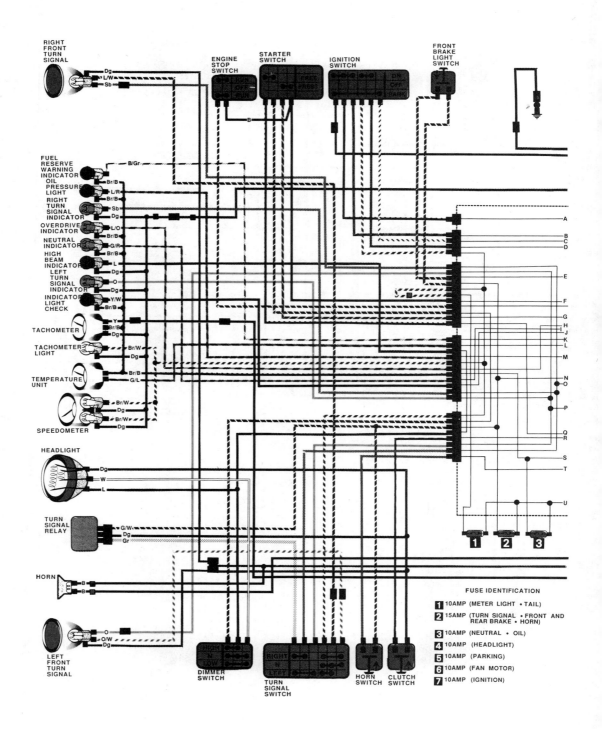

FUSE IDENTIFICATION

1	10AMP (METER LIGHT • TAIL)
2	15AMP (TURN SIGNAL • FRONT AND REAR BRAKE • HORN)
3	10AMP (NEUTRAL • OIL)
4	10AMP (HEADLIGHT)
5	10AMP (PARKING)
6	10AMP (FAN MOTOR)
7	10AMP (IGNITION)

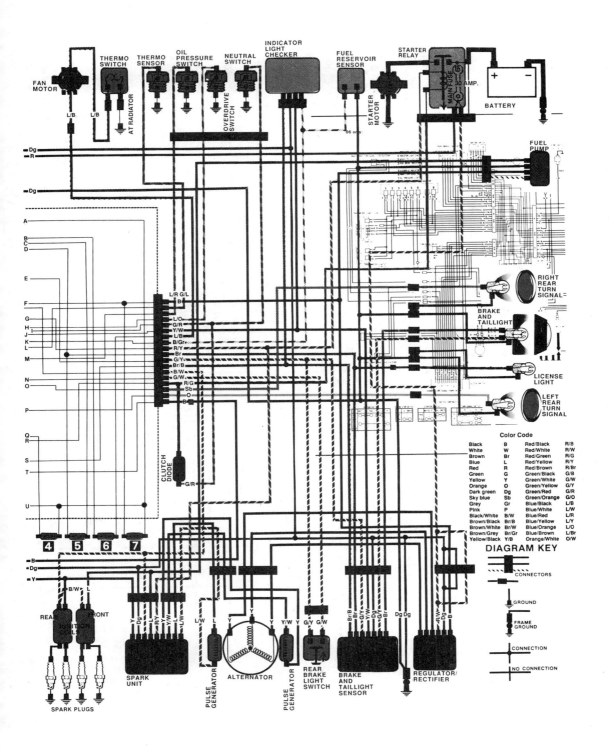

1987 HONDA VT700C SHADOW

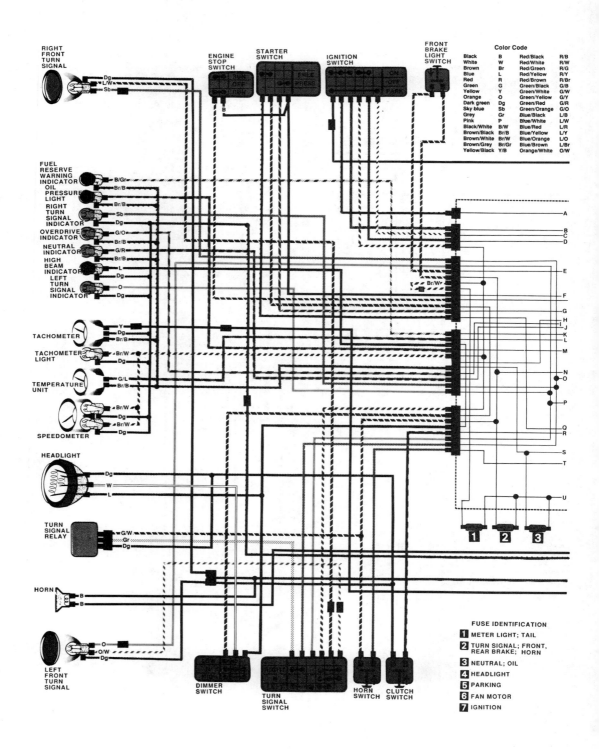

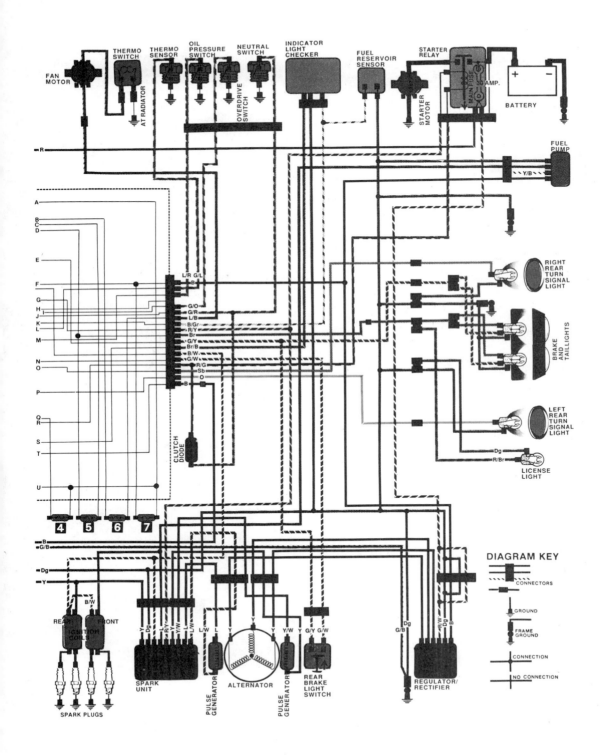

NOTES